Comprehensive Criminal Procedure
Third Edition

2014 Supplement

D1446503

2014 Supplement

Comprehensive Criminal Procedure

Third Edition

Ronald Jay Allen

John Henry Wigmore Professor of Law
Northwestern University

William J. Stuntz

Henry J. Friendly Professor of Law
Harvard University

Joseph L. Hoffmann

Harry Pratter Professor of Law
Indiana University Maurer School of Law

Debra A. Livingston

United States Circuit Judge, Second Circuit
Paul J. Kellner Professor of Law
Columbia University

Andrew D. Leipold

Edwin M. Adams Professor and Director,
Program in Criminal Law & Procedure
University of Illinois

Published by Wolters Kluwer Law & Business in New York.

Wolters Kluwer Law & Business serves customers worldwide with CCH, Aspen Publishers, and Kluwer Law International products. (www.wolterskluwerlb.com)

To contact Customer Service, e-mail customer.service@wolterskluwer.com, call 1-800-234-1660, fax 1-800-901-9075, or mail correspondence to:

Wolters Kluwer Law & Business
Attn: Order Department
PO Box 990
Frederick, MD 21705

Printed in the United States of America.

1 2 3 4 5 6 7 8 9 0

ISBN 978-1-4548-4166-1

Library of Congress Cataloging-in-Publication Data
Comprehensive criminal procedure / Ronald Jay Allen . . . [et al.]. — 3rd ed.
        p. cm.
    Includes bibliographical references and index.
    ISBN 978-0-7355-8778-6 (casebook)
    1. Criminal procedure — United States — Cases. 2. Criminal justice, Administration of — United States — Cases. I. Allen, Ronald J. (Ronald Jay), 1948-

KF9618.C66 2011
345.73'05 — dc22

                                                                    2010053400

About Wolters Kluwer Law & Business

Wolters Kluwer Law & Business is a leading global provider of intelligent information and digital solutions for legal and business professionals in key specialty areas, and respected educational resources for professors and law students. Wolters Kluwer Law & Business connects legal and business professionals as well as those in the education market with timely, specialized authoritative content and information-enabled solutions to support success through productivity, accuracy and mobility.

Serving customers worldwide, Wolters Kluwer Law & Business products include those under the Aspen Publishers, CCH, Kluwer Law International, Loislaw, ftwilliam. com and MediRegs family of products.

CCH products have been a trusted resource since 1913, and are highly regarded resources for legal, securities, antitrust and trade regulation, government contracting, banking, pension, payroll, employment and labor, and healthcare reimbursement and compliance professionals.

Aspen Publishers products provide essential information to attorneys, business professionals and law students. Written by preeminent authorities, the product line offers analytical and practical information in a range of specialty practice areas from securities law and intellectual property to mergers and acquisitions and pension/benefits. Aspen's trusted legal education resources provide professors and students with high-quality, up-to-date and effective resources for successful instruction and study in all areas of the law.

Kluwer Law International products provide the global business community with reliable international legal information in English. Legal practitioners, corporate counsel and business executives around the world rely on Kluwer Law journals, looseleafs, books, and electronic products for comprehensive information in many areas of international legal practice.

Loislaw is a comprehensive online legal research product providing legal content to law firm practitioners of various specializations. Loislaw provides attorneys with the ability to quickly and efficiently find the necessary legal information they need, when and where they need it, by facilitating access to primary law as well as state-specific law, records, forms and treatises.

ftwilliam.com offers employee benefits professionals the highest quality plan documents (retirement, welfare and non-qualified) and government forms (5500/ PBGC, 1099 and IRS) software at highly competitive prices.

MediRegs products provide integrated health care compliance content and software solutions for professionals in healthcare, higher education and life sciences, including professionals in accounting, law and consulting.

Wolters Kluwer Law & Business, a division of Wolters Kluwer, is headquartered in New York. Wolters Kluwer is a market-leading global information services company focused on professionals.

Contents

PART FOUR   THE ADJUDICATION PROCESS

Contents

Table of Cases

Italics indicate principal cases.

PART TWO

THE RIGHT TO COUNSEL— THE LINCHPIN OF CONSTITUTIONAL PROTECTION

Chapter 3

The Right to Counsel and Other Assistance

A. The Constitutional Requirements

1. The Right to the Assistance of Counsel at Trial

Insert the following paragraph at the end of Note 5 on page 146:

In Southern Union Co. v. United States, 132 S. Ct. 2344 (2012), the Court reaffirmed the view set forth in its earlier decision in International Union, United Mine Workers v. Bagwell, 512 U.S. 821 (1993), that a fine can be a sufficiently serious criminal sanction to trigger the constitutional right to a jury trial. Presumably, the same thing can be said with respect to the constitutional right to counsel. *Southern Union Co.* is discussed further in Chapter 15, infra, in connection with the application of Apprendi v. New Jersey, 530 U.S. 466 (2000), to criminal fines.

2. The Right to the Assistance of Counsel Before and After Trial

a. When Does the Right to Counsel Begin?

Insert the following note after Note 5 on page 166:

5a. Suppose a lineup or showup is highly suggestive, but there is no state action that caused the suggestiveness; does this violate due process? In Perry v. New Hampshire, 132 S. Ct. 716 (2012), the police responded to a report of a car break-in in an apartment parking lot. A suspect was found at the scene, and while one officer stayed with the suspect, a second officer went up into the apartments to speak to a witness. When the officer in the apartment asked the witness for a description of the perpetrator, the witness pointed out the window and said the suspect was the person standing next to the police officer in the parking lot. The suspect moved to suppress the witness's identification as being too suggestive, but the Supreme Court agreed there had been no due process violation. Justice Ginsburg's opinion for the Court reasoned that, consistent with other constitutional violations, some action by the police to make the lineup suggestive was necessary for a due process claim. The Court also noted that a contrary rule would render every eyewitness identification subject to potential challenge and judicial review, which was contrary to the normal rule that reliability decisions are to be made by juries, not judges.

b.   When Does the Right to Counsel End?

Insert the following note after Note 4 on page 199:

4a. Is an indigent who faces possible incarceration for civil contempt, in connection with an alleged violation of a court order to pay child support, constitutionally entitled to state-appointed counsel? The Court addressed this issue in Turner v. Rogers, 131 S. Ct. 2507 (2011). Justice Breyer, writing for a narrow five-Justice majority, noted that although the Sixth Amendment right to counsel applies to *criminal* contempts (other than summary proceedings), see United States v. Dixon, 509 U.S. 688, 696 (1993); Cooke v. United States, 267 U.S. 517, 537 (1925), that same right does not apply to *civil* proceedings, even where incarceration might result. But the Due Process Clause can be an alternative source for a right to counsel in such cases. Applying the multi-factor balancing test for due process set forth in Mathews v. Eldridge, see Medina v. California, 505 U.S. 437 (1992), supra at page 104, Justice Breyer concluded:

> The "private interest that will be affected" argues strongly for the right to counsel that Turner advocates. That interest consists of an indigent defendant's loss of personal liberty through imprisonment. . . .
> Given the importance of the interest at stake, it is obviously important to assure accurate decisionmaking in respect to the key "ability to pay" question. Moreover, the fact that ability to comply marks a dividing line between civil and criminal contempt . . . reinforces the need for accuracy. That is because an incorrect decision (wrongly classifying the contempt proceeding as civil) can increase the risk of wrongful incarceration by depriving the defendant of the procedural protections (including counsel) that the Constitution would demand in a criminal proceeding. *See, e.g., Dixon*, 509 U.S., at 696 (proof beyond a reasonable doubt, protection from double jeopardy). . . . And since 70% of child support arrears nationwide are owed by parents with either no reported income or income of $10,000 per year or less, the issue of ability to pay may arise fairly often. See E. Sorensen, L. Sousa, & S. Schaner, Assessing Child Support Arrears in Nine Large States and the Nation 22 (2007) (prepared by

The Urban Institute), online at *http://aspe.hhs.gov/hsp/07/assessing-CS-debt/report.pdf* (as visited June 16, 2011, and available in Clerk of Court's case file). . . .

On the other hand, the Due Process Clause does not always require the provision of counsel in civil proceedings where incarceration is threatened. . . . And in determining whether the Clause requires a right to counsel here, we must take account of opposing interests, as well as consider the probable value of "additional or substitute procedural safeguards." *Mathews*, supra, at 335.

Doing so, we find three related considerations that, when taken together, argue strongly against the Due Process Clause requiring the State to provide indigents with counsel in every proceeding of the kind before us.

First, the critical question likely at issue in these cases concerns, as we have said, the defendant's ability to pay. That question is often closely related to the question of the defendant's indigence. But when the right procedures are in place, indigence can be a question that in many — but not all — cases is sufficiently straightforward to warrant determination *prior* to providing a defendant with counsel, even in a criminal case. Federal law, for example, requires a criminal defendant to provide information showing that he is indigent, and therefore entitled to state-funded counsel, *before* he can receive that assistance. See 18 U.S.C. § 3006A(b).

Second, sometimes, as here, the person opposing the defendant at the hearing is not the government represented by counsel but the custodial parent *un*represented by counsel. See Dept. of Health and Human Services, Office of Child Support Enforcement, Understanding Child Support Debt: A Guide to Exploring Child Support Debt in Your State 5, 6 (2004) (51% of nationwide arrears, and 58% in South Carolina, are not owed to the government). The custodial parent, perhaps a woman with custody of one or more children, may be relatively poor, unemployed, and unable to afford counsel. Yet she may have encouraged the court to enforce its order through contempt. . . . And the proceeding is ultimately for her benefit.

A requirement that the State provide counsel to the noncustodial parent in these cases could create an asymmetry of representation. . . . Doing so could mean a degree of formality or delay that would unduly slow payment to those immediately in need. And, perhaps more important for present purposes, doing so could make the proceedings *less* fair overall, increasing the risk of a decision that would erroneously deprive a family of the support it is entitled to receive. The needs of such families play an important role in our analysis. . . .

Third, as the Solicitor General points out, there is available a set of "substitute procedural safeguards," *Mathews*, 424 U.S., at 335, which, if employed together, can significantly reduce the risk of an erroneous deprivation of liberty. They can do so, moreover, without incurring some of the drawbacks inherent in recognizing an automatic right to counsel. Those safeguards include (1) notice to the defendant that his "ability to pay" is a critical issue in the contempt proceeding; (2) the use of a form (or the equivalent) to elicit relevant financial information; (3) an opportunity at the hearing for the defendant to respond to statements and questions about his financial status, (*e.g.*, those triggered by his responses on the form); and (4) an express finding by the court that the defendant has the ability to pay. See Tr. of Oral Arg. 26-27; Brief for United States as *Amicus Curiae* 23-25. In presenting these alternatives, the Government draws upon considerable experience in helping to manage statutorily mandated federal-state efforts to enforce child support orders. It does not claim that they are the only possible alternatives, and this Court's cases suggest, for example, that sometimes assistance other than purely legal assistance (here, say, that of a neutral social worker) can prove constitutionally sufficient. . . . But the Government does claim that these alternatives can assure the "fundamental fairness" of the proceeding even where the State does not pay for counsel for an indigent defendant.

While recognizing the strength of Turner's arguments, we ultimately believe that the three considerations we have just discussed must carry the day. In our view, a categorical right to counsel in proceedings of the kind before us would carry with it disadvantages (in the form of unfairness and delay) that, in terms of ultimate fairness, would deprive it of significant superiority over the alternatives that we have mentioned. We consequently hold that the Due Process Clause does not *automatically* require the provision of counsel at civil contempt proceedings to an indigent individual who is subject to a child support order, even if that individual faces incarceration (for up to a year). In particular, that Clause does not require the provision of counsel where the opposing parent or other custodian (to whom support funds are owed) is not represented by counsel and the State provides alternative procedural safeguards equivalent to those we have mentioned (adequate notice of the importance of ability to pay, fair opportunity to present, and to dispute, relevant information, and court findings).

Turner, 131 S. Ct., at ___. Justice Breyer emphasized that a different result might obtain if the child support payment was owed to the state (an opposing party much more likely to be represented by counsel), or if the particular case was "unusually complex." Id. at ___.

B. *Effective Assistance of Counsel*

1. The Meaning of Effective Assistance

Insert the following paragraph at the end of this section on page 241:

And in Cullen v. Pinholster, 131 S. Ct. 1388 (2011), a narrow 5-4 majority of the Court reversed the Ninth Circuit and rejected a death-row inmate's claim of ineffective assistance of counsel based on his defense lawyer's alleged failure to investigate (and present) mitigating evidence. The Court reviewed in detail the state-court record of defense counsel's behavior, and concluded that — especially in light of the "doubly deferential" review standard applicable to ineffective-assistance claims in habeas corpus cases under AEDPA — the defense lawyer (1) pursued reasonable investigation of mitigation evidence, (2) acted reasonably in trying to exclude the prosecution's aggravation evidence rather than relying on dubious mitigation evidence, and (3) given the overall weakness of the defendant's case, chose a reasonable strategy based primarily on trying to evoke sympathy for the defendant's mother. The Court noted that the Ninth Circuit, after reviewing Terry Williams v. Taylor, Wiggins v. Smith, and Rompilla v. Beard, "drew from those cases a 'constitutional duty to investigate,' and the principle that '[i]t is prima facie ineffective assistance for counsel to "abandon[ ] their investigation of [the] petitioner's background after having acquired only rudimentary knowledge of his history from a narrow set of sources."'" This, according to the Court, was wrong:

> The Court of Appeals misapplied *Strickland* and overlooked "the constitutionally protected independence of counsel and . . . the wide latitude counsel must have in making tactical decisions." 466 U.S., at 689. Beyond the general requirement of reasonableness, "specific guidelines are not appropriate." Id., at 688. "No particular set of detailed rules for counsel's conduct can satisfactorily take account of the variety of circumstances faced by defense counsel or the range of legitimate decisions. . . ." Id., at 688-689. *Strickland* itself rejected the notion that the same investigation will be required in every case. Id., at 691 ("[C]ounsel has a duty to make reasonable investigations *or* to make a reasonable decision that makes particular investigations unnecessary." (emphasis added)). It is "[r]are" that constitutionally competent representation will require "any one technique or approach." Harrington v. Richter, 562 U.S. ___, ___, 131 S. Ct. 770 (2011). The Court of Appeals erred in attributing strict rules to this Court's recent case law.

Pinholster, 131 S. Ct., at 1406-1407.

SPECIAL EDITOR'S NOTE: The issue of ineffective assistance of counsel in the context of guilty pleas and plea bargaining has taken on much greater significance because of the Supreme Court's 2012 decisions in Missouri v. Frye and Lafler v. Cooper. For this reason, we assume that many teachers will want to cover this material, either as part of Chapter 3 (Right to Counsel), or as part of Chapter 13 (Guilty Pleas and Plea Bargaining). In this Supplement, we have included Missouri v. Frye and Lafler v. Cooper as main cases in Chapter 3, and the following instructions are meant for teachers who want to cover the new cases as part of Chapter 3. Teachers who want to cover the new cases as part of Chapter 3 may also want to incorporate the main case of Hill v. Lockhart, which now appears in Chapter 13 of the main volume, at pages 1251-1254, in place of Note 4 on page 235.

Insert the following new heading and materials after the end of Section 1 on page 241, and renumber Section 2 on page 241 as Section 3. Move the content of Notes 4, 5 (as revised below), and 6 on pages 235-238 to the beginning of the new Section 2, and renumber Note 7 on page 238 as Note 4. Replace the last paragraph of Note 5 with the following:

The Court remanded for a determination of whether or not Padilla suffered *Strickland* prejudice as a result of his attorney's mistaken advice. On remand, the Kentucky Court of Appeals found that Mr. Padilla had indeed been prejudiced, and vacated his conviction. 381 S.W.3d 322 (2012).

The importance of the immigration consequences on the defendant's decision to plead guilty — the deficient performance question in *Padilla* — is so great that the Federal Rules of Criminal Procedure were amended in 2013 to require district judges to inform a defendant that if he is not a U.S. citizen, a guilty plea could result in removal, denial of citizenship, and exclusion from the U.S. in the future. See Rule 11(b)(1)(O).

2.   Effective Assistance and Plea Bargaining

Insert the content of Notes 4, 5, and 6 on pages 235-238 here.

What about the flip side of *Hill* and *Padilla*? What about a case in which the defendant, due to poor advice from his defense lawyer, rejects a plea bargain offered by the prosecution and then later gets convicted, either after a trial or pursuant to a subsequent (but less favorable) plea bargain? Can this be a basis for a successful *Strickland* claim of ineffective assistance of counsel?

Lower courts split on this issue for a number of years. In 2012, the Supreme Court finally weighed in on the issue when it decided the companion cases of Missouri v. Frye and Lafler v. Cooper. Unfortunately, these two decisions raised at least as many new and difficult questions as they answered, and the Court explicitly acknowledged as much. Once again, as with Crawford v. Washington (which dramatically altered the application of the Confrontation Clause to hearsay evidence, see Chapter 14) and Apprendi v. New Jersey (which dramatically changed the constitutional rules applicable to criminal sentencing, see Chapter 15), we now face an extended period of uncertainty and instability in constitutional criminal procedure law, as lower courts struggle to respond and adapt to *Frye* and *Cooper*.

In reading these two companion cases, it is important for you to understand that — notwithstanding the pagination of the two cases — the Court majority treated *Frye* as the lead case, and then treated *Cooper* as a further iteration of the ruling in *Frye*. However, Justice Scalia — author of the lead dissents in both cases — treated them in the opposite order. Thus, Justice Scalia's principal dissent appears in the *Cooper* case, and his *Frye* dissent incorporates and builds upon his *Cooper* dissent. Given this anomaly, we strongly suggest reading the opinions in the following order: (1) the *Frye* majority opinion; (2) the *Cooper* majority opinion; (3) Justice Scalia's *Cooper* dissent; (4) Justice Alito's *Cooper* dissent; and, finally, (5) Justice Scalia's *Frye* dissent.

MISSOURI v. FRYE

Certiorari to the Court of Appeals of Missouri, Western District

132 S. Ct. 1399 (2012)

JUSTICE KENNEDY delivered the opinion of the Court.

The Sixth Amendment, applicable to the States by the terms of the Fourteenth Amendment, provides that the accused shall have the assistance of counsel in all criminal prosecutions. The right to counsel is the right to effective assistance of counsel. See Strickland v. Washington, 466 U.S. 668, 686 (1984). This case arises in the context of claimed ineffective assistance that led to the lapse of a prosecution offer of a plea bargain, a proposal that offered terms more lenient than the terms of the guilty plea entered later. The initial question is whether the constitutional right to counsel extends to the negotiation and consideration of plea offers that lapse or are rejected. If there is a right to effective assistance with respect to those offers, a further question is what a defendant must demonstrate in order to show that prejudice resulted from counsel's deficient performance. Other questions relating to ineffective assistance with respect to plea offers, including the question of proper remedies, are considered in a second case decided today. See Lafler v. Cooper, post, at 3-16.

I

[Here Justice Kennedy described the facts of the *Frye* case: Frye was charged with driving on a revoked license. Because he had three prior convictions for the same offense, he was subject to a felony charge with a possible maximum sentence of four years in prison. The prosecution sent a letter to Frye's defense lawyer, offering two possible plea bargains. One of those offers would have substituted a misdemeanor charge, with a recommendation of a 90-day sentence, for the felony charge. The defense lawyer never told Frye about the plea offers, and the offers expired. A few days before Frye's preliminary hearing, he was once again arrested for driving on a revoked license. Frye then pleaded guilty, with no plea bargain, to the original felony charge and was sentenced to three years in prison. In a state post-conviction motion, Frye alleged that his defense lawyer rendered him constitutionally ineffective assistance of counsel. Frye testified that he would have accepted the plea bargain to the misdemeanor charge if he had been told about it. The post-conviction court denied Frye's motion, but the Missouri Court of Appeals reversed, finding that Frye satisfied both the performance and prejudice prongs of *Strickland*. — EDS.]

II

A

It is well settled that the right to the effective assistance of counsel applies to certain steps before trial. The "Sixth Amendment guarantees a defendant the right to have counsel present at all 'critical' stages of the criminal proceedings." Montejo v. Louisiana, 556 U.S. 778, 786 (2009) (quoting United States v. Wade, 388 U.S. 218, 227-228 (1967)). Critical stages include arraignments, postindictment interrogations, postindictment lineups, and the entry of a guilty plea. See Hamilton v. Alabama, 368 U.S. 52 (1961) (arraignment); Massiah v. United States, 377 U.S. 201 (1964) (postindictment interrogation); *Wade*, supra (postindictment lineup); Argersinger v. Hamlin, 407 U.S. 25 (1972) (guilty plea).

With respect to the right to effective counsel in plea negotiations, a proper beginning point is to discuss two cases from this Court considering the role of counsel in advising a client about a plea offer and an ensuing guilty plea: Hill v. Lockhart, 474 U.S. 52 (1985); and Padilla v. Kentucky, 559 U.S. ___ (2010).

Hill established that claims of ineffective assistance of counsel in the plea bargain context are governed by the two-part test set forth in *Strickland*. See *Hill*, supra, at 57. As noted above, in Frye's case, the Missouri Court of Appeals, applying the two part test of *Strickland*, determined first that defense counsel had been ineffective and second that there was resulting prejudice.

In *Hill*, the decision turned on the second part of the *Strickland* test. There, a defendant who had entered a guilty plea claimed his counsel had misinformed him of the amount of time he would have to serve before he became eligible for parole. But the defendant had not alleged that, even if adequate advice and assistance had been given, he would have elected to plead not guilty and proceed to trial. Thus, the Court found that no prejudice from the inadequate advice had been shown or alleged. *Hill*, supra, at 60.

In *Padilla*, the Court again discussed the duties of counsel in advising a client with respect to a plea offer that leads to a guilty plea. *Padilla* held that a guilty plea, based on a plea offer, should be set aside because counsel misinformed the defendant of the immigration consequences of the conviction. The Court made clear that "the negotiation of a plea bargain is a critical phase of litigation for purposes of the Sixth Amendment right to effective assistance of counsel." 559 U.S., at ___. It also rejected the argument made by petitioner in this case that a knowing and voluntary plea supersedes errors by defense counsel. Cf. Brief for Respondent in Padilla v. Kentucky, O.T. 2009, No. 08-651, p. 27 (arguing Sixth Amendment's assurance of effective assistance "does not extend to collateral aspects of the prosecution" because "knowledge of the consequences that are collateral to the guilty plea is not a prerequisite to the entry of a knowing and intelligent plea").

In the case now before the Court the State, as petitioner, points out that the legal question presented is different from that in *Hill* and *Padilla*. In those cases the claim was that the prisoner's plea of guilty was invalid because counsel had provided incorrect advice pertinent to the plea. In the instant case, by contrast, the guilty plea that was accepted, and the plea proceedings concerning it in court, were all based on accurate advice and information from counsel. The challenge is not to the advice pertaining to the plea that was accepted but rather to the course of legal representation that preceded it with respect to other potential pleas and plea offers.

To give further support to its contention that the instant case is in a category different from what the Court considered in *Hill* and *Padilla*, the State urges that there is no right to a plea offer or a plea bargain in any event. See Weatherford v. Bursey, 429 U.S. 545, 561 (1977). It claims Frye therefore was not deprived of any legal benefit to which he was entitled. Under this view, any wrongful or mistaken action of counsel with respect to earlier plea offers is beside the point.

The State is correct to point out that *Hill* and *Padilla* concerned whether there was ineffective assistance leading to acceptance of a plea offer, a process involving a formal court appearance with the defendant and all counsel present. Before a guilty plea is entered the defendant's understanding of the plea and its consequences can be established on the record. This affords the State substantial protection against later claims that the plea was the result of inadequate advice. At the plea entry proceedings the trial court and all counsel have the opportunity to establish on the record that the defendant understands the process that led to any offer, the advantages and disadvantages of accepting it, and the sentencing consequences or possibilities that will ensue once a conviction is entered based upon the plea. See, e.g., Fed. Rule Crim. Proc.

11; Mo. Sup. Ct. Rule 24.02 (2004). *Hill* and *Padilla* both illustrate that, nevertheless, there may be instances when claims of ineffective assistance can arise after the conviction is entered. Still, the State, and the trial court itself, have had a substantial opportunity to guard against this contingency by establishing at the plea entry proceeding that the defendant has been given proper advice or, if the advice received appears to have been inadequate, to remedy that deficiency before the plea is accepted and the conviction entered.

When a plea offer has lapsed or been rejected, however, no formal court proceedings are involved. This underscores that the plea-bargaining process is often in flux, with no clear standards or timelines and with no judicial supervision of the discussions between prosecution and defense. Indeed, discussions between client and defense counsel are privileged. So the prosecution has little or no notice if something may be amiss and perhaps no capacity to intervene in any event. And, as noted, the State insists there is no right to receive a plea offer. For all these reasons, the State contends, it is unfair to subject it to the consequences of defense counsel's inadequacies, especially when the opportunities for a full and fair trial, or, as here, for a later guilty plea albeit on less favorable terms, are preserved.

The State's contentions are neither illogical nor without some persuasive force, yet they do not suffice to overcome a simple reality. Ninety-seven percent of federal convictions and ninety-four percent of state convictions are the result of guilty pleas. See Dept. of Justice, Bureau of Justice Statistics, Sourcebook of Criminal Justice Statistics Online, Table 5.22.2009, http://www.albany.edu/ sourcebook/pdf/t5222009.pdf (all Internet materials as visited Mar. 1, 2012, and available in Clerk of Court's case file); Dept. of Justice, Bureau of Justice Statistics, S. Rosenmerkel, M. Durose, & D. Farole, Felony Sentences in State Courts, 2006-Statistical Tables, p. 1 (NCJ226846, rev. Nov. 2010), http://bjs.ojp.usdoj.gov/content/pub/pdf/fssc06st.pdf; *Padilla*, supra, at ___, (recognizing pleas account for nearly 95% of all criminal convictions). The reality is that plea bargains have become so central to the administration of the criminal justice system that defense counsel have responsibilities in the plea bargain process, responsibilities that must be met to render the adequate assistance of counsel that the Sixth Amendment requires in the criminal process at critical stages. Because ours "is for the most part a system of pleas, not a system of trials," *Lafler*, post, at 11, it is insufficient simply to point to the guarantee of a fair trial as a backstop that inoculates any errors in the pretrial process. "To a large extent . . . horse trading [between prosecutor and defense counsel] determines who goes to jail and for how long. That is what plea bargaining is. It is not some adjunct to the criminal justice system; it *is* the criminal justice system." Scott & Stuntz, Plea Bargaining as Contract, 101 Yale L J. 1909, 1912 (1992). See also Barkow, Separation of Powers and the Criminal Law, 58 Stan. L. Rev. 989, 1034 (2006) ("[Defendants] who do take their case to trial and lose receive longer sentences than even Congress or the prosecutor might think appropriate, because the longer sentences exist on the books largely for bargaining purposes. This often results in individuals who accept a plea bargain receiving shorter sentences than other individuals who are less morally culpable but take a chance and go to trial" (footnote omitted)). In today's criminal justice system, therefore, the negotiation of a plea bargain, rather than the unfolding of a trial, is almost always the critical point for a defendant.

To note the prevalence of plea bargaining is not to criticize it. The potential to conserve valuable prosecutorial resources and for defendants to admit their crimes and receive more favorable terms at sentencing means that a plea agreement can benefit both parties. In order that these benefits can be realized, however, criminal defendants require effective counsel during plea negotiations. "Anything less . . . might deny a defendant 'effective representation by counsel at the only stage when legal aid and advice would help him.'" *Massiah*, 377 U.S., at 204 (quoting Spano v. New York, 360 U.S. 315, 326 (1959) (Douglas, J., concurring)).

B

The inquiry then becomes how to define the duty and responsibilities of defense counsel in the plea bargain process. This is a difficult question. "The art of negotiation is at least as nuanced as the art of trial advocacy and it presents questions farther removed from immediate judicial supervision." Premo v. Moore, 562 U.S. ___, ___ (2011). Bargaining is, by its nature, defined to a substantial degree by personal style. The alternative courses and tactics in negotiation are so individual that it may be neither prudent nor practicable to try to elaborate or define detailed standards for the proper discharge of defense counsel's participation in the process. Cf. ibid.

This case presents neither the necessity nor the occasion to define the duties of defense counsel in those respects, however. Here the question is whether defense counsel has the duty to communicate the terms of a formal offer to accept a plea on terms and conditions that may result in a lesser sentence, a conviction on lesser charges, or both.

This Court now holds that, as a general rule, defense counsel has the duty to communicate formal offers from the prosecution to accept a plea on terms and conditions that may be favorable to the accused. Any exceptions to that rule need not be explored here, for the offer was a formal one with a fixed expiration date. When defense counsel allowed the offer to expire without advising the defendant or allowing him to consider it, defense counsel did not render the effective assistance the Constitution requires.

Though the standard for counsel's performance is not determined solely by reference to codified standards of professional practice, these standards can be important guides. The American Bar Association recommends defense counsel "promptly communicate and explain to the defendant all plea offers made by the prosecuting attorney," ABA Standards for Criminal Justice, Pleas of Guilty 14-3.2(a) (3d ed. 1999), and this standard has been adopted by numerous state and federal courts over the last 30 years. . . . The standard for prompt communication and consultation is also set out in state bar professional standards for attorneys. See, e.g., Fla. Rule Regulating Bar 4-1.4 (2008); Ill. Rule Prof. Conduct 1.4 (2011); Kan. Rule Prof. Conduct 1.4 (2010); Ky. Sup. Ct. Rule 3.130, Rule Prof. Conduct 1.4 (2011); Mass. Rule Prof. Conduct 1.4 (2011-2012); Mich. Rule Prof. Conduct 1.4 (2011).

The prosecution and the trial courts may adopt some measures to help ensure against late, frivolous, or fabricated claims after a later, less advantageous plea offer has been accepted or after a trial leading to conviction with resulting harsh consequences. First, the fact of a formal offer means that its terms and its processing can be documented so that what took place in the negotiation process becomes more clear if some later inquiry turns on the conduct of earlier pretrial negotiations. Second, States may elect to follow rules that all offers must be in writing, again to ensure against later misunderstandings or fabricated charges. See N.J. Ct. Rule 3:9-1(b) (2012) ("Any plea offer to be made by the prosecutor shall be in writing and forwarded to the defendant's attorney"). Third, formal offers can be made part of the record at any subsequent plea proceeding or before a trial on the merits, all to ensure that a defendant has been fully advised before those further proceedings commence. At least one State often follows a similar procedure before trial. See Brief for National Association of Criminal Defense Lawyers et al. as Amici Curiae 20 (discussing hearings in Arizona conducted pursuant to State v. Donald, 198 Ariz. 406, 10 P.3d 1193 (App. 2000)). . . .

Here defense counsel did not communicate the formal offers to the defendant. As a result of that deficient performance, the offers lapsed.

Under *Strickland*, the question then becomes what, if any, prejudice resulted from the breach of duty.

C

To show prejudice from ineffective assistance of counsel where a plea offer has lapsed or been rejected because of counsel's deficient performance, defendants must demonstrate a reasonable probability they would have accepted the earlier plea offer had they been afforded effective assistance of counsel. Defendants must also demonstrate a reasonable probability the plea would have been entered without the prosecution canceling it or the trial court refusing to accept it, if they had the authority to exercise that discretion under state law. To establish prejudice in this instance, it is necessary to show a reasonable probability that the end result of the criminal process would have been more favorable by reason of a plea to a lesser charge or a sentence of less prison time. Cf. Glover v. United States, 531 U.S. 198, 203 (2001) ("[A]ny amount of [additional] jail time has Sixth Amendment significance").

This application of *Strickland* to the instances of an uncommunicated, lapsed plea does nothing to alter the standard laid out in *Hill*. In cases where a defendant complains that ineffective assistance led him to accept a plea offer as opposed to proceeding to trial, the defendant will have to show "a reasonable probability that, but for counsel's errors, he would not have pleaded guilty and would have insisted on going to trial." *Hill*, 474 U.S., at 59. *Hill* was correctly decided and applies in the context in which it arose. *Hill* does not, however, provide the sole means for demonstrating prejudice arising from the deficient performance of counsel during plea negotiations. Unlike the defendant in *Hill*, Frye argues that with effective assistance he would have accepted an earlier plea offer (limiting his sentence to one year in prison) as opposed to entering an open plea (exposing him to a maximum sentence of four years' imprisonment). In a case, such as this, where a defendant pleads guilty to less favorable terms and claims that ineffective assistance of counsel caused him to miss out on a more favorable earlier plea offer, *Strickland*'s inquiry into whether "the result of the proceeding would have been different," 466 U.S., at 694, requires looking not at whether the defendant would have proceeded to trial absent ineffective assistance but whether he would have accepted the offer to plead pursuant to the terms earlier proposed.

In order to complete a showing of *Strickland* prejudice, defendants who have shown a reasonable probability they would have accepted the earlier plea offer must also show that, if the prosecution had the discretion to cancel it or if the trial court had the discretion to refuse to accept it, there is a reasonable probability neither the prosecution nor the trial court would have prevented the offer from being accepted or implemented. This further showing is of particular importance because a defendant has no right to be offered a plea, see *Weatherford*, 429 U.S., at 561, nor a federal right that the judge accept it, Santobello v. New York, 404 U.S. 257, 262 (1971). In at least some States, including Missouri, it appears the prosecution has some discretion to cancel a plea agreement to which the defendant has agreed, see, e.g., 311 S.W.3d, at 359 (case below); Ariz. Rule Crim. Proc. 17.4(b) (Supp. 2011). The Federal Rules, some state rules including in Missouri, and this Court's precedents give trial courts some leeway to accept or reject plea agreements, see Fed. Rule Crim. Proc. 11(c)(3); see Mo. Sup. Ct. Rule 24.02(d)(4); Boykin v. Alabama, 395 U.S. 238, 243-244 (1969). It can be assumed that in most jurisdictions prosecutors and judges are familiar with the boundaries of acceptable plea bargains and sentences. So in most instances it should not be difficult to make an objective assessment as to whether or not a particular fact or intervening circumstance would suffice, in the normal course, to cause prosecutorial withdrawal or judicial nonapproval of a plea bargain. The determination that there is or is not a reasonable probability that the outcome of the proceeding would have been different absent counsel's errors can be conducted within that framework.

III

These standards must be applied to the instant case. As regards the deficient performance prong of *Strickland*, the Court of Appeals found the "record is void of *any* evidence of any effort by trial counsel to communicate the [formal] Offer to Frye during the Offer window, let alone any evidence that Frye's conduct interfered with trial counsel's ability to do so." 311 S.W.3d, at 356. On this record, it is evident that Frye's attorney did not make a meaningful attempt to inform the defendant of a written plea offer before the offer expired. See supra, at 2. The Missouri Court of Appeals was correct that "counsel's representation fell below an objective standard of reasonableness." *Strickland*, supra, at 688.

The Court of Appeals erred, however, in articulating the precise standard for prejudice in this context. As noted, a defendant in Frye's position must show not only a reasonable probability that he would have accepted the lapsed plea but also a reasonable probability that the prosecution would have adhered to the agreement and that it would have been accepted by the trial court. Frye can show he would have accepted the offer, but there is strong reason to doubt the prosecution and the trial court would have permitted the plea bargain to become final.

There appears to be a reasonable probability Frye would have accepted the prosecutor's original offer of a plea bargain if the offer had been communicated to him, because he pleaded guilty to a more serious charge, with no promise of a sentencing recommendation from the prosecutor. It may be that in some cases defendants must show more than just a guilty plea to a charge or sentence harsher than the original offer. For example, revelations between plea offers about the strength of the prosecution's case may make a late decision to plead guilty insufficient to demonstrate, without further evidence, that the defendant would have pleaded guilty to an earlier, more generous plea offer if his counsel had reported it to him. Here, however, that is not the case. The Court of Appeals did not err in finding Frye's acceptance of the less favorable plea offer indicated that he would have accepted the earlier (and more favorable) offer had he been apprised of it; and there is no need to address here the showings that might be required in other cases.

The Court of Appeals failed, however, to require Frye to show that the first plea offer, if accepted by Frye, would have been adhered to by the prosecution and accepted by the trial court. Whether the prosecution and trial court are required to do so is a matter of state law, and it is not the place of this Court to settle those matters. The Court has established the minimum requirements of the Sixth Amendment as interpreted in *Strickland*, and States have the discretion to add procedural protections under state law if they choose. A State may choose to preclude the prosecution from withdrawing a plea offer once it has been accepted or perhaps to preclude a trial court from rejecting a plea bargain. In Missouri, it appears "a plea offer once accepted by the defendant can be withdrawn without recourse" by the prosecution. 311 S.W.3d, at 359. The extent of the trial court's discretion in Missouri to reject a plea agreement appears to be in some doubt. Compare id., at 360, with Mo. Sup. Ct. Rule 24.02(d)(4).

We remand for the Missouri Court of Appeals to consider these state-law questions, because they bear on the federal question of *Strickland* prejudice. If, as the Missouri court stated here, the prosecutor could have canceled the plea agreement, and if Frye fails to show a reasonable probability the prosecutor would have adhered to the agreement, there is no *Strickland* prejudice. Likewise, if the trial court could have refused to accept the plea agreement, and if Frye fails to show a reasonable probability the trial court would have accepted the plea, there is no *Strickland* prejudice. In this case, given Frye's new offense for driving without a license on December 30, 2007, there is reason to doubt that the prosecution would have adhered to the agreement or that the trial court would have accepted it at the January 4, 2008, hearing, unless they were required by state law to do so.

It is appropriate to allow the Missouri Court of Appeals to address this question in the first instance. The judgment of the Missouri Court of Appeals is vacated, and the case is remanded for further proceedings not inconsistent with this opinion.

JUSTICE SCALIA, with whom CHIEF JUSTICE ROBERTS, JUSTICE THOMAS, and JUSTICE ALITO join, dissenting.

This is a companion case to Lafler v. Cooper, post, p.___. The principal difference between the cases is that the fairness of the defendant's conviction in *Lafler* was established by a full trial and jury verdict, whereas Frye's conviction here was established by his own admission of guilt, received by the court after the usual colloquy that assured it was voluntary and truthful. In *Lafler* all that could be said (and as I discuss there it was quite enough) is that the fairness of the conviction was clear, though a unanimous jury finding beyond a reasonable doubt can sometimes be wrong. Here it can be said not only that the process was fair, but that the defendant acknowledged the correctness of his conviction. Thus, as far as the reasons for my dissent are concerned, this is an a fortiori case. I will not repeat here the constitutional points that I discuss at length in *Lafler*, but I will briefly apply those points to the facts here and comment upon a few statements in the Court's analysis.

Galin Frye's attorney failed to inform him about a plea offer, and Frye ultimately pleaded guilty without the benefit of a deal. Counsel's mistake did not deprive Frye of any substantive or procedural right; only of the opportunity to accept a plea bargain to which he had no entitlement in the first place. So little entitlement that, had he known of and accepted the bargain, the prosecution would have been able to withdraw it right up to the point that his guilty plea pursuant to the bargain was accepted. See 311 S.W.3d 350, 359, and n. 4 (Mo. App. 2010).

The Court acknowledges, moreover, that Frye's conviction was untainted by attorney error: "[T]he guilty plea that was accepted, and the plea proceedings concerning it in court, were all based on accurate advice and information from counsel." Ante, at 5. Given the "ultimate focus" of our ineffective-assistance cases on "the fundamental fairness of the proceeding whose result is being challenged," Strickland v. Washington, 466 U.S. 668, 696 (1984), that should be the end of the matter. Instead, here, as in *Lafler*, the Court mechanically applies an outcome-based test for prejudice, and mistakes the possibility of a different result for constitutional injustice. As I explain in *Lafler*, post, p. ___ (dissenting opinion), that approach is contrary to our precedents on the right to effective counsel, and for good reason.

The Court announces its holding that "as a general rule, defense counsel has the duty to communicate formal offers from the prosecution" as though that resolves a disputed point; in reality, however, neither the State nor the Solicitor General argued that counsel's performance here was adequate. Ante, at 9. The only issue was whether the inadequacy deprived Frye of his constitutional right to a fair trial. In other cases, however, it will not be so clear that counsel's plea-bargaining skills, which must now meet a constitutional minimum, are adequate. "[H]ow to define the duty and responsibilities of defense counsel in the plea bargain process," the Court acknowledges, "is a difficult question," since "[b]argaining is, by its nature, defined to a substantial degree by personal style." Ante, at 8. Indeed. What if an attorney's "personal style" is to establish a reputation as a hard bargainer by, for example, advising clients to proceed to trial rather than accept anything but the most favorable plea offers? It seems inconceivable that a lawyer could compromise his client's *constitutional rights* so that he can secure better deals for other clients in the future; does a hard-bargaining "personal style" now violate the Sixth Amendment? The Court ignores such difficulties, however, since "[t]his case presents neither the necessity nor the occasion to define the duties of defense counsel in those respects." Ante, at 8. Perhaps not. But it does present the necessity of confronting the serious difficulties that will be created by constitutionalization of the plea-bargaining process. It will not do simply to announce that they will be solved in the sweet by-and-by.

While the inadequacy of counsel's performance in this case is clear enough, whether it was prejudicial (in the sense that the Court's new version of *Strickland* requires) is not. The Court's description of how that question is to be answered on remand is alone enough to show how unwise it is to constitutionalize the plea-bargaining process. Prejudice is to be determined, the Court tells us, by a process of retrospective crystal-ball gazing posing as legal analysis. First of all, of course, we must estimate whether the defendant *would have accepted* the earlier plea bargain. Here that seems an easy question, but as the Court acknowledges, ante, at 14, it will not always be. Next, since Missouri, like other States, permits accepted plea offers to be withdrawn by the prosecution (a reality which alone should suffice, one would think, to demonstrate that Frye had no entitlement to the plea bargain), we must estimate whether the prosecution *would have withdrawn* the plea offer. And finally, we must estimate whether the trial court *would have approved* the plea agreement. These last two estimations may seem easy in the present case, since Frye committed a new infraction before the hearing at which the agreement would have been presented; but they assuredly will not be easy in the mine run of cases.

The Court says "[i]t can be assumed that in most jurisdictions prosecutors and judges are familiar with the boundaries of acceptable plea bargains and sentences." Ante, at 13. Assuredly it can, just as it can be assumed that the sun rises in the west; but I know of no basis for the assumption. Virtually no cases deal with the standards for a prosecutor's withdrawal from a plea agreement beyond stating the general rule that a prosecutor may withdraw any time prior to, but not after, the entry of a guilty plea or other action constituting detrimental reliance on the defendant's part. See, e.g., United States v. Kuchinski, 469 F.3d 853, 857-858 (CA9 2006). And cases addressing trial courts' authority to accept or reject plea agreements almost universally observe that a trial court enjoys broad discretion in this regard. See, e.g., Missouri v. Banks, 135 S.W.3d 497, 500 (Mo. App. 2004) (trial court abuses its discretion in rejecting a plea only if the decision "is so arbitrary and unreasonable that it shocks the sense of justice and indicates a lack of careful consideration" (internal quotation marks omitted)). Of course after today's opinions there will be cases galore, so the Court's *assumption* would better be cast as an optimistic *prediction* of the certainty that will emerge, many years hence, from our newly created constitutional field of plea-bargaining law. Whatever the "boundaries" ultimately devised (if that were possible), a vast amount of discretion will still remain, and it is extraordinary to make a defendant's constitutional rights depend upon a series of retrospective mind-readings as to how that discretion, in prosecutors and trial judges, *would have been* exercised.

The plea-bargaining process is a subject worthy of regulation, since it is the means by which most criminal convictions are obtained. It happens not to be, however, a subject covered by the Sixth Amendment, which is concerned not with the fairness of bargaining but with the fairness of conviction. "The Constitution . . . is not an all-purpose tool for judicial construction of a perfect world; and when we ignore its text in order to make it that, we often find ourselves swinging a sledge where a tack hammer is needed." Padilla v. Kentucky, 559 U.S. ___, ___ (2010) (Scalia, J., dissenting). In this case and its companion, the Court's sledge may require the reversal of perfectly valid, eminently just, convictions. A legislature could solve the problems presented by these cases in a much more precise and efficient manner. It might begin, for example, by penalizing the attorneys who made such grievous errors. That type of sub-constitutional remedy is not available to the Court, which is limited to penalizing (almost) everyone else by reversing valid convictions or sentences. Because that result is inconsistent with the Sixth Amendment and decades of our precedent, I respectfully dissent.

LAFLER v. COOPER
Certiorari to the United States Court of Appeals for the Sixth Circuit
132 S. Ct. 1376 (2012)

JUSTICE KENNEDY delivered the opinion of the Court.

In this case, as in Missouri v. Frye, also decided today, a criminal defendant seeks a remedy when inadequate assistance of counsel caused nonacceptance of a plea offer and further proceedings led to a less favorable outcome. In *Frye*, defense counsel did not inform the defendant of the plea offer; and after the offer lapsed the defendant still pleaded guilty, but on more severe terms. Here, the favorable plea offer was reported to the client but, on advice of counsel, was rejected. In *Frye* there was a later guilty plea. Here, after the plea offer had been rejected, there was a full and fair trial before a jury. After a guilty verdict, the defendant received a sentence harsher than that offered in the rejected plea bargain. The instant case comes to the Court with the concession that counsel's advice with respect to the plea offer fell below the standard of adequate assistance of counsel guaranteed by the Sixth Amendment, applicable to the States through the Fourteenth Amendment.

I

[Here Justice Kennedy described the facts of the *Cooper* case: Cooper was charged with assault with intent to murder, along with three other offenses. The prosecution offered to dismiss two of the charges, and to recommend a sentence of 51 to 85 months in prison on the remaining two charges, in exchange for a guilty plea. Cooper communicated to the trial judge his willingness to accept the plea offer and admit his guilt. But he ultimately rejected the plea offer, allegedly because his defense counsel advised him that the prosecution would not be able to prove his intent to kill because the victim had been shot below the waist. At trial, Cooper was convicted on all counts and received a mandatory minimum sentence of 185 to 360 months in prison. In a post-conviction motion, Cooper alleged ineffective assistance of counsel in connection with his attorney's advice to reject the plea offer. The post-conviction court rejected the claim, and the Michigan Court of Appeals affirmed. Cooper then filed a federal habeas corpus petition raising the same claim of ineffective assistance. The federal district court found ineffective assistance, conditionally granted the writ of habeas corpus, and ordered specific performance of the original plea offer. The Sixth Circuit affirmed. — EDS.]

II

A

Defendants have a Sixth Amendment right to counsel, a right that extends to the plea-bargaining process. *Frye*, ante, at 8; see also Padilla v. Kentucky, 559 U.S. ___, ___ (2010) (slip op., at 16); *Hill*, supra, at 57. During plea negotiations defendants are "entitled to the effective assistance of competent counsel." McMann v. Richardson, 397 U.S. 759, 771 (1970). In *Hill*, the Court held "the two part Strickland v. Washington test applies to challenges to guilty pleas based on ineffective assistance of counsel." 474 U.S., at 58. The performance prong of *Strickland* requires a defendant to show "'that counsel's representation fell below an objective standard of reasonableness.'" 474 U.S., at 57 (quoting *Strickland*, 466 U.S., at 688). In this case all parties agree the performance of respondent's counsel was deficient when he advised respondent to reject the plea offer on the grounds he could not be convicted at trial. In light of this concession, it is unnecessary for this Court to explore the issue.

The question for this Court is how to apply *Strickland*'s prejudice test where ineffective assistance results in a rejection of the plea offer and the defendant is convicted at the ensuing trial.

B

To establish *Strickland* prejudice a defendant must "show that there is a reasonable probability that, but for counsel's unprofessional errors, the result of the proceeding would have been different." Id., at 694. In the context of pleas a defendant must show the outcome of the plea process would have been different with competent advice. See *Frye*, ante, at 12 (noting that *Strickland*'s inquiry, as applied to advice with respect to plea bargains, turns on "whether 'the result of the proceeding would have been different'" (quoting *Strickland*, supra, at 694)); see also *Hill*, 474 U.S., at 59 ("The . . . 'prejudice,' requirement . . . focuses on whether counsel's constitutionally ineffective performance affected the outcome of the plea process"). In *Hill*, when evaluating the petitioner's claim that ineffective assistance led to the improvident acceptance of a guilty plea, the Court required the petitioner to show "that there is a reasonable probability that, but for counsel's errors, [the defendant] would not have pleaded guilty and would have insisted on going to trial." Ibid.

In contrast to *Hill*, here the ineffective advice led not to an offer's acceptance but to its rejection. Having to stand trial, not choosing to waive it, is the prejudice alleged. In these circumstances a defendant must show that but for the ineffective advice of counsel there is a reasonable probability that the plea offer would have been presented to the court (i.e., that the defendant would have accepted the plea and the prosecution would not have withdrawn it in light of intervening circumstances), that the court would have accepted its terms, and that the conviction or sentence, or both, under the offer's terms would have been less severe than under the judgment and sentence that in fact were imposed. Here, the Court of Appeals for the Sixth Circuit agreed with that test for *Strickland* prejudice in the context of a rejected plea bargain. This is consistent with the test adopted and applied by other appellate courts without demonstrated difficulties or systemic disruptions. See 376 Fed. Appx., at 571-573; see also, e.g., United States v. Rodriguez Rodriguez, 929 F.2d 747, 753, n. 1 (CA1 1991) (per curiam); United States v. Gordon, 156 F.3d 376, 380-381 (CA2 1998) (per curiam); United States v. Day, 969 F.2d 39, 43-45 (CA3 1992); Beckham v. Wainwright, 639 F.2d 262, 267 (CA5 1981); Julian v. Bartley , 495 F.3d 487, 498-500 (CA7 2007); Wanatee v. Ault, 259 F.3d 700, 703-704 (CA8 2001); Nunes v. Mueller, 350 F.3d 1045, 1052-1053 (CA9 2003); Williams v. Jones, 571 F.3d 1086, 1094-1095 (CA10 2009) (per curiam); United States v. Gaviria, 116 F.3d 1498, 1512-1514, 325 U.S. App. D.C. 322 (CADC 1997) (per curiam).

Petitioner and the Solicitor General propose a different, far more narrow, view of the Sixth Amendment. They contend there can be no finding of *Strickland* prejudice arising from plea bargaining if the defendant is later convicted at a fair trial. The three reasons petitioner and the Solicitor General offer for their approach are unpersuasive.

First, petitioner and the Solicitor General claim that the sole purpose of the Sixth Amendment is to protect the right to a fair trial. Errors before trial, they argue, are not cognizable under the Sixth Amendment unless they affect the fairness of the trial itself. See Brief for Petitioner 12-21; Brief for United States as Amicus Curiae 10-12. The Sixth Amendment, however, is not so narrow in its reach. Cf. *Frye*, ante, at 11 (holding that a defendant can show prejudice under *Strickland* even absent a showing that the deficient performance precluded him from going to trial). The Sixth Amendment requires effective assistance of counsel at critical stages of a criminal proceeding. Its protections are not designed simply to protect the trial, even though "counsel's absence [in these stages] may derogate from the accused's right to a fair trial." United States v. Wade, 388 U.S. 218, 226 (1967). The constitutional guarantee applies to pretrial critical stages that are part of the whole course of a criminal proceeding, a proceeding in which defendants cannot be presumed to make critical decisions without counsel's advice. This is consistent, too, with the rule that defendants have a right to effective assistance of counsel on appeal, even though that cannot in any way be characterized as part of the trial. See, e.g., Halbert v. Michigan, 545 U.S. 605 (2005); Evitts v. Lucey, 469 U.S. 387 (1985). The precedents also establish that there exists a right to counsel during sentencing in both noncapital, see Glover v. United States, 531 U.S. 198, 203-204 (2001); Mempa v. Rhay, 389 U.S. 128 (1967), and capital cases, see Wiggins v. Smith, 539 U.S. 510, 538 (2003). Even though sentencing does not concern the defendant's guilt or innocence, ineffective assistance of counsel during a sentencing hearing can result in *Strickland* prejudice because "any amount of [additional] jail time has Sixth Amendment significance." *Glover*, supra, at 203.

The Court, moreover, has not followed a rigid rule that an otherwise fair trial remedies errors not occurring at the trial itself. It has inquired instead whether the trial cured the particular error at issue. Thus, in Vasquez v. Hillery, 474 U.S. 254 (1986), the deliberate exclusion of all African-Americans from a grand jury was prejudicial because a defendant may have been tried on charges that would not have been brought at all by a properly constituted grand jury. Id., at 263; see Ballard v. United States, 329 U.S. 187, 195 (1946) (dismissing an indictment returned by a grand jury from which women were excluded); see also Stirone v. United States, 361 U.S. 212, 218-219 (1960) (reversing a defendant's conviction because the jury may have based its verdict on acts not charged in the indictment). By contrast, in United States v. Mechanik, 475 U.S. 66 (1986), the complained-of error was a violation of a grand jury rule meant to ensure probable cause existed to believe a defendant was guilty. A subsequent trial, resulting in a verdict of guilt, cured this error. See id., at 72-73.

In the instant case respondent went to trial rather than accept a plea deal, and it is conceded this was the result of ineffective assistance during the plea negotiation process. Respondent received a more severe sentence at trial, one 3½ times more severe than he likely would have received by pleading guilty. Far from curing the error, the trial caused the injury from the error. Even if the trial itself is free from constitutional flaw, the defendant who goes to trial instead of taking a more favorable plea may be prejudiced from either a conviction on more serious counts or the imposition of a more severe sentence.

Second, petitioner claims this Court refined *Strickland*'s prejudice analysis in *Fretwell* to add an additional requirement that the defendant show that ineffective assistance of counsel led to his being denied a substantive or procedural right. Brief for Petitioner 12-13. The Court has rejected the argument that *Fretwell* modified *Strickland* before and does so again now. See Williams v. Taylor, 529 U.S. 362, 391 (2000) ("The Virginia Supreme Court erred in holding that our decision in Lockhart v. Fretwell, 506 U.S. 364 (1993), modified or in some way supplanted the rule set down in *Strickland*"); see also *Glover*, supra, at 203 ("The Court explained last Term [in *Williams*] that our holding in *Lockhart* does not supplant the *Strickland* analysis").

Fretwell could not show *Strickland* prejudice resulting from his attorney's failure to object to the use of a sentencing factor the Eighth Circuit had erroneously (and temporarily) found to be impermissible. *Fretwell*, 506 U.S., at 373. Because the objection upon which his ineffective-assistance-of-counsel claim was premised was meritless, Fretwell could not demonstrate an error entitling him to relief. The case presented the "unusual circumstance where the defendant attempts to demonstrate prejudice based on considerations that, as a matter of law, ought not inform the inquiry." Ibid. (O'Connor, J., concurring). See also ibid. (recognizing "[t]he determinative question—whether there is a reasonable probability that, but for counsel's unprofessional errors, the result of the proceeding would have been different—remains unchanged" (internal quotation marks and citation omitted)). It is for this same reason a defendant cannot show prejudice based on counsel's refusal to present perjured testimony, even if such testimony might have affected the outcome of the case. See Nix v. Whiteside, 475 U.S. 157, 175 (1986) (holding first that counsel's refusal to present perjured testimony breached no professional duty and second that it cannot establish prejudice under *Strickland*).

Both *Fretwell* and *Nix* are instructive in that they demonstrate "there are also situations in which it would be unjust to characterize the likelihood of a different outcome as legitimate 'prejudice,'" *Williams*, supra, at 391-392, because defendants would receive a windfall as a result of the application of an incorrect legal principle or a defense strategy outside the law. Here, however, the injured client seeks relief from counsel's failure to meet a valid legal standard, not from counsel's refusal to violate it. He maintains that, absent ineffective counsel, he would have accepted a plea offer for a sentence the prosecution evidently deemed consistent with the sound administration of criminal justice. The favorable sentence that eluded the defendant in the criminal proceeding appears to be the sentence he or others in his position would have received in the ordinary course, absent the failings of counsel. See Bibas, Regulating the Plea-Bargaining Market: From Caveat Emptor to Consumer Protection, 99 Cal. L. Rev. 1117, 1138 (2011) ("The expected posttrial sentence is imposed in only a few percent of cases. It is like the sticker price for cars: only an ignorant, ill-advised consumer would view full price as the norm and anything less a bargain"); see also *Frye*, ante, at 7-8. If a plea bargain has been offered, a defendant has the right to effective assistance of counsel in considering whether to accept it. If that right is denied, prejudice can be shown if loss of the plea opportunity led to a trial resulting in a conviction on more serious charges or the imposition of a more severe sentence.

It is, of course, true that defendants have "no right to be offered a plea . . . nor a federal right that the judge accept it." *Frye*, ante, at 12. In the circumstances here, that is beside the point. If no plea offer is made, or a plea deal is accepted by the defendant but rejected by the judge, the issue raised here simply does not arise. Much the same reasoning guides cases that find criminal defendants have a right to effective assistance of counsel in direct appeals even though the Constitution does not require States to provide a system of appellate review at all. See *Evitts*, 469 U.S. 387; see also Douglas v. California, 372 U.S. 353 (1963). As in those cases, "[w]hen a State opts to act in a field where its action has significant discretionary elements, it must nonetheless act in accord with the dictates of the Constitution." *Evitts*, supra, at 401.

Third, petitioner seeks to preserve the conviction obtained by the State by arguing that the purpose of the Sixth Amendment is to ensure "the reliability of [a] conviction following trial." Brief for Petitioner 13. This argument, too, fails to comprehend the full scope of the Sixth Amendment's protections; and it is refuted by precedent. *Strickland* recognized "[t]he benchmark for judging any claim of ineffectiveness must be whether counsel's conduct so undermined the proper function-ing of the adversarial process that the trial cannot be relied on as having produced a just result." 466 U.S., at 686. The goal of a just result is not divorced from the reliability of a conviction, see United States v. Cronic, 466 U.S. 648, 658 (1984); but here the question is not the fairness or reliability of the trial but the fairness and regularity of the processes that preceded it, which caused the defendant to lose benefits he would have received in the ordinary course but for counsel's ineffective assistance.

There are instances, furthermore, where a reliable trial does not fore-close relief when counsel has failed to assert rights that may have altered the outcome. In Kimmelman v. Morrison, 477 U.S. 365 (1986), the Court held that an attorney's failure to timely move to suppress evidence during trial could be grounds for federal habeas relief. The Court rejected the suggestion that the "failure to make a timely request for the exclusion of illegally seized evidence" could not be the basis for a Sixth Amendment violation because the evidence "is 'typically reliable and often the most probative information bearing on the guilt or innocence of the defendant.'" Id., at 379 (quoting Stone v. Powell, 428 U.S. 465, 490 (1976)). "The constitutional rights of criminal defendants," the Court observed, "are granted to the innocent and the guilty alike. Consequently, we decline to hold either that the guarantee of effective assistance of counsel belongs solely to the innocent or that it attaches only to matters affecting the determination of actual guilt." 477 U.S., at 380. The same logic applies here. The fact that respondent is guilty does not mean he was not entitled by the Sixth Amendment to effective assistance or that he suffered no prejudice from his attorney's deficient performance during plea bargaining.

In the end, petitioner's three arguments amount to one general contention: A fair trial wipes clean any deficient performance by defense counsel during plea bargaining. That position ignores the reality that criminal justice today is for the most part a system of pleas, not a system of trials. Ninety-seven percent of federal convictions and ninety-four percent of state convictions are the result of guilty pleas. See *Frye*, ante, at 7. As explained in *Frye*, the right to adequate assistance of counsel cannot be defined or enforced without taking account of the central role plea bargaining plays in securing convictions and determining sentences. Ibid. ("[I]t is insufficient simply to point to the guarantee of a fair trial as a backstop that inoculates any errors in the pretrial process").

C

Even if a defendant shows ineffective assistance of counsel has caused the rejection of a plea leading to a trial and a more severe sentence, there is the question of what constitutes an appropriate remedy. That question must now be addressed.

Sixth Amendment remedies should be "tailored to the injury suffered from the constitutional violation and should not unnecessarily infringe on competing interests." United States v. Morrison, 449 U.S. 361, 364 (1981). Thus, a remedy must "neutralize the taint" of a constitutional violation, id., at 365, while at the same time not grant a windfall to the defendant or needlessly squander the considerable resources the State properly invested in the criminal prosecution. See *Mechanik*, 475 U.S., at 72 ("The reversal of a conviction entails substantial social costs: it forces jurors, witnesses, courts, the prosecution, and the defendants to expend further time, energy, and other resources to repeat a trial that has already once taken place; victims may be asked to relive their disturbing experiences").

The specific injury suffered by defendants who decline a plea offer as a result of ineffective assistance of counsel and then receive a greater sentence as a result of trial can come in at least one of two forms. In some cases, the sole advantage a defendant would have received under the plea is a lesser sentence. This is typically the case when the charges that would have been admitted as part of the plea bargain are the same as the charges the defendant was convicted of after trial. In this situation the court may conduct an evidentiary hearing to determine whether the defendant has shown a reasonable probability that but for counsel's errors he would have accepted the plea. If the showing is made, the court may exercise discretion in determining whether the defendant should receive the term of imprisonment the government offered in the plea, the sentence he received at trial, or something in between.

In some situations it may be that resentencing alone will not be full redress for the constitutional injury. If, for example, an offer was for a guilty plea to a count or counts less serious than the ones for which a defendant was convicted after trial, or if a mandatory sentence confines a judge's sentencing discretion after trial, a resentencing based on the conviction at trial may not suffice. See, e.g., *Williams*, 571 F.3d, at 1088; Riggs v. Fairman, 399 F.3d 1179, 1181 (CA9 2005). In these circumstances, the proper exercise of discretion to remedy the constitutional injury may be to require the prosecution to reoffer the plea proposal. Once this has occurred, the judge can then exercise discretion in deciding whether to vacate the conviction from trial and accept the plea or leave the conviction undisturbed.

In implementing a remedy in both of these situations, the trial court must weigh various factors; and the boundaries of proper discretion need not be defined here. Principles elaborated over time in decisions of state and federal courts, and in statutes and rules, will serve to give more complete guidance as to the factors that should bear upon the exercise of the judge's discretion. At this point, however, it suffices to note two considerations that are of relevance.

First, a court may take account of a defendant's earlier expressed willingness, or unwillingness, to accept responsibility for his or her actions. Second, it is not necessary here to decide as a constitutional rule that a judge is required to prescind (that is to say disregard) any information concerning the crime that was discovered after the plea offer was made. The time continuum makes it difficult to restore the defendant and the prosecution to the precise positions they occupied prior to the rejection of the plea offer, but that baseline can be consulted in finding a remedy that does not require the prosecution to incur the expense of conducting a new trial.

Petitioner argues that implementing a remedy here will open the floodgates to litigation by defendants seeking to unsettle their convictions. See Brief for Petitioner 20. Petitioner's concern is misplaced. Courts have recognized claims of this sort for over 30 years, see supra, at 5, and yet there is no indication that the system is overwhelmed by these types of suits or that defendants are receiving windfalls as a result of strategically timed *Strickland* claims. See also *Padilla*, 559 U.S., at ___ ("We confronted a similar 'floodgates' concern in *Hill*," but "flood did not follow in that decision's wake"). In addition, the "prosecution and the trial courts may adopt some measures to help ensure against late, frivolous, or fabricated claims after a later, less advantageous plea offer has been accepted or after a trial leading to conviction." *Frye*, ante, at 10. See also ibid. (listing procedures currently used by various States). This, too, will help ensure against meritless claims.

III

The standards for ineffective assistance of counsel when a defendant rejects a plea offer and goes to trial must now be applied to this case. [Here Justice Kennedy concluded that the instant case was governed by the established legal rule set forth in Strickland v. Washington, and that the state court did not properly apply *Strickland* to the case, thus permitting a federal habeas court to review the state court's decision and provide appropriate relief. — Eds.]

Respondent has satisfied *Strickland*'s two-part test. Regarding performance, perhaps it could be accepted that it is unclear whether respondent's counsel believed respondent could not be convicted for assault with intent to murder as a matter of law because the shots hit [the victim] below the waist, or whether he simply thought this would be a persuasive argument to make to the jury to show lack of specific intent. And, as the Court of Appeals for the Sixth Circuit suggested, an erroneous strategic prediction about the outcome of a trial is not necessarily deficient performance. Here, however, the fact of deficient performance has been conceded by all parties. The case comes to us on that assumption, so there is no need to address this question.

As to prejudice, respondent has shown that but for counsel's deficient performance there is a reasonable probability he and the trial court would have accepted the guilty plea. See 376 Fed. Appx., at 571-572. In addition, as a result of not accepting the plea and being convicted at trial, respondent received a minimum sentence 3½ times greater than he would have received under the plea. The standard for ineffective assistance under *Strickland* has thus been satisfied.

As a remedy, the District Court ordered specific performance of the original plea agreement. The correct remedy in these circumstances, however, is to order the State to reoffer the plea agreement. Presuming respondent accepts the offer, the state trial court can then exercise its discretion in determining whether to vacate the convictions and resentence respondent pursuant to the plea agreement, to vacate only some of the convictions and resentence respondent accordingly, or to leave the convictions and sentence from trial undisturbed. See Mich. Ct. Rule 6.302(C)(3) (2011) ("If there is a plea agreement and its terms provide for the defendant's plea to be made in exchange for a specific sentence disposition or a prosecutorial sentence recommendation, the court may . . . reject the agreement"). Today's decision leaves open to the trial court how best to exercise that discretion in all the circumstances of the case.

The judgment of the Court of Appeals for the Sixth Circuit is vacated, and the case is remanded for further proceedings consistent with this opinion.

JUSTICE SCALIA, with whom JUSTICE THOMAS joins, and with whom CHIEF JUSTICE ROBERTS joins as to all but Part IV, dissenting.

"If a plea bargain has been offered, a defendant has the right to effective assistance of counsel in considering whether to accept it. If that right is denied, prejudice can be shown if loss of the plea opportunity led to a trial resulting in a conviction on more serious charges or the imposition of a more severe sentence." Ante, at 9.

"The inquiry then becomes how to define the duty and responsibilities of defense counsel in the plea bargain process. This is a difficult question. . . . Bargaining is, by its nature, defined to a substantial degree by personal style. . . . This case presents neither the necessity nor the occasion to define the duties of defense counsel in those respects. . . ." Missouri v. Frye, ante, at 8.

With those words from this and the companion case, the Court today opens a whole new field of constitutionalized criminal procedure: plea-bargaining law. The ordinary criminal process has become too long, too expensive, and unpredictable, in no small part as a consequence of an intricate federal Code of Criminal Procedure imposed on the States by this Court in pursuit of perfect justice. See Friendly, The Bill of Rights as a Code of Criminal Procedure, 53 Cal. L. Rev. 929 (1965). The Court now moves to bring perfection to the alternative in which prosecutors and defendants have sought relief. Today's opinions deal with only two aspects of counsel's plea-bargaining inadequacy, and leave other aspects (who knows what they might be?) to be worked out in further constitutional litigation that will burden the criminal process. And it would be foolish to think that "constitutional" rules governing *counsel's* behavior will not be followed by rules governing the *prosecution's* behavior in the plea-bargaining process that the Court today announces "'*is* the criminal justice system,'" *Frye*, ante, at 7 (quoting approvingly from Scott & Stuntz, Plea Bargaining as Contract, 101 Yale L.J. 1909, 1912 (1992) (hereinafter Scott)). Is it constitutional, for example, for the prosecution to withdraw a plea offer that has already been accepted? Or to withdraw an offer before the defense has had adequate time to consider and accept it? Or to make no plea offer at all, even though its case is weak — thereby excluding the defendant from "the criminal justice system"?

Anthony Cooper received a full and fair trial, was found guilty of all charges by a unanimous jury, and was given the sentence that the law prescribed. The Court nonetheless concludes that Cooper is entitled to some sort of habeas corpus relief (perhaps) because his attorney's allegedly incompetent advice regarding a plea offer *caused* him to receive a full and fair trial. That conclusion is foreclosed by our precedents. Even if it were not foreclosed, the constitutional right to effective plea-bargainers that it establishes is at least a new rule of law, which does not undermine the Michigan Court of Appeals' decision and therefore cannot serve as the basis for habeas relief. And the remedy the Court announces — namely, whatever the state trial court in its discretion prescribes, down to and including no remedy at all — is unheard-of and quite absurd for violation of a constitutional right. I respectfully dissent.

I

This case and its companion, Missouri v. Frye, raise relatively straightforward questions about the scope of the right to effective assistance of counsel. Our case law originally derived that right from the Due Process

Clause, and its guarantee of a fair trial, see United States v. Gonzalez-Lopez, 548 U.S. 140, 147 (2006), but the seminal case of Strickland v. Washington, 466 U.S. 668 (1984), located the right within the Sixth Amendment. As the Court notes, ante, at 6, the right to counsel does not begin at trial. It extends to "any stage of the prosecution, formal or informal, in court or out, where counsel's absence might derogate from the accused's right to a fair trial." United States v. Wade, 388 U.S. 218, 226 (1967). Applying that principle, we held that the "entry of a guilty plea, whether to a misdemeanor or a felony charge, ranks as a 'critical stage' at which the right to counsel adheres." Iowa v. Tovar, 541 U.S. 77, 81 (2004); see also Hill v. Lockhart, 474 U.S. 52, 58 (1985). And it follows from this that acceptance of a plea offer is a critical stage. That, and nothing more, is the point of the Court's observation in Padilla v. Kentucky, 559 U.S. ___, ___ (2010), that "the negotiation of a plea bargain is a critical phase of litigation for purposes of the Sixth Amendment right to effective assistance of counsel." The defendant in *Padilla* had accepted the plea bargain and pleaded guilty, abandoning his right to a fair trial; he was entitled to advice of competent counsel before he did so. The Court has never held that the rule articulated in *Padilla*, *Tovar*, and *Hill* extends to all aspects of plea negotiations, requiring not just advice of competent counsel before the defendant accepts a plea bargain and pleads guilty, but also the advice of competent counsel before the defendant rejects a plea bargain and stands on his constitutional right to a fair trial. The latter is a vast departure from our past cases, protecting not just the constitutionally prescribed right to a fair adjudication of guilt and punishment, but a judicially invented right to effective plea bargaining.

It is also apparent from *Strickland* that bad plea bargaining has nothing to do with ineffective assistance of counsel in the constitutional sense. *Strickland* explained that "[i]n giving meaning to the requirement [of effective assistance], . . . we must take its purpose—to ensure a fair trial—as the guide." 466 U.S., at 686. Since "the right to the effective assistance of counsel is recognized not for its own sake, but because of the effect it has on the ability of the accused to receive a fair trial," United States v. Cronic, 466 U.S. 648, 658 (1984), the "benchmark" inquiry in evaluating any claim of ineffective assistance is whether counsel's performance "so undermined the proper functioning of the adversarial process" that it failed to produce a reliably "just result." *Strickland*, 466 U.S., at 686. That is what *Strickland*'s requirement of "prejudice" consists of: Because the right to effective assistance has as its purpose the assurance of a fair trial, the right is not infringed unless counsel's mistakes call into question the basic justice of a defendant's conviction or sentence. That has been, until today, entirely clear. A defendant must show "that counsel's errors were so serious as to deprive the defendant of a fair trial, a trial whose result is reliable." Id., at 687. See also *Gonzalez-Lopez*, supra, at 147. Impairment of fair trial is how we distinguish between unfortunate attorney error and error of constitutional significance.[1]

To be sure, *Strickland* stated a rule of thumb for measuring prejudice which, applied blindly and out of context, could support the Court's holding today. . . . *Strickland* itself cautioned, however, that its test was not to be applied in a mechanical fashion, and that courts were not to divert their "ultimate focus" from "the fundamental fairness of the proceeding whose result is being challenged." Id., at 696. And until today we have followed that course. . . .

Those precedents leave no doubt about the answer to the question presented here. As the Court itself observes, a criminal defendant has no right to a plea bargain. Ante, at 9. "[T]here is no constitutional right to plea bargain; the prosecutor need not do so if he prefers to go to trial." Weatherford v. Bursey, 429 U.S. 545, 561 (1977). Counsel's mistakes in this case thus did not "deprive the defendant of a substantive or procedural right to which the law entitles him," Williams [v. Taylor, 529 U.S. 362,] 393 [(2000)]. Far from being "beside the point," ante, at 9, that is critical to correct application of our precedents. Like [Lockhart v.] Fretwell, [506 U.S. 364 (1993),] this case "concerns the unusual circumstance where the defendant attempts to demonstrate prejudice based on considerations that, as a matter of law, ought not inform the inquiry," 506 U.S., at 373 (O'Connor, J., concurring); he claims "that he might have been denied 'a right the law simply does not recognize,'" id., at 375 (same). *Strickland*, *Fretwell*, and *Williams* all instruct that the pure outcome-based test on which the Court relies is an erroneous measure of cognizable prejudice. In ignoring *Strickland*'s "ultimate focus . . . on the fundamental fairness of the proceeding whose result is being challenged," 466 U.S., at 696, the Court has lost the forest for the trees, leading it to accept what we have previously rejected, the "novel argument that constitutional rights are infringed by trying the defendant rather than accepting his plea of guilty." *Weatherford*, supra, at 561.

1. Rather than addressing the constitutional origins of the *right to effective counsel*, the Court responds to the broader claim (raised by no one) that "the sole purpose of the Sixth Amendment is to protect the right to a fair trial." . . . To destroy that straw man, the Court cites cases in which violations of rights *other* than the right to effective counsel — and, perplexingly, even rights found outside the Sixth Amendment and the Constitution entirely — were not cured by a subsequent trial. . . . Unlike the right to effective counsel, no showing of prejudice is required to make violations of the rights at issue in [such cases] complete. . . . Those cases are thus irrelevant to the question presented here, which is whether a defendant can establish *prejudice* under Strickland v. Washington, 466 U.S. 668 (1984), while conceding the fairness of his conviction, sentence, and appeal.

II

[Here, Justice Scalia argued that — even if the decision of the Michigan Court of Appeals was incorrect — that decision should not be subject to reversal by a federal court sitting in habeas, because the federal habeas corpus statute permits such a reversal only if the relevant state court decision was "contrary to, or involved an unreasonable application of, clearly established Federal law, as determined by the Supreme Court of the United States." 28 U.S.C. § 2254(d)(1). In Justice Scalia's view, the Michigan Court of Appeals faithfully interpreted and applied *Strickland's* performance and prejudice prongs, and thus its decision should have been insulated from federal habeas reversal. — EDS.]

III

It is impossible to conclude discussion of today's extraordinary opinion without commenting upon the remedy it provides for the unconstitutional conviction. It is a remedy unheard-of in American jurisprudence — and, I would be willing to bet, in the jurisprudence of any other country.

The Court requires Michigan to "reoffer the plea agreement" that was rejected because of bad advice from counsel. Ante, at 16. That would indeed be a powerful remedy — but for the fact that Cooper's acceptance of that reoffered agreement is not conclusive. Astoundingly, "the state trial court can then *exercise its discretion* in determining whether to vacate the convictions and resentence respondent pursuant to the plea agreement, to vacate only some of the convictions and resentence respondent accordingly, *or to leave the convictions and sentence from trial undisturbed.*" Ibid. (emphasis added).

Why, one might ask, require a "reoffer" of the plea agreement, and its acceptance by the defendant? If the district court finds (as a necessary element, supposedly, of *Strickland* prejudice) that Cooper *would have accepted* the original offer, and would thereby have avoided trial and conviction, why not skip the reoffer-and-reacceptance minuet and simply leave it to the discretion of the state trial court what the remedy shall be? The answer, of course, is camouflage. Trial courts, after all, *regularly* accept or reject plea agreements, so there seems to be nothing extraordinary about their accepting or rejecting the new one mandated by today's decision. But the acceptance or rejection of a plea agreement that has no status whatever under the United States Constitution is worlds apart from what this is: "discretionary" specification of a remedy for an unconstitutional criminal conviction.

To be sure, the Court asserts that there are "factors" which bear upon (and presumably limit) exercise of this discretion — factors that it is not prepared to specify in full, much less assign some determinative weight. "Principles elaborated over time in decisions of state and federal courts, and in statutes and rules" will (in the Court's rosy view) sort all that out. Ante, at 13. I find it extraordinary that "statutes and rules" can specify the remedy for a criminal defendant's unconstitutional conviction. Or that the remedy for an unconstitutional conviction should *ever* be subject *at all* to a trial judge's discretion. Or, finally, that the remedy could *ever* include no remedy at all.

I suspect that the Court's squeamishness in fashioning a remedy, and the incoherence of what it comes up with, is attributable to its realization, deep down, that there is no real constitutional violation here anyway. The defendant has been fairly tried, lawfully convicted, and properly sentenced, and *any* "remedy" provided for this will do nothing but undo the just results of a fair adversarial process.

IV

In many — perhaps most — countries of the world, American-style plea bargaining is forbidden in cases as serious as this one, even for the purpose of obtaining testimony that enables conviction of a greater malefactor, much less for the purpose of sparing the expense of trial. See, e.g., World Plea Bargaining 344, 363-366 (S. Thaman ed. 2010). In Europe, many countries adhere to what they aptly call the "legality principle" by requiring prosecutors to charge all prosecutable offenses, which is typically incompatible with the practice of charge-bargaining. See, e.g., id., at xxii; Langbein, Land Without Plea Bargaining: How the Germans Do It, 78 Mich. L. Rev. 204, 210-211 (1979) (describing the "Legalitätsprinzip," or rule of compulsory prosecution, in Germany). Such a system reflects an admirable belief that the law is the law, and those who break it should pay the penalty provided.

In the United States, we have plea bargaining aplenty, but until today it has been regarded as a necessary evil. It presents grave risks of prosecutorial overcharging that effectively compels an innocent defendant to avoid massive risk by pleading guilty to a lesser offense; and for guilty defendants it often — perhaps usually — results in a sentence well below what the law prescribes for the actual crime. But even so, we accept plea bargaining because many believe that without it our long and expensive process of criminal trial could not sustain the burden imposed on it, and our system of criminal justice would grind to a halt. See, e.g.,

Alschuler, Plea Bargaining and Its History, 79 Colum. L. Rev. 1, 38 (1979).

Today, however, the Supreme Court of the United States elevates plea bargaining from a necessary evil to a constitutional entitlement. It is no longer a somewhat embarrassing adjunct to our criminal justice system; rather, as the Court announces in the companion case to this one, "'it *is* the criminal justice system.'" *Frye*, ante, at 7 (quoting approvingly from Scott 1912). Thus, even though there is no doubt that the respondent here is guilty of the offense with which he was charged; even though he has received the exorbitant gold standard of American justice — a full-dress criminal trial with its innumerable constitutional and statutory limitations upon the evidence that the prosecution can bring forward, and (in Michigan as in most States) the requirement of a unanimous guilty verdict by impartial jurors; the Court says that his conviction is invalid because he was deprived of his *constitutional entitlement* to plea-bargain.

I am less saddened by the outcome of this case than I am by what it says about this Court's attitude toward criminal justice. The Court today embraces the sporting chance theory of criminal law, in which the State functions like a conscientious casino-operator, giving each player a fair chance to beat the house, that is, to serve less time than the law says he deserves. And when a player is excluded from the tables, his *constitutional rights* have been violated. I do not subscribe to that theory. No one should, least of all the Justices of the Supreme Court.

* * *

Today's decision upends decades of our cases, violates a federal statute, and opens a whole new boutique of constitutional jurisprudence ("plea-bargaining law") without even specifying the remedies the boutique offers. The result in the present case is the undoing of an adjudicatory process that worked *exactly* as it is supposed to. Released felon Anthony Cooper, who shot repeatedly and gravely injured a woman named Kali Mundy, was tried and convicted for his crimes by a jury of his peers, and given a punishment that Michigan's elected representatives have deemed appropriate. Nothing about that result is unfair or unconstitutional. To the contrary, it is wonderfully just, and infinitely superior to the trial-by-bargain that today's opinion affords constitutional status. I respectfully dissent.

JUSTICE ALITO, dissenting

... The weakness in the Court's analysis is highlighted by its opaque discussion of the remedy that is appropriate when a plea offer is rejected due to defective legal representation. If a defendant's Sixth Amendment rights are violated when deficient legal advice about a favorable plea offer causes the opportunity for that bargain to be lost, the only logical remedy is to give the defendant the benefit of the favorable deal. But such a remedy would cause serious injustice in many instances, as I believe the Court tacitly recognizes. The Court therefore eschews the only logical remedy and relies on the lower courts to exercise sound discretion in determining what is to be done.

Time will tell how this works out. The Court, for its part, finds it unnecessary to define "the boundaries of proper discretion" in today's opinion. Ante, at 13. In my view, requiring the prosecution to renew an old plea offer would represent an abuse of discretion in at least two circumstances: first, when important new information about a defendant's culpability comes to light after the offer is rejected, and, second, when the rejection of the plea offer results in a substantial expenditure of scarce prosecutorial or judicial resources.

The lower court judges who must implement today's holding may — and I hope, will — do so in a way that mitigates its potential to produce unjust results. But I would not depend on these judges to come to the rescue. The Court's interpretation of the Sixth Amendment right to counsel is unsound, and I therefore respectfully dissent.

NOTES AND QUESTIONS

1. Exactly how big of a deal are these two cases? The answer, as suggested by Justice Alito's *Cooper* dissent, may depend heavily on the way that lower courts give additional content to the bare-bones rule of law declared by the Court in *Frye* and *Cooper*.

For example, the Court in these two cases doesn't say very much at all about the performance prong of *Strickland* — in *Frye*, the deficiency of the defense lawyer's performance (i.e., not telling the client at all about two plea offers) was self-evident (even to Justice Scalia), whereas in *Cooper*, the Court was required to assume deficient performance because the state chose not to litigate the issue. In the future, what will constitute deficient performance in connection with plea bargaining?

The Court in *Cooper* hints that the scope of deficient performance in this context might turn out to be relatively narrow. Should it be limited to deficient advice about pure issues of law, or does it also extend to poor advice about matters that might be described as "strategic"? In *Cooper* itself (had the performance issue been litigated), would it have mattered whether Cooper's defense attorney mistakenly believed that state law would bar a finding of "intent to kill" where the victim was shot below the waist (i.e., if he made a pure error of law), or whether he simply believed that no jury would ever be likely to convict on such facts (i.e., if he made a "strategic" blunder)? Can these categories always be distinguished? Keep in mind that in the traditional *Strickland* context of errors committed by defense counsel at trial, characterizing the defense attorney's decision as "strategic" is usually the kiss of death for a *Strickland* claim. As Justice Kennedy notes in *Cooper*, "an erroneous strategic prediction about the outcome of a trial is not necessarily deficient performance."

If the scope of deficient performance, in connection with plea bargaining, is defined narrowly, then *Frye* and *Cooper* may turn out to have much less impact than Justice Scalia (for one) currently fears.

2. Turning to the prejudice prong of *Strickland*, does it seem strange that the required finding of prejudice in this context must take into account such unknowns as (1) whether the defendant would likely have accepted the plea offer, (2) whether the prosecution would likely have withdrawn the plea offer, and (3) whether the trial judge would likely have accepted the terms of the plea offer? Is it really possible for anyone to "unring the bell" and reconstruct what one would likely have done in a counter-factual scenario like this? In practice, does this mean that trial judges will be likely to find *Strickland* prejudice — or not — based largely on whatever they feel would be an appropriate disposition of the defendant's case, as of the time when the ineffective-assistance claim is being reviewed, typically on a motion for post-conviction relief?

3. Finally — and perhaps most interestingly — note the extraordinary nature of the remedial scheme created by Justice Kennedy (albeit a scheme that even he admits will have to evolve, based upon the experience of lower courts). How is a court supposed to decide whether or not a defendant is entitled to the benefit of a forgone plea bargain — especially after trial, when the remedial issue becomes even more convoluted than after a subsequent guilty plea?

What does Justice Kennedy mean when he says that, in cases involving only possible sentencing relief, "the court may exercise discretion in determining whether the defendant should receive the term of imprisonment the government offered in the plea, the sentence he received at trial, or something in between"? Or that, in cases involving possible reduction of charges, "the judge can then exercise discretion in deciding whether to vacate the conviction from trial and accept the plea or leave the conviction undisturbed"? How are judges supposed to "exercise discretion" in such situations, when a defendant has been deprived of a constitutional right?

And to make matters even worse, Justice Kennedy then adds the following: "In implementing a remedy in both of these situations, the trial court must weigh various factors; and the boundaries of proper discretion need not be defined here. Principles elaborated over time in decisions of state and federal courts, and in statutes and rules, will serve to give more complete guidance as to the factors that should bear upon the exercise of the judge's discretion." Judges across the land undoubtedly are shaking their heads—or pulling out their hair—over such Delphic opaqueness.

PART THREE

THE RIGHT TO BE LET ALONE — AN EXAMINATION OF THE FOURTH AND FIFTH AMENDMENTS AND RELATED AREAS

Chapter 5

The Fourth Amendment

B. The Scope of the Fourth Amendment

1. The Meaning of "Searches"

a. The Relationship Between Privacy and Property

Insert the following notes and main case after Note 7 on page 372:

7a. Recently the Court has made clear that trespass continues to play an important role in Fourth Amendment analysis, and that the *Katz* standard is not the only relevant test. In United States v. Jones, 132 S. Ct. 945 (2012), the police attached a GPS tracking device to a suspect's car, allowing them to continually monitor his travel habits. The government argued that no search had occurred, because the suspect had no expectation of privacy related to his movements on the public roads. But Justice Scalia's majority opinion was explicit: although *Katz* concluded that no physical intrusion is required for a search to occur, "*Katz* [also] did not erode the principle that, when the Government *does* engage in physical intrusion of a constitutionally protected area in order to obtain information, that intrusion may constitute a violation of the Fourth Amendment." By attaching the GPS device to Jones's car, the government "physically occupied private property for the purpose of obtaining information," and that, said the Court, was sufficient to make it a Fourth Amendment search. (*Jones* is set forth as a main case later in this Supplement, in the section on "Privacy and Technology.")

The revival of trespass notions as an independent basis for a Fourth Amendment violation, along with the issue of dog sniffs, was soon back before the Court.

FLORIDA v. JARDINES
Certiorari to the Supreme Court of Florida
133 S. Ct.1409 (2013)

JUSTICE SCALIA delivered the opinion of the Court.

We consider whether using a drug-sniffing dog on a homeowner's porch to investigate the contents of the home is a "search" within the meaning of the Fourth Amendment.

I

In 2006, Detective William Pedraja of the Miami–Dade Police Department received an unverified tip that marijuana was being grown in the home of respondent Joelis Jardines. One month later, the Department and the Drug Enforcement Administration sent a joint surveillance team to Jardines' home. Detective Pedraja was part of that team. He watched the home for fifteen minutes and saw no vehicles in the driveway or activity around the home, and could not see inside because the blinds were drawn. Detective Pedraja then approached Jardines' home accompanied by Detective Douglas Bartelt, a trained canine handler who had just arrived at the scene with his drug-sniffing dog. The dog was trained to detect the scent of marijuana, cocaine, heroin, and several other drugs, indicating the presence of any of these substances through particular behavioral changes recognizable by his handler.

Detective Bartelt had the dog on a six-foot leash, owing in part to the dog's "wild" nature, and tendency to dart around erratically while searching. As the dog approached Jardines' front porch, he apparently sensed one of the odors he had been trained to detect, and began energetically exploring the area for the strongest point source of that odor. . . .

After sniffing the base of the front door, the dog sat, which is the trained behavior upon discovering the odor's strongest point. Detective Bartelt then pulled the dog away from the door and returned to his vehicle. He left the scene after informing Detective Pedraja that there had been a positive alert for narcotics.

On the basis of what he had learned at the home, Detective Pedraja applied for and received a warrant to search the residence. When the warrant was executed later that day, Jardines attempted to flee and was arrested; the search revealed marijuana plants, and he was charged with trafficking in cannabis.

At trial, Jardines moved to suppress the marijuana plants on the ground that the canine investigation was an unreasonable search. The trial court granted the motion, and the Florida Third District Court of Appeal reversed. On a petition for discretionary review, the Florida Supreme Court quashed the decision of the Third District Court of Appeal and approved the trial court's decision to suppress, holding (as relevant here) that the use of the trained narcotics dog to investigate Jardines' home was a Fourth Amendment search unsupported by probable cause, rendering invalid the warrant based upon information gathered in that search.

We granted certiorari, limited to the question of whether the officers' behavior was a search within the meaning of the Fourth Amendment.

II

The Fourth Amendment provides in relevant part that the "right of the people to be secure in their persons, houses, papers, and effects, against unreasonable searches and seizures, shall not be violated." The Amendment establishes a simple baseline, one that for much of our history formed the exclusive basis for its protections: When "the Government obtains information by physically intruding" on persons, houses, papers, or effects, "a 'search' within the original meaning of the Fourth Amendment" has "undoubtedly occurred." United States v. Jones, 132 S. Ct. 945, n.3 (2012). By reason of our decision in Katz v. United States, 389 U.S. 347 (1967), property rights "are not the sole measure of Fourth Amendment violations" — but though *Katz* may add to the baseline, it does not subtract anything from the Amendment's protections "when the Government *does* engage in [a] physical intrusion of a constitutionally protected area." *Knotts*, 460 U.S. at 286 (Brennan, J.).

That principle renders this case a straightforward one. The officers were gathering information in an area belonging to Jardines and immediately surrounding his house — in the curtilage of the house, which we have held enjoys protection as part of the home itself. And they gathered that information by physically entering and occupying the area to engage in conduct not explicitly or implicitly permitted by the homeowner.

A

The Fourth Amendment "indicates with some precision the places and things encompassed by its protections": persons, houses, papers, and effects. The Fourth Amendment does not, therefore, prevent all investigations conducted on private property; for example, an officer may (subject to *Katz*) gather information in what we have called "open fields"—even if those fields are privately owned—because such fields are not enumerated in the Amendment's text.

But when it comes to the Fourth Amendment, the home is first among equals. At the Amendment's "very core" stands "the right of a man to retreat into his own home and there be free from unreasonable governmental intrusion." *Silverman*, 365 U.S. at 511. This right would be of little practical value if the State's agents could stand in a home's porch or side garden and trawl for evidence with impunity; the right to retreat would be significantly diminished if the police could enter a man's property to observe his repose from just outside the front window.

We therefore regard the area "immediately surrounding and associated with the home"—what our cases call the curtilage—as "part of the home itself for Fourth Amendment purposes." *Oliver*, 466 U.S. at 180. That principle has ancient and durable roots. Just as the distinction between the home and the open fields is "as old as the common law," so too is the identity of home and what Blackstone called the "curtilage or homestall," for the "house protects and privileges all its branches and appurtenants." 4 W. Blackstone, Commentaries on the Laws of England 223, 225 (1769). This area around the home is "intimately linked to the home, both physically and psychologically," and is where "privacy expectations are most heightened." *Ciraolo*, 476 U.S. at 213.

While the boundaries of the curtilage are generally "clearly marked," the "conception defining the curtilage" is at any rate familiar enough that it is "easily understood from our daily experience." Here there is no doubt that the officers entered it: The front porch is the classic exemplar of an area adjacent to the home and "to which the activity of home life extends." *Oliver*, 466 U.S. at 182, n.12.

B

Since the officers' investigation took place in a constitutionally protected area, we turn to the question of whether it was accomplished through an unlicensed physical intrusion. While law enforcement officers need not "shield their eyes" when passing by the home "on public thoroughfares," an officer's leave to gather information is sharply circumscribed when he steps off those thoroughfares and enters the Fourth Amendment's protected areas. In permitting, for example, visual observation of the home from "public navigable airspace," we were careful to note that it was done "in a physically nonintrusive manner." Entick v. Carrington, 2 Wils. K.B. 275, 95 Eng. Rep. 807 (K.B. 1765), a case "undoubtedly familiar" to "every American statesman" at the time of the Founding, states the general rule clearly: "[O]ur law holds the property of every man so sacred, that no man can set his foot upon his neighbour's close without his leave." Id., at 291. As it is undisputed that the detectives had all four of their feet and all four of their companion's firmly planted on the constitutionally protected extension of Jardines' home, the only question is whether he had given his leave (even implicitly) for them to do so. He had not.

"A license may be implied from the habits of the country," notwithstanding the "strict rule of the English common law as to entry upon a close." McKee v. Gratz, 260 U.S. 127, 136 (1922) (Holmes, J.). We have accordingly recognized that "the knocker on the front door is treated as an invitation or license to attempt an entry, justifying ingress to the home by solicitors, hawkers and peddlers of all kinds." Breard v. Alexandria, 341 U.S. 622, 626 (1951). This implicit license typically permits the visitor to approach the home by the front path, knock promptly, wait briefly to be received, and then (absent invitation to linger longer) leave. Complying with the terms of that traditional invitation does not require fine-grained legal knowledge; it is generally managed without incident by the Nation's Girl Scouts and trick-or-treaters. Thus, a police officer not armed with a warrant may approach a home and knock, precisely because that is no more than any private citizen might do.

But introducing a trained police dog to explore the area around the home in hopes of discovering incriminating evidence is something else. There is no customary invitation to do *that*. An invitation to engage in canine forensic investigation assuredly does not inhere in the very act of hanging a knocker.[3] To find a visitor knocking on the door is routine (even if sometimes unwelcome); to spot that same visitor exploring the front path with a metal detector, or marching his bloodhound into the garden before saying hello and asking permission, would inspire most of us to—well, call the police. The scope of a license—express or implied—is limited not only to a particular area but also to a specific purpose. Consent at a traffic stop to an officer's checking out an anonymous tip that there is a body in the trunk does not permit the officer to

---

3. The dissent insists that our argument must rest upon "the particular instrument that Detective Bartelt used to detect the odor of marijuana"—the dog. It is not the dog that is the problem, but the behavior that here involved use of the dog. We think a typical person would find it "'a cause for great alarm'" to find a stranger snooping about his front porch *with or without* a dog. The dissent would let the police do whatever they want by way of gathering evidence so long as they stay on the base-path, to use a baseball analogy—so long as they "stick to the path that is typically used to approach a front door, such as a paved walkway." From that vantage point they can presumably peer into the house through binoculars with impunity. That is not the law, as even the State concedes.

rummage through the trunk for narcotics. Here, the background social norms that invite a visitor to the front door do not invite him there to conduct a search.[4]

The State points to our decisions holding that the subjective intent of the officer is irrelevant. See Ashcroft v. al-Kidd, 131 S. Ct. 2074 (2011); Whren v. United States, 517 U.S. 806 (1996). But those cases merely hold that a stop or search *that is objectively reasonable* is not vitiated by the fact that the officer's real reason for making the stop or search has nothing to do with the validating reason. Thus, the defendant will not be heard to complain that although he was speeding the officer's real reason for the stop was racial harassment. Here, however, the question before the court is precisely *whether* the officer's conduct was an objectively reasonable search. As we have described, that depends upon whether the officers had an implied license to enter the porch, which in turn depends upon the purpose for which they entered. Here, their behavior objectively reveals a purpose to conduct a search, which is not what anyone would think he had license to do.

III

The State argues that investigation by a forensic narcotics dog by definition cannot implicate any legitimate privacy interest. The State cites for authority our decisions in United States v. Place, 462 U.S. 696 (1983), United States v. Jacobsen, 466 U.S. 109 (1984), and Illinois v. Caballes, 543 U.S. 405 (2005), which held, respectively, that canine inspection of luggage in an airport, chemical testing of a substance that had fallen from a parcel in transit, and canine inspection of an automobile during a lawful traffic stop, do not violate the "reasonable expectation of privacy" described in *Katz*.

Just last Term, we considered an argument much like this. [United States v.] Jones[, 132 S. Ct. 945 (2012)] held that tracking an automobile's whereabouts using a physically-mounted GPS receiver is a Fourth Amendment search. The Government argued that the *Katz* standard "show[ed] that no search occurred," as the defendant had "no 'reasonable expectation of privacy'" in his whereabouts on the public roads, a pro-

4. The dissent argues, citing Kentucky v. King, that "gathering evidence—even damning evidence—is a lawful activity that falls within the scope of the license to approach." *Post*, at ___. That is a false generalization. What Kentucky v. King establishes is that it is not a Fourth Amendment search to approach the home in order to speak with the occupant, *because all are invited to do that*. The mere "purpose of discovering information," in the course of engaging in that permitted conduct does not cause it to violate the Fourth Amendment. But no one is impliedly invited to enter the protected premises of the home in order to do nothing but conduct a search.

position with at least as much support in our case law as the one the State marshals here. But because the GPS receiver had been physically mounted on the defendant's automobile (thus intruding on his "effects"), we held that tracking the vehicle's movements was a search: a person's "Fourth Amendment rights do not rise or fall with the *Katz* formulation." The *Katz* reasonable-expectations test "has been *added to,* not *substituted for,*" the traditional property-based understanding of the Fourth Amendment, and so is unnecessary to consider when the government gains evidence by physically intruding on constitutionally protected areas.

Thus, we need not decide whether the officers' investigation of Jardines' home violated his expectation of privacy under *Katz.* One virtue of the Fourth Amendment's property-rights baseline is that it keeps easy cases easy. That the officers learned what they learned only by physically intruding on Jardines' property to gather evidence is enough to establish that a search occurred.

For a related reason we find irrelevant the State's argument (echoed by the dissent) that forensic dogs have been commonly used by police for centuries. This argument is apparently directed to our holding in Kyllo v. United States, 533 U.S. 27 (2001), that surveillance of the home is a search where "the Government uses a device that is not in general public use" to "explore details of the home that would previously have been unknowable *without physical intrusion.*" Id., at 40 (emphasis added). But the implication of that statement is that when the government uses a physical intrusion to explore details of the home (including its curtilage), the antiquity of the tools that they bring along is irrelevant.

* * *

The government's use of trained police dogs to investigate the home and its immediate surroundings is a "search" within the meaning of the Fourth Amendment. The judgment of the Supreme Court of Florida is therefore affirmed.

JUSTICE KAGAN, with whom JUSTICE Ginsburg and JUSTICE SOTOMAYOR join, concurring.

For me, a simple analogy clinches this case — and does so on privacy as well as property grounds. A stranger comes to the front door of your home carrying super-high-powered binoculars. He doesn't knock or say hello. Instead, he stands on the porch and uses the binoculars to peer through your windows, into your home's furthest corners. . . . Has your "visitor" trespassed on your property, exceeding the license you have granted to members of the public to, say, drop off the mail or distribute campaign flyers? Yes, he has. And has he also invaded your "reasonable expectation of privacy," by nosing into intimacies you sensibly thought protected from disclosure? Yes, of course, he has done that too.

That case is this case in every way that matters. Here, police officers came to Joelis Jardines' door with a super-sensitive instrument, which they deployed to detect things inside that they could not perceive unassisted. The equipment they used was animal, not mineral. But contra the dissent, that is of no significance in determining whether a search occurred. Detective Bartelt's dog was not your neighbor's pet, come to your porch on a leisurely stroll. As this Court discussed earlier this Term, drug-detection dogs are highly trained tools of law enforcement, geared to respond in distinctive ways to specific scents so as to convey clear and reliable information to their human partners. See Florida v. Harris, 133 S. Ct. 1050, 1053-1054, 1056-1057 (2013). They are to the poodle down the street as high-powered binoculars are to a piece of plain glass. Like the binoculars, a drug-detection dog is a specialized device for discovering objects not in plain view (or plain smell). . . .

. . . If we had decided this case on privacy grounds, we would have realized that Kyllo v. United States, 533 U.S. 27 (2001), already resolved it. The *Kyllo* Court held that police officers conducted a search when they used a thermal-imaging device to detect heat emanating from a private home, even though they committed no trespass. Highlighting our intention to draw both a "firm" and a "bright" line at "the entrance to the house," we announced the following rule:

> "Where, as here, the Government uses a device that is not in general public use, to explore details of the home that would previously have been unknowable without physical intrusion, the surveillance is a 'search' and is presumptively unreasonable without a warrant." *Ibid.*

That "firm" and "bright" rule governs this case: The police officers here conducted a search because they used a "device . . . not in general public use" (a trained drug-detection dog) to "explore details of the home" (the presence of certain substances) that they would not otherwise have discovered without entering the premises. . . .

With these further thoughts, suggesting that a focus on Jardines' privacy interests would make an "easy cas[e] easy" twice over, I join the Court's opinion in full.

JUSTICE ALITO, with whom CHIEF JUSTICE ROBERTS, JUSTICE KENNEDY, and JUSTICE BREYER join, dissenting.

The Court's decision in this important Fourth Amendment case is based on a putative rule of trespass law that is nowhere to be found in the annals of Anglo-American jurisprudence.

The law of trespass generally gives members of the public a license to use a walkway to approach the front door of a house and to remain there for a brief time. This license is not limited to persons who intend to speak to an occupant or who actually do so. (Mail carriers and persons delivering packages and flyers are examples of individuals who may lawfully approach a front door without intending to converse.) Nor is the license restricted to categories of visitors whom an occupant of the dwelling is likely to welcome; as the Court acknowledges, this license applies even to "solicitors, hawkers and peddlers of all kinds." And the license even extends to police officers who wish to gather evidence against an occupant (by asking potentially incriminating questions).

According to the Court, however, the police officer in this case, Detective Bartelt, committed a trespass because he was accompanied during his otherwise lawful visit to the front door of respondent's house by his dog, Franky. Where is the authority evidencing such a rule? Dogs have been domesticated for about 12,000 years; they were ubiquitous in both this country and Britain at the time of the adoption of the Fourth Amendment; and their acute sense of smell has been used in law enforcement for centuries. Yet the Court has been unable to find a single case—from the United States or any other common-law nation—that supports the rule on which its decision is based. Thus, trespass law provides no support for the Court's holding today.

The Court's decision is also inconsistent with the reasonable-expectations-of-privacy test that the Court adopted in Katz v. United States, 389 U.S. 347 (1967). A reasonable person understands that odors emanating from a house may be detected from locations that are open to the public, and a reasonable person will not count on the strength of those odors remaining within the range that, while detectible by a dog, cannot be smelled by a human.

For these reasons, I would hold that no search within the meaning of the Fourth Amendment took place in this case, and I would reverse the decision below.

I

. . .

A critical fact that the Court omits is that, as respondent's counsel explained at oral argument, this entire process—walking down the driveway and front path to the front door, waiting for Franky to find the strongest source of the odor, and walking back to the car — took approximately a minute or two. Thus, the amount of time that Franky and the detective remained at the front porch was even less. The Court also fails to mention that, while Detective Bartelt apparently did not personally smell the odor of marijuana coming from the house, another officer who subsequently stood on the front porch, Detective Pedraja, did notice that smell and was able to identify it.

II . . .

A

It is said that members of the public may lawfully proceed along a walkway leading to the front door of a house because custom grants them a license to do so. Breard v. Alexandria, 341 U.S. 622, 626 (1951). J. Bishop, Commentaries on the Non–Contract Law § 823, p. 378 (1889). This rule encompasses categories of visitors whom most homeowners almost certainly wish to allow to approach their front doors — friends, relatives, mail carriers, persons making deliveries. But it also reaches categories of visitors who are less universally welcome — "solicitors," "hawkers," "peddlers," and the like. The law might attempt to draw fine lines between categories of welcome and unwelcome visitors, distinguishing, for example, between tolerable and intolerable door-to-door peddlers (Girl Scouts selling cookies versus adults selling aluminum siding) or between police officers on agreeable and disagreeable missions (gathering information about a bothersome neighbor versus asking potentially incriminating questions). But the law of trespass has not attempted such a difficult taxonomy. . . .

Of course, this license has certain spatial and temporal limits. A visitor must stick to the path that is typically used to approach a front door, such as a paved walkway. A visitor cannot traipse through the garden, meander into the backyard, or take other circuitous detours that veer from the pathway that a visitor would customarily use. . . .

Similarly, a visitor may not linger at the front door for an extended period. The license is limited to the amount of time it would customarily take to approach the door, pause long enough to see if someone is home, and (if not expressly invited to stay longer), leave.

As I understand the law of trespass and the scope of the implied license, a visitor who adheres to these limitations is not necessarily required to ring the doorbell, knock on the door, or attempt to speak with an occupant. For example, mail carriers, persons making deliveries, and individuals distributing flyers may leave the items they are carrying and depart without making any attempt to converse. . . .

As the majority acknowledges, this implied license to approach the front door extends to the police. As we recognized in Kentucky v. King, 131 S. Ct. 1849 (2011), police officers do not engage in a search when they approach the front door of a residence and seek to engage in what is termed a "knock and talk," *i.e.*, knocking on the door and seeking to speak to an occupant for the purpose of gathering evidence. See id., at ____, 131 S. Ct., at 1862. Even when the objective of a "knock and talk" is to obtain evidence that will lead to the homeowner's arrest and prosecution, the license to approach still applies. In other words, gathering evidence — even damning evidence — is a lawful activity that falls within the scope of the license to approach. And when officers walk up to the front door of a house, they are permitted to see, hear, and smell whatever can be detected from a lawful vantage point.

B

. . . The Court concludes that Detective Bartelt went too far because he had the "*objectiv[e]* . . . purpose to conduct a search" (emphasis added). What this means, I take it, is that anyone aware of what Detective Bartelt did would infer that his subjective purpose was to gather evidence. But if this is the Court's point, then a standard "knock and talk" and most other police visits would likewise constitute searches. With the exception of visits to serve warrants or civil process, police almost always approach homes with a purpose of discovering information. That is certainly the objective of a "knock and talk." The Court offers no meaningful way of distinguishing the "objective purpose" of a "knock and talk" from the "objective purpose" of Detective Bartelt's conduct here.

The Court contends that a "knock and talk" is different because it involves talking, and "all are invited" to do that. But a police officer who approaches the front door of a house in accordance with the limitations already discussed may gather evidence by means other than talking. The officer may observe items in plain view and smell odors coming from the house. So the Court's "objective purpose" argument cannot stand.

What the Court must fall back on, then, is the particular instrument that Detective Bartelt used to detect the odor of marijuana, namely, his dog. But in the entire body of common-law decisions, the Court has not found a single case holding that a visitor to the front door of a home commits a trespass if the visitor is accompanied by a dog on a leash. . . .

The Court responds that "[i]t is not the dog that is the problem, but the behavior that here involved use of the dog." But where is the support in the law of trespass for *this* proposition? Dogs' keen sense of smell has been used in law enforcement for centuries. . . . If bringing a tracking dog to the front door of a home constituted a trespass, one would expect at least one case to have arisen during the past 800 years. But the Court has found none. . . .

III

The concurring opinion attempts to provide an alternative ground for today's decision, namely, that Detective Bartelt's conduct violated respondent's reasonable expectations of privacy. But we have already rejected a very similar, if not identical argument, see Illinois v. Caballes, 543 U.S. 405, 409-410 (2005), and in any event I see no basis for concluding that the occupants of a dwelling have a reasonable expectation of privacy in odors that emanate from the dwelling and reach spots where members of the public may lawfully stand.

It is clear that the occupant of a house has no reasonable expectation of privacy with respect to odors that can be smelled by human beings who are standing in such places. And I would not draw a line between odors that can be smelled by humans and those that are detectible only by dogs. . . .

In an attempt to show that respondent had a reasonable expectation of privacy in the odor of marijuana wafting from his house, the concurrence argues that this case is just like Kyllo v. United States, 533 U.S. 27 (2001), which held that police officers conducted a search when they used a thermal imaging device to detect heat emanating from a house. This Court, however, has already rejected the argument that the use of a drug-sniffing dog is the same as the use of a thermal imaging device. See *Caballes,* 543 U.S., at 409-410. The very argument now advanced by the concurrence appears in Justice Souter's *Caballes* dissent. See *id.,* at 413, and n. 3. But the Court was not persuaded.

Contrary to the interpretation propounded by the concurrence, *Kyllo* is best understood as a decision about the use of new technology. The *Kyllo* Court focused on the fact that the thermal imaging device was a form of "sense-enhancing technology" that was "not in general public use," and it expressed concern that citizens would be "at the mercy of advancing technology" if its use was not restricted. A dog, however, is not a new form of "technology" or a "device." . . .

... When the police used the thermal imaging device in *Kyllo,* they were on a public street, and "committed no trespass." Therefore, if a dog's nose is just like a thermal imaging device for Fourth Amendment purposes, a search would occur if a dog alerted while on a public sidewalk or in the corridor of an apartment building. And the same would be true if the dog was trained to sniff, not for marijuana, but for more dangerous quarry, such as explosives or for a violent fugitive or kidnapped child. I see no ground for hampering legitimate law enforcement in this way. . . .

NOTES AND QUESTIONS

1. Justice Scalia's majority opinion suggests that this is an easy case — the police entered the curtilage of defendant's home without permission or license to do so, and used Franky the police dog to gather information from inside the house. Thus, the dog sniff was a search governed by the Fourth Amendment.

Is the case really that easy? As the dissent points out and the majority acknowledges, people are permitted to come onto the porch of a home to ask directions, conduct an opinion poll, or sell cookies or salvation, all of which may involve gathering information and all of which may be unwelcomed by the homeowner. More pointedly, in Kentucky v. King, 131 S. Ct. 1849 (2011) (discussed below in this Supplement under the material on Exigent Circumstances) the Court said that when the police come to a home to engage in a "knock and talk" — "knocking on the door and seeking to speak to an occupant for the purpose of gathering evidence" — no search has occurred. Can you articulate why all of this conduct is permitted, but a dog sniff that does not even require the homeowner to open the front door does not?

2. The majority in *Jardines* distinguishes the knock-and-talk behavior in footnote 4 by saying that while "all are invited" to come to the front door and speak to the homeowner, "no one is impliedly invited to enter the protected premises of the home in order to do nothing but conduct a search." Suppose the police brought Franky the dog with them to the front door, knocked, and while they were talking to the homeowner, let Franky sniff around on the porch. Has a search occurred?

3. On a related point, how critical is the dog to the holding of *Jardines?* If the police officer had come on to the porch without a dog, and pressed his face against a window in the front door and peered inside, would the Fourth Amendment be violated if the officer saw an illegal weapon in the front hall? Bill collectors and nosy neighbors certainly peer into homes; should the police be different? Justice Kagan's concurring opinion says

that if the officer used "super-high-powered binoculars" to look through a window into a home from the porch, that would violate both the *Jardines* majority's trespass test and the *Katz* reasonable expectation of privacy test. Does peering through a window without binoculars violate the trespass test, the *Katz* test, both, or neither?

c. Privacy and Technology

Insert the following note and main case after the first paragraph of Note 4 on page 398, and omit the second paragraph of Note 4:

4a. The Supreme Court thereafter took up the question as a matter of Fourth Amendment law. Did the Court provide an answer?

UNITED STATES v. JONES
Certiorari to the United States Court of Appeals for the D.C. Circuit
132 S. Ct. 945 (2012)

JUSTICE SCALIA delivered the opinion of the Court.

We decide whether the attachment of a Global-Positioning-System (GPS) tracking device to an individual's vehicle, and subsequent use of that device to monitor the vehicle's movements on public streets, constitutes a search or seizure within the meaning of the Fourth Amendment.

I

In 2004 respondent Antoine Jones, owner and operator of a nightclub in the District of Columbia, came under suspicion of trafficking in narcotics and was made the target of an investigation by a joint FBI and Metropolitan Police Department task force. Officers employed various investigative techniques, including visual surveillance of the nightclub, installation of a camera focused on the front door of the club, and a pen register and wiretap covering Jones's cellular phone.

Based in part on information gathered from these sources, in 2005 the Government applied to the United States District Court for the District of Columbia for a warrant authorizing the use of an electronic tracking device on the Jeep Grand Cherokee registered to Jones's wife. A warrant issued, authorizing installation of the device in the District of Columbia and within 10 days.

On the 11th day, and not in the District of Columbia but in Maryland,[1] agents installed a GPS tracking device on the undercarriage of the Jeep while it was parked in a public parking lot. Over the next 28 days, the Government used the device to track the vehicle's movements, and once had to replace the device's battery when the vehicle was parked in a different public lot in Maryland. By means of signals from multiple satellites, the device established the vehicle's location within 50 to 100 feet, and communicated that location by cellular phone to a Government computer. It relayed more than 2,000 pages of data over the 4-week period.

The Government ultimately obtained a multiple-count indictment charging Jones . . . with . . . conspiracy to distribute and possess with intent to distribute five kilograms or more of cocaine and 50 grams or more of cocaine base. . . . Before trial, Jones filed a motion to suppress evidence obtained through the GPS device. The District Court granted the motion only in part. . . . Jones's trial in October 2006 produced a hung jury on the conspiracy count.

In March 2007, a grand jury returned another indictment, charging Jones and others with the same conspiracy. The Government introduced at trial the same GPS-derived locational data admitted in the first trial, which connected Jones to the alleged conspirators' stash house that contained $850,000 in cash, 97 kilograms of cocaine, and 1 kilogram of cocaine base. The jury returned a guilty verdict, and the District Court sentenced Jones to life imprisonment.

The United States Court of Appeals for the District of Columbia Circuit reversed the conviction because of admission of the evidence obtained by warrantless use of the GPS device which, it said, violated the Fourth Amendment. . . . We granted certiorari.

II

A

The Fourth Amendment provides in relevant part that "[t]he right of the people to be secure in their persons, houses, papers, and effects, against unreasonable searches and seizures, shall not be violated." It is beyond dispute that a vehicle is an "effect" as that term is used in the Amendment. We hold that the Government's installation of a GPS device

---

1. In this litigation, the Government has conceded noncompliance with the warrant and has argued only that a warrant was not required.

on a target's vehicle,[2] and its use of that device to monitor the vehicle's movements, constitutes a "search."

It is important to be clear about what occurred in this case: The Government physically occupied private property for the purpose of obtaining information. We have no doubt that such a physical intrusion would have been considered a "search" within the meaning of the Fourth Amendment when it was adopted. Entick v. Carrington, 95 Eng. Rep. 807 (C.P. 1765), is a "case we have described as a 'monument of English freedom' 'undoubtedly familiar' to 'every American statesman' at the time the Constitution was adopted, and considered to be 'the true and ultimate expression of constitutional law'" with regard to search and seizure. Brower v. County of Inyo, 489 U.S. 593, 596 (1989) (quoting Boyd v. United States, 116 U.S. 616, 626 (1886)). In that case, Lord Camden expressed in plain terms the significance of property rights in search-and-seizure analysis:

> "[O]ur law holds the property of every man so sacred, that no man can set his foot upon his neighbour's close without his leave; if he does he is a trespasser, though he does no damage at all; if he will tread upon his neighbour's ground, he must justify it by law." *Entick, supra,* at 817.

The text of the Fourth Amendment reflects its close connection to property, since otherwise it would have referred simply to "the right of the people to be secure against unreasonable searches and seizures"; the phrase "in their persons, houses, papers, and effects" would have been superfluous.

Consistent with this understanding, our Fourth Amendment jurisprudence was tied to common-law trespass, at least until the latter half of the 20th century. Thus, in Olmstead v. United States, 277 U.S. 438 (1928), we held that wiretaps attached to telephone wires on the public streets did not constitute a Fourth Amendment search because "[t]here was no entry of the houses or offices of the defendants," id., at 464.

Our later cases, of course, have deviated from that exclusively property-based approach. In Katz v. United States, 389 U.S. 347, 351 (1967), we said that "the Fourth Amendment protects people, not places," and

2. As we have noted, the Jeep was registered to Jones's wife. The Government acknowledged, however, that Jones was "the exclusive driver." If Jones was not the owner he had at least the property rights of a bailee. The Court of Appeals concluded that the vehicle's registration did not affect his ability to make a Fourth Amendment objection, and the Government has not challenged that determination here. We therefore do not consider the Fourth Amendment significance of Jones's status.

found a violation in attachment of an eavesdropping device to a public telephone booth. Our later cases have applied the analysis of Justice Harlan's concurrence in that case, which said that a violation occurs when government officers violate a person's "reasonable expectation of privacy," id., at 360.

The Government contends that the Harlan standard shows that no search occurred here, since Jones had no "reasonable expectation of privacy" in the area of the Jeep accessed by Government agents (its underbody) and in the locations of the Jeep on the public roads, which were visible to all. But we need not address the Government's contentions, because Jones's Fourth Amendment rights do not rise or fall with the *Katz* formulation. At bottom, we must "assur[e] preservation of that degree of privacy against government that existed when the Fourth Amendment was adopted. [Kyllo v. United States, 533 U.S. 27, 34 (2001).] As explained, for most of our history the Fourth Amendment was understood to embody a particular concern for government trespass upon the areas ("persons, houses, papers, and effects") it enumerates.[3] *Katz* did not repudiate that understanding. . . .

. . . *Katz* . . . established that "property rights are not the sole measure of Fourth Amendment violations," but did not "snuf[f] out the previously recognized protection for property," [Soldal v. Cook County, 506 U.S. 56, 64 (1992)]. As Justice Brennan explained in his concurrence in [United States v. Knotts, 460 U.S. 276 (1983)], *Katz* did not erode the principle "that, when the Government *does* engage in physical intrusion of a constitutionally protected area in order to obtain information, that intrusion may constitute a violation of the Fourth Amendment." 460 U.S., at 286 (opinion concurring in judgment). We have embodied that preservation of past rights in our very definition of "reasonable expectation of privacy" which we have said to be an expectation "that has a source outside of the Fourth Amendment, either by reference to concepts of real or personal property law or to understandings that are recognized and

---

3. Justice Alito's concurrence (hereinafter concurrence) doubts the wisdom of our approach because "it is almost impossible to think of late-18th-century situations that are analogous to what took place in this case." But in fact it posits a situation that is not far afield — a constable's concealing himself in the target's coach in order to track its movements. There is no doubt that the information gained by that trespassory activity would be the product of an unlawful search — whether that information consisted of the conversations occurring in the coach, or of the destinations to which the coach traveled.

In any case, it is quite irrelevant whether there was an 18th-century analog. Whatever new methods of investigation may be devised, our task, *at a minimum*, is to decide whether the action in question would have constituted a "search" within the original meaning of the Fourth Amendment. Where, as here, the Government obtains information by physically intruding on a constitutionally protected area, such a search has undoubtedly occurred.

permitted by society." Minnesota v. Carter, 525 U.S. 83, 88 (1998) (internal quotation marks omitted). *Katz* did not narrow the Fourth Amendment's scope.[5]

The Government contends that several of our post-*Katz* cases foreclose the conclusion that what occurred here constituted a search. It relies principally on two cases in which we rejected Fourth Amendment challenges to "beepers," electronic tracking devices that represent another form of electronic monitoring. The first case, *Knotts*, upheld against Fourth Amendment challenge the use of a "beeper" that had been placed in a container of chloroform, allowing law enforcement to monitor the location of the container. We said that there had been no infringement of Knotts' reasonable expectation of privacy since the information obtained — the location of the automobile carrying the container on public roads, and the location of the off-loaded container in open fields near Knotts' cabin — had been voluntarily conveyed to the public.[6] But as we have discussed, the *Katz* reasonable-expectation-of-privacy test has been *added to,* not *substituted for,* the common-law trespassory test. The holding in *Knotts* addressed only the former, since the latter was not at issue. The beeper had been placed in the container before it came into Knotts' possession, with the consent of the then-owner. Knotts did not challenge that installation, and we specifically declined to consider its effect on the Fourth Amendment analysis. *Knotts* would be relevant, perhaps, if the Government were making the argument that what would otherwise be an unconstitutional search is not such where it produces only public information. The Government does not make that argument, and we know of no case that would support it.

---

5. The concurrence notes that post-*Katz* we have explained that "'an actual trespass is neither necessary *nor sufficient* to establish a constitutional violation.'" Post, at 960 (quoting United States v. Karo, 468 U.S. 705, 713 (1984)). That is undoubtedly true, and undoubtedly irrelevant. *Karo* was considering whether a seizure occurred, and as the concurrence explains, a seizure of property occurs, not when there is a trespass, but "when there is some meaningful interference with an individual's possessory interests in that property." Likewise with a search. Trespass alone does not qualify, but there must be conjoined with that what was present here: an attempt to find something or to obtain information.

Related to this, and similarly irrelevant, is the concurrence's point that, if analyzed separately, neither the installation of the device nor its use would constitute a Fourth Amendment search. Of course not. A trespass on "houses" or "effects," or a *Katz* invasion of privacy, is not alone a search unless it is done to obtain information; and the obtaining of information is not alone a search unless it is achieved by such a trespass or invasion of privacy.

6. *Knotts* noted the "limited use which the government made of the signals from this particular beeper," 460 U.S., at 284; and reserved the question whether "different constitutional principles may be applicable" to "dragnet-type law enforcement practices" of the type that GPS tracking made possible here, ibid.

The second "beeper" case, United States v. Karo, 468 U.S. 705 (1984), does not suggest a different conclusion. There we addressed the question left open by *Knotts*, whether the installation of a beeper in a container amounted to a search or seizure. As in *Knotts*, at the time the beeper was installed the container belonged to a third party, and it did not come into possession of the defendant until later. Thus, the specific question we considered was whether the installation "*with the consent of the original owner* constitute[d] a search or seizure . . . when the container is delivered to a buyer having no knowledge of the presence of the beeper." Id., at 707 (emphasis added). We held not. The Government, we said, came into physical contact with the container only before it belonged to the defendant Karo; and the transfer of the container with the unmonitored beeper inside did not convey any information and thus did not invade Karo's privacy. That conclusion is perfectly consistent with the one we reach here. Karo accepted the container as it came to him, beeper and all, and was therefore not entitled to object to the beeper's presence, even though it was used to monitor the container's location. Jones, who possessed the Jeep at the time the Government trespassorily inserted the information-gathering device, is on much different footing. . . .

Finally, the Government's position gains little support from our conclusion in Oliver v. United States, 466 U.S. 170 (1984), that officers' information-gathering intrusion on an "open field" did not constitute a Fourth Amendment search even though it was a trespass at common law. Quite simply, an open field, unlike the curtilage of a home, is not one of those protected areas enumerated in the Fourth Amendment. The Government's physical intrusion on such an area — unlike its intrusion on the "effect" at issue here — is of no Fourth Amendment significance.[8]

B

The concurrence begins by accusing us of applying "18th-century tort law." That is a distortion. What we apply is an 18th-century guarantee against unreasonable searches, which we believe must provide *at a minimum* the degree of protection it afforded when it was adopted. The

---

8. Thus, our theory [unlike the suggestion of the concurrence] is *not* that the Fourth Amendment is concerned with "*any* technical trespass that led to the gathering of evidence" (emphasis added). The Fourth Amendment protects against trespassory searches only with regard to those items ("persons, houses, papers, and effects") that it enumerates. The trespass that occurred in *Oliver* may properly be understood as a "search," but not one "in the constitutional sense." 466 U.S., at 170.

concurrence does not share that belief. It would apply *exclusively Katz*'s reasonable-expectation-of-privacy test, even when that eliminates rights that previously existed.

The concurrence faults our approach for "present[ing] particularly vexing problems" in cases that do not involve physical contact, such as those that involve the transmission of electronic signals. We entirely fail to understand that point. For unlike the concurrence, which would make *Katz* the *exclusive* test, we do not make trespass the exclusive test. Situations involving merely the transmission of electronic signals without trespass would *remain* subject to *Katz* analysis.

In fact, it is the concurrence's insistence on the exclusivity of the *Katz* test that needlessly leads us into "particularly vexing problems" in the present case. This Court has to date not deviated from the understanding that mere visual observation does not constitute a search. We accordingly held in *Knotts* that "[a] person traveling in an automobile on public thoroughfares has no reasonable expectation of privacy in his movements from one place to another." 460 U.S., at 281. Thus, even assuming that the concurrence is correct to say that "[t]raditional surveillance" of Jones for a 4-week period "would have required a large team of agents, multiple vehicles, and perhaps aerial assistance," our cases suggest that such visual observation is constitutionally permissible. It may be that achieving the same result through electronic means, without an accompanying trespass, is an unconstitutional invasion of privacy, but the present case does not require us to answer that question.

And answering it affirmatively leads us needlessly into additional thorny problems. The concurrence posits that "relatively short-term monitoring of a person's movements on public streets" is okay, but that "the use of longer term GPS monitoring in investigations *of most offenses*" is no good. That introduces yet another novelty into our jurisprudence. There is no precedent for the proposition that whether a search has occurred depends on the nature of the crime being investigated. And even accepting that novelty, it remains unexplained why a 4-week investigation is "surely" too long and why a drug-trafficking conspiracy involving substantial amounts of cash and narcotics is not an "extraordinary offens[e]" which may permit longer observation. What of a 2-day monitoring of a suspected purveyor of stolen electronics? Or of a 6-month monitoring of a suspected terrorist? We may have to grapple with these "vexing problems" in some future case where a classic trespassory search is not involved and resort must be had to *Katz* analysis; but there is no reason for rushing forward to resolve them here.

III

The Government argues in the alternative that even if the attachment and use of the device was a search, it was reasonable — and thus lawful — under the Fourth Amendment because "officers had reasonable suspicion, and indeed probable cause, to believe that [Jones] was a leader in a large-scale cocaine distribution conspiracy." Brief for United States 50-51. We have no occasion to consider this argument. The Government did not raise it below, and the D.C. Circuit therefore did not address it. We consider the argument forfeited.

The judgment of the Court of Appeals for the D.C. Circuit is affirmed.

JUSTICE SOTOMAYOR, concurring.

I join the Court's opinion because I agree that a search within the meaning of the Fourth Amendment occurs, at a minimum, "[w]here, as here, the Government obtains information by physically intruding on a constitutionally protected area." In this case, the Government installed a Global Positioning System (GPS) tracking device on respondent Antoine Jones' Jeep without a valid warrant and without Jones' consent, then used that device to monitor the Jeep's movements over the course of four weeks. The Government usurped Jones' property for the purpose of conducting surveillance on him, thereby invading privacy interests long afforded, and undoubtedly entitled to, Fourth Amendment protection.

Of course, the Fourth Amendment is not concerned only with trespassory intrusions on property. . . . In [Katz v. United States, 389 U.S. 347, 353 (1967)], this Court enlarged its then-prevailing focus on property rights by announcing that the reach of the Fourth Amendment does not "turn upon the presence or absence of a physical intrusion." Id., at 353. As the majority's opinion makes clear, however, Katz's reasonable-expectation-of-privacy test augmented, but did not displace or diminish, the common-law trespassory test that preceded it. . . . Justice Alito's approach, which discounts altogether the constitutional relevance of the Government's physical intrusion on Jones' Jeep, erodes that longstanding protection for privacy expectations inherent in items of property that people possess or control. By contrast, the trespassory test applied in the majority's opinion reflects an irreducible constitutional minimum: When the Government physically invades personal property to gather information, a search occurs. The reaffirmation of that principle suffices to decide this case.

Nonetheless, as Justice Alito notes, physical intrusion is now unnecessary to many forms of surveillance. With increasing regularity, the Government will be capable of duplicating the monitoring undertaken in this case by enlisting factory- or owner-installed vehicle tracking devices or GPS-enabled smartphones. In cases of electronic or other novel modes of surveillance that do not depend upon a physical invasion on property, the majority opinion's trespassory test may provide little guidance. But "[s]ituations involving merely the transmission of electronic signals without trespass would *remain* subject to *Katz* analysis." As Justice Alito incisively observes, the same technological advances that have made possible nontrespassory surveillance techniques will also affect the *Katz* test by shaping the evolution of societal privacy expectations. Under that rubric, I agree with Justice Alito that, at the very least, "longer term GPS monitoring in investigations of most offenses impinges on expectations of privacy."

In cases involving even short-term monitoring, some unique attributes of GPS surveillance relevant to the *Katz* analysis will require particular attention. GPS monitoring generates a precise, comprehensive record of a person's public movements that reflects a wealth of detail about her familial, political, professional, religious, and sexual associations. The Government can store such records and efficiently mine them for information years into the future. And because GPS monitoring is cheap in comparison to conventional surveillance techniques and, by design, proceeds surreptitiously, it evades the ordinary checks that constrain abusive law enforcement practices: "limited police resources and community hostility." Illinois v. Lidster, 540 U.S. 419, 426 (2004).

Awareness that the Government may be watching chills associational and expressive freedoms. And the Government's unrestrained power to assemble data that reveal private aspects of identity is susceptible to abuse. The net result is that GPS monitoring—by making available at a relatively low cost such a substantial quantum of intimate information about any person whom the Government, in its unfettered discretion, chooses to track—may "alter the relationship between citizen and government in a way that is inimical to democratic society." United States v. Cuevas-Perez, 640 F.3d 272, 285 (C.A.7 2011) (Flaum, J., concurring).

I would take these attributes of GPS monitoring into account when considering the existence of a reasonable societal expectation of privacy in the sum of one's public movements. I would ask whether people reasonably expect that their movements will be recorded and aggregated in a manner that enables the Government to ascertain, more or less at will, their political and religious beliefs, sexual habits, and so on. I do not regard as dispositive the fact that the Government might obtain the fruits of GPS monitoring through lawful conventional surveillance techniques. I would also consider the appropriateness of entrusting to the Executive, in the absence of any oversight from a coordinate branch, a tool so amenable to misuse, especially in light of the Fourth Amendment's goal to curb arbitrary exercises of police power and prevent "a too permeating police surveillance," United States v. Di Re, 332 U.S. 581, 595 (1948).

More fundamentally, it may be necessary to reconsider the premise that an individual has no reasonable expectation of privacy in information voluntarily disclosed to third parties. This approach is ill suited to the digital age, in which people reveal a great deal of information about themselves to third parties in the course of carrying out mundane tasks. People disclose the phone numbers that they dial or text to their cellular providers; the URLs that they visit and the e-mail addresses with which they correspond to their Internet service providers; and the books, groceries, and medications they purchase to online retailers. Perhaps, as Justice Alito notes, some people may find the "tradeoff" of privacy for convenience "worthwhile," or come to accept this "diminution of privacy" as "inevitable," and perhaps not. I for one doubt that people would accept without complaint the warrantless disclosure to the Government of a list of every Web site they had visited in the last week, or month, or year. But whatever the societal expectations, they can attain constitutionally protected status only if our Fourth Amendment jurisprudence ceases to treat secrecy as a prerequisite for privacy. I would not assume that all information voluntarily disclosed to some member of the public for a limited purpose is, for that reason alone, disentitled to Fourth Amendment protection.

Resolution of these difficult questions in this case is unnecessary, however, because the Government's physical intrusion on Jones' Jeep supplies a narrower basis for decision. I therefore join the majority's opinion.

JUSTICE ALITO, with whom JUSTICE GINSBURG, JUSTICE BREYER, and JUSTICE KAGAN join, concurring in the judgment.

This case requires us to apply the Fourth Amendment's prohibition of unreasonable searches and seizures to a 21st-century surveillance technique, the use of a Global Positioning System (GPS) device to monitor a vehicle's movements for an extended period of time. Ironically, the Court has chosen to decide this case based on 18th-century tort law. By attaching a small GPS device to the underside of the vehicle that respondent drove, the law enforcement officers in this case engaged in conduct that might have provided grounds in 1791 for a suit for trespass to chattels. And for this reason, the Court concludes, the installation and use of the GPS device constituted a search.

This holding, in my judgment, is unwise. It strains the language of the Fourth Amendment; it has little if any support in current Fourth Amendment case law; and it is highly artificial.

I would analyze the question presented in this case by asking whether respondent's reasonable expectations of privacy were violated by the long-term monitoring of the movements of the vehicle he drove.

I

A

The Fourth Amendment prohibits "unreasonable searches and seizures," and the Court makes very little effort to explain how the attachment or use of the GPS device fits within these terms. The Court does not contend that there was a seizure. A seizure of property occurs when there is "some meaningful interference with an individual's possessory interests in that property," United States v. Jacobsen, 466 U.S. 109, 113 (1984), and here there was none. Indeed, the success of the surveillance technique that the officers employed was dependent on the fact that the GPS did not interfere in any way with the operation of the vehicle, for if any such interference had been detected, the device might have been discovered.

The Court does claim that the installation and use of the GPS constituted a search, but this conclusion is dependent on the questionable proposition that these two procedures cannot be separated for purposes of Fourth Amendment analysis. If these two procedures are analyzed separately, it is not at all clear from the Court's opinion why either should be regarded as a search. It is clear that the attachment of the GPS device was not itself a search; if the device had not functioned or if the officers had not used it, no information would have been obtained. And the Court does not contend that the use of the device constituted a search either. On the contrary, the Court accepts the holding in United States v. Knotts, 460 U.S. 276 (1983), that the use of a surreptitiously planted electronic device to monitor a vehicle's movements on public roads did not amount to a search.

The Court argues — and I agree — that "we must 'assur[e] preservation of that degree of privacy against government that existed when the Fourth Amendment was adopted.'" (quoting Kyllo v. United States, 533 U.S. 27, 34 (2001)). But it is almost impossible to think of late–18th-century situations that are analogous to what took place in this case. (Is it possible to imagine a case in which a constable secreted himself somewhere in a coach and remained there for a period of time in order to monitor the movements of the coach's owner?[3]) The Court's theory seems to be that the concept of a search, as originally understood, comprehended any technical trespass that led to the gathering of evidence, but we know that this is incorrect. At common law, any unauthorized intrusion on private property was actionable, but a trespass on open fields, as opposed to the "curtilage" of a home, does not fall within the scope of the Fourth Amendment because private property outside the curtilage is not part of a "hous[e]" within the meaning of the Fourth Amendment.

B

The Court's reasoning in this case is very similar to that in the Court's early decisions involving wiretapping and electronic eavesdropping, namely, that a technical trespass followed by the gathering of evidence constitutes a search. In the early electronic surveillance cases, the Court concluded that a Fourth Amendment search occurred when private conversations were monitored as a result of an "unauthorized physical penetration into the premises occupied" by the defendant. Silverman v. United States, 365 U.S. 505, 509 (1961). In *Silverman,* police officers listened to conversations in an attached home by inserting a "spike mike" through the wall that this house shared with the vacant house next door. Id., at 506. This procedure was held to be a search because the mike made contact with a heating duct on the other side of the wall and thus "usurp[ed] . . . an integral part of the premises." Id., at 511.

By contrast, in cases in which there was no trespass, it was held that there was no search. Thus, in Olmstead v. United States, 277 U.S. 438 (1928), the Court found that the Fourth Amendment did not apply because "[t]he taps from house lines were made in the streets near the houses." Id., at 457. . . .

This trespass-based rule was repeatedly criticized. In *Olmstead,* Justice Brandeis wrote that it was "immaterial where the physical connection with the telephone wires was made." 277 U.S., at 479 (dissenting opinion). Although a private conversation transmitted by wire did not fall within the literal words of the Fourth Amendment, he argued, the Amendment should be understood as prohibiting "every unjustifiable intrusion by the government upon the privacy of the individual." Id., at 478. . . .

Katz v. United States, 389 U.S. 347 (1967), finally did away with the old approach, holding that a trespass was not required for a Fourth

---

3. The Court suggests that something like this might have occurred in 1791, but this would have required either a gigantic coach, a very tiny constable, or both—not to mention a constable with incredible fortitude and patience.

Amendment violation. *Katz* involved the use of a listening device that was attached to the outside of a public telephone booth and that allowed police officers to eavesdrop on one end of the target's phone conversation. This procedure did not physically intrude on the area occupied by the target, but the *Katz* Court "repudiate[ed]" the old doctrine, Rakas v. Illinois, 439 U.S. 128, 143 (1978), and held that "[t]he fact that the electronic device employed . . . did not happen to penetrate the wall of the booth can have no constitutional significance," 389 U.S., at 353. What mattered, the Court now held, was whether the conduct at issue "violated the privacy upon which [the defendant] justifiably relied while using the telephone booth." *Katz*, supra, at 353.

Under this approach, as the Court later put it when addressing the relevance of a technical trespass, "an actual trespass is neither necessary *nor sufficient* to establish a constitutional violation." United States v. Karo, 468 U.S. 705, 713 (emphasis added). In Oliver [v. United States, 466 U.S. 170 (1984)] the Court wrote:

> "The existence of a property right is but one element in determining whether expectations of privacy are legitimate. 'The premise that property interests control the right of the Government to search and seize has been discredited.' *Katz*, 389 U.S., at 353 (quoting Warden v. Hayden, 387 U.S. 294, 304 (1967); some internal quotation marks omitted)." 466 U.S., at 183. . . .

III

Disharmony with a substantial body of existing case law is only one of the problems with the Court's approach in this case.

I will briefly note four others. First, the Court's reasoning largely disregards what is really important (the *use* of a GPS for the purpose of long-term tracking) and instead attaches great significance to something that most would view as relatively minor (attaching to the bottom of a car a small, light object that does not interfere in any way with the car's operation). Attaching such an object is generally regarded as so trivial that it does not provide a basis for recovery under modern tort law. But under the Court's reasoning, this conduct may violate the Fourth Amendment. By contrast, if long-term monitoring can be accomplished without committing a technical trespass — suppose, for example, that the Federal Government required or persuaded auto manufacturers to include a GPS tracking device in every car — the Court's theory would provide no protection.

Second, the Court's approach leads to incongruous results. If the police attach a GPS device to a car and use the device to follow the car for even a brief time, under the Court's theory, the Fourth Amendment applies. But if the police follow the same car for a much longer period using unmarked cars and aerial assistance, this tracking is not subject to any Fourth Amendment constraints.

In the present case, the Fourth Amendment applies, the Court concludes, because the officers installed the GPS device after respondent's wife, to whom the car was registered, turned it over to respondent for his exclusive use. But if the GPS had been attached prior to that time, the Court's theory would lead to a different result. The Court proceeds on the assumption that respondent "had at least the property rights of a bailee," but a bailee may sue for a trespass to chattel only if the injury occurs during the term of the bailment. See 8A Am. Jur. 2d, Bailment § 166, pp. 685-686 (2009). So if the GPS device had been installed before respondent's wife gave him the keys, respondent would have no claim for trespass—and, presumably, no Fourth Amendment claim either.

Third, under the Court's theory, the coverage of the Fourth Amendment may vary from State to State. If the events at issue here had occurred in a community property State or a State that has adopted the Uniform Marital Property Act, respondent would likely be an owner of the vehicle, and it would not matter whether the GPS was installed before or after his wife turned over the keys. In non-community-property States, on the other hand, the registration of the vehicle in the name of respondent's wife would generally be regarded as presumptive evidence that she was the sole owner.

Fourth, the Court's reliance on the law of trespass will present particularly vexing problems in cases involving surveillance that is carried out by making electronic, as opposed to physical, contact with the item to be tracked. For example, suppose that the officers in the present case had followed respondent by surreptitiously activating a stolen vehicle detection system that came with the car when it was purchased. Would the sending of a radio signal to activate this system constitute a trespass to chattels? Trespass to chattels has traditionally required a physical touching of the property. In recent years, courts have wrestled with the application of this old tort in cases involving unwanted electronic contact with computer systems, and some have held that even the transmission of electrons that occurs when a communication is sent from one computer to another is enough. But may such decisions be followed in applying the Court's trespass theory? Assuming that what matters under the Court's theory is the law of trespass as it existed at the time of the adoption of the Fourth Amendment, do these recent decisions represent a change in the law or simply the application of the old tort to new situations?

IV

A

The *Katz* expectation-of-privacy test avoids the problems and complications noted above, but it is not without its own difficulties. It involves a degree of circularity, see *Kyllo*, 533 U.S., at 34, and judges are apt to confuse their own expectations of privacy with those of the hypothetical reasonable person to which the *Katz* test looks. In addition, the *Katz* test rests on the assumption that this hypothetical reasonable person has a well-developed and stable set of privacy expectations. But technology can change those expectations. Dramatic technological change may lead to periods in which popular expectations are in flux and may ultimately produce significant changes in popular attitudes. New technology may provide increased convenience or security at the expense of privacy, and many people may find the tradeoff worthwhile. And even if the public does not welcome the diminution of privacy that new technology entails, they may eventually reconcile themselves to this development as inevitable.

On the other hand, concern about new intrusions on privacy may spur the enactment of legislation to protect against these intrusions. This is what ultimately happened with respect to wiretapping. After *Katz*, Congress did not leave it to the courts to develop a body of Fourth Amendment case law governing that complex subject. Instead, Congress promptly enacted a comprehensive statute, see 18 U.S.C. §§ 2510-2522 (2006 ed. and Supp. IV), and since that time, the regulation of wiretapping has been governed primarily by statute and not by case law. In an ironic sense, although *Katz* overruled *Olmstead*, Chief Justice Taft's suggestion in the latter case that the regulation of wiretapping was a matter better left for Congress, has been borne out.

B

Recent years have seen the emergence of many new devices that permit the monitoring of a person's movements. In some locales, closed-circuit television video monitoring is becoming ubiquitous. On toll roads, automatic toll collection systems create a precise record of the movements of motorists who choose to make use of that convenience. Many motorists purchase cars that are equipped with devices that permit a central station to ascertain the car's location at any time so that roadside assistance may be provided if needed and the car may be found if it is stolen.

Perhaps most significant, cell phones and other wireless devices now permit wireless carriers to track and record the location of users — and as of June 2011, it has been reported, there were more than 322 million wireless devices in use in the United States. For older phones, the accuracy of the location information depends on the density of the tower network, but new "smart phones," which are equipped with a GPS device, permit more precise tracking. For example, when a user activates the GPS on such a phone, a provider is able to monitor the phone's location and speed of movement and can then report back real-time traffic conditions after combining ("crowdsourcing") the speed of all such phones on any particular road. Similarly, phone-location-tracking services are offered as "social" tools, allowing consumers to find (or to avoid) others who enroll in these services. The availability and use of these and other new devices will continue to shape the average person's expectations about the privacy of his or her daily movements.

V

In the pre-computer age, the greatest protections of privacy were neither constitutional nor statutory, but practical. Traditional surveillance for any extended period of time was difficult and costly and therefore rarely undertaken. The surveillance at issue in this case — constant monitoring of the location of a vehicle for four weeks — would have required a large team of agents, multiple vehicles, and perhaps aerial assistance. Only an investigation of unusual importance could have justified such an expenditure of law enforcement resources. Devices like the one used in the present case, however, make long-term monitoring relatively easy and cheap. In circumstances involving dramatic technological change, the best solution to privacy concerns may be legislative. A legislative body is well situated to gauge changing public attitudes, to draw detailed lines, and to balance privacy and public safety in a comprehensive way.

To date, however, Congress and most States have not enacted statutes regulating the use of GPS tracking technology for law enforcement purposes. The best that we can do in this case is to apply existing Fourth Amendment doctrine and to ask whether the use of GPS tracking in a particular case involved a degree of intrusion that a reasonable person would not have anticipated.

Under this approach, relatively short-term monitoring of a person's movements on public streets accords with expectations of privacy that our society has recognized as reasonable. But the use of longer term GPS monitoring in investigations of most offenses impinges on expectations of privacy. For such offenses, society's expectation has been that law enforcement agents and others would not—and indeed, in the main, simply could not—secretly monitor and catalogue every single movement of an individual's car for a very long period. In this case, for four weeks, law enforcement agents tracked every movement that respondent made in the vehicle he was driving. We need not identify with precision the point at which the tracking of this vehicle became a search, for the line was surely crossed before the 4-week mark. Other cases may present more difficult questions. But where uncertainty exists with respect to whether a certain period of GPS surveillance is long enough to constitute a Fourth Amendment search, the police may always seek a warrant. We also need not consider whether prolonged GPS monitoring in the context of investigations involving extraordinary offenses would similarly intrude on a constitutionally protected sphere of privacy. In such cases, long-term tracking might have been mounted using previously available techniques.

For these reasons, I conclude that the lengthy monitoring that occurred in this case constituted a search under the Fourth Amendment. I therefore agree with the majority that the decision of the Court of Appeals must be affirmed.

NOTES AND QUESTIONS

1. The Justices in *Jones* were unanimous that the defendant's conviction was properly reversed due to the admission of the GPS evidence at his criminal trial. But how wide was their agreement as to the reasons why?

2. There are two major lines of analysis. First, Justice Scalia, asserting the Fourth Amendment's "close connection" to property, looks to precedent largely predating *Katz* to conclude that because the agents investigating Jones trespassed on private property protected in the text of the Fourth Amendment for the purpose of obtaining information, a search took place within the meaning of that Amendment. (He declines to address whether a warrant was necessary for that search to be reasonable because the government did not raise this point below.) Given his conclusion that the conduct here would have constituted a Fourth Amendment intrusion on protected property interests at common law, and that *Katz* in no way narrowed the scope of Fourth Amendment protection, Justice Scalia finds it unnecessary to address *Katz*'s reasonable expectations approach. (For a more complete understanding of the traditional property-oriented approach to the Fourth Amendment, and its corresponding relationship with the Fifth Amendment, see Chapter 4, supra, and the extensive discussion therein of *Boyd* and its progeny.)

But not so Justice Alito. Deeming the majority's approach both "unwise" and "artificial," Justice Alito addresses the question whether Jones was subjected to a Fourth Amendment intrusion by applying *Katz*. He concludes that the answer to this question is yes because "the use of longer term GPS monitoring in investigations of most offenses impinges on expectations of privacy" and the line between short-term and long-term monitoring "was surely crossed before the 4-week mark."

3. So which approach is preferable? Justice Alito charges that the majority's approach will produce "incongruous results" based, *inter alia*, on the vagaries of bailment and family law, and on whether a given surveillance is effected with a GPS device or via unmarked cars. Justice Scalia says that Justice Alito, by failing to recognize that the *Katz* test in no way displaced the common law trespass approach, unnecessarily opens up a host of thorny questions such as the line between short-term and long-term monitoring, and the difference between those offenses in which long-term monitoring is and is not permissible. Who has the better of this argument?

4. And to which test must law enforcement agents look in planning for the use of surveillance techniques to track a suspect's public movements? Consider that Justice Sotomayor joins the majority opinion (thus giving Justice Scalia a majority for the proposition that *Katz* did not displace the common law's trespass approach). But she does so while also expressly agreeing with Justice Alito that regardless whether a physical trespass is necessary to install a GPS device, "longer term" GPS monitoring in investigations of "most" offenses constitutes a search. For the record, Justices Ginsburg, Breyer, and Kagan joined in Justice Alito's opinion. Counting noses, isn't it clear that now *both* tests are potentially implicated whenever a suspect's movements are tracked?

5. Your view of the two approaches might depend on what tack you think the Court should take in dealing with rapid technological advances that implicate the scope of personal privacy. The majority's approach is in some ways the more modest — putting off, until another day, the question of new modes of surveillance that do not depend on any physical invasion of constitutionally protected property. On the other hand, doesn't Justice Alito have a point in contending that the majority is disregarding what is *important* about the advent of GPS monitoring — namely, the vast amount of information it permits the government to acquire at low cost — in favor of an approach that will provide *no* guidance for future cases not involving a trespass?

6. The majority is *very* clear on one point — that the Court's task is, at a minimum, to ensure that the Fourth Amendment provides the degree of protection against government that it afforded when adopted. The

majority does not address this point at any length, since it deems it obvious that the physical trespass and information gathering at stake in *Jones* would have constituted a search at this relevant point. However, the meaning of the Court's affirmation that "we must 'assur[e] preservation of that degree of privacy against government that existed when the Fourth Amendment was adopted'" (a proposition with which Justice Alito, by the way, also agrees) is not clear, at least as regards new technology. Consider the following case, also involving technological advance that makes possible the acquisition by government of information perhaps not previously available — but this time concerning not a suspect's public movements, but activity within his home.

Insert the following note after Note 5 on page 405:

5a. On a related note, how "technological" does the police practice have to be? In Florida v. Jardines, 133 S. Ct. 1409 (2013) (set forth as a main case earlier in this Supplement), the Court concluded that a warrantless dog sniff that took place inside the curtilage of the home violated the Fourth Amendment. Although the majority did not really discuss the issue, Justice Kagan's concurring opinion and Justice Alito's dissent provided different views on the meaning of *Kyllo*. Justice Kagan said that a trained drug-detection dog was precisely the type of "device that is not in general public use" that could be used to gather information from inside the home, which *Kyllo* condemned. Justice Alito, on the other hand, said that "*Kyllo* is best understood as a decision about the use of new technology," and that a dog, "is not a new form of 'technology' or a 'device.'" Which is the better reading of *Kyllo*? More importantly, is there something distinctive about gathering information with technology? Or does "technological" just serve as a proxy for "not in general public use?"

C. Probable Cause and Warrants

1. The Warrant "Requirement"

Insert the following note after Note 9 on page 432:

10. In Bailey v. United States, 133 S. Ct. 1031 (2013), the Court returned to the *Summers* holding to make clear that it establishes a categorical rule permitting the detention of those on the premises at

which a proper search is being conducted, but that it does not extend further — no matter how reasonable such a detention might be, given the facts of a particular case. Police first observed Chunon Bailey and a male companion as they were departing from the area of a basement apartment that police intended to search pursuant to a warrant authorizing search for an illegal handgun. Bailey matched the description of "Polo," a man described by a confidential informant as selling drugs at the location. Detectives surreptitiously followed the men, who departed by car, for about a mile before stopping their vehicle. Bailey initially admitted to living at the apartment before denying residence there upon learning that it was being searched by police. Detectives recovered a key from Bailey during a patdown, however, which was later found to unlock the apartment's door. The men were handcuffed and driven in a patrol car back to the apartment, where a search team had already recovered narcotics and a gun. The district court denied a motion to suppress the apartment key and Bailey's statements, holding, *inter alia*, that Bailey's detention was justified pursuant to *Summers*. The Second Circuit affirmed, interpreting the Court's decision in *Summers* "to 'authoriz[e] law enforcement to detain the occupant of premises subject to a valid search warrant when that person is seen leaving those premises and the detention is effected *as soon as reasonably practicable*.'" 133 S. Ct. at 1037. The Supreme Court, in a majority opinion authored by Justice Kennedy, disagreed with this characterization of *Summers'* scope:

> *Summers* recognized that a rule permitting the detention of occupants on the premises during the execution of a search warrant, even absent individualized suspicion, was reasonable and necessary in light of the law enforcement interests in conducting a safe and efficient search. Because this exception grants substantial authority to police officers to detain outside of the traditional rules of the Fourth Amendment, it must be circumscribed.
>
> A spatial constraint defined by the immediate vicinity of the premises to be searched is therefore required for detentions incident to the execution of a search warrant. . . . Limiting the rule in *Summers* to the area in which an occupant poses a real threat to the safe and efficient execution of a search warrant ensures that the scope of the detention incident to a search is confined to its underlying justification. Once an occupant is beyond the immediate vicinity of the premises to be searched, the search-related law enforcement interests are diminished and the intrusiveness of the detention is more severe. Id. at 1041-42.

Justice Breyer, joined by Justices Alito and Thomas in dissent, argued that police had acted reasonably in effecting the detention 0.7 mile from the scene because, among other reasons, detention in open view of the residence would have added to the dangers of executing the search, as well as the risk of evidence destruction. The dissenters endorsed the Second Circuit's approach, concluding that requiring that any detention pursuant to *Summers* be effected as soon as reasonably practicable was superior to a rule based on whether the individual leaving a residence to be searched was still within the "immediate vicinity," a line "inviting case-by-case litigation" without "clear case-by-case guidance." Id. at 1047. In Justice Breyer's words, "I believe that the majority has substituted a line based on indeterminate geography for a line based on realistic considerations related to basic Fourth Amendment concerns such as privacy, safety, evidence destruction, and flight." Id. at 1049.

Finally, Justice Scalia authored a concurrence in which Justices Ginsburg and Kagan joined. He agreed with the majority that *Summers* is a categorical, bright-line rule applying only to the detention of "occupants," properly described in the majority opinion as "persons within 'the immediate vicinity of the premises to be searched.'" Id. at 1043. He wrote separately to make clear his view that the Second Circuit and the dissenters went astray in focusing, not on whether Bailey's detention fit within this rule, but on open-ended balancing: "Weighing the equities—Bailey 'posed a risk of harm to the officers,' his detention 'was not unreasonably prolonged,' and so forth—the Court of Appeals proclaimed the officers' conduct, 'in the circumstances presented, reasonable and prudent.'" Id. Justice Scalia concluded "[t]hat may be so, but it is irrelevant to whether *Summers* authorized the officers to seize Bailey without probable cause." Id.

Assume the officers did act reasonably. (And Justice Breyer stressed in his dissent that the officers prudently delayed detention, not only to minimize the threat of evidence destruction and flight, but also the danger posed by the fact that Bailey, his companion, or others inside the residence could have been armed.) Do you think the Court properly determined that the reasonableness of the officers' conduct was simply not germane to whether *Summers* should apply? Why or why not?

2. The Probable Cause Standard

Insert the following note after Note 1 on page 443:

1a. At the start, why did the *Gates* majority deem it so important to replace the "two-pronged test"? In a portion of the opinion not excerpted here, Justice Rehnquist noted that "[u]nlike a totality-of-the-circumstances analysis, which permits a balanced assessment of the relative weights of all the various indicia of reliability (and unreliability) attending an informant's tip, the 'two-pronged test' ha[d] encouraged an excessively technical dissection of informants' tips, with undue attention being focused on isolated issues that cannot sensibly be divorced from the other facts presented to the magistrate." In a footnote, he provided the following support for this proposition:

> 9. Some lower court decisions, brought to our attention by the State, reflect a rigid application of such rules. In Bridger v. State, 503 S.W.2d 801 (Tex. Cr. App. 1974), the affiant had received a confession of armed robbery from one of two suspects in the robbery; in addition, the suspect had given the officer $800 in cash stolen during the robbery. The suspect also told the officer that the gun used in the robbery was hidden in the other suspect's apartment. A warrant issued on the basis of this was invalidated on the ground that the affidavit did not satisfactorily describe how the accomplice had obtained his information regarding the gun.
>
> Likewise, in People v. Balanza, 55 Ill. App. 3d 1028, 371 N.E.2d 687 (1978), the affidavit submitted in support of an application for a search warrant stated that an informant of proven and uncontested reliability had seen, in specifically described premises, "a quantity of a white crystalline substance which was represented to the informant by a white male occupant of the premises to be cocaine. Informant has observed cocaine on numerous occasions in the past and is thoroughly familiar with its appearance. The informant states that the white crystalline powder he observed in the above described premises appeared to him to be cocaine." Id., at 1029, 371 N.E.2d, at 688. The warrant issued on the basis of the affidavit was invalidated because "[t]here is no indication as to how the informant or for that matter any other person could tell whether a white substance was cocaine and not some other substance such as sugar or salt." Id., at 1030, 371 N.E.2d, at 689.
>
> Finally, in People v. Brethauer, 174 Colo. 29, 482 P.2d 369 (1971), an informant, stated to have supplied reliable information in the past, claimed that L.S.D. and marihuana were located on certain premises. The informant supplied police with drugs, which were tested by police and confirmed to be illegal substances. The affidavit setting forth these, and other, facts was found defective under both prongs of Spinelli.

Do these cases suggest that the two-pronged test was being applied in an "excessively technical" way? If so, was this a flaw in the test or in its application in individual cases?

Insert the following note after Note 3 on page 444:

3a. Notice, however, that while the Court has consistently reaffirmed the fact-specific nature of the probable cause, it has recently provided guidance (and comfort) to law enforcement in one frequently-recurring fact pattern: dog sniffs that alert the police to the presence of drugs or explosives. In Florida v. Harris, 133 S. Ct. 1050 (2013), the Court overturned a Florida Supreme Court decision that imposed strict rules for determining whether dog sniffs were sufficiently reliable to constitute probable cause. The Florida Court said, among other things, that before a judge could base probable cause on a dog sniff, the prosecutor must introduce field performance records that provide "comprehensive documentation of the dog's prior 'hits' and 'misses' in the field." The U.S. Supreme Court unanimously rejected the requirement, finding it inconsistent with the flexible, commonsense determination required by *Gates* and subsequent cases. Instead, said the Court, "If a bona fide organization has certified a dog after testing his reliability in a controlled setting, a court can presume (subject to any conflicting evidence offered) that the dog's alert provides probable cause to search."

3. "Exceptions" to the Warrant "Requirement"

a. *Exigent Circumstances*

Insert the following note and main case after Note 4 on page 454:

4a. The so-called created exigency doctrine in the lower courts varied considerably across jurisdictions until May 2011, when the Supreme Court took up the question whether police may rely on exigent circumstances to dispense with the need for a warrant when they themselves have caused suspects to attempt evidence destruction. Does the Court successfully resolve the confusion? Is anything left of the "created exigency" doctrine?

KENTUCKY v. KING

Certiorari to the Supreme Court of Kentucky

131 S. Ct. 1849 (2011)

JUSTICE ALITO delivered the opinion of the Court.

It is well established that "exigent circumstances," including the need to prevent the destruction of evidence, permit police officers to conduct an otherwise permissible search without first obtaining a warrant. In this case, we consider whether this rule applies when police, by knocking on the door of a residence and announcing their presence, cause the occupants to attempt to destroy evidence. . . .

I

A

This case concerns the search of an apartment in Lexington, Kentucky. Police officers set up a controlled buy of crack cocaine outside an apartment complex. Undercover Officer Gibbons watched the deal take place from an unmarked car in a nearby parking lot. After the deal occurred, Gibbons radioed uniformed officers to move in on the suspect. He told the officers that the suspect was moving quickly toward the breezeway of an apartment building, and he urged them to "hurry up and get there" before the suspect entered an apartment.

In response to the radio alert, the uniformed officers drove into the nearby parking lot, left their vehicles, and ran to the breezeway. Just as they entered the breezeway, they heard a door shut and detected a very strong odor of burnt marijuana. At the end of the breezeway, the officers saw two apartments, one on the left and one on the right, and they did not know which apartment the suspect had entered. . . . Because they smelled marijuana smoke emanating from the apartment on the left, they approached the door of that apartment.

Officer Steven Cobb, one of the uniformed officers who approached the door, testified that the officers banged on the left apartment door "as loud as [they] could" and announced, "'This is the police'" or "'Police, police, police.'" Cobb said that "[a]s soon as [the officers] started banging on the door," they "could hear people inside moving," and "[i]t sounded as [though] things were being moved inside the apartment." These noises, Cobb testified, led the officers to believe that drug-related evidence was about to be destroyed.

At that point, the officers announced that they "were going to make entry inside the apartment." Cobb then kicked in the door, the officers entered the apartment, and they found three people in the front room: respondent Hollis King, respondent's girlfriend, and a guest who was smoking marijuana. The officers performed a protective sweep of the apartment during which they saw marijuana and powder cocaine in plain view. In a subsequent search, they also discovered crack cocaine, cash, and drug paraphernalia.

Police eventually entered the apartment on the right. Inside, they found the suspected drug dealer who was the initial target of their investigation.

B

[A] grand jury charged respondent. . . . Respondent filed a motion to suppress the evidence from the warrantless search, but the Circuit Court denied the motion. . . . The Kentucky Court of Appeals affirmed. . . . The Supreme Court of Kentucky reversed. As a preliminary matter, the court observed that there was "certainly some question as to whether the sound of persons moving [inside the apartment] was sufficient to establish that evidence was being destroyed." But the court did not answer that question. Instead, it "assume[d] for the purpose of argument that exigent circumstances existed."

. . . To determine whether police impermissibly created the exigency, the Supreme Court of Kentucky announced a two-part test. First, the court held, police cannot "deliberately creat[e] the exigent circumstances with the bad faith intent to avoid the warrant requirement." Second, even absent bad faith, the court concluded, police may not rely on exigent circumstances if "it was reasonably foreseeable that the investigative tactics employed by the police would create the exigent circumstances." Although the court found no evidence of bad faith, it held that exigent circumstances could not justify the search because it was reasonably foreseeable that the occupants would destroy evidence when the police knocked on the door and announced their presence.

We granted certiorari. . . .

II

A

. . . Although the text of the Fourth Amendment does not specify when a search warrant must be obtained, this Court has inferred that a warrant must generally be secured. "It is a 'basic principle of Fourth Amendment law,'" we have often said, "'that searches and seizures inside a home without a warrant are presumptively unreasonable.'" Brigham City v. Stuart, 547 U.S. 398, 403 (2006) (quoting Groh v. Ramirez, 540 U.S. 551, 559 (2004)). But we have also recognized that this presumption may be overcome in some circumstances because "[t]he ultimate touchstone of the Fourth Amendment is 'reasonableness.'" Brigham City, supra, at 403. Accordingly, the warrant requirement is subject to certain reasonable exceptions.

One well-recognized exception applies when "'the exigencies of the situation' make the needs of law enforcement so compelling that [a] warrantless search is objectively reasonable under the Fourth Amendment." Mincey v. Arizona, 437 U.S. 385, 394 (1978).

This Court has identified several exigencies that may justify a warrantless search of a home. See Brigham City, 547 U.S., at 403. . . . [W]hat is relevant here — the need "to prevent the imminent destruction of evidence" has long been recognized as a sufficient justification for a warrantless search. . . .

B

Over the years, lower courts have developed an exception to the exigent circumstances rule, the so-called "police-created exigency" doctrine. Under this doctrine, police may not rely on the need to prevent destruction of evidence when that exigency was "created" or "manufactured" by the conduct of the police. See, e.g., United States v. Chambers, 395 F.3d 563, 566 (CA6 2005) ("[F]or a warrantless search to stand, law enforcement officers must be responding to an unanticipated exigency rather than simply creating the exigency for themselves"); United States v. Gould, 364 F.3d 578, 590 (CA5 2004) (en banc) ("[A]lthough exigent circumstances may justify a warrantless probable cause entry into the home, they will not do so if the exigent circumstances were manufactured by the agents" (internal quotation marks omitted)).

In applying this exception for the "creation" or "manufacturing" of an exigency by the police, courts require something more than mere proof that fear of detection by the police caused the destruction of evidence. An additional showing is obviously needed because, as the Eighth Circuit has recognized, "in some sense the police always create the exigent circumstances." United States v. Duchi, 906 F.2d 1278, 1284 (CA8 1990). That is to say, in the vast majority of cases in which evidence is destroyed by persons who are engaged in illegal conduct, the reason for the destruction is fear that the evidence will fall into the hands of law enforcement. Destruction of evidence issues probably occur most frequently in drug cases because drugs may be easily destroyed by flushing them down a toilet or rinsing them down a drain. Persons in possession of valuable drugs are unlikely to destroy them unless they fear discovery by the police. Consequently, a rule that precludes the police from making a warrantless entry to prevent the destruction of evidence whenever their conduct causes the exigency would unreasonably shrink the reach of this well-established exception to the warrant requirement.

Presumably for the purpose of avoiding such a result, the lower courts have held that the police-created exigency doctrine requires more than simple causation, but the lower courts have not agreed on the test to be applied. Indeed, the petition in this case maintains that "[t]here are currently five different tests being used by the United States Courts of Appeals," and that some state courts have crafted additional tests.

III

A

Despite the welter of tests devised by the lower courts, the answer to the question presented in this case follows directly and clearly from the principle that permits warrantless searches in the first place. As previously noted, warrantless searches are allowed when the circumstances make it reasonable, within the meaning of the Fourth Amendment, to dispense with the warrant requirement. Therefore, the answer to the question before us is that the exigent circumstances rule justifies a warrantless search when the conduct of the police preceding the exigency is reasonable in the same sense. Where, as here, the police did not create the exigency by engaging or threatening to engage in conduct that violates the Fourth Amendment, warrantless entry to prevent the destruction of evidence is reasonable and thus allowed.[4] . . .

B

Some lower courts have adopted a rule that is similar to the one that we recognize today. But others, including the Kentucky Supreme Court, have imposed additional requirements that are unsound and that we now reject.

Bad faith. Some courts, including the Kentucky Supreme Court, ask whether law enforcement officers "'deliberately created the exigent circumstances with the bad faith intent to avoid the warrant requirement.'"

This approach is fundamentally inconsistent with our Fourth Amendment jurisprudence. "Our cases have repeatedly rejected" a subjective approach, asking only whether "the circumstances, viewed *objectively,* justify the action." *Brigham City,* 547 U.S., at 404. Indeed, we have never held, outside limited contexts such as an "inventory search or administrative inspection . . . , that an officer's motive invalidates objectively justifiable behavior under the Fourth Amendment." *Whren v. United States,* 517 U.S. 806, 812 (1996). . . .

Reasonable foreseeability. Some courts, again including the Kentucky Supreme Court, hold that police may not rely on an exigency if "'it was reasonably foreseeable that the investigative tactics employed by the police would create the exigent circumstances.'" Courts applying this test have

4. There is a strong argument to be made that, at least in most circumstances, the exigent circumstances rule should not apply where the police, without a warrant or any legally sound basis for a warrantless entry, threaten that they will enter without permission unless admitted. In this case, however, no such actual threat was made, and therefore we have no need to reach that question.

invalidated warrantless home searches on the ground that it was reasonably foreseeable that police officers, by knocking on the door and announcing their presence, would lead a drug suspect to destroy evidence.

Contrary to this reasoning, however, we have rejected the notion that police may seize evidence without a warrant only when they come across the evidence by happenstance. In Horton [v. California, 496 U.S. 128, 138 (1990)] . . . we held that the police may seize evidence in plain view even though the officers may be "interested in an item of evidence and fully expec[t] to find it in the course of a search."

Adoption of a reasonable foreseeability test would also introduce an unacceptable degree of unpredictability. For example, whenever law enforcement officers knock on the door of premises occupied by a person who may be involved in the drug trade, there is *some* possibility that the occupants may possess drugs and may seek to destroy them. Under a reasonable foreseeability test, it would be necessary to quantify the degree of predictability that must be reached before the police-created exigency doctrine comes into play.

A simple example illustrates the difficulties that such an approach would produce. Suppose that the officers in the present case did not smell marijuana smoke and thus knew only that there was a 50% chance that the fleeing suspect had entered the apartment on the left rather than the apartment on the right. Under those circumstances, would it have been reasonably foreseeable that the occupants of the apartment on the left would seek to destroy evidence upon learning that the police were at the door? Or suppose that the officers knew only that the suspect had disappeared into one of the apartments on a floor with 3, 5, 10, or even 20 units? If the police chose a door at random and knocked for the purpose of asking the occupants if they knew a person who fit the description of the suspect, would it have been reasonably foreseeable that the occupants would seek to destroy evidence?

We have noted that "[t]he calculus of reasonableness must embody allowance for the fact that police officers are often forced to make split-second judgments—in circumstances that are tense, uncertain, and rapidly evolving." Graham v. Connor, 490 U.S. 386, 396-397 (1989). The reasonable foreseeability test would create unacceptable and unwarranted difficulties for law enforcement officers who must make quick decisions in the field, as well as for judges who would be required to determine after the fact whether the destruction of evidence in response to a knock on the door was reasonably foreseeable based on what the officers knew at the time.

Probable cause and time to secure a warrant. Some courts, in applying the police-created exigency doctrine, fault law enforcement officers if, after acquiring evidence that is sufficient to establish probable cause to search particular premises, the officers do not seek a warrant but instead knock on the door and seek either to speak with an occupant or to obtain consent to search.

This approach unjustifiably interferes with legitimate law enforcement strategies. There are many entirely proper reasons why police may not want to seek a search warrant as soon as the bare minimum of evidence needed to establish probable cause is acquired. Without attempting to provide a comprehensive list of these reasons, we note a few.

First, the police may wish to speak with the occupants of a dwelling before deciding whether it is worthwhile to seek authorization for a search. They may think that a short and simple conversation may obviate the need to apply for and execute a warrant. Second, the police may want to ask an occupant of the premises for consent to search because doing so is simpler, faster, and less burdensome than applying for a warrant. A consensual search also "may result in considerably less inconvenience" and embarrassment to the occupants than a search conducted pursuant to a warrant. Third, law enforcement officers may wish to obtain more evidence before submitting what might otherwise be considered a marginal warrant application. Fourth, prosecutors may wish to wait until they acquire evidence that can justify a search that is broader in scope than the search that a judicial officer is likely to authorize based on the evidence then available. And finally, in many cases, law enforcement may not want to execute a search that will disclose the existence of an investigation because doing so may interfere with the acquisition of additional evidence against those already under suspicion or evidence about additional but as yet unknown participants in a criminal scheme.

We have said that "[l]aw enforcement officers are under no constitutional duty to call a halt to criminal investigation the moment they have the minimum evidence to establish probable cause." Hoffa v. United States, 385 U.S. 293, 310 (1966). Faulting the police for failing to apply for a search warrant at the earliest possible time after obtaining probable cause imposes a duty that is nowhere to be found in the Constitution.

Standard or good investigative tactics. Finally, some lower court cases suggest that law enforcement officers may be found to have created or manufactured an exigency if the court concludes that the course of their investigation was "contrary to standard or good law enforcement practices (or to the policies or practices of their jurisdictions)." This approach fails to provide clear guidance for law enforcement officers and authorizes courts to make judgments on matters that are the province of those who are responsible for federal and state law enforcement agencies.

C

Respondent argues for a rule that differs from those discussed above, but his rule is also flawed. Respondent contends that law enforcement officers impermissibly create an exigency when they "engage in conduct that would cause a reasonable person to believe that entry is imminent and inevitable." In respondent's view, relevant factors include the officers' tone of voice in announcing their presence and the forcefulness of their knocks. But the ability of law enforcement officers to respond to an exigency cannot turn on such subtleties.

Police officers may have a very good reason to announce their presence loudly and to knock on the door with some force. A forceful knock may be necessary to alert the occupants that someone is at the door. Furthermore, unless police officers identify themselves loudly enough, occupants may not know who is at their doorstep. Officers are permitted — indeed, encouraged — to identify themselves to citizens, and "in many circumstances this is cause for assurance, not discomfort." Citizens who are startled by an unexpected knock on the door or by the sight of unknown persons in plain clothes on their doorstep may be relieved to learn that these persons are police officers. Others may appreciate the opportunity to make an informed decision about whether to answer the door to the police.

If respondent's test were adopted, it would be extremely difficult for police officers to know how loudly they may announce their presence or how forcefully they may knock on a door without running afoul of the police-created exigency rule. And in most cases, it would be nearly impossible for a court to determine whether that threshold had been passed. The Fourth Amendment does not require the nebulous and impractical test that respondent proposes.[5]

---

5. Contrary to respondent's argument, Johnson v. United States, 333 U.S. 10 (1948), does not require affirmance in this case. In *Johnson*, officers noticed the smell of burning opium emanating from a hotel room. They then knocked on the door and demanded entry. Upon seeing that Johnson was the only occupant of the room, they placed her under arrest, searched the room, and discovered opium and drug paraphernalia. Id., at 11.

Defending the legality of the search, the Government attempted to justify the warrantless search of the room as a valid search incident to a lawful arrest. See Brief for United States in Johnson v. United States, O.T. 1947, No. 329. The Government did not contend that the officers entered the room in order to prevent the destruction of evidence. Although the officers said that they heard a "'shuffling'" noise inside the room after they knocked on the door, 333 U.S., at 12, the Government did not claim that this particular noise was a noise that would have led a reasonable officer to think that evidence was about to be destroyed. Thus, *Johnson* is simply not a case about exigent circumstances. See id., at 14-15 (noting that if "exceptional circumstances" existed — for example, if a "suspect was fleeing or likely to take flight" or if "evidence or contraband was threatened with removal or destruction" — then "it may be contended that a magistrate's warrant for search may be dispensed with").

D

For these reasons, we conclude that the exigent circumstances rule applies when the police do not gain entry to premises by means of an actual or threatened violation of the Fourth Amendment. This holding provides ample protection for the privacy rights that the Amendment protects.

When law enforcement officers who are not armed with a warrant knock on a door, they do no more than any private citizen might do. And whether the person who knocks on the door and requests the opportunity to speak is a police officer or a private citizen, the occupant has no obligation to open the door or to speak. . . . And even if an occupant chooses to open the door and speak with the officers, the occupant need not allow the officers to enter the premises and may refuse to answer any questions at any time.

Occupants who choose not to stand on their constitutional rights but instead elect to attempt to destroy evidence have only themselves to blame for the warrantless exigent-circumstances search that may ensue.

IV

We now apply our interpretation of the police-created exigency doctrine to the facts of this case.

A

We need not decide whether exigent circumstances existed in this case. Any warrantless entry based on exigent circumstances must, of course, be supported by a genuine exigency. The trial court and the Kentucky Court of Appeals found that there was a real exigency in this case, but the Kentucky Supreme Court expressed doubt on this issue. . . .

We . . . assume for purposes of argument that an exigency existed. We decide only the question on which the Kentucky Supreme Court ruled and on which we granted certiorari: Under what circumstances do police impermissibly create an exigency? Any question about whether an exigency actually existed is better addressed by the Kentucky Supreme Court on remand.

B

In this case, we see no evidence that the officers either violated the Fourth Amendment or threatened to do so prior to the point when they entered the apartment. Officer Cobb testified without contradiction that the officers "banged on the door as loud as [they] could" and announced either "'Police,

police, police'" or "'This is the police.'" This conduct was entirely consistent with the Fourth Amendment, and we are aware of no other evidence that might show that the officers either violated the Fourth Amendment or threatened to do so (for example, by announcing that they would break down the door if the occupants did not open the door voluntarily). . . .

* * *

Like the court below, we assume for purposes of argument that an exigency existed. Because the officers in this case did not violate or threaten to violate the Fourth Amendment prior to the exigency, we hold that the exigency justified the warrantless search of the apartment. The judgment of the Kentucky Supreme Court is reversed. . . .

[JUSTICE GINSBURG's dissenting opinion is omitted.]

NOTES AND QUESTIONS

1. The Kentucky Supreme Court expressed doubt as to whether the sounds of persons moving inside the apartment, coupled with what police otherwise knew about the circumstances, provided a sufficient basis on which the police here could conclude that evidence was being destroyed. Justice Alito, writing for the majority, assumed, without deciding, that an exigency existed. What do you think? Did police have an adequate basis to believe that immediate action was necessary — even before we turn to the question whether it makes a difference that police may have created any exigency that was present? How much evidence of exigency do police need? Probable cause to believe evidence is being destroyed? Something less? Something more?

2. Let's assume there was an exigency here. Do you agree that police were entitled to rely on this exigency to dispense with a warrant even when they caused the imminent need for action by knocking on the door? Note that Justice Ginsburg was the sole Justice who dissented from this position. Is it simply obvious that police are entitled to presume when announcing their presence in the way any citizen might that suspects will not respond by seeking to destroy evidence?

3. Of course, most citizens don't announce their presence by shouting and banging on the door as loudly as possible — precisely what these police did, according to their own testimony. Assume police have been conducting surveillance of a brownstone they believe to be a crack house. Despite their best efforts, police have been unable to establish probable cause to support this belief. Police surround the residence and then loudly announce their presence, using a bullhorn and pounding on the

front door. Officers move in when they observe suspects throwing drugs and weapons out the windows. Is this permissible after *King* — at least so long as police do not also shout out, "We're coming in!" as they surround the home?

4. Finally, is *King* really a case of police-created exigency? Why wasn't the smell of marijuana smoke, standing alone, sufficient to establish an exigency — an exigency existing even before police knocked on the door? After all, the smell provided a strong basis to believe not only that marijuana would be found in the apartment, but that it was literally being consumed. Does probable cause to believe that marijuana is being smoked in a home and that evidence of this conduct may dissipate, in the time it takes to get a warrant, provide an adequate reason for dispensing with the warrant requirement?

Insert the following at the end of Note 4 on page 459:

In Stanton v. Sims, 134 S. Ct. ___ (2013), the Court held that a police officer who, while in hot pursuit of a fleeing misdemeanor suspect, kicked open a gate to chase the suspect into the curtilage of a home and thereby injured an innocent third party, was nevertheless entitled to qualified immunity from a Section 1983 lawsuit because any possible Fourth Amendment violation was, at a minimum, not "clearly established" under prevailing law. The Court noted that *Welsh* "did not lay down a categorical rule for all cases involving minor offenses," and furthermore that "nothing in the [*Welsh*] opinion establishes that the seriousness of the crime is equally important *in cases of hot pursuit*." The Court also pointed out that in United States v. Santana, 427 U.S. 38 (1976), which upheld the warrantless entry into a home in "hot pursuit" of a suspect who had committed a felony, "we did not expressly limit our holding based on that fact." The questions asked in the preceding paragraph are, apparently, still open.

4a. In Missouri v. McNeely, 133 S. Ct. 1552 (2013), the Supreme Court had occasion to consider the subject of testing for blood alcohol content ("BAC") in drunk-driving cases again — albeit in a matter not involving entry into the home. Recall that in Schmerber v. California, 384 U.S. 757 (1966), which we examined in Chapter Four, the Supreme Court determined that where a suspect had suffered injuries in an automobile accident and was at the hospital receiving treatment, the police officer who arrested him acted consistently with the Fourth Amendment in ordering a warrantless blood test to be performed over the suspect's objection, given that the officer might reasonably have believed he confronted an emergency in which delaying to obtain a warrant threatened the destruction of the blood alcohol evidence. McNeely, stopped for speeding and crossing the centerline, refused to take a breath test, and was arrested and taken to the hospital for blood testing. The State argued for a *per se* rule in drunk-driving cases, that "whenever an officer has probable cause to believe an individual has been driving under the influence of alcohol, exigent circumstances will necessarily exist," excusing the officer from obtaining a warrant for the testing itself, "because the BAC evidence is inherently evanescent." *McNeely*, 133 S. Ct. at 1560. The majority rejected this claim:

> In those drunk-driving investigations where police officers can reasonably obtain a warrant before a blood sample can be drawn without significantly undermining the efficacy of the search, the Fourth Amendment mandates that they do so. We do not doubt that some circumstances will make obtaining a warrant impractical such that the dissipation of alcohol from the bloodstream will support an exigency justifying a properly conducted warrantless blood test. That, however, is a reason to decide each case on its facts, as we did in *Schmerber*. . . .
>
> The State's proposed *per se* rule . . . fails to account for advances in the 47 years since *Schmerber* was decided that allow for the more expeditious processing of warrant applications, particularly in contexts like drunk-driving investigations where the evidence offered to establish probable cause is simple. . . . Well over a majority of States allow police officers or prosecutors to apply for search warrants remotely through various means, including telephonic or radio communication, electronic communication such as e-mail, and video conferencing. And in addition to technology-based developments, jurisdictions have found other ways to streamline the warrant process, such as by using standard-form applications for drunk-driving investigations.
>
> We by no means claim that telecommunications innovations have, will, or should eliminate all delay from the warrant-application process. . . . But technological developments that enable police officers to secure warrants more quickly, and do so without undermining the neutral magistrate judge's essential role as a check on police discretion, are relevant to an assessment of exigency. That is particularly so in this context, where BAC evidence is lost gradually and relatively predictably. . . .
>
> In short, while the natural dissipation of alcohol in the blood may support a finding of exigency in a specific case, as it did in *Schmerber*, it does not do so categorically. Whether a warrantless blood test of a drunk-driving suspect is

reasonable must be determined case by case based on the totality of the circumstances.

Id. at 1561-63. Do you agree? Should technological advances be considered more systematically in thinking about the scope of the exigency exception?

NOTES ON PUNITIVE AND PROTECTIVE POLICING

Insert the following notes after Note 2 on page 464:

2a. Perhaps reasonableness, pure and simple? Consider Ryburn v. Huff, 132 S. Ct. 987 (2012), a per curiam opinion from a unanimous Court.

In *Ryburn*, police went to the home of Vincent Huff, a high school student, after the principal of the school informed them that Vincent was rumored to have written a letter threatening to "shoot up" the school, resulting in many parents deciding to keep their children at home. One of Vincent's classmates told police that Vincent was capable of carrying out such a threat. (Vincent, who had been absent from school for two days, was reported to be the victim of bullying.) Officers went to Vincent's home and knocked on the door, announcing they were police, but received no response. They then called the home and heard the telephone ringing inside, but it was not answered. Finally, when police called the cell phone of Vincent's mother, she answered and, upon being asked her location, admitted that she and Vincent were inside the home. An officer requested to speak with her, but she hung up, only to walk outside with Vincent a few minutes later. When the officers advised Vincent that they were there to speak with him about the threat, he responded, "I can't believe you're here for that."

Sergeant Darin Ryburn next asked Mrs. Huff if the officers might come inside. She said no. He then asked if there were any guns in the house. Mrs. Huff responded by running inside. Sergeant Ryburn, who later testified that he was "scared because [he] didn't know what was in that house," followed her, as did Vincent and another officer who did not want Sergeant Ryburn to enter the home alone. Two additional officers followed, believing that Mrs. Huff had given her consent to entry.

The officers were in the home between five and 10 minutes. During that time, Mr. Huff appeared in the living room. The officers conducted no search, but merely spoke with Vincent and Mr. Huff during this period, before concluding that the rumor about Vincent's alleged threat was false. The officers thereafter departed, and the Huffs brought suit under 42 U.S.C. § 1983, alleging violation of their Fourth Amendment rights.

After a two-day bench trial, the district court concluded that the officers were entitled to qualified immunity because Mrs. Huff's odd behavior, combined with the information they had obtained from the school, could have led reasonable officers to conclude "that there could be weapons inside the house, and that family members or the officers themselves were in danger." The Ninth Circuit affirmed as to the officers who entered the home believing that Mrs. Huff had consented, but reversed as to Sergeant Ryburn and the officer who first entered with him. The divided panel concluded that any belief that the situation threatened imminent harm was objectively unreasonable, because Mrs. Huff had merely asserted her right to end the conversation.

The Supreme Court disagreed — and in emphatic terms:

> The panel majority — far removed from the scene and with the opportunity to dissect the elements of the situation — confidently concluded that the officers really had no reason to fear for their safety or that of anyone else. As the panel majority saw things, it was irrelevant that the Huffs did not respond when the officers knocked on the door and announced their presence and when they called the home phone because the Huffs had no legal obligation to respond to a knock on the door or to answer the phone. The majority attributed no significance to the fact that when the officers finally reached Mrs. Huff on her cell phone, she abruptly hung up in the middle of their conversation. And, according to the majority, the officers should not have been concerned by Mrs. Huff's reaction when they asked her if there were any guns in the house because Mrs. Huff "merely asserted her right to end her conversation with the officers and returned to her home."

The panel majority erred, the Court concluded, by apparently taking the view "that conduct cannot be regarded as a matter of concern so long as it is lawful," and by analyzing each event transpiring at the Huffs' residence in isolation, in an "entirely unrealistic" way. "Judged from the proper perspective of a reasonable police officer forced to make a split-second decision in response to a rapidly unfolding chain of events that culminated with Mrs. Huff turning and running into the house after refusing to answer a question about guns," the Court said, "petitioners' belief that entry was necessary to avoid injury to themselves or others was eminently reasonable."

2b. As discussed at pages 353-355 of the main volume, because *Ryburn* was a qualified immunity case, the Court was formally addressing *not*

whether the officers violated the Fourth Amendment by entering the
Huffs' home, but instead whether officers in their position might make
a reasonable mistake as to the legality of their entry. The Court's analysis
strongly suggests, however, that the Justices believed the officers' conduct
was lawful. Thus, the Justices asserted that "[n]o decision of this Court has
found a Fourth Amendment violation on facts even roughly comparable
to those present in this case. On the contrary, some of our opinions may
be read as pointing in the opposite direction." The Court cited *Stuart* as
one of those opinions, and pointed out that "[a] reasonable police officer"
could read it to mean "that the Fourth Amendment permits an officer to
enter a residence if the officer has a reasonable basis for concluding that
there is an imminent threat of violence."

2c. That last sentence is worth pondering. A "reasonable basis" is quite
different from probable cause — and in *Ryburn*, arose from something
much less definitive than the situation in *Stuart*, where officers actually
observed one person inside the home striking another person in the face.
Was the entry in *Ryburn* nonetheless "reasonable"? If so, why? In that
sense, might *Ryburn* represent a significant extension of the Court's
ruling in *Stuart*? And what does *Ryburn* signal — if anything — about the
Huffs' right to decline to cooperate with police?

2d. As set forth in Note 3 on page 464, perhaps Fourth Amendment
rules *should* differ, depending upon whether police target and search
suspects they are attempting to prosecute, as opposed to intruding on
Fourth Amendment interests for the purpose of protecting life and limb.
If so, on which side of that line should *Ryburn* fall? How about *Stuart*?

d. Arrests

Insert the following note after Note 3 on page 514:

3a. Now consider what may happen when a person in Atwater's situation is not released within a few hours, "without assignment to the
general jail population and without substantial contact with other detainees," see Florence v. Burlington County, 132 S. Ct. 1510, 1522 (2012),
but is instead committed to the general population. Does the decision in
Florence constitute an argument that *Atwater* was incorrectly decided?

In connection with a 1998 arrest, Albert Florence pleaded guilty and
was sentenced to pay a fine in monthly installments. In 2003, a bench
warrant issued for his arrest when he fell behind in payments and
neglected to appear at a hearing. Although Florence paid the outstand-

ing balance a few days later, the warrant somehow remained in the statewide police database in New Jersey. Florence was arrested two years later when the warrant appeared in the database during a traffic stop. He was admitted to and held in two separate detention facilities over a period of approximately one week before the charges were dismissed upon determination that the fine had been paid.

Florence was searched before being admitted to each facility. At the first jail, he was required to shower with a delousing agent and was visually examined by officers for scars, marks, gang tattoos, and contraband as he disrobed. He alleged that he was also instructed "to open his mouth, lift his tongue, hold out his arms, turn around, and lift his genitals." Id. at 1514. At the second facility, he was again required to remove his clothing while an officer inspected for markings, wounds, and contraband. He alleged that "he was required to lift his genitals, turn around, and cough in a squatting position." Id.

After his release, Florence filed a 42 U.S.C. § 1983 action, asserting Fourth Amendment violations. Florence argued that a person arrested for a minor offense cannot be required to remove his clothing and expose his body to close visual inspection as a routine part of intake, but should only be subjected to this treatment when officials have reason to suspect him of concealing a weapon, drugs, or other contraband. The Supreme Court, in an opinion authored by Justice Kennedy and joined in relevant part by Chief Justice Roberts and Justices Scalia, Alito, and Thomas, disagreed:

> *Atwater* did not address whether the Constitution imposes special restrictions on the searches of offenders suspected for committing minor offenses once they are taken to jail. . . .
> Correctional officials have a significant interest in conducting a thorough search as a standard part of the intake process. The admission of inmates creates numerous risks for facility staff, for the existing detainee population, and for a new detainee himself or herself. The danger of introducing lice or contagious infections, for example, is well documented. . . .
> Jails and prisons also face grave threats posed by the increasing number of gang members who go through the intake process. . . . The identification and isolation of gang members before they are admitted protects everyone in the facility. Detecting contraband concealed by new detainees, furthermore, is a most serious responsibility. . . . Correctional officers have had to confront arrestees concealing knives, scissors, razor blades, glass shards, and other prohibited items on their person, including in their body cavities. . . .
> It is not surprising that correctional officials have sought to perform thorough searches at intake for disease, gang affiliation, and contraband. Jails are

often crowded, unsanitary, and dangerous places. There is a substantial interest in preventing any new inmate, either of his own will or as a result of coercion, from putting all who live or work at these institutions at even greater risk when he is admitted to the general population. . . .

Experience shows that people arrested for minor offenses have tried to smuggle prohibited items into jail, sometimes by using their rectal cavities or genitals for the concealment. . . .

Even if people arrested for a minor offense do not themselves wish to introduce contraband into a jail, they may be coerced into doing so by others. . . .

It also may be difficult, as a practical matter, to classify inmates by their current and prior offenses before the intake search. Jails can be even more dangerous than prisons because officials there know so little about the people they admit at the outset. . . .

One of the central principles in *Atwater* applies with equal force here. Officers who interact with those suspected of violating the law have an "essential interest in readily administrable rules." The officials in charge of the jails in this case urge the Court to reject any complicated constitutional scheme requiring them to conduct less thorough inspections of some detainees based on their behavior, suspected offense, criminal history, and other factors. They offer significant reasons why the Constitution must not prevent them from conducting the same search on any suspected offender who will be admitted to the general population in their facilities. The restrictions suggested by petitioner would limit the intrusion on the privacy of some detainees but at the risk of increased danger to everyone in the facility, including the less serious offenders themselves. . . .

Even assuming all the facts in favor of petitioner, the search procedures [here] struck a reasonable balance between inmate privacy and the needs of the institution.

Do you agree? Note that Chief Justice Roberts and Justice Alito joined the majority opinion while also writing separately to note that the circumstances before the Court presented no occasion to consider whether an exception might exist for cases in which arrestees need not be held in the general jail population. Further, in Justice Alito's words, "[t]he Court does not address whether it is always reasonable, without regard to the offense or the reason for detention, to strip search an arrestee before the arrestee's detention has been reviewed by a judicial officer." Id. at 1525. Accordingly, Justice Breyer, in a dissent joined by Justices Ginsburg, Sotomayor, and Kagan, noted that "[i]n an appropriate case . . . it remains open for the Court to consider whether it would be reasonable to admit an arrestee for a minor offense to the general jail population, and to subject her to the humiliation of a strip search, prior to any review by a judicial officer." Id. at 1532 (internal quotation omitted).

e. Searches Incident to Arrest

Insert the following note and main case after Note 5 on page 535:

6. Can you think of any objects, commonly found on or near the person of an arrestee, that are so imbued with privacy interests — and so unlikely to trigger the concerns that motivated *Chimel* — that the police should *not* be allowed to search them without a warrant pursuant to the search incident doctrine? What about cell phones, which today can (and often do) contain virtually a person's entire life story? In the following companion cases, *Riley* and *Wurie*, the Court considered this important question — and issued a unanimous decision that, although relatively limited in scope, immediately will impact large numbers of criminal investigations and prosecutions, and eventually could turn out to have broader implications for the future of technology searches under the Fourth Amendment.

RILEY v. CALIFORNIA
Certiorari to the Court of Appeal of California, Fourth Appellate District
134 S. Ct. ___ (2014)

CHIEF JUSTICE ROBERTS delivered the opinion of the Court.

These two cases raise a common question: whether the police may, without a warrant, search digital information on a cell phone seized from an individual who has been arrested.

I

A

In the first case, petitioner David Riley was stopped by a police officer for driving with expired registration tags. In the course of the stop, the officer also learned that Riley's license had been suspended. The officer impounded Riley's car, pursuant to department policy, and another officer conducted an inventory search of the car. Riley was arrested for possession of concealed and loaded firearms when that search turned up two handguns under the car's hood. See Cal. Penal Code Ann. § § 12025(a)(1), 12031(a)(1) (West 2009).

An officer searched Riley incident to the arrest and found items associated with the "Bloods" street gang. He also seized a cell phone from Riley's pants pocket. According to Riley's uncontradicted assertion, the phone was a "smart phone," a cell phone with a broad range of other functions based on advanced computing capability, large storage capacity, and Internet connectivity. The officer accessed information on the phone and noticed that some words (presumably in text messages or a contacts list) were preceded by the letters "CK"—a label that, he believed, stood for "Crip Killers," a slang term for members of the Bloods gang.

At the police station about two hours after the arrest, a detective specializing in gangs further examined the contents of the phone. The detective testified that he "went through" Riley's phone "looking for evidence, because . . . gang members will often video themselves with guns or take pictures of themselves with the guns." Although there was "a lot of stuff" on the phone, particular files that "caught [the detective's] eye" included videos of young men sparring while someone yelled encouragement using the moniker "Blood." The police also found photographs of Riley standing in front of a car they suspected had been involved in a shooting a few weeks earlier.

Riley was ultimately charged, in connection with that earlier shooting, with firing at an occupied vehicle, assault with a semiautomatic firearm, and attempted murder. The State alleged that Riley had committed those crimes for the benefit of a criminal street gang, an aggravating factor that carries an enhanced sentence. Compare Cal. Penal Code Ann. § 246 (2008) with § 186.22(b)(4)(B) (2014). Prior to trial, Riley moved to suppress all evidence that the police had obtained from his cell phone. He contended that the searches of his phone violated the Fourth Amendment, because they had been performed without a warrant and were not otherwise justified by exigent circumstances. The trial court rejected that argument. At Riley's trial, police officers testified about the photographs and videos found on the phone, and some of the photographs were admitted into evidence. Riley was convicted on all three counts and received an enhanced sentence of 15 years to life in prison.

The California Court of Appeal affirmed. The court relied on the California Supreme Court's decision in People v. Diaz, 51 Cal. 4th 84, 244 P. 3d 501 (2011), which held that the Fourth Amendment permits a warrantless search of cell phone data incident to an arrest, so long as the cell phone was immediately associated with the arrestee's person. See id., at 93, 244 P. 3d, at 505-506.

The California Supreme Court denied Riley's petition for review, and we granted certiorari.

B

In the second case, [United States v. Wurie, No. 13-212,] a police officer performing routine surveillance observed respondent Brima

Wurie make an apparent drug sale from a car. Officers subsequently arrested Wurie and took him to the police station. At the station, the officers seized two cell phones from Wurie's person. The one at issue here was a "flip phone," a kind of phone that is flipped open for use and that generally has a smaller range of features than a smart phone. Five to ten minutes after arriving at the station, the officers noticed that the phone was repeatedly receiving calls from a source identified as "my house" on the phone's external screen. A few minutes later, they opened the phone and saw a photograph of a woman and a baby set as the phone's wallpaper. They pressed one button on the phone to access its call log, then another button to determine the phone number associated with the "my house" label. They next used an online phone directory to trace that phone number to an apartment building.

When the officers went to the building, they saw Wurie's name on a mailbox and observed through a window a woman who resembled the woman in the photograph on Wurie's phone. They secured the apartment while obtaining a search warrant and, upon later executing the warrant, found and seized 215 grams of crack cocaine, marijuana, drug paraphernalia, a firearm and ammunition, and cash.

Wurie was charged with distributing crack cocaine, possessing crack cocaine with intent to distribute, and being a felon in possession of a firearm and ammunition. See 18 U.S.C. § 922(g); 21 U.S.C. § 841(a). He moved to suppress the evidence obtained from the search of the apartment, arguing that it was the fruit of an unconstitutional search of his cell phone. The District Court denied the motion. 612 F. Supp. 2d 104 (Mass. 2009). Wurie was convicted on all three counts and sentenced to 262 months in prison.

A divided panel of the First Circuit reversed the denial of Wurie's motion to suppress and vacated Wurie's convictions for possession with intent to distribute and possession of a firearm as a felon. 728 F. 3d 1 (2013). The court held that cell phones are distinct from other physical possessions that may be searched incident to arrest without a warrant, because of the amount of personal data cell phones contain and the negligible threat they pose to law enforcement interests.

We granted certiorari.

II

The Fourth Amendment provides:

> "The right of the people to be secure in their persons, houses, papers, and effects, against unreasonable searches and seizures, shall not be violated, and

no Warrants shall issue, but upon probable cause, supported by Oath or affirmation, and particularly describing the place to be searched, and the persons or things to be seized."

As the text makes clear, "the ultimate touchstone of the Fourth Amendment is 'reasonableness.'" Brigham City v. Stuart, 547 U.S. 398, 403 (2006). Our cases have determined that "[w]here a search is undertaken by law enforcement officials to discover evidence of criminal wrongdoing, . . . reasonableness generally requires the obtaining of a judicial warrant." Vernonia School Dist. 47J v. Acton, 515 U.S. 646, 653 (1995). Such a warrant ensures that the inferences to support a search are "drawn by a neutral and detached magistrate instead of being judged by the officer engaged in the often competitive enterprise of ferreting out crime." Johnson v. United States, 333 U.S. 10, 14 (1948). In the absence of a warrant, a search is reasonable only if it falls within a specific exception to the warrant requirement. See Kentucky v. King, 563 U.S. ___, ___ (2011).

The two cases before us concern the reasonableness of a warrantless search incident to a lawful arrest. In 1914, this Court first acknowledged in dictum "the right on the part of the Government, always recognized under English and American law, to search the person of the accused when legally arrested to discover and seize the fruits or evidences of crime." Weeks v. United States, 232 U.S. 383, 392 (1914). Since that time, it has been well accepted that such a search constitutes an exception to the warrant requirement. Indeed, the label "exception" is something of a misnomer in this context, as warrantless searches incident to arrest occur with far greater frequency than searches conducted pursuant to a warrant. See 3 W. LaFave, Search and Seizure §5.2(b), p. 132, and n. 15 (5th ed. 2012).

Although the existence of the exception for such searches has been recognized for a century, its scope has been debated for nearly as long. See Arizona v. Gant, 556 U.S. 332, 350 (2009) (noting the exception's "checkered history"). That debate has focused on the extent to which officers may search property found on or near the arrestee. Three related precedents set forth the rules governing such searches:

The first, Chimel v. California, 395 U.S. 752 (1969), laid the groundwork for most of the existing search incident to arrest doctrine. Police officers in that case arrested Chimel inside his home and proceeded to search his entire three-bedroom house, including the attic and garage. In particular rooms, they also looked through the contents of drawers. Id., at 753-754.

The Court crafted the following rule for assessing the reasonableness of a search incident to arrest:

> "When an arrest is made, it is reasonable for the arresting officer to search the person arrested in order to remove any weapons that the latter might seek to use in order to resist arrest or effect his escape. Otherwise, the officer's safety might well be endangered, and the arrest itself frustrated. In addition, it is entirely reasonable for the arresting officer to search for and seize any evidence on the arrestee's person in order to prevent its concealment or destruction. . . . There is ample justification, therefore, for a search of the arrestee's person and the area 'within his immediate control' — construing that phrase to mean the area from within which he might gain possession of a weapon or destructible evidence." Id., at 762-763.

The extensive warrantless search of Chimel's home did not fit within this exception, because it was not needed to protect officer safety or to preserve evidence. Id., at 763, 768.

Four years later, in United States v. Robinson, 414 U.S. 218 (1973), the Court applied the *Chimel* analysis in the context of a search of the arrestee's person. A police officer had arrested Robinson for driving with a revoked license. The officer conducted a patdown search and felt an object that he could not identify in Robinson's coat pocket. He removed the object, which turned out to be a crumpled cigarette package, and opened it. Inside were 14 capsules of heroin. Id., at 220, 223.

The Court of Appeals concluded that the search was unreasonable because Robinson was unlikely to have evidence of the crime of arrest on his person, and because it believed that extracting the cigarette package and opening it could not be justified as part of a protective search for weapons. This Court reversed, rejecting the notion that "case-by-case adjudication" was required to determine "whether or not there was present one of the reasons supporting the authority for a search of the person incident to a lawful arrest." Id., at 235. As the Court explained, "[t]he authority to search the person incident to a lawful custodial arrest, while based upon the need to disarm and to discover evidence, does not depend on what a court may later decide was the probability in a particular arrest situation that weapons or evidence would in fact be found upon the person of the suspect." Ibid. Instead, a "custodial arrest of a suspect based on probable cause is a reasonable intrusion under the Fourth Amendment; that intrusion being lawful, a search incident to the arrest requires no additional justification." Ibid.

The Court thus concluded that the search of Robinson was reasonable even though there was no concern about the loss of evidence, and the

arresting officer had no specific concern that Robinson might be armed. Id.,
at 236. In doing so, the Court did not draw a line between a search of
Robinson's person and a further examination of the cigarette pack found
during that search. It merely noted that, "[h]aving in the course of a lawful
search come upon the crumpled package of cigarettes, [the officer] was
entitled to inspect it." Ibid. A few years later, the Court clarified that this
exception was limited to "personal property . . . immediately associated with
the person of the arrestee." United States v. Chadwick, 433 U.S. 1, 15 (1977)
(200-pound, locked footlocker could not be searched incident to
arrest), abrogated on other grounds by California v. Acevedo, 500 U.S. 565
(1991).

The search incident to arrest trilogy concludes with *Gant*, which analyzed searches of an arrestee's vehicle. *Gant*, like *Robinson*, recognized
that the *Chimel* concerns for officer safety and evidence preservation
underlie the search incident to arrest exception. See 556 U.S., at 338.
As a result, the Court concluded that *Chimel* could authorize police to
search a vehicle "only when the arrestee is unsecured and within reaching
distance of the passenger compartment at the time of the search." 556
U.S., at 343. *Gant* added, however, an independent exception for a
warrantless search of a vehicle's passenger compartment "when it is
'reasonable to believe evidence relevant to the crime of arrest might be
found in the vehicle.'" Ibid. (quoting Thornton v. United States, 541 U.S.
615, 632 (2004) (Scalia, J., concurring in judgment)). That exception
stems not from *Chimel*, the Court explained, but from "circumstances
unique to the vehicle context." 556 U.S., at 343.

III

These cases require us to decide how the search incident to arrest doctrine applies to modern cell phones, which are now such a pervasive and
insistent part of daily life that the proverbial visitor from Mars might
conclude they were an important feature of human anatomy. A smart
phone of the sort taken from Riley was unheard of ten years ago; a
significant majority of American adults now own such phones. See A.
Smith, Pew Research Center, Smartphone Ownership — 2013 Update
(June 5, 2013). Even less sophisticated phones like Wurie's, which have
already faded in popularity since Wurie was arrested in 2007, have been
around for less than 15 years. Both phones are based on technology
nearly inconceivable just a few decades ago, when *Chimel* and *Robinson*
were decided.

Absent more precise guidance from the founding era, we generally determine whether to exempt a given type of search from the warrant requirement "by assessing, on the one hand, the degree to which it intrudes upon an individual's privacy and, on the other, the degree to which it is needed for the promotion of legitimate governmental interests." Wyoming v. Houghton, 526 U.S. 295, 300 (1999). Such a balancing of interests supported the search incident to arrest exception in *Robinson*, and a mechanical application of *Robinson* might well support the warrantless searches at issue here.

But while *Robinson's* categorical rule strikes the appropriate balance in the context of physical objects, neither of its rationales has much force with respect to digital content on cell phones. On the government interest side, *Robinson* concluded that the two risks identified in *Chimel* — harm to officers and destruction of evidence — are present in all custodial arrests. There are no comparable risks when the search is of digital data. In addition, *Robinson* regarded any privacy interests retained by an individual after arrest as significantly diminished by the fact of the arrest itself. Cell phones, however, place vast quantities of personal information literally in the hands of individuals. A search of the information on a cell phone bears little resemblance to the type of brief physical search considered in *Robinson*.

We therefore decline to extend *Robinson* to searches of data on cell phones, and hold instead that officers must generally secure a warrant before conducting such a search.

A

We first consider each *Chimel* concern in turn. In doing so, we do not overlook *Robinson's* admonition that searches of a person incident to arrest, "while based upon the need to disarm and to discover evidence," are reasonable regardless of "the probability in a particular arrest situation that weapons or evidence would in fact be found." 414 U.S., at 235. Rather than requiring the "case-by-case adjudication" that *Robinson* rejected, ibid., we ask instead whether application of the search incident to arrest doctrine to this particular category of effects would "untether the rule from the justifications underlying the *Chimel* exception," *Gant*, supra, at 343. See also Knowles v. Iowa, 525 U.S. 113, 119 (1998) (declining to extend *Robinson* to the issuance of citations, "a situation where the concern for officer safety is not present to the same extent and the concern for destruction or loss of evidence is not present at all").

1

Digital data stored on a cell phone cannot itself be used as a weapon to harm an arresting officer or to effectuate the arrestee's escape. Law enforcement officers remain free to examine the physical aspects of a phone to ensure that it will not be used as a weapon—say, to determine whether there is a razor blade hidden between the phone and its case. Once an officer has secured a phone and eliminated any potential physical threats, however, data on the phone can endanger no one.

Perhaps the same might have been said of the cigarette pack seized from Robinson's pocket. Once an officer gained control of the pack, it was unlikely that Robinson could have accessed the pack's contents. But unknown physical objects may always pose risks, no matter how slight, during the tense atmosphere of a custodial arrest. The officer in *Robinson* testified that he could not identify the objects in the cigarette pack but knew they were not cigarettes. See 414 U.S., at 223, 236, n. 7. Given that, a further search was a reasonable protective measure. No such unknowns exist with respect to digital data. As the First Circuit explained, the officers who searched Wurie's cell phone "knew exactly what they would find therein: data. They also knew that the data could not harm them." 728 F. 3d, at 10.

The United States and California both suggest that a search of cell phone data might help ensure officer safety in more indirect ways, for example by alerting officers that confederates of the arrestee are headed to the scene. There is undoubtedly a strong government interest in warning officers about such possibilities, but neither the United States nor California offers evidence to suggest that their concerns are based on actual experience. The proposed consideration would also represent a broadening of *Chimel's* concern that an *arrestee himself* might grab a weapon and use it against an officer "to resist arrest or effect his escape." 395 U.S., at 763. And any such threats from outside the arrest scene do not "lurk[ ] in all custodial arrests." *Chadwick*, 433 U.S., at 14-15. Accordingly, the interest in protecting officer safety does not justify dispensing with the warrant requirement across the board. To the extent dangers to arresting officers may be implicated in a particular way in a particular case, they are better addressed through consideration of case-specific exceptions to the warrant requirement, such as the one for exigent circumstances. See, e.g., Warden, Md. Penitentiary v. Hayden, 387 U.S. 294, 298-299 (1967) ("The Fourth Amendment does not require police officers to delay in the course of an investigation if to do so would gravely endanger their lives or the lives of others.").

2

The United States and California focus primarily on the second *Chimel* rationale: preventing the destruction of evidence.

Both Riley and Wurie concede that officers could have seized and secured their cell phones to prevent destruction of evidence while seeking a warrant. That is a sensible concession. See Illinois v. McArthur, 531 U.S. 326, 331-333 (2001); *Chadwick*, supra, at 13, and n. 8. And once law enforcement officers have secured a cell phone, there is no longer any risk that the arrestee himself will be able to delete incriminating data from the phone.

The United States and California argue that information on a cell phone may nevertheless be vulnerable to two types of evidence destruction unique to digital data — remote wiping and data encryption. Remote wiping occurs when a phone, connected to a wireless network, receives a signal that erases stored data. This can happen when a third party sends a remote signal or when a phone is preprogrammed to delete data upon entering or leaving certain geographic areas (so-called "geofencing"). See Dept. of Commerce, National Institute of Standards and Technology, R. Ayers, S. Brothers, & W. Jansen, Guidelines on Mobile Device Forensics (Draft) 29, 31 (SP 800-101 Rev. 1, Sept. 2013) (hereinafter Ayers). Encryption is a security feature that some modern cell phones use in addition to password protection. When such phones lock, data becomes protected by sophisticated encryption that renders a phone all but "unbreakable" unless police know the password. Brief for United States as Amicus Curiae in No. 13-132, p. 11.

As an initial matter, these broader concerns about the loss of evidence are distinct from *Chimel's* focus on a defendant who responds to arrest by trying to conceal or destroy evidence within his reach. See 395 U.S., at 763-764. With respect to remote wiping, the Government's primary concern turns on the actions of third parties who are not present at the scene of arrest. And data encryption is even further afield. There, the Government focuses on the ordinary operation of a phone's security features, apart from *any* active attempt by a defendant or his associates to conceal or destroy evidence upon arrest.

We have also been given little reason to believe that either problem is prevalent. The briefing reveals only a couple of anecdotal examples of remote wiping triggered by an arrest. See Brief for Association of State Criminal Investigative Agencies et al. as Amici Curiae in No. 13-132, pp. 9-10; see also Tr. of Oral Arg. in No. 13-132, p. 48. Similarly, the opportunities for officers to search a password-protected phone before data becomes encrypted are quite limited. Law enforcement officers are very unlikely to come upon such a phone in an unlocked state because most phones lock at the touch of a button or, as a default, after some very short period of inactivity. See, e.g., iPhone User Guide for iOS 7.1 Software 10 (2014) (default lock after about one minute). This may explain why the encryption argument was not made until the merits stage in this Court, and has never been considered by the Courts of Appeals.

Moreover, in situations in which an arrest might trigger a remote-wipe attempt or an officer discovers an unlocked phone, it is not clear that the ability to conduct a warrantless search would make much of a difference. The need to effect the arrest, secure the scene, and tend to other pressing matters means that law enforcement officers may well not be able to turn their attention to a cell phone right away. See Tr. of Oral Arg. in No. 13-132, at 50; see also Brief for United States as Amicus Curiae in No. 13-132, at 19. Cell phone data would be vulnerable to remote wiping from the time an individual anticipates arrest to the time any eventual search of the phone is completed, which might be at the station house hours later. Likewise, an officer who seizes a phone in an unlocked state might not be able to begin his search in the short time remaining before the phone locks and data becomes encrypted.

In any event, as to remote wiping, law enforcement is not without specific means to address the threat. Remote wiping can be fully pre-vented by disconnecting a phone from the network. There are at least two simple ways to do this: First, law enforcement officers can turn the phone off or remove its battery. Second, if they are concerned about encryption or other potential problems, they can leave a phone powered on and place it in an enclosure that isolates the phone from radio waves. See Ayers 30-31. Such devices are commonly called "Faraday bags," after the English scientist Michael Faraday. They are essentially sandwich bags made of aluminum foil: cheap, lightweight, and easy to use. See Brief for Criminal Law Professors as Amici Curiae 9. They may not be a complete answer to the problem, see Ayers 32, but at least for now they provide a reasonable response. In fact, a number of law enforcement agencies around the country already encourage the use of Faraday bags. See, e.g., Dept. of Justice, National Institute of Justice, Electronic Crime Scene Investigation: A Guide for First Responders 14, 32 (2d ed. Apr. 2008); Brief for Criminal Law Professors as Amici Curiae 4-6.

To the extent that law enforcement still has specific concerns about the potential loss of evidence in a particular case, there remain more tar-geted ways to address those concerns. If "the police are truly confronted with a 'now or never' situation," — for example, circumstances suggesting that a defendant's phone will be the target of an imminent remote-wipe attempt—they may be able to rely on exigent circumstances to search the phone immediately. Missouri v. McNeely, 569 U.S. ___, ___ (2013) (quoting Roaden v. Kentucky, 413 U.S. 496, 505 (1973); some internal quotation marks omitted). Or, if officers happen to seize a phone in an unlocked state, they may be able to disable a phone's automatic-lock feature in order to prevent the phone from locking and encrypting data. See App. to Reply Brief in No. 13-132, p. 3a (diagramming the few necessary steps). Such a preventive measure could be analyzed under the principles set forth in our decision in *McArthur*, 531 U.S. 326, which approved officers' reasonable steps to secure a scene to preserve evidence while they awaited a warrant. See id., at 331-333.

B

The search incident to arrest exception rests not only on the heightened government interests at stake in a volatile arrest situation, but also on an arrestee's reduced privacy interests upon being taken into police custody. *Robinson* focused primarily on the first of those rationales. But it also quoted with approval then-Judge Cardozo's account of the historical basis for the search incident to arrest exception: "Search of the person becomes lawful when grounds for arrest and accusation have been discovered, and the law is in the act of subjecting the body of the accused to its physical dominion." 414 U.S., at 232 (quoting People v. Chiagles, 237 N. Y. 193, 197, 142 N. E. 583, 584 (1923)); see also 414 U.S., at 237 (Powell, J., concurring) ("an individual lawfully subjected to a custodial arrest retains no significant Fourth Amendment interest in the privacy of his person"). Put simply, a patdown of Robinson's clothing and an inspection of the cigarette pack found in his pocket constituted only minor additional intrusions compared to the substantial government authority exercised in taking Robinson into custody. See *Chadwick*, 433 U.S., at 16, n. 10 (searches of a person are justified in part by "reduced expectations of privacy caused by the arrest").

The fact that an arrestee has diminished privacy interests does not mean that the Fourth Amendment falls out of the picture entirely. Not every search "is acceptable solely because a person is in custody." Maryland v. King, 569 U.S. ___, ___ (2013). To the contrary, when "privacy-related concerns are weighty enough" a "search may require a warrant, notwithstanding the diminished expectations of privacy of the arrestee." Ibid. One such example, of course, is *Chimel*. *Chimel* refused to "characteriz[e] the invasion of privacy that results from a top-to-bottom search of a man's house as 'minor.'" 395 U.S., at 766-767, n. 12. Because a search of the arrestee's entire house was a substantial invasion beyond the arrest itself, the Court concluded that a warrant was required.

Robinson is the only decision from this Court applying *Chimel* to a search of the contents of an item found on an arrestee's person. In an earlier case, this Court had approved a search of a zipper bag carried by an arrestee, but the Court analyzed only the validity of the arrest itself. See Draper v. United States, 358 U.S. 307, 310-311 (1959). Lower courts applying *Robinson* and *Chimel*, however, have approved searches of a variety of personal items carried by an arrestee. See, e.g., United States v. Carrion, 809 F. 2d 1120, 1123, 1128 (CA5 1987) (billfold and address book); United States v. Watson, 669 F. 2d 1374, 1383-1384 (CA11 1982) (wallet); United States v. Lee, 501 F. 2d 890, 892, 163 U.S. App. D.C. 330 (CADC 1974) (purse).

The United States asserts that a search of all data stored on a cell phone is "materially indistinguishable" from searches of these sorts of physical items. That is like saying a ride on horseback is materially indistinguishable from a flight to the moon. Both are ways of getting from point A to point B, but little else justifies lumping them together. Modern cell phones, as a category, implicate privacy concerns far beyond those implicated by the search of a cigarette pack, a wallet, or a purse. A conclusion that inspecting the contents of an arrestee's pockets works no substantial additional intrusion on privacy beyond the arrest itself may make sense as applied to physical items, but any extension of that reasoning to digital data has to rest on its own bottom.

1

Cell phones differ in both a quantitative and a qualitative sense from other objects that might be kept on an arrestee's person. The term "cell phone" is itself misleading shorthand; many of these devices are in fact minicomputers that also happen to have the capacity to be used as a telephone. They could just as easily be called cameras, video players, rolodexes, calendars, tape recorders, libraries, diaries, albums, televisions, maps, or newspapers.

One of the most notable distinguishing features of modern cell phones is their immense storage capacity. Before cell phones, a search of a person was limited by physical realities and tended as a general matter to constitute only a narrow intrusion on privacy. See Kerr, Foreword: Accounting for Technological Change, 36 Harv. J. L. & Pub. Pol'y 403, 404-405 (2013). Most people cannot lug around every piece of mail they have received for the past several months, every picture they have taken, or every book or article they have read — nor would they have any reason to attempt to do so. And if they did, they would have to drag behind them a trunk of the sort held to require a search warrant in *Chadwick*, supra, rather than a container the size of the cigarette package in *Robinson*.

But the possible intrusion on privacy is not physically limited in the same way when it comes to cell phones. The current top-selling smart phone has a standard capacity of 16 gigabytes (and is available with up to 64 gigabytes). Sixteen gigabytes translates to millions of pages of text, thousands of pictures, or hundreds of videos. Cell phones couple that capacity with the ability to store many different types of information: Even the most basic phones that sell for less than $20 might hold photographs, picture messages, text messages, Internet browsing history, a calendar, a thousand-entry phone book, and so on. We expect that the gulf between physical practicability and digital capacity will only continue to widen in the future.

The storage capacity of cell phones has several interrelated consequences for privacy. First, a cell phone collects in one place many distinct types of information — an address, a note, a prescription, a bank statement, a video — that reveal much more in combination than any isolated record. Second, a cell phone's capacity allows even just one type of information to convey far more than previously possible. The sum of an individual's private life can be reconstructed through a thousand photographs labeled with dates, locations, and descriptions; the same cannot be said of a photograph or two of loved ones tucked into a wallet. Third, the data on a phone can date back to the purchase of the phone, or even earlier. A person might carry in his pocket a slip of paper reminding him to call Mr. Jones; he would not carry a record of all his communications with Mr. Jones for the past several months, as would routinely be kept on a phone.[1]

Finally, there is an element of pervasiveness that characterizes cell phones but not physical records. Prior to the digital age, people did not typically carry a cache of sensitive personal information with them as they went about their day. Now it is the person who is not carrying a cell phone, with all that it contains, who is the exception. According to one poll, nearly three-quarters of smart phone users report being within five feet of their phones most of the time, with 12% admitting that they even use their phones in the shower. See Harris Interactive, 2013 Mobile

---

1. Because the United States and California agree that these cases involve *searches* incident to arrest, these cases do not implicate the question whether the collection or inspection of aggregated digital information amounts to a search under other circumstances.

Consumer Habits Study (June 2013). A decade ago police officers searching an arrestee might have occasionally stumbled across a highly personal
item such as a diary. See, e.g., United States v. Frankenberry, 387 F. 2d
337 (CA2 1967) (per curiam). But those discoveries were likely to be few
and far between. Today, by contrast, it is no exaggeration to say that
many of the more than 90% of American adults who own a cell phone
keep on their person a digital record of nearly every aspect of their
lives—from the mundane to the intimate. See Ontario v. Quon, 560
U.S. 746, 760 (2010). Allowing the police to scrutinize such records on
a routine basis is quite different from allowing them to search a personal
item or two in the occasional case.

Although the data stored on a cell phone is distinguished from physical records by quantity alone, certain types of data are also qualitatively
different. An Internet search and browsing history, for example, can be
found on an Internet-enabled phone and could reveal an individual's
private interests or concerns—perhaps a search for certain symptoms of
disease, coupled with frequent visits to WebMD. Data on a cell phone can
also reveal where a person has been. Historic location information is a
standard feature on many smart phones and can reconstruct someone's
specific movements down to the minute, not only around town but also
within a particular building. See United States v. Jones, 565 U.S. ___, ___
(2012) (Sotomayor, J., concurring) ("GPS monitoring generates a precise,
comprehensive record of a person's public movements that reflects a
wealth of detail about her familial, political, professional, religious, and
sexual associations.").

Mobile application software on a cell phone, or "apps," offer a range
of tools for managing detailed information about all aspects of a person's
life. There are apps for Democratic Party news and Republican Party
news; apps for alcohol, drug, and gambling addictions; apps for sharing
prayer requests; apps for tracking pregnancy symptoms; apps for planning your budget; apps for every conceivable hobby or pastime; apps for
improving your romantic life. There are popular apps for buying or
selling just about anything, and the records of such transactions may be
accessible on the phone indefinitely. There are over a million apps
available in each of the two major app stores; the phrase "there's an
app for that" is now part of the popular lexicon. The average smart
phone user has installed 33 apps, which together can form a revealing
montage of the user's life. See Brief for Electronic Privacy Information
Center as Amicus Curiae in No. 13-132, p. 9.

In 1926, Learned Hand observed (in an opinion later quoted in
Chimel) that it is "a totally different thing to search a man's pockets and

use against him what they contain, from ransacking his house for every-thing which may incriminate him." United States v. Kirschenblatt, 16 F. 2d 202, 203 (CA2). If his pockets contain a cell phone, however, that is no longer true. Indeed, a cell phone search would typically expose to the government far *more* than the most exhaustive search of a house: A phone not only contains in digital form many sensitive records previously found in the home; it also contains a broad array of private information never found in a home in any form — unless the phone is.

2

To further complicate the scope of the privacy interests at stake, the data a user views on many modern cell phones may not in fact be stored on the device itself. Treating a cell phone as a container whose contents may be searched incident to an arrest is a bit strained as an initial matter. See New York v. Belton, 453 U.S. 454, 460, n. 4 (1981) (describing a "container" as "any object capable of holding another object"). But the analogy crumbles entirely when a cell phone is used to access data located elsewhere, at the tap of a screen. That is what cell phones, with increasing frequency, are designed to do by taking advantage of "cloud computing." Cloud computing is the capacity of Internet-connected devices to display data stored on remote servers rather than on the device itself. Cell phone users often may not know whether particular information is stored on the device or in the cloud, and it generally makes little difference. Moreover, the same type of data may be stored locally on the device for one user and in the cloud for another.

The United States concedes that the search incident to arrest excep-tion may not be stretched to cover a search of files accessed remotely — that is, a search of files stored in the cloud. Such a search would be like finding a key in a suspect's pocket and arguing that it allowed law enforcement to unlock and search a house. But officers searching a phone's data would not typically know whether the information they are viewing was stored locally at the time of the arrest or has been pulled from the cloud.

Although the Government recognizes the problem, its proposed solu-tions are unclear. It suggests that officers could disconnect a phone from the network before searching the device — the very solution whose feasi-bility it contested with respect to the threat of remote wiping. Alternatively, the Government proposes that law enforcement agencies "develop protocols to address" concerns raised by cloud computing. Reply Brief in No. 13-212, pp. 14-15. Probably a good idea, but the

Founders did not fight a revolution to gain the right to government agency protocols. The possibility that a search might extend well beyond papers and effects in the physical proximity of an arrestee is yet another reason that the privacy interests here dwarf those in *Robinson*.

C

Apart from their arguments for a direct extension of *Robinson*, the United States and California offer various fallback options for permitting warrantless cell phone searches under certain circumstances. Each of the proposals is flawed and contravenes our general preference to provide clear guidance to law enforcement through categorical rules. "[I]f police are to have workable rules, the balancing of the competing interests . . . 'must in large part be done on a categorical basis — not in an ad hoc, case-by-case fashion by individual police officers.'" Michigan v. Summers, 452 U.S. 692, 705, n. 19 (1981) (quoting Dunaway v. New York, 442 U.S. 200, 219-220 (1979) (White, J., concurring)).

The United States first proposes that the *Gant* standard be imported from the vehicle context, allowing a warrantless search of an arrestee's cell phone whenever it is reasonable to believe that the phone contains evidence of the crime of arrest. But *Gant* relied on "circumstances unique to the vehicle context" to endorse a search solely for the purpose of gathering evidence. 556 U.S., at 343. Justice Scalia's *Thornton* opinion, on which *Gant* was based, explained that those unique circumstances are "a reduced expectation of privacy" and "heightened law enforcement needs" when it comes to motor vehicles. 541 U.S., at 631; see also Wyoming v. Houghton, 526 U.S., at 303-304. For reasons that we have explained, cell phone searches bear neither of those characteristics.

At any rate, a *Gant* standard would prove no practical limit at all when it comes to cell phone searches. In the vehicle context, *Gant* generally protects against searches for evidence of past crimes. See 3 W. LaFave, Search and Seizure § 7.1(d), at 709, and n. 191. In the cell phone context, however, it is reasonable to expect that incriminating information will be found on a phone regardless of when the crime occurred. Similarly, in the vehicle context *Gant* restricts broad searches resulting from minor crimes such as traffic violations. See id., § 7.1(d), at 713, and n. 204. That would not necessarily be true for cell phones. It would be a particularly inexperienced or unimaginative law enforcement officer who could not come up with several reasons to suppose evidence of just about any crime could be found on a cell phone. Even an individual pulled over for something as basic as speeding might well have locational data dispositive of guilt on his phone. An individual pulled over for reckless driving might have evidence on the phone that shows whether he was texting while driving. The sources of potential pertinent information are virtually unlimited, so applying the *Gant* standard to cell phones would in effect give "police officers unbridled discretion to rummage at will among a person's private effects." 556 U.S., at 345.

The United States also proposes a rule that would restrict the scope of a cell phone search to those areas of the phone where an officer reasonably believes that information relevant to the crime, the arrestee's identity, or officer safety will be discovered. See Brief for United States in No. 13-212, at 51-53. This approach would again impose few meaningful constraints on officers. The proposed categories would sweep in a great deal of information, and officers would not always be able to discern in advance what information would be found where.

We also reject the United States' final suggestion that officers should always be able to search a phone's call log, as they did in Wurie's case. The Government relies on Smith v. Maryland, 442 U.S. 735 (1979), which held that no warrant was required to use a pen register at telephone company premises to identify numbers dialed by a particular caller. The Court in that case, however, concluded that the use of a pen register was not a "search" at all under the Fourth Amendment. See id., at 745-746. There is no dispute here that the officers engaged in a search of Wurie's cell phone. Moreover, call logs typically contain more than just phone numbers; they include any identifying information that an individual might add, such as the label "my house" in Wurie's case.

Finally, at oral argument California suggested a different limiting principle, under which officers could search cell phone data if they could have obtained the same information from a pre-digital counterpart. See Tr. of Oral Arg. in No. 13-132, at 38-43; see also *Flores-Lopez*, 670 F. 3d, at 807 ("If police are entitled to open a pocket diary to copy the owner's address, they should be entitled to turn on a cell phone to learn its number."). But the fact that a search in the pre-digital era could have turned up a photograph or two in a wallet does not justify a search of thousands of photos in a digital gallery. The fact that someone could have tucked a paper bank statement in a pocket does not justify a search of every bank statement from the last five years. And to make matters worse, such an analogue test would allow law enforcement to search a range of items contained on a phone, even though people would be unlikely to carry such a variety of information in physical form. In Riley's case, for example, it is implausible that he would have strolled around with video tapes, photo albums, and an address book all crammed into his pockets. But because each of those items has a pre-digital analogue, police under California's proposal would be able to search a phone for all of those items — a significant diminution of privacy.

In addition, an analogue test would launch courts on a difficult line-drawing expedition to determine which digital files are comparable to physical records. Is an e-mail equivalent to a letter? Is a voicemail equivalent to a phone message slip? It is not clear how officers could make these kinds of decisions before conducting a search, or how courts would apply the proposed rule after the fact. An analogue test would "keep defendants and judges guessing for years to come." Sykes v. United States, 564 U.S. 1, ___ (2011) (Scalia, J., dissenting) (discussing the Court's analogue test under the Armed Career Criminal Act).

IV

We cannot deny that our decision today will have an impact on the ability of law enforcement to combat crime. Cell phones have become important tools in facilitating coordination and communication among members of criminal enterprises, and can provide valuable incriminating information about dangerous criminals. Privacy comes at a cost.

Our holding, of course, is not that the information on a cell phone is immune from search; it is instead that a warrant is generally required before such a search, even when a cell phone is seized incident to arrest. Our cases have historically recognized that the warrant requirement is "an important working part of our machinery of government," not merely "an inconvenience to be somehow 'weighed' against the claims of police efficiency." Coolidge v. New Hampshire, 403 U.S. 443, 481 (1971). Recent technological advances similar to those discussed here have, in addition, made the process of obtaining a warrant itself more efficient. See McNeely, 569 U.S., at ___; id., at ___ (Roberts, C.J., concurring in part and dissenting in part) (describing jurisdiction where "police officers can e-mail warrant requests to judges' iPads [and] judges have signed such warrants and e-mailed them back to officers in less than 15 minutes").

Moreover, even though the search incident to arrest exception does not apply to cell phones, other case-specific exceptions may still justify a warrantless search of a particular phone. "One well-recognized exception applies when ' "the exigencies of the situation" make the needs of law enforcement so compelling that [a] warrantless search is objectively reasonable under the Fourth Amendment.'" Kentucky v. King, 563 U.S., at ___ (quoting Mincey v. Arizona, 437 U.S. 385, 394 (1978)). Such exigencies could include the need to prevent the imminent destruction of evidence in individual cases, to pursue a fleeing suspect, and to assist persons who are seriously injured or are threatened with imminent injury. In *Chadwick*, for example, the Court held that the exception for searches incident to arrest did not justify a search of the trunk at issue, but noted that "if officers have reason to believe that luggage contains some immediately dangerous instrumentality, such as explosives, it would be foolhardy to transport it to the station house without opening the luggage." 433 U.S., at 15, n. 9.

In light of the availability of the exigent circumstances exception, there is no reason to believe that law enforcement officers will not be able to address some of the more extreme hypotheticals that have been suggested: a suspect texting an accomplice who, it is feared, is preparing to detonate a bomb, or a child abductor who may have information about the child's location on his cell phone. The defendants here recognize — indeed, they stress — that such fact-specific threats may justify a warrant-less search of cell phone data. See Reply Brief in No. 13-132, at 8-9; Brief for Respondent in No. 13-212, at 30, 41. The critical point is that, unlike the search incident to arrest exception, the exigent circumstances excep-tion requires a court to examine whether an emergency justified a warrantless search in each particular case. See *McNeely*, supra, at ___.[2]

* * *

Our cases have recognized that the Fourth Amendment was the found-ing generation's response to the reviled "general warrants" and "writs of assistance" of the colonial era, which allowed British officers to rummage through homes in an unrestrained search for evidence of criminal activ-ity. Opposition to such searches was in fact one of the driving forces behind the Revolution itself. In 1761, the patriot James Otis delivered a speech in Boston denouncing the use of writs of assistance. A young John Adams was there, and he would later write that "[e]very man of a crowded audience appeared to me to go away, as I did, ready to take arms against writs of assistance." 10 Works of John Adams 247-248 (C. Adams ed. 1856). According to Adams, Otis's speech was "the first scene of the first act of opposition to the arbitrary claims of Great Britain. Then and there

---

2. In Wurie's case, for example, the dissenting First Circuit judge argued that exigent circumstances could have justified a search of Wurie's phone. See 728 F. 3d 1, 17 (2013) (opinion of Howard, J.) (discussing the repeated unanswered calls from "my house," the suspected location of a drug stash). But the majority concluded that the Government had not made an exigent circumstances argument. See id., at 1. The Government acknowledges the same in this Court. See Brief for United States in No. 13-212, p. 28, n. 8.

the child Independence was born." Id., at 248 (quoted in Boyd v. United States, 116 U.S. 616, 625 (1886)).

Modern cell phones are not just another technological convenience. With all they contain and all they may reveal, they hold for many Americans "the privacies of life," *Boyd*, supra, at 630. The fact that technology now allows an individual to carry such information in his hand does not make the information any less worthy of the protection for which the Founders fought. Our answer to the question of what police must do before searching a cell phone seized incident to an arrest is accordingly simple — get a warrant.

We reverse the judgment of the California Court of Appeal in No. 13-132 and remand the case for further proceedings not inconsistent with this opinion. We affirm the judgment of the First Circuit in No. 13-212.

JUSTICE ALITO, concurring in part and concurring in the judgment.

I agree with the Court that law enforcement officers, in conducting a lawful search incident to arrest, must generally obtain a warrant before searching information stored or accessible on a cell phone. I write separately to address two points.

I

A

First, I am not convinced at this time that the ancient rule on searches incident to arrest is based exclusively (or even primarily) on the need to protect the safety of arresting officers and the need to prevent the destruction of evidence. Cf. ante, at 9. This rule antedates the adoption of the Fourth Amendment by at least a century. See T. Clancy, The Fourth Amendment: Its History and Interpretation 340 (2008); T. Taylor, Two Studies in Constitutional Interpretation 28 (1969); Amar, Fourth Amendment First Principles, 107 Harv. L. Rev. 757, 764 (1994). In Weeks v. United States, 232 U.S. 383, 392 (1914), we held that the Fourth Amendment did not disturb this rule. See also Taylor, supra, at 45; Stuntz, The Substantive Origins of Criminal Procedure, 105 Yale L. J. 393, 401 (1995) ("The power to search incident to arrest — a search of the arrested suspect's person . . . — was well established in the mid-eighteenth century, and nothing in . . . the Fourth Amendment changed that"). And neither in *Weeks* nor in any of the authorities discussing the old common-law rule have I found any suggestion that it was based exclusively or primarily on the need to protect arresting officers or to prevent the destruction of evidence. . . .

B

Despite my view on the point discussed above, I agree that we should not mechanically apply the rule used in the predigital era to the search of a cell phone. Many cell phones now in use are capable of storing and accessing a quantity of information, some highly personal, that no person would ever have had on his person in hard-copy form. This calls for a new balancing of law enforcement and privacy interests.

The Court strikes this balance in favor of privacy interests with respect to all cell phones and all information found in them, and this approach leads to anomalies. For example, the Court's broad holding favors information in digital form over information in hard-copy form. Suppose that two suspects are arrested. Suspect number one has in his pocket a monthly bill for his land-line phone, and the bill lists an incriminating call to a long-distance number. He also has in his a wallet a few snapshots, and one of these is incriminating. Suspect number two has in his pocket a cell phone, the call log of which shows a call to the same incriminating number. In addition, a number of photos are stored in the memory of the cell phone, and one of these is incriminating. Under established law, the police may seize and examine the phone bill and the snapshots in the wallet without obtaining a warrant, but under the Court's holding today, the information stored in the cell phone is out.

While the Court's approach leads to anomalies, I do not see a workable alternative. Law enforcement officers need clear rules regarding searches incident to arrest, and it would take many cases and many years for the courts to develop more nuanced rules. And during that time, the nature of the electronic devices that ordinary Americans carry on their persons would continue to change.

II

This brings me to my second point. While I agree with the holding of the Court, I would reconsider the question presented here if either Congress or state legislatures, after assessing the legitimate needs of law enforcement and the privacy interests of cell phone owners, enact legislation that draws reasonable distinctions based on categories of information or perhaps other variables.

The regulation of electronic surveillance provides an instructive example. After this Court held that electronic surveillance constitutes a search even when no property interest is invaded, see Katz v. United States, 389 U.S. 347, 353-359 (1967), Congress responded by enacting Title III of the Omnibus Crime Control and Safe Streets Act of 1968, 82

Stat. 211. See also 18 U.S.C. § 2510 et seq. Since that time, electronic surveillance has been governed primarily, not by decisions of this Court, but by the statute, which authorizes but imposes detailed restrictions on electronic surveillance. See ibid.

Modern cell phones are of great value for both lawful and unlawful purposes. They can be used in committing many serious crimes, and they present new and difficult law enforcement problems. At the same time, because of the role that these devices have come to play in contemporary life, searching their contents implicates very sensitive privacy interests that this Court is poorly positioned to understand and evaluate. Many forms of modern technology are making it easier and easier for both government and private entities to amass a wealth of information about the lives of ordinary Americans, and at the same time, many ordinary Americans are choosing to make public much information that was seldom revealed to outsiders just a few decades ago.

In light of these developments, it would be very unfortunate if privacy protection in the 21st century were left primarily to the federal courts using the blunt instrument of the Fourth Amendment. Legislatures, elected by the people, are in a better position than we are to assess and respond to the changes that have already occurred and those that almost certainly will take place in the future.

NOTES AND QUESTIONS

1. The immediate impact of *Riley* is that police must stop using the search incident doctrine as authority for conducting warrantless searches of the contents of cell phones found on or near arrestees. Given that about 12 million Americans are arrested each year, and the vast majority of them carry cell phones, that's a pretty big deal. Certainly the Court was well aware that its decision could impede police investigations—but as Chief Justice Roberts succinctly put it: "Privacy comes at a cost."

How high is that cost? According to Lt. Andy Neiman of the Los Angeles Police Department, maybe not all that high: "Prior to this decision, officers and investigators were able to access some of the information in a phone that could be critical to an investigation. . . . But now, we'll do what the courts say, as we always do, and we'll abide by their recommendations, and we'll just have to obtain search warrants from this point forward." See "LAPD Reacts to Supreme Court Ruling on Cellphone Searches," CBS Los Angeles, June 25, 2014, available online at http://losangeles.cbslocal.com/2014/06/25/lapd-reacts-to-supreme-court-ruling-on-smartphone-searches/.

Given the fact of an arrest that, in order to be legal, must be based on probable cause, isn't it pretty likely that police will be able to obtain search warrants in most circumstances — at least those involving arrests for relatively serious crimes? But what about *Atwater*-type misdemeanor crimes? Or, much more significantly, what about pretext arrests for traffic or other low-level offenses, where police reasonably suspect (but can't yet establish at the level of probable cause) the arrestee to be guilty of something much worse? In such situations, *Riley* probably means no police access to the arrestee's cell phone. Which means that Lieutenant Neiman might be whistling in the dark when he implies that the *Riley* decision won't have that much impact on police investigations.

In many jurisdictions, police have long been using search-incident authority to search the cell phones of arrestees on a routine basis. This raises another concern: Will all of the past criminal convictions that were based in part on information found during a cell phone search incident to arrest now have to be overturned and those cases retried? For cases in which the conviction had already become "final" (because the conviction was affirmed on direct appeal, and the Supreme Court also either affirmed or denied certiorari) before June 25, 2014 (the date on which *Riley* was decided), the answer is almost surely no; the Supreme Court has long held that Fourth Amendment issues cannot be litigated in habeas corpus, see Stone v. Powell, 428 U.S. 465 (1976). But for cases that were still pending on direct appeal as of June 25, 2014, the answer is almost certainly yes, because new Supreme Court constitutional rulings *do* apply to direct appeals, see Griffith v. Kentucky, 479 U.S. 314 (1979).

2. More broadly, what does *Riley* mean for the general subject of technology searches under the Fourth Amendment? The decision would seem to extend logically to other similar kinds of electronic devices, such as iPads and laptop computers, that could be found on or near an arrestee at the time of the arrest and that could contain large amounts of personal information. But does *Riley* tell us anything at all about the future of technology searches *beyond* the relatively narrow context of searches incident to arrest?

Some commentators think so. According to Professor Orin Kerr, a well-known expert on technology searches: "*Riley* may just be the tip of the iceberg. Computers have now generated a very different rule for searches incident to arrest: The police have to follow one rule for physical evidence and a different rule for digital evidence. If that's true for searches incident to arrest, what other rules are also going to change?" See Orin Kerr, "The Significance of *Riley*," The Volokh Conspiracy, Washington Post, June 25, 2014, available online at http://www.washingtonpost.com/news/volokh-conspiracy/wp/2014/06/25/the-significance-of-riley/.

Is Professor Kerr right? Does *Riley* suggest that the Court will soon rule that police need a warrant to obtain from an ISP and read e-mail messages sent or received by persons under investigation? Or to use stealth technology to listen in on cell phone calls made by suspects? Or to track the location of a cell phone carried by a suspect? What about the current controversy over the widespread NSA collection of Internet data and eavesdropping on cell phone calls—even of persons who are not suspected of any crime at all? Doesn't *Riley* seem to indicate that such practices are now suspect, and likely to be invalidated?

3. Are you so sure? As Professor Kerr also points out in the same article, the Court emphasizes in footnote 1 of *Riley*: "Because the United States and California agree that these cases involve *searches* incident to arrest, these cases do not implicate the question whether the collection or inspection of aggregated digital information amounts to a search under other circumstances" (emphasis in original). What does *that* mean? Return to the start of this chapter, and ask yourself whether some or all of the practices mentioned in the preceding paragraph might not be a "search" at all, within the meaning of the Fourth Amendment—because the digital information sought by the government is already being shared with *someone* (an ISP, the cell phone provider, the person on the other end of the cell phone call), thus triggering the doctrine of "knowing exposure" as set forth in United States v. White, 401 U.S. 745 (1971), and other cases (see supra pages 379-390). Maybe we will need more than the *Riley* decision to tell us exactly where the Court really wants to go with respect to the general subject of technology searches and the Fourth Amendment.

D. Reasonableness

1. Stops and Frisks

Insert the following note and main case after Note 3 on page 562, and renumber Note 4 on page 562 as Note 7:

4. Perhaps. Over a decade *after* September 11, the Court again took up the subject of reasonable suspicion in the context of anonymous tips. Note in the following case that the standards articulated in *Florida v. J.L.* for a unanimous Court remain the same. But two things are different: first, the police conduct is deemed reasonable; and, second, application of the *J.L.* standards now produces a sharply divided Court.

NAVARETTE v. CALIFORNIA
Certiorari to the California Court of Appeal, First Appellate District
134 S. Ct. 1683 (2014)

JUSTICE THOMAS delivered the opinion of the Court.

After a 911 caller reported that a vehicle had run her off the road, a police officer located the vehicle she identified during the call and executed a traffic stop. We hold that the stop complied with the Fourth Amendment because, under the totality of the circumstances, the officer had reasonable suspicion that the driver was intoxicated.

I

On August 23, 2008, a Mendocino County 911 dispatch team for the California Highway Patrol (CHP) received a call from another CHP dispatcher in neighboring Humboldt County. The Humboldt County dispatcher relayed a tip from a 911 caller, which the Mendocino County team recorded as follows: "'Showing southbound Highway 1 at mile marker 88, Silver Ford 150 pickup. Plate of 8-David-94925. Ran the reporting party off the roadway and was last seen approximately five [minutes] ago.'" The Mendocino County team then broadcast that information to CHP officers at 3:47 p.m.

A CHP officer heading northbound toward the reported vehicle responded to the broadcast. At 4:00 p.m., the officer passed the truck near mile marker 69. At about 4:05 p.m., after making a U-turn, he pulled the truck over. A second officer, who had separately responded to the broadcast, also arrived on the scene. As the two officers approached the truck, they smelled marijuana. A search of the truck bed revealed 30 pounds of marijuana. The officers arrested the driver, petitioner Lorenzo Prado Navarette, and the passenger, petitioner José Prado Navarette.

Petitioners moved to suppress the evidence, arguing that the traffic stop violated the Fourth Amendment because the officer lacked reasonable suspicion of criminal activity. Both the magistrate who presided over the suppression hearing and the Superior Court disagreed.[1] Petitioners

---

1. At the suppression hearing, counsel for petitioners did not dispute that the reporting party identified herself by name in the 911 call recording. Because neither the caller nor the Humboldt County dispatcher who received the call was present at the hearing, however, the prosecution did not introduce the recording into evidence. The prosecution proceeded to treat the tip as anonymous, and the lower courts followed suit.

pleaded guilty to transporting marijuana and were sentenced to 90 days in jail plus three years of probation.

The California Court of Appeal affirmed, concluding that the officer had reasonable suspicion to conduct an investigative stop. . . . The California Supreme Court denied review. We granted certiorari, and now affirm.

II

The Fourth Amendment permits brief investigative stops — such as the traffic stop in this case — when a law enforcement officer has "a particularized and objective basis for suspecting the particular person stopped of criminal activity." United States v. Cortez, 449 U.S. 411, 417-418 (1981); see also Terry v. Ohio, 392 U.S. 1, 21-22 (1968). The "reasonable suspicion" necessary to justify such a stop "is dependent upon both the content of information possessed by police and its degree of reliability." Alabama v. White, 496 U.S. 325, 330 (1990). The standard takes into account "the totality of the circumstances — the whole picture." Cortez, supra, at 417. Although a mere "'hunch'" does not create reasonable suspicion, Terry, supra, at 27, the level of suspicion the standard requires is "considerably less than proof of wrongdoing by a preponderance of the evidence," and "obviously less" than is necessary for probable cause, United States v. Sokolow, 490 U.S. 1, 7 (1989).

A

These principles apply with full force to investigative stops based on information from anonymous tips. We have firmly rejected the argument "that reasonable cause for a[n investigative stop] can only be based on the officer's personal observation, rather than on information supplied by another person." Adams v. Williams, 407 U.S. 143, 147 (1972). Of course, "an anonymous tip *alone* seldom demonstrates the informant's basis of knowledge or veracity." White, 496 U.S., at 329 (emphasis added). That is because "ordinary citizens generally do not provide extensive recitations of the basis of their everyday observations," and an anonymous tipster's veracity is "'by hypothesis largely unknown, and unknowable.'" Ibid. But under appropriate circumstances, an anonymous tip can demonstrate "sufficient indicia of reliability to provide reasonable suspicion to make [an] investigatory stop." Id., at 327.

Our decisions in Alabama v. White, 496 U.S. 325 (1990), and Florida v. J. L., 529 U.S. 266 (2000), are useful guides. In *White*, an anonymous tipster told the police that a woman would drive from a particular apartment building to a particular motel in a brown Plymouth station wagon with a broken right tail light. The tipster further asserted that the woman would be transporting cocaine. 496 U.S., at 327. After confirming the innocent details, officers stopped the station wagon as it neared the motel and found cocaine in the vehicle. Id., at 331. We held that the officers' corroboration of certain details made the anonymous tip sufficiently reliable to create reasonable suspicion of criminal activity. By accurately predicting future behavior, the tipster demonstrated "a special familiarity with respondent's affairs," which in turn implied that the tipster had "access to reliable information about that individual's illegal activities." Id., at 332. We also recognized that an informant who is proved to tell the truth about some things is more likely to tell the truth about other things, "including the claim that the object of the tip is engaged in criminal activity." Id., at 331 (citing Illinois v. Gates, 462 U.S. 213, 244 (1983)).

In *J. L.*, by contrast, we determined that no reasonable suspicion arose from a bare-bones tip that a young black male in a plaid shirt standing at a bus stop was carrying a gun. 529 U.S., at 268. The tipster did not explain how he knew about the gun, nor did he suggest that he had any special familiarity with the young man's affairs. Id., at 271. As a result, police had no basis for believing "that the tipster ha[d] knowledge of concealed criminal activity." Id., at 272. Furthermore, the tip included no predictions of future behavior that could be corroborated to assess the tipster's credibility. Id., at 271. We accordingly concluded that the tip was insufficiently reliable to justify a stop and frisk.

B

The initial question in this case is whether the 911 call was sufficiently reliable to credit the allegation that petitioners' truck "ran the [caller] off the roadway." Even assuming for present purposes that the 911 call was anonymous, see n. 1, supra, we conclude that the call bore adequate indicia of reliability for the officer to credit the caller's account. The officer was therefore justified in proceeding from the premise that the truck had, in fact, caused the caller's car to be dangerously diverted from the highway.

By reporting that she had been run off the road by a specific vehicle — a silver Ford F-150 pickup, license plate 8D94925 — the caller necessarily claimed eyewitness knowledge of the alleged dangerous driving. That basis of knowledge lends significant support to the tip's reliability. See *Gates*, supra, at 234 ("[An informant's] explicit and detailed description of alleged wrongdoing, along with a statement that the event was observed firsthand, entitles his tip to greater weight than might otherwise be the case"); Spinelli v. United States, 393 U.S. 410, 416 (1969) (a tip of illegal gambling is less reliable when "it is not alleged that the informant personally observed [the defendant] at work or that he had ever placed a bet with him"). This is in contrast to *J. L.*, where the tip provided no basis for concluding that the tipster had actually seen the gun. 529 U.S., at 271. Even in *White*, where we upheld the stop, there was scant evidence that the tipster had actually observed cocaine in the station wagon. We called *White* a "'close case'" because "[k]nowledge about a person's future movements indicates some familiarity with that person's affairs, but having such knowledge does not necessarily imply that the informant knows, in particular, whether that person is carrying hidden contraband." 529 U.S., at 271. A driver's claim that another vehicle ran her off the road, however, necessarily implies that the informant knows the other car was driven dangerously.

There is also reason to think that the 911 caller in this case was telling the truth. Police confirmed the truck's location near mile marker 69 (roughly 19 highway miles south of the location reported in the 911 call) at 4:00 p.m. (roughly 18 minutes after the 911 call). That timeline of events suggests that the caller reported the incident soon after she was run off the road. That sort of contemporaneous report has long been treated as especially reliable. In evidence law, we generally credit the proposition that statements about an event and made soon after perceiving that event are especially trustworthy because "substantial contemporaneity of event and statement negate the likelihood of deliberate or conscious misrepresentation." Advisory Committee's Notes on Fed. Rule Evid. 803(1) (describing the rationale for the hearsay exception for "present sense impression[s]"). A similar rationale applies to a "statement relating to a startling event" — such as getting run off the road — "made while the declarant was under the stress of excitement that it caused." Fed. Rule Evid. 803(2) (hearsay exception for "excited utterances"). Unsurprisingly, 911 calls that would otherwise be inadmissible hearsay have often been admitted on those grounds. See D. Binder, Hearsay Handbook § 8.1, pp. 257-259 (4th ed. 2013-2014) (citing cases admitting 911 calls as present sense impressions); id., § 9.1, at 274-275 (911 calls admitted as excited utterances). There was no indication that the tip in *J. L.* (or even in *White*) was contemporaneous with the observation of criminal activity or made under the stress of excitement caused by a startling event, but those considerations weigh in favor of the caller's veracity here.

Another indicator of veracity is the caller's use of the 911 emergency system. A 911 call has some features that allow for identifying and tracing callers, and thus provide some safeguards against making false reports with immunity. See *J. L.,* supra, at 276 (Kennedy, J., concurring). As this case illustrates, see n. 1, supra, 911 calls can be recorded, which provides victims with an opportunity to identify the false tipster's voice and subject him to prosecution, see, e.g., Cal. Penal Code Ann. § 653x (West 2010) (makes "telephon[ing] the 911 emergency line with the intent to annoy or harass" punishable by imprisonment and fine); see also § 148.3 (2014 West Cum. Supp.) (prohibits falsely reporting "that an 'emergency' exists"); § 148.5 (prohibits falsely reporting "that a felony or misdemeanor has been committed"). The 911 system also permits law enforcement to verify important information about the caller. In 1998, the Federal Communications Commission (FCC) began to require cellular carriers to relay the caller's phone number to 911 dispatchers. 47 CFR § 20.18(d)(1) (2013) (FCC's "Phase I enhanced 911 services" requirements). Beginning in 2001, carriers have been required to identify the caller's geographic location with increasing specificity. §§ 20.18(e)-(h) ("Phase II enhanced 911 service" requirements). And although callers may ordinarily block call recipients from obtaining their identifying information, FCC regulations exempt 911 calls from that privilege. §§ 64.1601(b), (d)(4)(ii) ("911 emergency services" exemption from rule that, when a caller so requests, "a carrier may not reveal that caller's number or name"). None of this is to suggest that tips in 911 calls are *per se* reliable. Given the foregoing technological and regulatory developments, however, a reasonable officer could conclude that a false tipster would think twice before using such a system. The caller's use of the 911 system is therefore one of the relevant circumstances that, taken together, justified the officer's reliance on the information reported in the 911 call.

C

Even a reliable tip will justify an investigative stop only if it creates reasonable suspicion that "criminal activity may be afoot." *Terry,* 392 U.S., at 30. We must therefore determine whether the 911 caller's report of being run off the roadway created reasonable suspicion of an ongoing crime such as drunk driving as opposed to an isolated episode of past recklessness. See *Cortez,* 449 U.S., at 417 ("An investigatory stop must be justified by some objective manifestation that the person stopped is, or is about to be, engaged in criminal activity"). We conclude that the behavior alleged by the 911 caller, "viewed from the standpoint of an objectively reasonable police officer, amount[s] to reasonable suspicion" of drunk driving. Ornelas v. United States, 517 U.S. 690, 696 (1996). The stop was therefore proper.[2]

Reasonable suspicion depends on ""'the factual and practical considerations of everyday life on which reasonable and prudent men, not legal technicians, act.'"" Id., at 695. Under that commonsense approach, we can appropriately recognize certain driving behaviors as sound indicia of drunk driving. See, e.g., People v. Wells, 38 Cal.4th 1078, 1081 (2006) ("'weaving all over the roadway'"); State v. Prendergast, 103 Hawai'i 451, 452-453 (2004) ("cross[ing] over the center line" on a highway and "almost caus[ing] several head-on collisions"); State v. Golotta, 178 N.J. 205, 209 (2003) (driving "'all over the road'" and "'weaving back and forth'"); State v. Walshire, 634 N.W.2d 625, 626 (Iowa 2001) ("driving in the median"). Indeed, the accumulated experience of thousands of officers suggests that these sorts of erratic behaviors are strongly correlated with drunk driving. See Nat. Highway Traffic Safety Admin., The Visual Detection of DWI Motorists 4-5 (Mar. 2010), online at http://nhtsa.gov/staticfiles/nti/pdf/808677.pdf (as visited Apr. 18, 2014, and available in Clerk of Court's case file). Of course, not all traffic infractions imply intoxication. Unconfirmed reports of driving without a seatbelt or slightly over the speed limit, for example, are so tenuously connected to drunk driving that a stop on those grounds alone would be constitutionally suspect. But a reliable tip alleging the dangerous behaviors discussed above generally would justify a traffic stop on suspicion of drunk driving.

The 911 caller in this case reported more than a minor traffic infraction and more than a conclusory allegation of drunk or reckless driving. Instead, she alleged a specific and dangerous result of the driver's conduct: running another car off the highway. That conduct bears too great a resemblance to paradigmatic manifestations of drunk driving to be dismissed as an isolated example of recklessness. Running another vehicle off the road suggests lane-positioning problems, decreased vigilance, impaired judgment, or some combination of those recognized drunk driving cues. See Visual Detection of DWI Motorists 4-5. And the experience of many officers suggests that a driver who almost strikes a vehicle or another object — the exact scenario that ordinarily causes "running [another vehicle] off the roadway" — is likely intoxicated. See id., at 5, 8.

---

2. Because we conclude that the 911 call created reasonable suspicion of an ongoing crime, we need not address under what circumstances a stop is justified by the need to investigate completed criminal activity. Cf. United States v. Hensley, 469 U.S. 221, 229 (1985).

As a result, we cannot say that the officer acted unreasonably under these circumstances in stopping a driver whose alleged conduct was a significant indicator of drunk driving.

Petitioners' attempts to second-guess the officer's reasonable suspicion of drunk driving are unavailing. It is true that the reported behavior might also be explained by, for example, a driver responding to "an unruly child or other distraction." Brief for Petitioners 21. But we have consistently recognized that reasonable suspicion "need not rule out the possibility of innocent conduct." United States v. Arvizu, 534 U.S. 266, 277 (2002).

Nor did the absence of additional suspicious conduct, after the vehicle was first spotted by an officer, dispel the reasonable suspicion of drunk driving. It is hardly surprising that the appearance of a marked police car would inspire more careful driving for a time. Cf. Arvizu, supra, at 275 ("'[s]lowing down after spotting a law enforcement vehicle'" does not dispel reasonable suspicion of criminal activity). Extended observation of an allegedly drunk driver might eventually dispel a reasonable suspicion of intoxication, but the 5-minute period in this case hardly sufficed in that regard. Of course, an officer who already has such a reasonable suspicion need not surveil a vehicle at length in order to personally observe suspicious driving. See Adams v. Williams, 407 U.S., at 147 (repudiating the argument that "reasonable cause for a[n investigative stop] can only be based on the officer's personal observation"). Once reasonable suspicion of drunk driving arises, "[t]he reasonableness of the officer's decision to stop a suspect does not turn on the availability of less intrusive investigatory techniques." Sokolow, 490 U.S., at 11. This would be a particularly inappropriate context to depart from that settled rule, because allowing a drunk driver a second chance for dangerous conduct could have disastrous consequences.

III

Like *White*, this is a "close case." 496 U.S., at 332. As in that case, the indicia of the 911 caller's reliability here are stronger than those in *J. L.*, where we held that a bare-bones tip was unreliable. 529 U.S., at 271. Although the indicia present here are different from those we found sufficient in *White*, there is more than one way to demonstrate "a particularized and objective basis for suspecting the particular person stopped of criminal activity." *Cortez*, 449 U.S., at 417-418. Under the totality of the circumstances, we find the indicia of reliability in this case sufficient to provide the officer with reasonable suspicion that the driver of the reported vehicle had run another vehicle off the road. That made it reasonable under the circumstances for the officer to execute a traffic stop. We accordingly affirm. . . .

JUSTICE SCALIA, with whom JUSTICE GINSBURG, JUSTICE SOTOMAYOR, and JUSTICE KAGAN join, dissenting.

The California Court of Appeal in this case relied on jurisprudence from the California Supreme Court (adopted as well by other courts) to the effect that "an anonymous and uncorroborated tip regarding a possibly intoxicated highway driver" provides without more the reasonable suspicion necessary to justify a stop. People v. Wells, 38 Cal.4th 1078, 1082 (2006). See also, e.g., United States v. Wheat, 278 F.3d 722, 729-730 (C.A.8 2001); State v. Walshire, 634 N.W.2d 625, 626-627, 630 (Iowa 2001). Today's opinion does not explicitly adopt such a departure from our normal Fourth Amendment requirement that anonymous tips must be corroborated; it purports to adhere to our prior cases, such as Florida v. J. L., 529 U.S. 266 (2000), and Alabama v. White, 496 U.S. 325 (1990). Be not deceived.

Law enforcement agencies follow closely our judgments on matters such as this, and they will identify at once our new rule: So long as the caller identifies where the car is, anonymous claims of a single instance of possibly careless or reckless driving, called in to 911, will support a traffic stop. This is not my concept, and I am sure would not be the Framers', of a people secure from unreasonable searches and seizures. I would reverse the judgment of the Court of Appeal of California.

I

The California Highway Patrol in this case knew nothing about the tipster on whose word—and that alone—they seized Lorenzo and José Prado Navarette. They did not know her name.[1] They did not know her phone number or address. They did not even know where she called from (she may have dialed in from a neighboring county).

The tipster said the truck had "[run her] off the roadway," id., at 36a, but the police had no reason to credit that charge and many reasons to doubt it, beginning with the peculiar fact that the accusation was anonymous. "[E]liminating accountability . . . is ordinarily the very purpose of anonymity." McIntyre v. Ohio Elections Comm'n, 514 U.S. 334, 385, (1995) (Scalia, J., dissenting). The unnamed tipster "can lie with

---

1. There was some indication below that the tipster was a woman. Beyond that detail, we must, as the Court notes, assume that the identity of the tipster was unknown.

impunity," *J. L.*, supra, at 275 (Kennedy, J., concurring). Anonymity is especially suspicious with respect to the call that is the subject of the present case. When does a victim complain to the police about an arguably criminal act (running the victim off the road) without giving his identity, so that he can accuse and testify when the culprit is caught?

The question before us, the Court agrees, is whether the "content of information possessed by police and its degree of reliability," *White*, 496 U.S. at 330, gave the officers reasonable suspicion that the driver of the truck (Lorenzo) was committing an ongoing crime. When the only source of the government's information is an informant's tip, we ask whether the tip bears sufficient "'indicia of reliability,'" id., at 328, to establish "a particularized and objective basis for suspecting the particular person stopped of criminal activity," United States v. Cortez, 449 U.S. 411, 417-418 (1981).

The most extreme case, before this one, in which an anonymous tip was found to meet this standard was *White*, supra. There the reliability of the tip was established by the fact that it predicted the target's behavior in the finest detail — a detail that could be known only by someone familiar with the target's business: She would, the tipster said, leave a particular apartment building, get into a brown Plymouth station wagon with a broken right tail light, and drive immediately to a particular motel. Id., at 327. Very few persons would have such intimate knowledge, and hence knowledge of the unobservable fact that the woman was carrying unlawful drugs was plausible. Id., at 332. Here the Court makes a big deal of the fact that the tipster was dead right about the fact that a silver Ford F-150 truck (license plate 8D94925) was traveling south on Highway 1 somewhere near mile marker 88. But everyone in the world who saw the car would have that knowledge, and anyone who wanted the car stopped would have to provide that information. Unlike the situation in *White*, that generally available knowledge in no way makes it plausible that the tipster saw the car run someone off the road.

The Court says that "[b]y reporting that she had been run off the road by a specific vehicle . . . the caller necessarily claimed eyewitness knowledge." So what? The issue is not how she claimed to know, but whether what she claimed to know was true. The claim to "eyewitness knowledge" of being run off the road supports *not at all* its veracity; nor does the amazing, mystifying prediction (so far short of what existed in *White*) that the petitioners' truck *would be heading south on Highway 1.*

The Court finds "reason to think" that the informant "was telling the truth" in the fact that police observation confirmed that the truck had been driving near the spot at which, and at the approximate time at which, the tipster alleged she had been run off the road. According to the Court, the statement therefore qualifies as a "'present sense impression'" or "'excited utterance,'" kinds of hearsay that the law deems categorically admissible given their low likelihood of reflecting "'deliberate or conscious misrepresentation.'" Ibid. (quoting Advisory Committee's Notes on Fed. Rule Evid. 803(1)). So, the Court says, we can fairly suppose that the accusation was true.

No, we cannot. To begin with, it is questionable whether either the "present sense impression" or the "excited utterance" exception to the hearsay rule applies here. The classic "present sense impression" is the recounting of an event that is occurring before the declarant's eyes, as the declarant is speaking ("I am watching the Hindenburg explode!"). See 2 K. Broun, McCormick on Evidence 362 (7th ed. 2013) (hereinafter McCormick). And the classic "excited utterance" is a statement elicited, almost involuntarily, by the shock of what the declarant is immediately witnessing ("My God, those people will be killed!"). See id., at 368-369. It is the immediacy that gives the statement some credibility; the declarant has not had time to dissemble or embellish. There is no such immediacy here. The declarant had time to observe the license number of the offending vehicle, 8D94925 (a difficult task if she was forced off the road and the vehicle was speeding away), to bring her car to a halt, to copy down the observed license number (presumably), and (if she was using her own cell phone) to dial a call to the police from the stopped car. Plenty of time to dissemble or embellish.

Moreover, even assuming that less than true immediacy will suffice for these hearsay exceptions to apply, the tipster's statement would run into additional barriers to admissibility and acceptance. According to the very Advisory Committee's Notes from which the Court quotes, cases addressing an unidentified declarant's present sense impression "indicate hesitancy in upholding the statement alone as sufficient" proof of the reported event. 28 U.S. C. App., at 371; see also 7 M. Graham, Handbook of Federal Evidence 19-20 (7th ed.2012). For excited utterances as well, the "knotty theoretical" question of statement-alone admissibility persists—seemingly even when the declarant is known. 2 McCormick 368. "Some courts . . . have taken the position that an excited utterance is admissible only if other proof is presented which supports a finding of fact that the exciting event did occur. The issue has not yet been resolved under the Federal Rules." Id., at 367-368 (footnote omitted). It is even unsettled whether excited utterances of an unknown declarant are *ever* admissible. A leading treatise reports that "the courts have been reluctant to admit such statements, principally because of uncertainty that foundational requirements, including the impact of the event on the declarant, have been satisfied." Id., at 372. In sum, it is unlikely that the law of evidence would deem the mystery caller in this case "especially trustworthy."

Finally, and least tenably, the Court says that another "indicator of veracity" is the anonymous tipster's mere "use of the 911 emergency system." Because, you see, recent "technological and regulatory developments" suggest that the identities of unnamed 911 callers are increasingly less likely to remain unknown. Indeed, the systems are able to identify "the caller's geographic location with increasing specificity." *Amici* disagree with this, see Brief for National Association of Criminal Defense Lawyers et. al. 8-12, and the present case surely suggests that *amici* are right—since we know neither the identity of the tipster nor even the county from which the call was made. But assuming the Court is right about the ease of identifying 911 callers, it proves absolutely nothing in the present case unless the anonymous caller was *aware* of that fact. "It is the tipster's *belief* in anonymity, not its *reality*, that will control his behavior." Id., at 10 (emphasis added). There is no reason to believe that your average anonymous 911 tipster is aware that 911 callers are readily identifiable.

II

All that has been said up to now assumes that the anonymous caller made, at least in effect, an accusation of drunken driving. But in fact she did not. She said that the petitioners' truck "'[r]an [me] off the roadway.'" App. 36a. That neither asserts that the driver was drunk nor even raises the *likelihood* that the driver was drunk. The most it conveys is that the truck did some apparently nontypical thing that forced the tipster off the roadway, whether partly or fully, temporarily or permanently. Who really knows what (if anything) happened? The truck might have swerved to avoid an animal, a pothole, or a jaywalking pedestrian.

But let us assume the worst of the many possibilities: that it was a careless, reckless, or even intentional maneuver that forced the tipster off the road. Lorenzo might have been distracted by his use of a hands-free cell phone, see Strayer, Drews, & Crouch, A Comparison of the Cell Phone Driver and the Drunk Driver, 48 Human Factors 381, 388 (2006), or distracted by an intense sports argument with Jose, see D. Strayer et al., AAA Foundation for Traffic Safety, Measuring Cognitive Distraction in the Automobile 28 (June 2013), online at https://www.aaafoundation.org/sites/default/files/MeasuringCognitiveDistractions.pdf as visited Apr. 17, 2014, and available in Clerk of Court's case file). Or, indeed, he might have intentionally forced the tipster off the road because of some personal animus, or hostility to her "Make Love, Not War" bumper sticker. I fail to see how reasonable suspicion of a *discrete instance* of irregular or hazardous driving generates a reasonable suspicion of *ongoing intoxicated driving*. What proportion of the hundreds of thousands — perhaps millions — of careless, reckless, or intentional traffic violations committed each day is attributable to drunken drivers? I say 0.1 percent. I have no basis for that except my own guesswork. But unless the Court has some basis in reality to believe that the proportion is many orders of magnitude above that — say 1 in 10 or at least 1 in 20 — it has no grounds for its unsupported assertion that the tipster's report in this case gave rise to a *reasonable suspicion* of drunken driving.

Bear in mind that that is the only basis for the stop that has been asserted in this litigation.[3] The stop required suspicion of an ongoing crime, not merely suspicion of having run someone off the road earlier. And driving while being a careless or reckless person, unlike driving while being a drunk person, is not an ongoing crime. In other words, in order to stop the petitioners the officers here not only had to assume without basis the accuracy of the anonymous accusation but also had to posit an unlikely reason (drunkenness) for the accused behavior.

In sum, at the moment the police spotted the truck, it was more than merely "*possib[le]*" that the petitioners were not committing an ongoing traffic crime. United States v. Arvizu, 534 U.S. 266, 277 (2002) (emphasis added). It was overwhelmingly likely that they were not.

III

It gets worse. Not only, it turns out, did the police have no good reason *at first* to believe that Lorenzo was driving drunk, they had very good reason *at last* to know that he was not. The Court concludes that the tip, plus confirmation of the truck's location, produced reasonable suspicion that the truck not only had been *but still was* barreling dangerously and drunkenly down Highway 1. In fact, alas, it was not, and the officers knew it. They followed the truck for five minutes, presumably to see if it was being operated recklessly. And *that* was good police work. While the anonymous tip was not enough to support a stop for drunken driving

---

3. The circumstances that may justify a stop under Terry v. Ohio, 392 U.S. 1 (1968), to investigate past criminal activity are far from clear, see United States v. Hensley, 469 U.S. 221, 229 (1985), and have not been discussed in this litigation. Hence, the Court says it "need not address" that question. I need not either. This case has been litigated on the assumption that only suspicion of ongoing intoxicated or reckless driving could have supported this stop.

under Terry v. Ohio, 392 U.S. 1 (1968), it was surely enough to counsel observation of the truck to see if it was driven by a drunken driver. But the pesky little detail left out of the Court's reasonable-suspicion equation is that, for the five minutes that the truck was being followed (five minutes is a *long* time), Lorenzo's driving was irreproachable. Had the officers witnessed the petitioners violate a single traffic law, they would have had cause to stop the truck, Whren v. United States, 517 U.S. 806, 810 (1996), and this case would not be before us. And not only was the driving *irreproachable*, but the State offers no evidence to suggest that the petitioners even did anything *suspicious*, such as suddenly slowing down, pulling off to the side of the road, or turning somewhere to see whether they were being followed. Cf. *Arvizu*, supra, at 270-271, 277 (concluding that an officer's suspicion of criminality was enhanced when the driver, upon seeing that he was being followed, "slowed dramatically," "appeared stiff," and "seemed to be trying to pretend" that the patrol car was not there). Consequently, the tip's suggestion of ongoing drunken driving (if it could be deemed to suggest that) not only went uncorroborated; it was affirmatively undermined.

A hypothetical variation on the facts of this case illustrates the point. Suppose an anonymous tipster reports that, while following near mile marker 88 a silver Ford F-150, license plate 8D949925, traveling southbound on Highway 1, she saw in the truck's open cab several five-foot-tall stacks of what was unmistakably baled cannabis. Two minutes later, a highway patrolman spots the truck exactly where the tip suggested it would be, begins following it, but sees nothing in the truck's cab. It is not enough to say that the officer's observation merely failed to corroborate the tipster's accusation. It is more precise to say that the officer's observation *discredited* the informant's accusation: The crime was supposedly occurring (and would continue to occur) in plain view, but the police saw nothing. Similarly, here, the crime supposedly suggested by the tip was ongoing intoxicated driving, the hallmarks of which are many, readily identifiable, and difficult to conceal. That the officers witnessed nary a minor traffic violation nor any other "sound indici[um] of drunk driving," ante, at 1690, strongly suggests that the suspected crime was *not* occurring after all. The tip's implication of continuing criminality, already weak, grew even weaker.

Resisting this line of reasoning, the Court curiously asserts that, since drunk drivers who see marked squad cars in their rearview mirrors may evade detection simply by driving "more careful[ly]," the "absence of additional suspicious conduct" is "hardly surprising" and thus largely irrelevant. Whether a drunk driver drives drunkenly, the Court seems

to think, is up to him. That is not how I understand the influence of
alcohol. I subscribe to the more traditional view that the dangers of
intoxicated driving are the intoxicant's impairing effects on the body —
effects that no mere act of the will can resist. See, *e.g.,* A. Dasgupta, The
Science of Drinking: How Alcohol Affects Your Body and Mind 39
(explaining that the physiological effect of a blood alcohol content
between 0.08 and 0.109, for example, is "sever[e] impair[ment]" of
"[b]alance, speech, hearing, and reaction time," as well as one's general
"ability to drive a motor vehicle"). Consistent with this view, I take it as a
fundamental premise of our intoxicated-driving laws that a driver soused
enough to swerve once can be expected to swerve again — and soon. If he
does not, and if the only evidence of his first episode of irregular driving
is a mere inference from an uncorroborated, vague, and nameless tip,
then the Fourth Amendment requires that he be left alone.

* * *

The Court's opinion serves up a freedom-destroying cocktail consist-
ing of two parts patent falsity: (1) that anonymous 911 reports of traffic
violations are reliable so long as they correctly identify a car and its
location, and (2) that a single instance of careless or reckless driving
necessarily supports a reasonable suspicion of drunkenness. All the mal-
evolent 911 caller need do is assert a traffic violation, and the targeted
car will be stopped, forcibly if necessary, by the police. If the driver turns
out not to be drunk (which will almost always be the case), the caller need
fear no consequences, even if 911 knows his identity. After all, he never
alleged drunkenness, but merely called in a traffic violation — and on
that point his word is as good as his victim's.

Drunken driving is a serious matter, but so is the loss of our freedom
to come and go as we please without police interference. To prevent and
detect murder we do not allow searches without probable cause or tar-
geted *Terry* stops without reasonable suspicion. We should not do so for
drunken driving either. After today's opinion all of us on the road, and
not just drug dealers, are at risk of having our freedom of movement
curtailed on suspicion of drunkenness, based upon a phone tip, true or
false, of a single instance of careless driving. I respectfully dissent.

NOTES AND QUESTIONS

1. Are you persuaded by the majority's reasoning? Does this anonymous tip — that a Silver Ford-150 pickup, bearing a particular plate and
at a particular location, just ran the tipster off the road — bear more

indicia of reliability than another anonymous tip that "a young black male standing at a particular bus stop and wearing a plaid shirt" is carrying a gun? Why?

2. The majority gives three reasons: (1) The tipster in *Navarette* claimed to be an eyewitness to the reckless driving, unlike the tipster in *J.L.*, who never claimed to have seen the gun; (2) Her report was made contemporaneously; and (3) She used the 911 emergency system. Is *that* persuasive? As to the first rationale, it's true that by asserting that she was run off the road, the tipster implicitly tells us that her basis of knowledge is strong: she was there, and she saw it. But as Justice Scalia points out in dissent, this hardly supports the proposition that she is telling the truth. And as to veracity (which is also relevant, after all) is it really enough that the tipster's report was made contemporaneously, and to 911? Would the result in *J.L.* have been different if the anonymous tipster there had called 911 to say he had just observed a gun in J.L.'s waistband?

3. If the majority's analysis seems thin, what about the dissent's? Justice Scalia starts off with the proposition that everything about the tip provides reason to doubt it, "beginning with the peculiar fact that the accusation was anonymous." But the majority says (and the dissent does not disagree) that the tipster identified herself by name on the 911 tape—a fact that it must disregard, simply because the tape was not put in evidence. Isn't *this* a peculiar way to elaborate constitutional rules—in the context of a set of facts that everyone seems to agree did not actually occur?

4. But let's assume the tipster *was* anonymous. Do you think it more or less likely that an anonymous tipster would provide false information in *Navarette*, as opposed to *J.L.* or Illinois v. Gates? Perhaps Justice Scalia is correct that a tipster would have "[p]lenty of time to dissemble or embellish" in reporting that a passing vehicle had forced her off the road. But isn't there something to the notion that a deceptive tipster attempting maliciously to set police on a false trail must go to considerably more trouble when the intended victim is in a moving car? Or is Justice Scalia operating on the assumption that deceptive tipsters pick their victims at random?

5. Finally, return to the observation in *J.L.* that the facts there "do not require us to speculate about the circumstances under which the danger alleged in an anonymous tip might be so great as to justify a search even without showing of reliability." To the extent that this observation suggests that reasonable suspicion and probable cause may amount to a more flexible requirement that police act reasonably under the circumstances (as suggested in the notes following *J.L.*), could *Navarette* be an

instance of this? After all, police are responsible for roadway safety — an interest that the Court deems distinct from police interest in ordinary crime control. See, e.g., Indianapolis v. Edmond, 531 U.S. 32 (2000), infra main text, at page 599. The police conduct here, moreover, involved the stop of a car, not the frisk of a person, as in *J.L.* And as the majority says, "allowing a drunk driver a second chance for dangerous conduct could have disastrous consequences." Perhaps it is simply reasonable, in the majority's judgment, to act upon an anonymous tip that a roadster has run another car off the road by stopping the car in question, to ascertain that the driver is not impaired.

6. Or maybe not. What about the dissent's point that police observed nothing wrong with Navarette's driving during the five minutes that he was under their surveillance?

2. Police Discretion and Profiling

Insert the following notes after Note 7 on page 583:

NOTES ON PRETEXT AND MATERIAL WITNESS DETENTIONS

1. In May 2011, the Court again reaffirmed its distaste for inquiries into the subjective intent of government officials in adjudicating Fourth Amendment claims — and in an unusual context in which the arrest power may exist even *without* probable cause to believe the arrestee has committed an infraction, much less a crime.

In Ashcroft v. al-Kidd, 131 S. Ct. 2074 (2011), the plaintiff, in a *Bivens* complaint, see Bivens v. Six Unknown Fed. Narcotics Agents, 403 U.S. 388 (1971), alleged that after the September 11 terrorist attacks, then-Attorney General Ashcroft authorized federal officials to detain terrorism suspects pursuant to the federal material witness statute. This statute authorizes judges to order the arrest of persons whose testimony "is material in a criminal proceeding . . . if it is shown that it may become impracticable to secure the presence of the person by subpoena." 18 U.S.C. § 3144. As Justice Scalia noted, writing for the majority, "[m]aterial witnesses enjoy the same constitutional right to pretrial release as other federal detainees, and federal law requires release if their testimony 'can adequately be secured by deposition, and if further detention is not necessary to prevent a failure of justice.'" (quoting 18 U.S.C. § 3144). The Court's opinion succinctly recaps plaintiff's allegations regarding his arrest as a material witness:

> The complaint alleges that, in the aftermath of the September 11th terrorist attacks, then-Attorney General John Ashcroft authorized federal prosecutors and law enforcement officials to use the material-witness statute to detain individuals with suspected ties to terrorist organizations. It is alleged that federal officials had no intention of calling most of these individuals as witnesses, and that they were detained, at Ashcroft's direction, because federal officials suspected them of supporting terrorism but lacked sufficient evidence to charge them with a crime.
>
> It is alleged that this pretextual detention policy led to the material-witness arrest of al-Kidd, a native-born United States citizen. FBI agents apprehended him in March 2003 as he checked in for a flight to Saudi Arabia. Two days earlier, federal officials had informed a Magistrate Judge that, if al-Kidd boarded his flight, they believed information "crucial" to the prosecution of Sami Omar al-Hussayen would be lost. Al-Kidd remained in federal custody for 16 days and on supervised release until al-Hussayen's trial concluded 14 months later. Prosecutors never called him as a witness.

2. Al-Kidd's Fourth Amendment claim was that he had been improperly seized and detained as a material witness by government officials who actually suspected him of terrorism, but who lacked probable cause to arrest. The Supreme Court declined the invitation to inquire into the purpose or motivation behind his detention. The Court noted that it had "almost uniformly rejected invitations to probe subjective intent." It acknowledged limited exceptions to this rule, noting in particular its decision in Indianapolis v. Edmond, 531 U.S. 32 (2000), found in the casebook at page 599, invalidating a suspicionless vehicle checkpoint set up for the "programmatic purpose" of detecting illegal narcotics. The Court observed that programmatic purpose may be relevant to assessing the validity of Fourth Amendment intrusions undertaken "pursuant to a general scheme *without* individualized suspicion" (emphasis added). But it found al-Kidd's situation to be far removed from that of a motorist who is stopped at a checkpoint in the absence of any reason to believe he has committed a crime:

> Needless to say, warrantless, "suspicionless intrusions pursuant to a general scheme," are far removed from the facts of this case. A warrant issued by a neutral Magistrate Judge authorized al-Kidd's arrest. The affidavit accompanying the warrant application (as al-Kidd concedes) gave individualized reasons to believe that he was a material witness and that he would soon disappear. . . .
>
> A warrant based on individualized suspicion in fact grants more protection against the malevolent and the incompetent than existed in most of our cases eschewing inquiries into intent. In *Whren*, 517 U.S. [806, 813 (1996)], . . . we

declined to probe the motive[ ] behind [a] seizure[ ] supported by probable cause but lacking a warrant approved by a detached magistrate. Terry v. Ohio, 392 U.S. 1, 21-22 (1968), . . . applied an objective standard to warrantless searches justified by a lesser showing of reasonable suspicion. . . . If concerns about improper motives and pretext do not justify subjective inquiries in those less protective contexts, we see no reason to adopt that inquiry here.

Al-Kidd would read our cases more narrowly. He asserts that *Whren* establishes that we ignore subjective intent only when there exists "probable cause to believe that a violation of law has occurred" — which was not the case here. That is a distortion of *Whren*. Our unanimous opinion held that we would not look behind an objectively reasonable traffic stop to determine whether racial profiling or a desire to investigate other potential crimes was the real motive. . . .

. . . We referred to probable cause to believe that a violation of law had occurred because that was the legitimating factor [validating the stop] in the case at hand. But the analysis of our opinion swept broadly to reject inquiries into motive generally. . . .

Because al-Kidd concedes that individualized suspicion supported the issuance of the material-witness arrest warrant; and does not assert that his arrest would have been unconstitutional absent the alleged pretextual use of the warrant; we find no Fourth Amendment violation. Efficient and evenhanded application of the law demands that we look to whether the arrest is objectively justified, rather than to the motive of the arresting officer.

3. Do you find this reasoning persuasive? Justice Ginsburg, joined by Justices Breyer and Sotomayor, concurred in the judgment on the ground that the defendant was entitled to qualified immunity but questioned the assumption that a valid warrant had issued:

> In addressing al-Kidd's Fourth Amendment claim against Ashcroft, the Court assumes at the outset the existence of a validly obtained material witness warrant. That characterization is puzzling. Is a warrant "validly obtained" when the affidavit on which it is based fails to inform the issuing Magistrate Judge that "the Government has no intention of using [al-Kidd as a witness] at [another's] trial," and does not disclose that al-Kidd had cooperated with FBI agents each of the several times they had asked to interview him?
>
> Casting further doubt on the assumption that the warrant was validly obtained, the Magistrate Judge was not told that al-Kidd's parents, wife, and children were all citizens and residents of the United States. In addition, the affidavit misrepresented that al-Kidd was about to take a one-way flight to Saudi Arabia, with a first-class ticket costing approximately $5,000; in fact, al-Kidd had a round-trip, coach-class ticket that cost $1,700. Given these omissions and misrepresentations, there is strong cause to question the Court's opening assumption — a valid material-witness warrant — and equally strong reason to conclude that a merits determination was neither necessary nor proper.

Justice Ginsburg also questioned whether the arrest warrant here was really based on individualized suspicion, as the majority opinion asserts:

> The word "suspicion" . . . ordinarily indicates that the person suspected has engaged in wrongdoing. Material witness status does not "involv[e] suspicion, or lack of suspicion," of the individual so identified. See Illinois v. Lidster, 540 U.S. 419, 424-425 (2004).
> This Court's decisions, until today, have uniformly used the term "individualized suspicion" to mean "individualized suspicion *of wrongdoing.*" See Indianapolis v. Edmond, 531 U.S. 32, 37 (2000) (emphasis added).

Justice Sotomayor, also concurring in the judgment, noted that "[a]lthough the majority is correct that a government official's subjective intent is generally 'irrelevant in determining whether that officer's actions violate the Fourth Amendment,' Bond v. United States, 529 U.S. 334, 338, n.2 (2000), none of our prior cases recognizing that principle involved prolonged detention of an individual without probable cause to believe he had committed any criminal offense."

Given these observations, is it really so obvious, as Justice Scalia suggests, that the concern about pretext here is less serious than in *Whren* and *Terry*?

4. The material witness statute authorizes judges to issue arrest warrants for the seizure of individuals in circumstances where probable cause to arrest for some crime has not been established. Note, finally, that Justice Kennedy, who joined the Court's opinion in full, also wrote separately to make clear that the Court's holding addressed *only* the argument put forth by al-Kidd—that alleged pretextual use of the material witness procedure had violated his Fourth Amendment rights—and not any other question regarding the legality of use of the material witness statute:

> Under the statute, a Magistrate Judge may issue a warrant to arrest someone as a material witness upon a showing by affidavit that "the testimony of a person is material in a criminal proceeding" and "that it may become impracticable to secure the presence of the person by subpoena." 18 U.S.C. § 3144. The scope of the statute's lawful authorization is uncertain. For example, a law-abiding citizen might observe a crime during the days or weeks before a scheduled flight abroad. It is unclear whether those facts alone might allow police to obtain a material witness warrant on the ground that it "may become impracticable" to secure the person's presence by subpoena. The question becomes more difficult if one further assumes the traveler would be willing to testify if asked; and more difficult still if one supposes that authorities delay obtaining or executing the warrant until the traveler has arrived at the airport. These possibilities resemble the facts in this case.

In considering these issues, it is important to bear in mind that the Material Witness Statute might not provide for the issuance of warrants within the meaning of the Fourth Amendment's Warrant Clause. The typical arrest warrant is based on probable cause that the arrestee has committed a crime; but that is not the standard for the issuance of warrants under the Material Witness Statute. If material witness warrants do not qualify as "Warrants" under the Fourth Amendment, then material witness arrests might still be governed by the Fourth Amendment's separate reasonableness requirement for seizures of the person. Given the difficulty of these issues, the Court is correct to address only the legal theory before it, without further exploring when material witness arrests might be consistent with statutory and constitutional requirements.

What do you think? Is it consistent with the text of the Fourth Amendment for judges to issue material witness arrest warrants on something other than probable cause to believe a person has committed a crime? Assuming the truth of the plaintiff's allegations, was he subjected to an unlawful seizure even apart from the alleged motivation of the seizing officials?

3. "Special Needs"

Insert the following note and main case after Note 4 on page 614:

5. The roadblock cases raised — but seemingly failed to answer — two questions that are extremely important to understanding the "all-the-circumstances reasonableness" approach to Fourth Amendment case law. First, what role does individualized suspicion play in Fourth Amendment analysis? When is it required and when may be it be dispensed with? Second, when is interest balancing appropriate? The following case, proclaimed by Justice Alito at oral argument to be "perhaps the most important criminal procedure case" that the Court has heard in decades, circles back to these questions, albeit in a new context. Consider whether the sharply divided Court provides any clearer answers. Consider, as well, the increasing importance — even dominance(?) — of the reasonableness approach to Fourth Amendment analysis.

MARYLAND v. KING
Certiorari to the Court of Appeals of Maryland
133 S. Ct. 1958 (2013)

JUSTICE KENNEDY delivered the opinion of the Court.

In 2003 a man concealing his face and armed with a gun broke into a woman's home in Salisbury, Maryland. He raped her. The police were unable to identify or apprehend the assailant based on any detailed description or other evidence they then had, but they did obtain from the victim a sample of the perpetrator's DNA.

In 2009 Alonzo King was arrested in Wicomico County, Maryland, and charged with first- and second-degree assault for menacing a group of people with a shotgun. As part of a routine booking procedure for serious offenses, his DNA sample was taken by applying a cotton swab or filter paper — known as a buccal swab — to the inside of his cheeks. The DNA was found to match the DNA taken from the Salisbury rape victim. King was tried and convicted for the rape. . . .

The Court of Appeals of Maryland, on review of King's rape conviction, ruled that the DNA taken when King was booked for the 2009 charge was an unlawful seizure because obtaining and using the cheek swab was an unreasonable search of the person. It set the rape conviction aside. This Court granted certiorari and now reverses the judgment of the Maryland court.

I

When King was arrested on April 10, 2009, for menacing a group of people with a shotgun and charged in state court with both first- and second-degree assault, he was processed for detention in custody at the Wicomico County Central Booking facility. Booking personnel used a cheek swab to take the DNA sample from him pursuant to provisions of the Maryland DNA Collection Act (or Act).

On July 13, 2009, King's DNA record was uploaded to the Maryland DNA database, and three weeks later, on August 4, 2009, his DNA profile was matched to the DNA sample collected in the unsolved 2003 rape case. Once the DNA was matched to King, detectives presented the forensic evidence to a grand jury, which indicted him for the rape. Detectives obtained a search warrant and took a second sample of DNA from King, which again matched the evidence from the rape. He moved to suppress the DNA match on the grounds that Maryland's DNA collection law violated the Fourth Amendment. The Circuit Court Judge upheld the statute as constitutional. King pleaded not guilty to the rape charges but was convicted and sentenced to life in prison without the possibility of parole.

In a divided opinion, the Maryland Court of Appeals struck down the portions of the Act authorizing collection of DNA from felony arrestees as unconstitutional. . . .

Both federal and state courts have reached differing conclusions as to whether the Fourth Amendment prohibits the collection and analysis of a DNA sample from persons arrested, but not yet convicted, on felony charges. This Court granted certiorari to address the question. King is the respondent here.

II

The advent of DNA technology is one of the most significant scientific advancements of our era. The full potential for use of genetic markers in medicine and science is still being explored, but the utility of DNA identification in the criminal justice system is already undisputed. Since the first use of forensic DNA analysis to catch a rapist and murderer in England in 1986, see J. Butler, Fundamentals of Forensic *DNA Typing* 5 (2009) (hereinafter Butler), law enforcement, the defense bar, and the courts have acknowledged DNA testing's "unparalleled ability both to exonerate the wrongly convicted and to identify the guilty. It has the potential to significantly improve both the criminal justice system and police investigative practices." District Attorney's Office for Third Judicial Dist. v. Osborne, 557 U.S. 52, 55 (2009).

A

The current standard for forensic DNA testing relies on a analysis of the chromosomes located within the nucleus of all human cells. "The DNA material in chromosomes is composed of 'coding' and 'noncoding' regions. The coding regions are known as *genes* and contain the information necessary for a cell to make proteins. . . . Non-protein-coding regions . . . are not related directly to making proteins, [and] have been referred to as 'junk' DNA." Butler 25. The adjective "junk" may mislead the layperson, for in fact this is the DNA region used with near certainty to identify a person. The term apparently is intended to indicate that this particular noncoding region, while useful and even dispositive for purposes like identity, does not show more far-reaching and complex characteristics like genetic traits.

Many of the patterns found in DNA are shared among all people, so forensic analysis focuses on "repeated DNA sequences scattered throughout the human genome," known as "short tandem repeats" (STRs). Id., at

147-148. The alternative possibilities for the size and frequency of these STRs at any given point along a strand of DNA are known as "alleles," id., at 25; and multiple alleles are analyzed in order to ensure that a DNA profile matches only one individual. Future refinements may improve present technology, but even now STR analysis makes it "possible to determine whether a biological tissue matches a suspect with near certainty." *Osborne*, supra, at 62.

The Act authorizes Maryland law enforcement authorities to collect DNA samples from "an individual who is charged with . . . a crime of violence or an attempt to commit a crime of violence; or . . . burglary or an attempt to commit burglary." Md. Pub. Saf. Code Ann. § 2-504(a)(3)(i) (Lexis 2011). Maryland law defines a crime of violence to include murder, rape, first-degree assault, kidnaping, arson, sexual assault, and a variety of other serious crimes. Once taken, a DNA sample may not be processed or placed in a database before the individual is arraigned (unless the individual consents). It is at this point that a judicial officer ensures that there is probable cause to detain the arrestee on a qualifying serious offense. If "all qualifying criminal charges are determined to be unsupported by probable cause . . . the DNA sample shall be immediately destroyed." § 2-504(d)(2)(I). DNA samples are also destroyed if "a criminal action begun against the individual . . . does not result in a conviction," "the conviction is finally reversed or vacated and no new trial is permitted," or "the individual is granted an unconditional pardon." § 2-511(a)(1).

The Act also limits the information added to a DNA database and how it may be used. Specifically, "[o]nly DNA records that directly relate to the identification of individuals shall be collected and stored." § 2-505(b)(1). No purpose other than identification is permissible: "A person may not willfully test a DNA sample for information that does not relate to the identification of individuals as specified in this subtitle." § 2-512(c). Tests for familial matches are also prohibited. See § 2-506(d) ("A person may not perform a search of the statewide DNA data base for the purpose of identification of an offender in connection with a crime for which the offender may be a biological relative of the individual from whom the DNA sample was acquired"). The officers involved in taking and analyzing respondent's DNA sample complied with the Act in all respects.

Respondent's DNA was collected in this case using a common procedure known as a "buccal swab." "Buccal cell collection involves wiping a small piece of filter paper or a cotton swab similar to a Q-tip against the inside cheek of an individual's mouth to collect some skin cells." Butler 86. The procedure is quick and painless. The swab touches inside an arrestee's mouth, but it requires no "surgical intrusio[n] beneath the skin," Winston v. Lee, 470 U.S. 753, 760 (1985), and it poses no "threa[t] to the health or safety" of arrestees, id., at 763.

B

Respondent's identification as the rapist resulted in part through the operation of a national project to standardize collection and storage of DNA profiles. Authorized by Congress and supervised by the Federal Bureau of Investigation, the Combined DNA Index System (CODIS) connects DNA laboratories at the local, state, and national level. Since its authorization in 1994, the CODIS system has grown to include all 50 States and a number of federal agencies. CODIS collects DNA profiles provided by local laboratories taken from arrestees, convicted offenders, and forensic evidence found at crime scenes. To participate in CODIS, a local laboratory must sign a memorandum of understanding agreeing to adhere to quality standards and submit to audits to evaluate compliance with the federal standards for scientifically rigorous DNA testing.

One of the most significant aspects of CODIS is the standardization of the points of comparison in DNA analysis. The CODIS database is based on 13 loci at which the STR alleles are noted and compared. These loci make possible extreme accuracy in matching individual samples, with a "random match probability of approximately 1 in 100 trillion (assuming unrelated individuals)." Ibid. The CODIS loci are from the non-protein coding junk regions of DNA, and "are not known to have any association with a genetic disease or any other genetic predisposition. Thus, the information in the database is only useful for human identity testing." Id., at 279. STR information is recorded only as a "string of numbers"; and the DNA identification is accompanied only by information denoting the laboratory and the analyst responsible for the submission. Id., at 270. In short, CODIS sets uniform national standards for DNA matching and then facilitates connections between local law enforcement agencies who can share more specific information about matched STR profiles.

All 50 States require the collection of DNA from felony convicts, and respondent does not dispute the validity of that practice. Twenty-eight States and the Federal Government have adopted laws similar to the Maryland Act authorizing the collection of DNA from some or all arrestees. Although those statutes vary in their particulars, such as what charges require a DNA sample, their similarity means that this case implicates more than the specific Maryland law. At issue is a standard, expanding technology already in widespread use throughout the Nation.

III

A

Although the DNA swab procedure used here presents a question the Court has not yet addressed, the framework for deciding the issue is well established. The Fourth Amendment, binding on the States by the Fourteenth Amendment, provides that "[t]he right of the people to be secure in their persons, houses, papers, and effects, against unreasonable searches and seizures, shall not be violated." It can be agreed that using a buccal swab on the inner tissues of a person's cheek in order to obtain DNA samples is a search. Virtually any "intrusio[n] into the human body," Schmerber v. California, 384 U.S. 757, 770 (1966), will work an invasion of "'cherished personal security' that is subject to constitutional scrutiny," Cupp v. Murphy, 412 U.S. 291, 295 (1973) (quoting Terry v. Ohio, 392 U.S. 1, 24-25 (1968)). The Court has applied the Fourth Amendment to police efforts to draw blood, see *Schmerber*, supra, scraping an arrestee's fingernails to obtain trace evidence, see *Cupp*, supra, and even to "a breathalyzer test, which generally requires the production of alveolar or 'deep lung' breath for chemical analysis," Skinner v. Railway Labor Executives' Assn., 489 U.S. 602, 616 (1989).

A buccal swab is a far more gentle process than a venipuncture to draw blood. It involves but a light touch on the inside of the cheek; and although it can be deemed a search within the body of the arrestee, it requires no "surgical intrusions beneath the skin." *Winston*, 470 U.S., at 760. The fact that an intrusion is negligible is of central relevance to determining reasonableness, although it is still a search as the law defines that term.

B

To say that the Fourth Amendment applies here is the beginning point, not the end of the analysis. . . . "As the text of the Fourth Amendment indicates, the ultimate measure of the constitutionality of a governmental search is 'reasonableness.' "Vernonia School Dist. 47J v. Acton, 515 U.S. 646, 652 (1995). In giving content to the inquiry whether an intrusion is reasonable, the Court has preferred "some quantum of individualized suspicion . . . [as] a prerequisite to a constitutional search or seizure. But the Fourth Amendment imposes no irreducible requirement of such suspicion." United States v. Martinez-Fuerte, 428 U.S. 543, 560-561 (1976) (citation and footnote omitted).

In some circumstances, such as "[w]hen faced with special law enforcement needs, diminished expectations of privacy, minimal intrusions, or the like, the Court has found that certain general, or individual, circumstances may render a warrantless search or seizure reasonable." Illinois v. McArthur, 531 U.S. 326, 330 (2001). Those circumstances diminish the need for a warrant, either because "the public interest is such that neither a warrant nor probable cause is required," Maryland v. Buie, 494 U.S. 325, 331 (1990), or because an individual is already on notice, for instance because of his employment, see *Skinner*, supra, or the conditions of his release from government custody, see Samson v. California, 547 U.S. 843 (2006), that some reasonable police intrusion on his privacy is to be expected. The need for a warrant is perhaps least when the search involves no discretion that could properly be limited by the "interpo[lation of] a neutral magistrate between the citizen and the law enforcement officer." Treasury Employees v. Von Raab, 489 U.S. 656, 667 (1989).

The instant case can be addressed with this background. The Maryland DNA Collection Act provides that, in order to obtain a DNA sample, all arrestees charged with serious crimes must furnish the sample on a buccal swab applied, as noted, to the inside of the cheeks. The arrestee is already in valid police custody for a serious offense supported by probable cause. The DNA collection is not subject to the judgment of officers whose perspective might be "colored by their primary involvement in 'the often competitive enterprise of ferreting out crime.'" *Terry*, supra, at 12 (quoting Johnson v. United States, 333 U.S. 10, 14 (1948)). As noted by this Court in a different but still instructive context involving blood testing, "[b]oth the circumstances justifying toxicological testing and the permissible limits of such intrusions are defined narrowly and specifically in the regulations that authorize them. . . . Indeed, in light of the standardized nature of the tests and the minimal discretion vested in those charged with administering the program, there are virtually no facts for a neutral magistrate to evaluate." *Skinner*, supra, at 622. Here, the search effected by the buccal swab of respondent falls within the category of cases this Court has analyzed by reference to the proposition that the "touchstone of the Fourth Amendment is reasonableness, not individualized suspicion." *Samson*, supra, at 855, n. 4.

Even if a warrant is not required, a search is not beyond Fourth Amendment scrutiny; for it must be reasonable in its scope and manner of execution. . . . To say that no warrant is required is merely to acknowledge that "rather than employing a *per se* rule of unreasonableness, we balance the privacy-related and law enforcement-related concerns to determine if the intrusion was reasonable." *McArthur*, supra, at 331.

This application of "traditional standards of reasonableness" requires a court to weigh "the promotion of legitimate governmental interests" against "the degree to which [the search] intrudes upon an individual's privacy." Wyoming v. Houghton, 526 U.S. 295, 300 (1999). An assessment of reasonableness to determine the lawfulness of requiring this class of arrestees to provide a DNA sample is central to the instant case.

IV

A

The legitimate government interest served by the Maryland DNA Collection Act is one that is well established: the need for law enforcement officers in a safe and accurate way to process and identify the persons and possessions they must take into custody. It is beyond dispute that "probable cause provides legal justification for arresting a person suspected of crime, and for a brief period of detention to take the administrative steps incident to arrest." Gerstein v. Pugh, 420 U.S. 103, 113-114 (1975). Also uncontested is the "right on the part of the Government, always recognized under English and American law, to search the person of the accused when legally arrested." Weeks v. United States, 232 U.S. 383, 392 (1914), overruled on other grounds, Mapp v. Ohio, 367 U.S. 643 (1961). "The validity of the search of a person incident to a lawful arrest has been regarded as settled from its first enunciation, and has remained virtually unchallenged." United States v. Robinson, 414 U.S. 218, 224 (1973). Even in that context, the Court has been clear that individual suspicion is not necessary, because "[t]he constitutionality of a search incident to an arrest does not depend on whether there is any indication that the person arrested possesses weapons or evidence. The fact of a lawful arrest, standing alone, authorizes a search." Michigan v. DeFillippo, 443 U.S. 31, 35 (1979).

The "routine administrative procedure[s] at a police station house incident to booking and jailing the suspect" derive from different origins and have different constitutional justifications than, say, the search of a place, Illinois v. Lafayette, 462 U.S. 640, 643 (1983); for the search of a place not incident to an arrest depends on the "fair probability that contraband or evidence of a crime will be found in a particular place," Illinois v. Gates, 462 U.S. 213, 238 (1983). The interests are further different when an individual is formally processed into police custody. Then "the law is in the act of subjecting the body of the accused to its physical dominion." People v. Chiagles, 237 N.Y. 193, 197 (1923) (Cardozo, J.). When probable cause exists to remove an individual from the normal channels of society and hold him in legal custody, DNA identification plays a critical role in serving those interests.

First, "[i]n every criminal case, it is known and must be known who has been arrested and who is being tried." Hiibel v. Sixth Judicial Dist. Court of Nev., Humboldt Cty., 542 U.S. 177, 191 (2004). An individual's identity is more than just his name or Social Security number, and the government's interest in identification goes beyond ensuring that the proper name is typed on the indictment. Identity has never been considered limited to the name on the arrestee's birth certificate. In fact, a name is of little value compared to the real interest in identification at stake when an individual is brought into custody. "It is a well recognized aspect of criminal conduct that the perpetrator will take unusual steps to conceal not only his conduct, but also his identity. Disguises used while committing a crime may be supplemented or replaced by changed names, and even changed physical features." Jones v. Murray, 962 F.2d 302, 307 (C.A. 4 1992). An "arrestee may be carrying a false ID or lie about his identity," and "criminal history records . . . can be inaccurate or incomplete." Florence v. Board of Chosen Freeholders of County of Burlington, 132 S. Ct. 1510, 1521 (2012).

A suspect's criminal history is a critical part of his identity that officers should know when processing him for detention. It is a common occurrence that "[p]eople detained for minor offenses can turn out to be the most devious and dangerous criminals. Hours after the Oklahoma City bombing, Timothy McVeigh was stopped by a state trooper who noticed he was driving without a license plate. Police stopped serial killer Joel Rifkin for the same reason. One of the terrorists involved in the September 11 attacks was stopped and ticketed for speeding just two days before hijacking Flight 93." Id., at 1520 (citations omitted). Police already seek this crucial identifying information. They use routine and accepted means as varied as comparing the suspect's booking photograph to sketch artists' depictions of persons of interest, showing his mugshot to potential witnesses, and of course making a computerized comparison of the arrestee's fingerprints against electronic databases of known criminals and unsolved crimes. In this respect the only difference between DNA analysis and the accepted use of fingerprint databases is the unparalleled accuracy DNA provides.

The task of identification necessarily entails searching public and police records based on the identifying information provided by the arrestee to see what is already known about him. The DNA collected from arrestees is an irrefutable identification of the person from whom it was taken. Like a fingerprint, the 13 CODIS loci are not themselves evidence of any particular crime, in the way that a drug test can by itself be evidence of illegal narcotics use. A DNA profile is useful to the police because it gives them a form of identification to search the records already in their valid possession. In this respect the use of DNA for identification is no different than matching an arrestee's face to a wanted poster of a previously unidentified suspect; or matching tattoos to known gang symbols to reveal a criminal affiliation; or matching the arrestee's fingerprints to those recovered from a crime scene. DNA is another metric of identification used to connect the arrestee with his or her public persona, as reflected in records of his or her actions that are available to the police. Those records may be linked to the arrestee by a variety of relevant forms of identification, including name, alias, date and time of previous convictions and the name then used, photograph, Social Security number, or CODIS profile. These data, found in official records, are checked as a routine matter to produce a more comprehensive record of the suspect's complete identity. Finding occurrences of the arrestee's CODIS profile in outstanding cases is consistent with this common practice. It uses a different form of identification than a name or fingerprint, but its function is the same.

Second, law enforcement officers bear a responsibility for ensuring that the custody of an arrestee does not create inordinate "risks for facility staff, for the existing detainee population, and for a new detainee." *Florence*, supra, at 1518. DNA identification can provide untainted information to those charged with detaining suspects and detaining the property of any felon. For these purposes officers must know the type of person whom they are detaining, and DNA allows them to make critical choices about how to proceed.

Third, looking forward to future stages of criminal prosecution, "the Government has a substantial interest in ensuring that persons accused of crimes are available for trials." Bell v. Wolfish, 441 U.S. 520, 534 (1979). A person who is arrested for one offense but knows that he has yet to answer for some past crime may be more inclined to flee the instant charges, lest continued contact with the criminal justice system expose one or more other serious offenses. For example, a defendant who had committed a prior sexual assault might be inclined to flee on a burglary charge, knowing that in every State a DNA sample would be taken from him after his conviction on the burglary charge that would tie him to the more serious charge of rape. In addition to subverting the administration of justice with respect to the crime of arrest, this ties back to the interest in safety; for a detainee who absconds from custody presents a risk to law enforcement officers, other detainees, victims of previous crimes, witnesses, and society at large.

Fourth, an arrestee's past conduct is essential to an assessment of the danger he poses to the public, and this will inform a court's determination whether the individual should be released on bail. . . . DNA identification of a suspect in a violent crime provides critical information to the police and judicial officials in making a determination of the arrestee's future dangerousness. This inquiry always has entailed some scrutiny beyond the name on the defendant's driver's license. For example, Maryland law requires a judge to take into account not only "the nature and circumstances of the offense charged" but also "the defendant's family ties, employment status and history, financial resources, reputation, character and mental condition, length of residence in the community." 1 Md. Rules 4-216(f)(1)(A), (C) (2013). Knowing that the defendant is wanted for a previous violent crime based on DNA identification is especially probative of the court's consideration of "the danger of the defendant to the alleged victim, another person, or the community." Rule 4-216(f)(1)(G).

This interest is not speculative. In considering laws to require collecting DNA from arrestees, government agencies around the Nation found evidence of numerous cases in which felony arrestees would have been identified as violent through DNA identification matching them to previous crimes but who later committed additional crimes because such identification was not used to detain them. . . .

Present capabilities make it possible to complete a DNA identification that provides information essential to determining whether a detained suspect can be released pending trial. See, e.g., States Brief 18, n. 10 ("DNA identification database samples have been processed in as few as two days in California, although around 30 days has been average"). Regardless of when the initial bail decision is made, release is not appropriate until a further determination is made as to the person's identity in the sense not only of what his birth certificate states but also what other records and data disclose to give that identity more meaning in the whole context of who the person really is. And even when release is permitted, the background identity of the suspect is necessary for determining what conditions must be met before release is allowed. If release is authorized, it may take time for the conditions to be met, and so the time before actual release can be substantial. For example, in the federal system, defendants released conditionally are detained on average for 112 days; those released on unsecured bond for 37 days; on personal recognizance for 36 days; and on other financial conditions for 27 days. See Dept. of

Justice, Bureau of Justice Statistics, Compendium of Federal Justice Statistics 45 (NCJ-213476, Dec. 2006) online at http://bjs.gov/content/pub/pdf/cfjs04.pdf. During this entire period, additional and supplemental data establishing more about the person's identity and background can provide critical information relevant to the conditions of release and whether to revisit an initial release determination. The facts of this case are illustrative. Though the record is not clear, if some thought were being given to releasing the respondent on bail on the gun charge, a release that would take weeks or months in any event, when the DNA report linked him to the prior rape, it would be relevant to the conditions of his release. The same would be true with a supplemental fingerprint report.

Even if an arrestee is released on bail, development of DNA identification revealing the defendant's unknown violent past can and should lead to the revocation of his conditional release. Pretrial release of a person charged with a dangerous crime is a most serious responsibility. It is reasonable in all respects for the State to use an accepted database to determine if an arrestee is the object of suspicion in other serious crimes, suspicion that may provide a strong incentive for the arrestee to escape and flee.

Finally, in the interests of justice, the identification of an arrestee as the perpetrator of some heinous crime may have the salutary effect of freeing a person wrongfully imprisoned for the same offense. "[P]rompt [DNA] testing . . . would speed up apprehension of criminals before they commit additional crimes, and prevent the grotesque detention of . . . innocent people." J. Dwyer, P. Neufeld, & B. Scheck, Actual Innocence 245 (2000).

Because proper processing of arrestees is so important and has consequences for every stage of the criminal process, the Court has recognized that the "governmental interests underlying a station-house search of the arrestee's person and possessions may in some circumstances be even greater than those supporting a search immediately following arrest." *Lafayette*, 462 U.S., at 645. Thus, the Court has been reluctant to circumscribe the authority of the police to conduct reasonable booking searches. For example, "[t]he standards traditionally governing a search incident to lawful arrest are not . . . commuted to the stricter *Terry* standards." *Robinson*, 414 U.S., at 234. Nor are these interests in identification served only by a search of the arrestee himself. "[I]nspection of an arrestee's personal property may assist the police in ascertaining or verifying his identity." *Lafayette*, supra, at 646. And though the Fifth Amendment's protection against self-incrimination is not, as a general rule, governed by a reasonableness standard, the Court has held that "questions . . . reasonably related to the police's adminis-trative concerns . . . fall outside the protections of Miranda [v. Arizona, 384 U.S. 436 (1966)] and the answers thereto need not be suppressed." Pennsylvania v. Muniz, 496 U.S. 582, 601-602 (1990).

B

DNA identification represents an important advance in the techniques used by law enforcement to serve legitimate police concerns for as long as there have been arrests, concerns the courts have acknowledged and approved for more than a century. Law enforcement agencies routinely have used scientific advancements in their standard procedures for the identification of arrestees. "Police had been using photography to cap-ture the faces of criminals almost since its invention." S. Cole, Suspect Identities 20 (2001). Courts did not dispute that practice, concluding that a "sheriff in making an arrest for a felony on a warrant has the right to exercise a discretion . . . , [if] he should deem it necessary to the safe-keeping of a prisoner, and to prevent his escape, or to enable him the more readily to retake the prisoner if he should escape, to take his photograph." State ex rel. Bruns v. Clausmier, 154 Ind. 599, 601, 603 (1990). By the time that it had become "the daily practice of the police officers and detectives of crime to use photographic pictures for the discovery and identification of criminals," the courts likewise had come to the conclusion that "it would be [a] matter of regret to have its use unduly restricted upon any fanciful theory or constitutional privilege." Shaffer v. United States, 24 App. D.C. 417, 426 (1904).

Beginning in 1887, some police adopted more exacting means to identify arrestees, using the system of precise physical measurements pioneered by the French anthropologist Alphonse Bertillon. Bertillon identification consisted of 10 measurements of the arrestee's body, along with a "scientific analysis of the features of the face and an exact anatomical localization of the various scars, marks, &c., of the body." Defense of the Bertillon System, N.Y. Times, Jan. 20, 1896, p. 3. "[W]hen a prisoner was brought in, his photograph was taken according to the Bertillon system, and his body measurements were then made. The measurements were made . . . and noted down on the back of a card or a blotter, and the photograph of the prisoner was expected to be placed on the card. This card, therefore, furnished both the likeness and descrip-tion of the prisoner, and was placed in the rogues' gallery, and copies were sent to various cities where similar records were kept." People ex rel. Jones v. Diehl, 53 A.D. 645, 646 (1990). As in the present case, the point of taking this information about each arrestee was not limited to verifying that the proper name was on the indictment. These procedures were used to "facilitate the recapture of escaped prisoners," to aid "the investigation of their past records and personal history," and "to preserve the means of identification for . . . future supervision after discharge." Hodgeman v. Olsen, 86 Wash. 615, 619 (1915).

Perhaps the most direct historical analogue to the DNA technology used to identify respondent is the familiar practice of fingerprinting arrestees. From the advent of this technique, courts had no trouble determining that fingerprinting was a natural part of "the administrative steps incident to arrest." County of Riverside v. McLaughlin, 500 U.S. 44, 58 (1991). In the seminal case of United States v. Kelly, 55 F.2d 67 (C.A.2 1932), Judge Augustus Hand wrote that routine fingerprinting did not violate the Fourth Amendment precisely because it fit within the accepted means of processing an arrestee into custody:

> "Finger printing seems to be no more than an extension of methods of identification long used in dealing with persons under arrest for real or supposed violations of the criminal laws. It is known to be a very certain means devised by modern science to reach the desired end, and has become especially important in a time when increased population and vast aggregations of people in urban centers have rendered the notoriety of the individual in the community no longer a ready means of identification. . . .
>
> "We find no ground in reason or authority for interfering with a method of identifying persons charged with crime which has now become widely known and frequently practiced." Id. at 69-70.

By the middle of the 20th century, it was considered "elementary that a person in lawful custody may be required to submit to photographing and fingerprinting as part of routine identification processes." Smith v. United States, 324 F.2d 879, 882 (C.A.D.C. 1963) (Burger, J.) (citations omitted).

DNA identification is an advanced technique superior to fingerprinting in many ways, so much so that to insist on fingerprints as the norm would make little sense to either the forensic expert or a layperson. . . .

The respondent's primary objection to this analogy is that DNA identification is not as fast as fingerprinting, and so it should not be considered to be the 21st-century equivalent. But rapid analysis of fingerprints is itself of recent vintage. The FBI's vaunted Integrated Automated Fingerprint Identification System (IAFIS) was only "launched on July 28, 1999. Prior to this time, the processing of . . . fingerprint submissions was largely a manual, labor-intensive process, taking weeks or months to process a single submission." Federal Bureau of Investigation, Integrated Automated Fingerprint Identification System, online at http://www.fbi.gov/about-us/cjis/fingerprints_biometrics/iafis/iafis. It was not the advent of this technology that rendered fingerprint analysis constitutional in a single moment. The question of how long it takes to process identifying information obtained from a valid search goes only to the efficacy of the search for its purpose of prompt identification, not the constitutionality of the search. Given the importance of DNA in the identification of police records pertaining to arrestees and the need to refine and confirm that identity for its important bearing on the decision to continue release on bail or to impose of new conditions, DNA serves an essential purpose despite the existence of delays such as the one that occurred in this case. Even so, the delay in processing DNA from arrestees is being reduced to a substantial degree by rapid technical advances. See, e.g., Attorney General DeWine Announces Significant Drop in DNA Turnaround Time (Jan. 4, 2013) (DNA processing time reduced from 125 days in 2010 to 20 days in 2012); Gov. Jindal Announces Elimination of DNA Backlog, DNA Unit Now Operating in Real Time (Nov. 17, 2011) (average DNA report time reduced from a year or more in 2009 to 20 days in 2011). And the FBI has already begun testing devices that will enable police to process the DNA of arrestees within 90 minutes. . . . Just as fingerprinting was constitutional for generations prior to the introduction of IAFIS, DNA identification of arrestees is a permissible tool of law enforcement today. New technology will only further improve its speed and therefore its effectiveness. And, as noted above, actual release of a serious offender as a routine matter takes weeks or months in any event. . . .

In sum, there can be little reason to question "the legitimate interest of the government in knowing for an absolute certainty the identity of the person arrested, in knowing whether he is wanted elsewhere, and in ensuring his identification in the event he flees prosecution." 3 W. LaFave, Search and Seizure § 5.3(c), p. 216 (5th ed. 2012). . . . DNA identification of arrestees, of the type approved by the Maryland statute here at issue, is "no more than an extension of methods of identification long used in dealing with persons under arrest." *Kelly*, 55 F.2d, at 69. In the balance of reasonableness required by the Fourth Amendment, therefore, the Court must give great weight both to the significant government interest at stake in the identification of arrestees and to the unmatched potential of DNA identification to serve that interest.

V

A

By comparison to this substantial government interest and the unique effectiveness of DNA identification, the intrusion of a cheek swab to obtain a DNA sample is a minimal one. True, a significant government interest does not alone suffice to justify a search. The government interest must outweigh the degree to which the search invades an individual's legitimate expectations of privacy. In considering those expectations in this case, however, the necessary predicate of a valid arrest for a serious offense is fundamental. . . .

The expectations of privacy of an individual taken into police custody "necessarily [are] of a diminished scope." *Bell*, 441 U.S., at 557. "[B]oth the person and the property in his immediate possession may be searched at the station house." United States v. Edwards, 415 U.S. 800, 803 (1974). A search of the detainee's person when he is booked into custody may "'involve a relatively extensive exploration,'" *Robinson*, 414 U.S., at 227, including "requir[ing] at least some detainees to lift their genitals or cough in a squatting position," *Florence*, 132 S. Ct., at 1520.

In this critical respect, the search here at issue differs from the sort of programmatic searches of either the public at large or a particular class of regulated but otherwise law-abiding citizens that the Court has previously labeled as "'special needs'" searches. When the police stop a motorist at a checkpoint, see Indianapolis v. Edmond, 531 U.S. 32 (2000), or test a political candidate for illegal narcotics, see Chandler [v. Miller, 520 U.S. 305, 314 (1997)], they intrude upon substantial expectations of privacy. So the Court has insisted on some purpose other than "to detect evidence of ordinary criminal wrongdoing" to justify these searches in the absence of individualized suspicion. *Edmond*, supra, at 38. Once an individual has been arrested on probable cause for a dangerous offense that may require detention before trial, however, his or her expectations of privacy and freedom from police scrutiny are reduced. DNA identification like that at issue here thus does not require consideration of any unique needs that would be required to justify searching the average citizen. The special needs cases, though in full accord with the result reached here, do not have a direct bearing on the issues presented in this case, because unlike the search of a citizen who has not been suspected of a wrong, a detainee has a reduced expectation of privacy.

The reasonableness inquiry here considers two other circumstances in which the Court has held that particularized suspicion is not categorically required: "diminished expectations of privacy [and] minimal intrusions." *McArthur*, 531 U.S., at 330. This is not to suggest that any search is acceptable solely because a person is in custody. Some searches, such as invasive surgery, see *Winston*, 470 U.S. 753, or a search of the arrestee's home, see Chimel v. California, 395 U.S. 752 (1969), involve either greater intrusions or higher expectations of privacy than are present in this case. In those situations, when the Court must "balance the privacy-related and law enforcement-related concerns to determine if the intrusion was reasonable," *McArthur*, supra, at 331, the privacy-related concerns are weighty enough that the search may require a warrant, notwithstanding the diminished expectations of privacy of the arrestee.

Here, by contrast to the approved standard procedures incident to any arrest detailed above, a buccal swab involves an even more brief and still minimal intrusion. A gentle rub along the inside of the cheek does not break the skin, and it "involves virtually no risk, trauma, or pain." *Schmerber*, 384 U.S., at 771. "A crucial factor in analyzing the magnitude of the intrusion . . . is the extent to which the procedure may threaten the safety or health of the individual," *Winston*, supra, at 761, and nothing suggests that a buccal swab poses any physical danger whatsoever. A brief intrusion of an arrestee's person is subject to the Fourth Amendment, but a swab of this nature does not increase the indignity already attendant to normal incidents of arrest.

B

In addition the processing of respondent's DNA sample's 13 CODIS loci did not intrude on respondent's privacy in a way that would make his DNA identification unconstitutional.

First, as already noted, the CODIS loci come from noncoding parts of the DNA that do not reveal the genetic traits of the arrestee. While science can always progress further, and those progressions may have Fourth Amendment consequences, alleles at the CODIS loci "are not at present revealing information beyond identification." Katsanis & Wagner, Characterization of the Standard and Recommended CODIS Markers, 58 J. Forensic Sci. S169, S171 (2013). The argument that the testing at issue in this case reveals any private medical information at all is open to dispute.

And even if non-coding alleles could provide some information, they are not in fact tested for that end. It is undisputed that law enforcement officers analyze DNA for the sole purpose of generating a unique identifying number against which future samples may be matched. This parallels a similar safeguard based on actual practice in the school drug-testing context, where the Court deemed it "significant that the tests at issue here look only for drugs, and not for whether the student is, for example, epileptic, pregnant, or diabetic." *Vernonia School Dist. 47J*, 515 U.S., at 658. If in the future police analyze samples to determine, for instance, an arrestee's predisposition for a particular disease or other hereditary factors not relevant to identity, that case would present additional privacy concerns not present here.

Finally, the Act provides statutory protections that guard against further invasion of privacy. As noted above, the Act requires that "[o]nly DNA records that directly relate to the identification of individuals shall be collected and stored." Md. Pub. Saf. Code Ann. § 2-505(b)(1). No purpose other than identification is permissible: "A person may not willfully test a DNA sample for information that does not relate to the identification of individuals as specified in this subtitle." § 2-512(c). This Court has noted often that "a 'statutory or regulatory duty to avoid unwarranted disclosures' generally allays . . . privacy concerns." NASA v. Nelson, 131 S. Ct. 746, 750 (2011) (quoting Whalen v. Roe, 429 U.S. 589, 605 (1977)). The Court need not speculate about the risks posed "by a system that did not contain comparable security provisions." Id., at 606. In light of the scientific and statutory safeguards, once respondent's DNA was lawfully collected the STR analysis of respondent's DNA pursuant to CODIS procedures did not amount to a significant invasion of privacy that would render the DNA identification impermissible under the Fourth Amendment.

* * *

In light of the context of a valid arrest supported by probable cause respondent's expectations of privacy were not offended by the minor intrusion of a brief swab of his cheeks. By contrast, that same context of arrest gives rise to significant state interests in identifying respondent not only so that the proper name can be attached to his charges but also so that the criminal justice system can make informed decisions concerning pretrial custody. Upon these considerations the Court concludes that DNA identification of arrestees is a reasonable search that can be considered part of a routine booking procedure. When officers make an arrest supported by probable cause to hold for a serious offense and they bring the suspect to the station to be detained in custody, taking and analyzing a cheek swab of the arrestee's DNA is, like fingerprinting and photographing, a legitimate police booking procedure that is reasonable under the Fourth Amendment.

The judgment of the Court of Appeals of Maryland is reversed.

JUSTICE SCALIA, with whom JUSTICE GINSBURG, JUSTICE SOTOMAYOR, and JUSTICE KAGAN join, dissenting.

The Fourth Amendment forbids searching a person for evidence of a crime when there is no basis for believing the person is guilty of the crime or is in possession of incriminating evidence. That prohibition is categorical and without exception; it lies at the very heart of the Fourth Amendment. Whenever this Court has allowed a suspicionless search, it has insisted upon a justifying motive apart from the investigation of crime.

It is obvious that no such noninvestigative motive exists in this case. The Court's assertion that DNA is being taken, not to solve crimes, but to *identify* those in the State's custody, taxes the credulity of the credulous. And the Court's comparison of Maryland's DNA searches to other techniques, such as fingerprinting, can seem apt only to those who know no more than today's opinion has chosen to tell them about how those DNA searches actually work.

A

At the time of the Founding, Americans despised the British use of so-called "general warrants"—warrants not grounded upon a sworn oath of a specific infraction by a particular individual, and thus not limited in scope and application. The first Virginia Constitution declared that "general warrants, whereby any officer or messenger may be commanded to search suspected places without evidence of a fact committed," or to search a person "whose offence is not particularly described and supported by evidence," "are grievous and oppressive, and ought not be granted." Va. Declaration of Rights § 10 (1776), in 1 B. Schwartz, The Bill of Rights: A Documentary History 234, 235 (1971). The Maryland Declaration of Rights similarly provided that general warrants were "illegal." Md. Declaration of Rights § XXIII (1776), in id., at 280, 282.

In the ratification debates, Antifederalists sarcastically predicted that the general, suspicionless warrant would be among the Constitution's "blessings." Blessings of the New Government, Independent Gazetteer, Oct. 6, 1787, in 13 Documentary History of the Ratification of the Constitution 345 (J. Kaminski & G. Saladino eds. 1981). "Brutus" of New York asked why the Federal Constitution contained no provision like Maryland's, Brutus II, N.Y. Journal, Nov. 1, 1787, in *id.*, at 524, and Patrick Henry warned that the new Federal Constitution would expose the citizenry to searches and seizures "in the most arbitrary manner, without any evidence or reason." 3 Debates on the Federal Constitution 588 (J. Elliot 2d ed. 1854).

Madison's draft of what became the Fourth Amendment answered these charges by providing that the "rights of the people to be secured in their persons . . . from all unreasonable searches and seizures, shall not be violated by warrants issued without probable cause . . . or not particularly describing the places to be searched." 1 Annals of Cong. 434-435 (1789). As ratified, the Fourth Amendment's Warrant Clause forbids a warrant to "issue" except "upon probable cause," and requires that it be "particula[r]" (which is to say, *individualized*) to "the place to be searched, and the persons or things to be seized." And we have held that, even when a warrant is not constitutionally necessary, the Fourth Amendment's general prohibition of "unreasonable" searches imports the same requirement of individualized suspicion. See Chandler v. Miller, 520 U.S. 305, 308 (1997).

Although there is a "closely guarded category of constitutionally permissible suspicionless searches," id., at 309, that has never included searches designed to serve "the normal need for law enforcement," Skinner v. Railway Labor Executives' Assn., 489 U.S. 602, 619 (1989) (internal quotation marks omitted). Even the common name for suspicionless searches — "special needs" searches — itself reflects that they must be justified, *always,* by concerns "other than crime detection." *Chandler*, supra, at 313-314. We have approved random drug tests of railroad employees, yes — but only because the Government's need to "regulat[e] the conduct of railroad employees to ensure safety" is distinct from "normal law enforcement." *Skinner*, supra, at 620. So too we have approved suspicionless searches in public schools — but only because there the government acts in furtherance of its "responsibilities . . . as guardian and tutor of children entrusted to its care." Vernonia School Dist. 47J v. Acton, 515 U.S. 646, 665 (1995).

So while the Court is correct to note that there are instances in which we have permitted searches without individualized suspicion, "[i]n none of these cases . . . did we indicate approval of a [search] whose primary purpose was to detect evidence of ordinary criminal wrongdoing." Indianapolis v. Edmond, 531 U.S. 32, 28 (2000). That limitation is crucial. It is only when a governmental purpose aside from crime-solving is at stake that we engage in the free-form "reasonableness" inquiry that the Court indulges at length today. To put it another way, both the legitimacy of the Court's method and the correctness of its outcome hinge entirely on the truth of a single proposition: that the primary purpose of these DNA searches is something other than simply discovering evidence of criminal wrongdoing. As I detail below, that proposition is wrong.

B

The Court alludes at several points to the fact that King was an arrestee, and arrestees may be validly searched incident to their arrest. But the Court does not really *rest* on this principle, and for good reason: The objects of a search incident to arrest must be either (1) weapons or evidence that might easily be destroyed, or (2) evidence relevant to the crime of arrest. See Arizona v. Gant, 556 U.S. 332, 343-344 (2009). Neither is the object of the search at issue here. The Court hastens to clarify that it does not mean to approve invasive surgery on arrestees or warrantless searches of their homes. That the Court feels the need to disclaim these consequences is as damning a criticism of its suspicionless-search regime as any I can muster. And the Court's attempt to distinguish those hypothetical searches from this real one is unconvincing. We are told that the "privacy-related concerns" in the search of a home "are weighty enough that the search may require a warrant, notwithstanding the diminished expectations of privacy of the arrestee." But why are the "privacy-related concerns" not also "weighty" when an intrusion into the *body* is at stake? (The Fourth Amendment lists "persons" *first* among the entities protected against unreasonable searches and seizures.) And could the police engage, without any suspicion of wrongdoing, in a "brief and . . . minimal" intrusion into the home of an arrestee — perhaps just peeking around the curtilage a bit? Obviously not.

At any rate, all this discussion is beside the point. No matter the degree of invasiveness, suspicionless searches are *never* allowed if their principal end is ordinary crime-solving. A search incident to arrest either serves other ends (such as officer safety, in a search for weapons) or is not suspicionless (as when there is reason to believe the arrestee possesses evidence relevant to the crime of arrest).

Sensing (correctly) that it needs more, the Court elaborates at length the ways that the search here served the special purpose of "identifying" King. But that seems to me quite wrong — unless what one means by "identifying" someone is "searching for evidence that he has committed crimes unrelated to the crime of his arrest." At points the Court does appear to use "identifying" in that peculiar sense — claiming, for example, that knowing "an arrestee's past conduct is essential to an assessment of the danger he poses." If identifying someone means finding out what unsolved crimes he has committed, then identification is indistinguish-able from the ordinary law-enforcement aims that have never been thought to justify a suspicionless search. Searching every lawfully stopped car, for example, might turn up information about unsolved crimes the driver had committed, but no one would say that such a search was aimed at "identifying" him, and no court would hold such a search lawful. I will therefore assume that the Court means that the DNA search at issue here was useful to "identify" King in the normal sense of that word — in the sense that would identify the author of Introduction to the Principles of Morals and Legislation as Jeremy Bentham.

1

The portion of the Court's opinion that explains the identification rationale is strangely silent on the actual workings of the DNA search at issue here. To know those facts is to be instantly disabused of the notion that what happened had anything to do with identifying King.

King was arrested on April 10, 2009, on charges unrelated to the case before us. That same day, April 10, the police searched him and seized the DNA evidence at issue here. What happened next? Reading the Court's opinion, particularly its insistence that the search was necessary to know "who [had] been arrested," one might guess that King's DNA was swiftly processed and his identity thereby confirmed — perhaps against some master database of known DNA profiles, as is done for fingerprints. After all, was not the suspicionless search here crucial to avoid "inordinate risks for facility staff" or to "existing detainee population"? Surely, then — *surely* — the State of Maryland got cracking on those grave risks immediately, by rushing to identify King with his DNA as soon as possible.

Nothing could be further from the truth. Maryland officials did not even begin the process of testing King's DNA that day. Or, actually, the next day. Or the day after that. And that was for a simple reason: Maryland law forbids them to do so. A "DNA sample collected from an individual charged with a crime . . . *may not* be tested or placed in the statewide DNA data base system prior to the first scheduled arraignment date." Md. Pub. Saf. Code Ann. § 2-504(d)(1) (Lexis 2011) (emphasis added). And King's first appearance in court was not until three days after his arrest. (I suspect, though, that they did not wait three days to ask his name or take his fingerprints.)

This places in a rather different light the Court's solemn declaration that the search here was necessary so that King could be identified at "every stage of the criminal process." I hope that the Maryland officials who read the Court's opinion do not take it seriously. Acting on the Court's misperception of Maryland law could lead to jail time. See Md. Pub. Saf. Code Ann. § 2-512(c)-(e) (punishing by up to five years' imprisonment anyone who obtains or tests DNA information except as provided by statute). Does the Court really believe that Maryland did not know whom it was arraigning? The Court's response is to imagine that release on bail could take so long that the DNA results are returned in time, or perhaps that bail could be revoked if the DNA test turned up incriminating information. That is no answer at all. If the purpose of this Act is to assess "whether [King] should be released on bail," why would it *possibly* forbid the DNA testing process to *begin* until King was arraigned? Why would Maryland resign itself to simply hoping that the bail decision will drag out long enough that the "identification" can succeed before the arrestee is released? The truth, known to Maryland and increasingly to the reader: this search had nothing to do with establishing King's identity.

It gets worse. King's DNA sample was not received by the Maryland State Police's Forensic Sciences Division until April 23, 2009 — two weeks after his arrest. It sat in that office, ripening in a storage area, until the custodians got around to mailing it to a lab for testing on June 25, 2009 — two months after it was received, and nearly *three* since King's arrest. After it was mailed, the data from the lab tests were not available for several more weeks, until July 13, 2009, which is when the test results were entered into Maryland's DNA database, *together with information identifying the person from whom the sample was taken*. Meanwhile, bail had been set, King had engaged in discovery, and he had requested a speedy trial — presumably not a trial of John Doe. It was not until August 4, 2009 — four months after King's arrest — that the forwarded sample transmitted (*without* identifying information) from the Maryland DNA database to the Federal Bureau of Investigation's national database was matched with a sample taken from the scene of an unrelated crime years earlier.

A more specific description of exactly what happened at this point illustrates why, by definition, King could not have been *identified* by this match. The FBI's DNA database (known as CODIS) consists of two distinct collections. One of them, the one to which King's DNA was submitted, consists of DNA samples taken from known convicts or arrestees. I will refer to this as the "Convict and Arrestee Collection." The other collection consists of samples taken from crime scenes; I will refer to this as the "Unsolved Crimes Collection." The Convict and Arrestee Collection stores "no names or other personal identifiers of the offenders, arrestees, or detainees." Rather, it contains only the DNA profile itself, the name of the agency that submitted it, the laboratory personnel who analyzed it, and an identification number for the specimen. This is because the submitting state laboratories are expected *already* to know the identities of the convicts and arrestees from whom samples are taken. (And, of course, they do.)

Moreover, the CODIS system works by checking to see whether any of the samples in the Unsolved Crimes Collection match any of the samples in the Convict and Arrestee Collection. That is sensible, if what one wants to do is solve those cold cases, but note what it requires: that the identity of the people whose DNA has been entered in the Convict and Arrestee Collection *already be known*.[1] If one wanted to identify someone in custody using his DNA, the logical thing to do would be to compare that DNA against the Convict and Arrestee Collection: to search, in other words, the collection that could be used (by checking back with the submitting state agency) to identify people, rather than the collection of evidence from unsolved crimes, whose perpetrators are by definition unknown. But that is not what was done. And that is because this search had nothing to do with identification.

In fact, if anything was "identified" at the moment that the DNA database returned a match, it was not King—his identity was already known. (The docket for the original criminal charges lists his full name, his race, his sex, his height, his weight, his date of birth, and his address.) Rather, what the August 4 match "identified" was *the previously-taken sample from the earlier crime*. That sample was genuinely mysterious to Maryland; the State knew that it had probably been left by the victim's attacker, but nothing else. King was not identified by his association with the sample; rather, the sample was identified by its association with King. The Court effectively destroys its own "identification" theory when it acknowledges that the object of this search was "to see what [was] already known about [King]." King was who he was, and volumes of his biography could not make him any more or any less King. No minimally competent speaker of English would say, upon noticing a known arrestee's similarity "to a wanted poster of a previously unidentified suspect," that the *arrestee* had thereby been identified. It was the previously unidentified suspect who had been identified—just as, here, it was the previously unidentified rapist.

2

That taking DNA samples from arrestees has nothing to do with identifying them is confirmed not just by actual practice (which the Court ignores) but by the enabling statute itself (which the Court also

---

1. By the way, this procedure has nothing to do with exonerating the wrongfully convicted, as the Court soothingly promises. The FBI CODIS database includes DNA from *unsolved* crimes. I know of no indication (and the Court cites none) that it also includes DNA from all—or even any—crimes whose perpetrators have already been convicted.

ignores). The Maryland Act at issue has a section helpfully entitled "Purpose of collecting and testing DNA samples." Md. Pub. Saf. Code Ann. § 2-505. (One would expect such a section to play a somewhat larger role in the Court's analysis of the Act's purpose — which is to say, at least *some* role.) That provision lists five purposes for which DNA samples may be tested. By this point, it will not surprise the reader to learn that the Court's imagined purpose is not among them.

Instead, the law provides that DNA samples are collected and tested, as a matter of Maryland law, "as part of an official investigation into a crime." § 2-505(a)(2). (Or, as our suspicionless-search cases would put it: for ordinary law-enforcement purposes.) That is certainly how everyone has always understood the Maryland Act until today. The Governor of Maryland, in commenting on our decision to hear this case, said that he was glad, because "[a]llowing law enforcement to collect DNA samples . . . is absolutely critical to our efforts to continue driving down crime," and "bolsters our efforts to resolve open investigations and bring them to a resolution." Marbella, Supreme Court Will Review Md. DNA Law, Baltimore Sun, Nov. 10, 2012, pp. 1, 14. The attorney general of Maryland remarked that he "look[ed] forward to the opportunity to defend this important crime-fighting tool," and praised the DNA database for helping to "bring to justice violent perpetrators." Even this Court's order staying the decision below states that the statute "provides a valuable tool for investigating unsolved crimes and thereby helping to remove violent offenders from the general population" — with, unsurprisingly, no mention of identity. 133 S. Ct. 1, 3 (2012) (Roberts, C.J., in chambers).

More devastating still for the Court's "identification" theory, the statute *does* enumerate two instances in which a DNA sample may be tested for the purpose of identification: "to help identify *human remains*," § 2-505(a)(3) (emphasis added), and "to help identify *missing individuals*," § 2-505(a)(4) (emphasis added). No mention of identifying arrestees. *Inclusio unius est exclusio alterius.* And note again that Maryland forbids using DNA records "for any purposes other than those specified" — it is actually a crime to do so.

The Maryland regulations implementing the Act confirm what is now monotonously obvious: These DNA searches have nothing to do with identification. For example, if someone is arrested and law enforcement determines that "a convicted offender Statewide DNA Data Base sample already exists" for that arrestee, "the agency is not required to obtain a new sample." Code of Md. Regs., tit. 29, § 05.01.04(B)(4) (2011). But how could the State know if an arrestee has already had his DNA sample collected, if the point of the sample is to identify who he is? Of course, if the DNA sample is instead taken in order to investigate crimes, this restriction makes perfect sense: Having previously placed an identified someone's DNA on file to check against available crime-scene evidence, there is no sense in going to the expense of taking a new sample. Maryland's regulations further require that the "individual collecting a sample . . . verify the identity of the individual from whom a sample is taken by name and, if applicable, State identification (SID) number." § 05.01.04(K). (But how?) And after the sample is taken, it continues to be identified *by* the individual's name, fingerprints, etc., see § 05.01.07(B) — rather than (as the Court believes) being used *to identify* individuals. See § 05.01.07(B)(2) ("Records and specimen information shall *be identified by* . . . [the] [n]ame of the donor" (emphasis added)).

So, to review: DNA testing does not even begin until after arraignment and bail decisions are already made. The samples sit in storage for months, and take weeks to test. When they are tested, they are checked against the Unsolved Crimes Collection — rather than the Convict and Arrestee Collection, which could be used to identify them. The Act forbids the Court's purpose (identification), but prescribes as its purpose what our suspicionless-search cases forbid ("official investigation into a crime"). Against all of that, it is safe to say that if the Court's identification theory is not wrong, there is no such thing as error.

II

The Court also attempts to bolster its identification theory with a series of inapposite analogies.

Is not taking DNA samples the same, asks the Court, as taking a person's photograph? No — because that is not a Fourth Amendment search at all. It does not involve a physical intrusion onto the person, and we have never held that merely taking a person's photograph invades any recognized "expectation of privacy," see Katz v. United States, 389 U.S. 347 (1967). Thus, it is unsurprising that the cases the Court cites as authorizing photo-taking do not even mention the Fourth Amendment. See State ex rel. Bruns v. Clausmier, 154 Ind. 599 (1900) (libel), Shaffer v. United States, 24 App. D.C. 417 (1904) (Fifth Amendment privilege against self-incrimination).

But is not the practice of DNA searches, the Court asks, the same as taking "Bertillon" measurements — noting an arrestee's height, shoe size, and so on, on the back of a photograph? No, because that system was not, in the ordinary case, used to solve unsolved crimes. It is possible, I suppose, to imagine situations in which such measurements might be useful to generate leads. (If witnesses described a very tall burglar, all the "tall man" cards could then be pulled.) But the obvious primary purpose of such measurements, as the Court's description of them makes clear, was to verify that, for example, the person arrested today is the same person that was arrested a year ago. Which is to say, Bertillon measurements were *actually* used as a system of identification, and drew their primary usefulness from that task.[3]

It is on the fingerprinting of arrestees, however, that the Court relies most heavily. The Court does not actually say whether it believes that taking a person's fingerprints is a Fourth Amendment search, and our cases provide no ready answer to that question. Even assuming so, however, law enforcement's post-arrest use of fingerprints could not be more different from its post-arrest use of DNA. Fingerprints of arrestees are taken primarily to identify them (though that process sometimes solves crimes); the DNA of arrestees is taken to solve crimes (and nothing else). Contrast CODIS, the FBI's nationwide DNA database, with IAFIS, the FBI's Integrated Automated Fingerprint Identification System.

Fingerprints	DNA Samples
The "average response time for an electronic criminal fingerprint submission is about 27 minutes." *IAFIS*.	DNA analysis can take months — far too long to be useful for identifying someone.
IAFIS includes detailed identification information, including "criminal histories; mug shots; scars and tattoo photos; physical characteristics like height, weight, and hair and eye color."	CODIS contains "[n]o names or other personal identifiers of the offenders, arrestees, or detainees." See CODIS and NDIS Fact Sheet.
"Latent prints" recovered from crime scenes are not systematically compared against the database of known fingerprints, since that requires further forensic work.	The entire *point* of the DNA database is to check crime scene evidence against the profiles of arrestees and convicts as they come in.

The Court asserts that the taking of fingerprints was "constitutional for generations prior to the introduction" of the FBI's rapid computer-

3. Puzzlingly, the Court's discussion of photography and Bertillon measurements repeatedly cites state cases (such as *Clausmier*) that were decided before the Fourth Amendment was held to be applicable to the States. Why the Court believes them relevant to the meaning of that Amendment is therefore something of a mystery.

matching system. This bold statement is bereft of citation to authority because there is none for it. The "great expansion in fingerprinting came before the modern era of Fourth Amendment jurisprudence," and so we were never asked to decide the legitimacy of the practice. United States v. Kincade, 379 F.3d 813, 874 (C.A.9 2004) (Kozinski, J., dissenting). As fingerprint databases expanded from convicted criminals, to arrestees, to civil servants, to immigrants, to everyone with a driver's license, Americans simply "became accustomed to having our fingerprints on file in some government database." Ibid. But it is wrong to suggest that this was uncontroversial at the time, or that this Court blessed universal fingerprinting for "generations" before it was possible to use it effectively for identification.

The Court also assures us that "the delay in processing DNA from arrestees is being reduced to a substantial degree by rapid technical advances." The idea, presumably, is that the snail's pace in this case is atypical, so that DNA is now readily usable for identification. The Court's proof, however, is nothing but a pair of press releases — each of which turns out to undercut this argument. We learn in them that reductions in backlog have enabled Ohio and Louisiana crime labs to analyze a submitted DNA sample in twenty days. But that is *still longer* than the *eighteen* days that Maryland needed to analyze King's sample, once it worked its way through the State's labyrinthine bureaucracy. What this illustrates is that these times do not take into account the many other sources of delay. So if the Court means to suggest that Maryland is unusual, that may be right — it may qualify in this context as a paragon of efficiency. . . . Meanwhile, the Court's holding will result in the dumping of a large number of arrestee samples — many from minor offenders — onto an already overburdened system: Nearly one-third of Americans will be arrested for some offense by age 23. See Brame, Turner, Paternoster, & Bushway, Cumulative Prevalence of Arrest From Ages 8 to 23 in a National Sample, 129 Pediatrics 21 (2011).

The Court also accepts uncritically the Government's representation at oral argument that it is developing devices that will be able to test DNA in mere minutes. At most, this demonstrates that it may one day be possible to design a program that uses DNA for a purpose other than crime-solving — not that Maryland has in fact designed such a program today. And that is the main point, which the Court's discussion of the brave new world of instant DNA analysis should not obscure. The issue before us is not whether DNA can *some day* be used for identification; nor even whether it can *today* be used for identification; but whether it *was used for identification here.*

Today, it can fairly be said that fingerprints really are used to identify people — so well, in fact, that there would be no need for the expense of a separate, wholly redundant DNA confirmation of the same information. What DNA adds — what makes it a valuable weapon in the law-enforcement arsenal — is the ability to solve unsolved crimes, by matching old crime-scene evidence against the profiles of people whose identities are already known. That is what was going on when King's DNA was taken, and we should not disguise the fact. Solving unsolved crimes is a noble objective, but it occupies a lower place in the American pantheon of noble objectives than the protection of our people from suspicionless law-enforcement searches. The Fourth Amendment must prevail.

* * *

The Court disguises the vast (and scary) scope of its holding by promising a limitation it cannot deliver. The Court repeatedly says that DNA testing, and entry into a national DNA registry, will not befall thee and me, dear reader, but only those arrested for "serious offense[s]." I cannot imagine what principle could possibly justify this limitation, and the Court does not attempt to suggest any. If one believes that DNA will "identify" someone arrested for assault, he must believe that it will "identify" someone arrested for a traffic offense. This Court does not base its judgments on senseless distinctions. At the end of the day, *logic will out.* When there comes before us the taking of DNA from an arrestee for a traffic violation, the Court will predictably (and quite rightly) say, "We can find no significant difference between this case and *King.*" Make no mistake about it: As an entirely predictable consequence of today's decision, your DNA can be taken and entered into a national DNA database if you are ever arrested, rightly or wrongly, and for whatever reason.

The most regrettable aspect of the suspicionless search that occurred here is that it proved to be quite unnecessary. All parties concede that it would have been entirely permissible, as far as the Fourth Amendment is concerned, for Maryland to take a sample of King's DNA as a consequence of his conviction for second-degree assault. So the ironic result of the Court's error is this: The only arrestees to whom the outcome here will ever make a difference are those who *have been acquitted* of the crime of arrest (so that their DNA could not have been taken upon conviction). In other words, this Act manages to burden uniquely the sole group for whom the Fourth Amendment's protections ought to be most jealously guarded: people who are innocent of the State's accusations.

Today's judgment will, to be sure, have the beneficial effect of solving more crimes; then again, so would the taking of DNA samples from anyone who flies on an airplane (surely the Transportation Security

Administration needs to know the "identity" of the flying public), applies for a driver's license, or attends a public school. Perhaps the construction of such a genetic panopticon is wise. But I doubt that the proud men who wrote the charter of our liberties would have been so eager to open their mouths for royal inspection. I therefore dissent, and hope that today's incursion upon the Fourth Amendment, like an earlier one,[6] will some day be repudiated.

NOTES AND QUESTIONS

1. What light does *King* shed on the relationship between reasonableness analysis and traditional Fourth Amendment analysis? Think first about the role of individualized suspicion. Justice Kennedy says that "[i]n giving content to the inquiry whether an intrusion is reasonable," the Court has preferred "some quantum" of individualized suspicion as a precondition to the constitutionality of a search or seizure, but that the Fourth Amendment "imposes no irreducible requirement of such suspicion." True, so far as it goes. The roadblock cases (setting aside *Edmond*) are a good example of this. To Justice Scalia, however, this observation has nothing to do with *King*. Justice Scalia says that "[t]he Fourth Amendment forbids searching a person for evidence of a crime when there is no basis for believing the person is guilty of the crime or is in possession of incriminating evidence. That prohibition is categorical and without exception; it lies at the very heart of the Fourth Amendment." And Justice Scalia apparently believes quite strongly that this prohibition applies in the case of *King*: employing a device used infrequently by the Justices, he chose to read his strongly worded dissent from the bench.

2. So who has the better of the argument? Let's assume that Justice Scalia is correct that while the Court has permitted searches without individualized suspicion, it has never done so where the primary purpose of the search is to detect evidence of ordinary wrongdoing. Was King searched for evidence of crime? Or was he merely subject to a procedure commonly used to identify a person taken into custody? And how do we know? Would Justice Scalia's vote change if King's DNA had been obtained for prompt testing against the Convict and Arrestee Collection? If it had also been tested against the Unsolved Crimes Collection, but the Maryland law stated that the purpose of such testing was not to solve

6. Compare New York v. Belton, 453 U.S. 454 (1981) (suspicionless search of a car permitted upon arrest of the driver), with Arizona v. Gant, 556 U.S. 332 (2009) (on second thought, no).

crimes, but to aid in making proper provision for the arrestee while detained and to ensure appropriate bail determinations?

3. Suppose that instead of being an arrestee charged with a serious crime, King was one of 20 houseguests who became murder suspects when the home's owner turned up dead during the party. If King (and all the other guests) had been subject to a buccal swab so that their DNA could be matched against DNA taken from the scene, would Justice Kennedy's vote change? What about Justice Scalia's? You may want to consider this question again after reading United States v. Dionisio in Chapter 10, and thinking about grand jury investigations. The Court has now determined that a buccal swab, unlike the obtaining of a voice exemplar, is a search for Fourth Amendment purposes. What difference might this make to obtaining a DNA sample from a suspect who has *not* been arrested? And for whom there may — or may not — be "individualized" suspicion?

4. *Is* Justice Scalia right in contending that the Fourth Amendment forbids searching a person for evidence of a crime "when there is no basis for believing the person is guilty of the crime or is in possession of incriminating evidence"? Suppose police have probable cause to arrest one of the 20 houseguests from the previous example because the other houseguests have identified him as the person who brought cocaine to the party. Couldn't he be arrested and searched pursuant to United States v. Robinson, 414 U.S. 218 (1973), even if the police are in fact seeking evidence related to the homicide? Is *this* consistent with Justice Scalia's position?

5. *Terry* involved interest balancing in the context of individualized suspicion. The majority in *King* found such balancing appropriate in determining the lawfulness of providing a DNA sample even absent such suspicion, in light of a number of factors, including the class of people required to furnish the sample. Does the dissent have a point in arguing that such balancing will lead, inexorably, to a "genetic panopticon" in which arrestees for even minor offenses — if not all those attending public school or flying on airplanes — will have their DNA taken and cataloged? And if so, is this a problem with interest balancing *per se*, or with any balance that doesn't stop at cataloging DNA samples from convicted persons only?

6. Does the majority shed any light on how the Court might approach an issue that is increasingly coming to occupy the public's attention — namely, the impact on personal privacy of technological advances that have made the storage and search of vast amounts of information ever cheaper and easier to accomplish? Justice Kennedy asserts that "junk" DNA does not reveal "complex characteristics like genetic traits." Will

this continue to be the case? And if in the future it is possible to discern significant personal information from such DNA (including a person's susceptibility to various medical conditions) is it enough to say, as Justice Kennedy does, that Maryland law prohibits testing for such purposes and that "even if non-coding alleles could provide some information, they are not in fact tested for that end"?

7. Consider *King* in light of recent reports that the National Security Agency ("NSA") has collected the call records of millions of Verizon and other phone carrier customers within the United States pursuant to periodic orders of the Foreign Intelligence Surveillance Court. It is open to dispute, according to the majority in *King*, whether testing the DNA samples at issue there "reveals any private medical information at all." While the scope of the NSA surveillance may not now be fully known, it is clear, in contrast, that various "searches" of the NSA's database *could* reveal significant personal information about an individual's habits, tastes, and correspondents — and even if the information itself (such as the records of calls to and from various numbers) has not historically been treated as a subject of Fourth Amendment concern. As you recall, the majority in *Jones* put off until another day the question how to treat privacy concerns emanating from the acquisition, storage, and use of GPS monitoring information not obtained via any physical invasion of constitutionally protected property. Some might say that the *King* majority similarly sidestepped many questions that might arise from the storage and acquisition of genetic information outside the context of the particular scientific limitations and statutory protections surrounding the Maryland program. Does *King* raise anew the question whether it is time for the Court to begin to tackle the issues surrounding new technological advances? Or is the Court already (if cautiously) doing so?

8. Does the preceding suggest that Professor Hal Krent may have been prescient, indeed, when he wrote, in 1995, that "[c]oncern for individual privacy has too often ended with the government's search for and seizure of evidence. Little attention has focused on what law enforcement officers [or other government officials] can do with property and information after a legitimate search and seizure. . . . Can government administrative authorities release information legitimately seized from a company during a regulatory search to its customers or competitors? Similarly, although the government may have a valid interest in requiring hospitals to extract a blood sample from newborns to test for genetic defects, can the government then analyze the blood for its DNA characteristics and store that information in a law enforcement data bank? Rapidly developing technology has thrust the use issue to the forefront: what the

government does with information may now threaten privacy more than the collection itself." Harold J. Krent, *Of Diaries and Data Banks: Use Restrictions Under the Fourth Amendment*, 74 Tex. L. Rev. 49, 50-51 (1995).

E. Consent Searches

Delete Note 1 on page 656, and renumber Notes 2 and 3 as Notes 1 and 2, respectively. Replace Note 4 on page 656 with the following note and main case, and renumber Note 5 on page 657 as Note 3:

3. Don't the dissenters have a point when they question exactly what interest is served by safeguarding the right of a home's occupant to override any consent to search given by his co-occupant — if, but only if, the objecting party happens to be at the door when the search is to take place? Is there any principled way to square the result in *Randolph* with the Court's decision in United States v. Matlock, 415 U.S. 164 (1974)?

4. Near the end of the majority opinion in *Randolph*, the Court suggests that its holding might be limited to cases where "there is no evidence that the police have removed the potentially objecting tenant from the entrance *for the sake of* avoiding a possible objection" (emphasis added). But how does one tell whether the police acted *for the sake of* avoiding an objection, or for some other reason? Isn't such an inquiry inconsistent with the general thrust of most Fourth Amendment case law, which rejects focusing on the subjective intent of the police (see, e.g., Kentucky v. King, 131 S. Ct. 1849 (2011), discussed earlier in this Supplement)?

Moreover, what happens if the police remove the objecting party from the scene *after* an objection is no longer merely *possible*, but has already been raised? Does the objecting party's express refusal to consent to the search remain in effect even after that party is no longer on the premises? Consider the Court's recent answer to this last question:

FERNANDEZ v. CALIFORNIA
Certiorari to the Court of Appeal of California, Second Appellate District
134 S. Ct. 1126 (2014)

JUSTICE ALITO delivered the opinion of the Court.

Our cases firmly establish that police officers may search jointly occupied premises if one of the occupants consents. See United States v. Matlock, 415 U.S. 164 (1974). In Georgia v. Randolph, 547 U.S. 103

(2006), we recognized a narrow exception to this rule, holding that the consent of one occupant is insufficient when another occupant is present and objects to the search. In this case, we consider whether *Randolph* applies if the objecting occupant is absent when another occupant consents. Our opinion in *Randolph* took great pains to emphasize that its holding was limited to situations in which the objecting occupant is physically present. We therefore refuse to extend *Randolph* to the very different situation in this case, where consent was provided by an abused woman well after her male partner had been removed from the apartment they shared.

I

A

. . . After observing Abel Lopez cash a check, petitioner Walter Fernandez approached Lopez and asked about the neighborhood in which he lived. When Lopez responded that he was from Mexico, Fernandez laughed and told Lopez that he was in territory ruled by the "D.F.S.," *i.e.,* the "Drifters" gang. Petitioner then pulled out a knife and pointed it at Lopez' chest. Lopez raised his hand in self-defense, and petitioner cut him on the wrist.

Lopez ran from the scene and called 911 for help, but petitioner whistled, and four men emerged from a nearby apartment building and attacked Lopez. After knocking him to the ground, they hit and kicked him and took his cell phone and his wallet, which contained $400 in cash. A police dispatch reported the incident and mentioned the possibility of gang involvement, and two Los Angeles police officers, Detective Clark and Officer Cirrito, drove to an alley frequented by members of the Drifters. A man who appeared scared walked by the officers and said: "'[T]he guy is in the apartment.'" The officers then observed a man run through the alley and into the building to which the man was pointing. A minute or two later, the officers heard sounds of screaming and fighting coming from that building.

After backup arrived, the officers knocked on the door of the apartment unit from which the screams had been heard. Roxanne Rojas answered the door. She was holding a baby and appeared to be crying. Her face was red, and she had a large bump on her nose. The officers also saw blood on her shirt and hand from what appeared to be a fresh injury. Rojas told the police that she had been in a fight. Officer Cirrito asked if anyone else was in the apartment, and Rojas said that her 4-year-old son was the only other person present.

After Officer Cirrito asked Rojas to step out of the apartment so that he could conduct a protective sweep, petitioner appeared at the door wearing only boxer shorts. Apparently agitated, petitioner stepped forward and said, "'You don't have any right to come in here. I know my rights.'" Suspecting that petitioner had assaulted Rojas, the officers removed him from the apartment and then placed him under arrest. Lopez identified petitioner as his initial attacker, and petitioner was taken to the police station for booking.

Approximately one hour after petitioner's arrest, Detective Clark returned to the apartment and informed Rojas that petitioner had been arrested. Detective Clark requested and received both oral and written consent from Rojas to search the premises.[2] In the apartment, the police found Drifters gang paraphernalia, a butterfly knife, clothing worn by the robbery suspect, and ammunition. Rojas' young son also showed the officers where petitioner had hidden a sawed-off shotgun.

B

Petitioner was charged with robbery, infliction of corporal injury on a spouse, cohabitant, or child's parent, possession of a firearm by a felon, possession of a short-barreled shotgun, and felony possession of ammunition.

Before trial, petitioner moved to suppress the evidence found in the apartment, but after a hearing, the court denied the motion. . . . The California Court of Appeal affirmed [the denial of the motion to suppress] . . . [and the] California Supreme Court denied the petition for review.

II

A

. . . While it is clear that a warrantless search is reasonable when the sole occupant of a house or apartment consents, what happens when there are two or more occupants? Must they all consent? Must they all be asked? Is consent by one occupant enough? The Court faced that problem 40 years ago in United States v. Matlock, 415 U.S. 164 (1974). . . . As the Court put it [in that case], "the consent of one who possesses common

---

2. Both petitioner and the dissent suggest that Rojas' consent was coerced. *Post*, at 9, n. 5 (opinion of Ginsburg, J.). But the trial court found otherwise, App. 152, and the correctness of that finding is not before us. . . .

authority over premises or effects is valid as against the absent, noncon-
senting person with whom that authority is shared." . . .

B

While consent by one resident of jointly occupied premises is generally
sufficient to justify a warrantless search, we recognized a narrow exception to
this rule in Georgia v. Randolph, 547 U.S. 103 (2006). In that case, police
officers responded to the Randolphs' home after receiving a report of a
domestic dispute. When the officers arrived, Janet Randolph informed the
officers that her estranged husband, Scott Randolph, was a cocaine user and
that there were "items of drug evidence" in the house. The officers first
asked Scott for consent to search, but he "unequivocally refused." The
officers then turned to Janet, and she consented to the search, which produced evidence that was later used to convict Scott for possession of cocaine.
     . . . [T]his Court held that Janet Randolph's consent was insufficient
under the circumstances to justify the warrantless search. The Court
reiterated the proposition that a person who shares a residence with
others assumes the risk that "any one of them may admit visitors, with
the consequence that a guest obnoxious to one may nevertheless be
admitted in his absence by another." But the Court held that "*a physically
present inhabitant's* express refusal of consent to a police search [of his
home] is dispositive as to him, regardless of the consent of a fellow
occupant." Id., at 122-123 (emphasis added).
     The Court's opinion went to great lengths to make clear that its holding
was limited to situations in which the objecting occupant is present. Again
and again, the opinion of the Court stressed this controlling factor. . . .
The Court's opinion could hardly have been clearer on this point, and the
separate opinion filed by Justice Breyer, whose vote was decisive, was
equally unambiguous. . . .

III

In this case, petitioner was not present when Rojas consented, but petitioner still contends that *Randolph* is controlling. He advances two main
arguments. First, he claims that his absence should not matter since he
was absent only because the police had taken him away. Second, he
maintains that it was sufficient that he objected to the search while he
was still present. Such an objection, he says, should remain in effect until
the objecting party "no longer wishes to keep the police out of his home."
Neither of these arguments is sound.

A

. . . In *Randolph*, the Court suggested in dictum that consent by one occupant might not be sufficient if "there is evidence that the police have removed the potentially objecting tenant from the entrance for the sake of avoiding a possible objection." 547 U.S., at 121. We do not believe the statement should be read to suggest that improper motive may invalidate objectively justified removal. Hence, it does not govern here.

The *Randolph* dictum is best understood not to require an inquiry into the subjective intent of officers who detain or arrest a potential objector but instead to refer to situations in which the removal of the potential objector is not objectively reasonable. As petitioner acknowledges, our Fourth Amendment cases "have repeatedly rejected" a subjective approach. Brigham City [v. Stuart,] 547 U.S. [398,] 404. "Indeed, we have never held, outside limited contexts such as an 'inventory search or administrative inspection . . . , that an officer's motive invalidates objectively justifiable behavior under the Fourth Amendment.'" [Kentucky v. King, 131 S. Ct., 1849, 1859 (2011)].

Petitioner does not claim that the *Randolph* Court meant to break from this consistent practice, and we do not think that it did. And once it is recognized that the test is one of objective reasonableness, petitioner's argument collapses. He does not contest the fact that the police had reasonable grounds for removing him from the apartment so that they could speak with Rojas, an apparent victim of domestic violence, outside of petitioner's potentially intimidating presence. In fact, he does not even contest the existence of probable cause to place him under arrest. We therefore hold that an occupant who is absent due to a lawful detention or arrest stands in the same shoes as an occupant who is absent for any other reason. . . .

B

This brings us to petitioner's second argument, viz., that his objection, made at the threshold of the premises that the police wanted to search, remained effective until he changed his mind and withdrew his objection. This argument is inconsistent with *Randolph*'s reasoning in at least two important ways. First, the argument cannot be squared with the "widely shared social expectations" or "customary social usage" upon which the *Randolph* holding was based. See 547 U.S., at 111, 121. Explaining why consent by one occupant could not override an objection by a physically present occupant, the *Randolph* Court stated:

"[I]t is fair to say that a caller standing at the door of shared premises would have no confidence that one occupant's invitation was a sufficiently good reason to enter when a fellow tenant stood there saying, 'stay out.' Without some very good reason, no sensible person would go inside under those conditions." Id., at 113.

It seems obvious that the calculus of this hypothetical caller would likely be quite different if the objecting tenant was not standing at the door. When the objecting occupant is standing at the threshold saying "stay out," a friend or visitor invited to enter by another occupant can expect at best an uncomfortable scene and at worst violence if he or she tries to brush past the objector. But when the objector is not on the scene (and especially when it is known that the objector will not return during the course of the visit), the friend or visitor is much more likely to accept the invitation to enter.[5] Thus, petitioner's argument is inconsistent with *Randolph*'s reasoning.

Second, petitioner's argument would create the very sort of practical complications that *Randolph* sought to avoid. The *Randolph* Court recognized that it was adopting a "formalis[tic]" rule, but it did so in the interests of "simple clarity" and administrability. Id., at 121, 122.

The rule that petitioner would have us adopt would produce a plethora of practical problems. For one thing, there is the question of duration. Petitioner argues that an objection, once made, should last until it is withdrawn by the objector, but such a rule would be unreasonable. Suppose that a husband and wife owned a house as joint tenants and that the husband, after objecting to a search of the house, was convicted and sentenced to a 15-year prison term. Under petitioner's proposed rule, the wife would be unable to consent to a search of the house 10 years after the date on which her husband objected. We refuse to stretch *Randolph* to such strange lengths.

Nor are we persuaded to hold that an objection lasts for a "reasonable" time. "[I]t is certainly unusual for this Court to set forth precise time limits governing police action," Maryland v. Shatzer, 559 U.S. 98, 110 (2010), and what interval of time would be reasonable in this context? A week? A month? A year? Ten years? . . .

---

5. . . . In the present case, for example, suppose that Rojas had called a relative, a friend, a supportive neighbor, or a person who works for a group that aids battered women and had invited that individual to enter and examine the premises while petitioner was in jail. Would any of those invitees have felt that it was beyond Rojas' authority to extend that invitation over petitioner's objection? . . .

Another problem concerns the procedure needed to register a continuing objection. Would it be necessary for an occupant to object while police
officers are at the door? If presence at the time of consent is not needed,
would an occupant have to be present at the premises when the objection
was made? Could an objection be made pre-emptively? Could a person like
Scott Randolph, suspecting that his estranged wife might invite the police
to view his drug stash and paraphernalia, register an objection in advance?
Could this be done by posting a sign in front of the house? Could a standing
objection be registered by serving notice on the chief of police?

Finally, there is the question of the particular law enforcement officers
who would be bound by an objection. Would this set include just the
officers who were present when the objection was made? . . .

If *Randolph* is taken at its word — that it applies only when the objector
is standing in the door saying "stay out" when officers propose to make a
consent search — all of these problems disappear. . . .

C

Petitioner argues strenuously that his expansive interpretation of *Randolph* would not hamper law enforcement because in most cases where
officers have probable cause to arrest a physically present objector they
also have probable cause to search the premises that the objector does
not want them to enter, but this argument misunderstands the constitutional status of consent searches. A warrantless consent search is
reasonable and thus consistent with the Fourth Amendment irrespective
of the availability of a warrant. Even with modern technological advances,
the warrant procedure imposes burdens on the officers who wish to
search, the magistrate who must review the warrant application, and the
party willing to give consent. When a warrantless search is justified,
requiring the police to obtain a warrant may "unjustifiably interfer[e]
with legitimate law enforcement strategies." *King,* 131 S. Ct., at 1860.
Such a requirement may also impose an unmerited burden on the person
who consents to an immediate search, since the warrant application
procedure entails delay. Putting the exception the Court adopted in
Randolph to one side, the lawful occupant of a house or apartment should
have the right to invite the police to enter the dwelling and conduct a
search. Any other rule would trample on the rights of the occupant who is
willing to consent. Such an occupant may want the police to search in
order to dispel "suspicion raised by sharing quarters with a criminal." 547
U.S., at 116; see also *Schneckloth,* 412 U.S., at 243, 93 S. Ct. 2041
(evidence obtained pursuant to a consent search "may insure that a

wholly innocent person is not wrongly charged with a criminal offense"). And an occupant may want the police to conduct a thorough search so that any dangerous contraband can be found and removed. In this case, for example, the search resulted in the discovery and removal of a sawed-off shotgun to which Rojas' 4-year-old son had access.

Denying someone in Rojas' position the right to allow the police to enter *her* home would also show disrespect for her independence. Having beaten Rojas, petitioner would bar her from controlling access to her own home until such time as he chose to relent. The Fourth Amendment does not give him that power.

* * *

The judgment of the California Court of Appeal is affirmed.

[The concurring opinions of Justice Scalia and Justice Thomas are omitted]

JUSTICE GINSBURG, with whom JUSTICE SOTOMAYOR and JUSTICE KAGAN join, dissenting.

. . . Instead of adhering to the warrant requirement, today's decision tells the police they may dodge it, nevermind ample time to secure the approval of a neutral magistrate. Suppressing the warrant requirement, the Court shrinks to petite size our holding in Georgia v. Randolph, 547 U.S. 103 (2006). . . .

I

This case calls for a straightforward application of *Randolph*. . . . After Walter Fernandez, while physically present at his home, rebuffed the officers' request to come in, the police removed him from the premises and then arrested him, albeit with cause to believe he had assaulted his cohabitant, Roxanne Rojas. At the time of the arrest, Rojas said nothing to contradict Fernandez' refusal. About an hour later, however, and with no attempt to obtain a search warrant, the police returned to the apartment and prevailed upon Rojas to sign a consent form authorizing search of the premises.

The circumstances triggering "the Fourth Amendment's traditional hostility to police entry into a home without a warrant," 547 U.S., at 126 (Breyer, J., concurring), are at least as salient here as they were in *Randolph*. In both cases, "[t]he search at issue was a search solely for evidence"; "[t]he objecting party," while on the premises, "made his objection [to police entry] known clearly and directly to the officers seeking to enter the [residence]"; and "the officers might easily have secured the premises and sought a warrant permitting them to enter."

Id., at 125-126. Here, moreover, with the objector in custody, there was scant danger to persons on the premises, or risk that evidence might be destroyed or concealed, pending request for, and receipt of, a warrant.

Despite these marked similarities, the Court removes this case from *Randolph*'s ambit. . . .

The Court tells us that the "widely shared social expectations" and "customary social usage" undergirding *Randolph*'s holding apply only when the objector remains physically present. *Randolph*'s discussion of social expectations, however, does not hinge on the objector's physical presence *vel non* at the time of the search. "[W]hen people living together disagree over the use of their common quarters," *Randolph* observes, "a resolution must come through voluntary accommodation, not by appeals to authority." 547 U.S., at 113-114. See also id., at 114 ("[T]here is no common understanding that one co-tenant generally has a right or authority to prevail over the express wishes of another, whether the issue is the color of the curtains or invitations to outsiders.") . . . *Randolph* thus trained on whether a joint occupant had conveyed an objection to a visitor's entry, and did not suggest that the objection could be ignored if the police reappeared post the objector's arrest.

A visitor might be less reluctant to enter over a joint occupant's objection, the Court speculates, if that visitor knows the objector will not be there. "Only in a Hobbesian world," however, "would one person's social obligations to another be limited to what the other[, because of his presence,] is . . . able to enforce." United States v. Henderson, 536 F.3d 776, 787 (CA7 2008) (Rovner, J., dissenting). Such conjectures about social behavior, at any rate, shed little light on the constitutionality of this warrantless home search, given the marked distinctions between private interactions and police investigations. Police, after all, have power no private person enjoys. They can, as this case illustrates, put a tenant in handcuffs and remove him from the premises.

Moreover, as the Court comprehended just last Term, "the background social norms that invite a visitor to the front door do not invite him there to conduct a search." Florida v. Jardines, 569 U.S. 1, ___ (2013). Similarly here, even if shared tenancy were understood to entail the prospect of visits by unwanted social callers while the objecting resident was gone, that unwelcome visitor's license would hardly include free rein to rummage through the dwelling in search of evidence and contraband. . . .

II

In its zeal to diminish *Randolph*, today's decision overlooks the warrant requirement's venerable role as the "bulwark of Fourth Amendment protection." Franks v. Delaware, 438 U.S. 154, 164 (1978). Reducing *Randolph* to a "narrow exception," the Court declares the main rule to be that "consent by one resident of jointly occupied premises is generally sufficient to justify a warrantless search." That declaration has it backwards, for consent searches themselves are a "'jealously and carefully drawn' exception" to "the Fourth Amendment rule ordinarily prohibiting the warrantless entry of a person's house as unreasonable *per se*." *Randolph*, 547 U.S., at 109. . . .

In this case, the police could readily have obtained a warrant to search the shared residence. The Court does not dispute this, but instead disparages the warrant requirement as inconvenient, burdensome, entailing delay "[e]ven with modern technological advances." Shut from the Court's sight is the ease and speed with which search warrants nowadays can be obtained. . . . With these developments in view, dilution of the warrant requirement should be vigilantly resisted. . . .

A final word is in order about the Court's reference to Rojas' autonomy, which, in its view, is best served by allowing her consent to trump an abusive cohabitant's objection. . . .[5] If a person's health and safety are threatened by a domestic abuser, exigent circumstances would justify immediate removal of the abuser from the premises, as happened here. . . . As the Court understood in *Randolph*, however, the specter of domestic abuse hardly necessitates the diminution of the Fourth Amendment rights at stake here. . . .

NOTES AND QUESTIONS

1. One of the risks created by *Fernandez* is that now, whenever the police face a situation where one party objects and the other consents, the officers will find some reason to remove a non-consenting party from the premises so they will be free to search. How realistic is this concern? Suppose the police remove Smith, the non-consenting party, and then get permission to search from Jones, the remaining co-tenant. The police search the house and find contraband that they want to use against Smith. If it turns out that the police did not have probable cause to remove Smith from the scene, should the contraband be excluded as the fruit of an illegal arrest? Or does Jones's consent still make the seizure valid?

---

5. Although the validity of Rojas' consent is not before us, the record offers cause to doubt that her agreement to the search was, in fact, an unpressured exercise of self-determination. . . . Rojas testified that the police, upon returning to the residence about an hour after Fernandez' arrest, began questioning her four-year-old son without her permission. Rojas asked to remain present during that questioning, but the police officer told her that their investigation was "going to determine whether or not we take your kids from you right now or not." Rojas thus maintained that she felt "pressured" into giving consent. . . .

2. In both *Fernandez* and *Randolph*, the Court identifies and then relies upon — with little or no citation to authority — "widely shared social expectations" and prevailing social norms as a basis for its interpretation of the Fourth Amendment. See also Florida v. Jardines, 569 U.S. 1 (2013) (the dog-sniff-on-the-front-porch case, discussed earlier in this Supplement). Are Supreme Court Justices the right people to be identifying what is customary social behavior? Perhaps this is an inevitable consequence of the Fourth Amendment's focus on reasonableness, but if you were a lawyer, how would you argue to the Court about what these prevailing social norms are?

F. The Scope of the Exclusionary Rule

1. The "Good Faith" Exception

Insert the following note and main case after Note 3 on page 673:

4. *Herring* extended the good-faith exception into new territory by making clear that the analysis in *Evans* applies whether an isolated negligent data entry was made by the court clerk or by someone within the police department. That said, the instances in which the Supreme Court has found the good-faith exception to apply remained fairly limited even after *Herring*. These instances included cases in which: (1) a magistrate erroneously issued a warrant; (2) an unconstitutional statute purported to authorize a Fourth Amendment intrusion; and (3) a database erroneously contained the information that a warrant existed. Now consider whether the following case, which again expands the reach of *Leon*, is similarly limited, or whether it might instead signal that the good-faith exception will not remain as strictly cabined as it has been in the 25-plus years since *Leon* was decided:

DAVIS v. UNITED STATES
Certiorari to the United States Court of Appeals for the Eleventh Circuit
131 S. Ct. 2419 (2011)

JUSTICE ALITO delivered the opinion of the Court.

The Fourth Amendment protects the right to be free from "unreasonable searches and seizures," but it is silent about how this right is to be enforced. To supplement the bare text, this Court created the exclusionary rule, a deterrent sanction that bars the prosecution from introducing evidence obtained by way of a Fourth Amendment violation. The question here is whether to apply this sanction when the police conduct a search in compliance with binding precedent that is later overruled. Because suppression would do nothing to deter police misconduct in these circumstances, and because it would come at a high cost to both the truth and the public safety, we hold that searches conducted in objectively reasonable reliance on binding appellate precedent are not subject to the exclusionary rule.

I

The question presented arises in this case as a result of a shift in our Fourth Amendment jurisprudence on searches of automobiles incident to arrests of recent occupants.

A

Under this Court's decision in Chimel v. California, 395 U.S. 752 (1969), a police officer who makes a lawful arrest may conduct a warrantless search of the arrestee's person and the area "within his immediate control." Id., at 763 (internal quotation marks omitted). This rule "may be stated clearly enough," but in the early going after *Chimel* it proved difficult to apply, particularly in cases that involved searches "inside [of] automobile[s] after the arrestees [we]re no longer in [them]." See New York v. Belton, 453 U.S. 454, 458-459 (1981). . . .

In *Belton*, a police officer conducting a traffic stop lawfully arrested four occupants of a vehicle and ordered the arrestees to line up, un-handcuffed, along the side of the thruway. The officer then searched the vehicle's passenger compartment and found cocaine inside a jacket that lay on the backseat. This Court upheld the search as reasonable incident to the occupants' arrests. In an opinion that repeatedly stressed the need for a "straightforward," "workable rule" to guide police conduct, the Court announced "that when a policeman has made a lawful custodial arrest of the occupant of an automobile, he may, as a contemporaneous incident of that arrest, search the passenger compartment of that automobile." Id., at 459-460 (footnote omitted).

For years, *Belton* was widely understood to have set down a simple, bright-line rule. Numerous courts read the decision to authorize automobile searches incident to arrests of recent occupants, regardless of whether the arrestee in any particular case was within reaching distance of the vehicle at the time of the search. Even after the arrestee had stepped out of the vehicle and had been subdued by police, the prevailing understanding was that *Belton* still authorized a substantially contemporaneous search of the automobile's passenger compartment.

Not every court, however, agreed with this reading of *Belton*. In State v. Gant, 216 Ariz. 1 (2007), the Arizona Supreme Court considered an automobile search conducted after the vehicle's occupant had been arrested, handcuffed, and locked in a patrol car. The court distinguished *Belton* as a case in which "four unsecured" arrestees "presented an immediate risk of loss of evidence and an obvious threat to [a] lone officer's safety." 216 Ariz., at 4. The court held that where no such "exigencies exis[t]"—where the arrestee has been subdued and the scene secured—the rule of *Belton* does not apply.

This Court granted certiorari in *Gant*, and affirmed in a 5-to-4 decision. Four of the Justices in the majority agreed with the Arizona Supreme Court that *Belton*'s holding applies only where "the arrestee is unsecured and within reaching distance of the passenger compartment at the time of the search." The four dissenting Justices, by contrast, understood *Belton* to have explicitly adopted the simple, bright-line rule stated in the *Belton* Court's opinion. To limit *Belton* to cases involving unsecured arrestees, the dissenters thought, was to overrule the decision's clear holding. Justice Scalia, who provided the fifth vote to affirm in *Gant*, agreed with the dissenters' understanding of *Belton*'s holding. Justice Scalia favored a more explicit and complete overruling of *Belton*, but he joined what became the majority opinion to avoid "a 4-to-1-to-4" disposition. As a result, the Court adopted a new, two-part rule under which an automobile search incident to a recent occupant's arrest is constitutional (1) if the arrestee is within reaching distance of the vehicle during the search, or (2) if the police have reason to believe that the vehicle contains "evidence relevant to the crime of arrest."

B

The search at issue in this case took place a full two years before this Court announced its new rule in *Gant*. On an April evening in 2007, police officers in Greenville, Alabama, conducted a routine traffic stop that eventually resulted in the arrests of driver Stella Owens (for driving while intoxicated) and passenger Willie Davis (for giving a false name to police). The police handcuffed both Owens and Davis, and they placed the arrestees in the back of separate patrol cars. The police then searched the passenger compartment of Owens's vehicle and found a revolver inside Davis's jacket pocket.

Davis was indicted in the Middle District of Alabama on one count of possession of a firearm by a convicted felon. In his motion to suppress the revolver, Davis acknowledged that the officers' search fully complied with "existing Eleventh Circuit precedent." Like most courts, the Eleventh Circuit had long read *Belton* to establish a bright-line rule authorizing substantially contemporaneous vehicle searches incident to arrests of recent occupants. Davis recognized that the District Court was obligated to follow this precedent, but he raised a Fourth Amendment challenge to preserve "the issue for review" on appeal. The District Court denied the motion, and Davis was convicted on the firearms charge.

While Davis's appeal was pending, this Court decided *Gant*. The Eleventh Circuit, in the opinion below, applied *Gant*'s new rule and held that the vehicle search incident to Davis's arrest "violated [his] Fourth Amendment rights." As for whether this constitutional violation warranted suppression, the Eleventh Circuit viewed that as a separate issue that turned on "the potential of exclusion to deter wrongful police conduct." Id., at 1265 (quoting Herring v. United States, 555 U.S. 135, 137 (2009); internal quotation marks omitted). The court concluded that "penalizing the [arresting] officer" for following binding appellate precedent would do nothing to "dete[r] . . . Fourth Amendment violations." It therefore declined to apply the exclusionary rule and affirmed Davis's conviction. We granted certiorari.

II

The Fourth Amendment protects the "right of the people to be secure in their persons, houses, papers, and effects, against unreasonable searches and seizures." The Amendment says nothing about suppressing evidence obtained in violation of this command. . . . Exclusion is "not a personal constitutional right," nor is it designed to "redress the injury" occasioned by an unconstitutional search. Stone v. Powell, 428 U.S. 465, 486 (1976). The rule's sole purpose, we have repeatedly held, is to deter future Fourth Amendment violations. . . .

Real deterrent value is a "necessary condition for exclusion," but it is not "a sufficient" one. Hudson v. Michigan, 547 U.S. 586, 596 (2006). The analysis must also account for the "substantial social costs" generated by the rule. Exclusion exacts a heavy toll on both the judicial system and society at large. It almost always requires courts to ignore reliable, trustworthy evidence bearing on guilt or innocence. And its bottom-line effect, in many cases, is to suppress the truth and set the criminal loose in the community without punishment. Our cases hold that society must swallow this bitter pill when necessary, but only as a "last resort." *Hudson*, supra, at 591. For exclusion to be appropriate, the deterrence benefits of suppression must outweigh its heavy costs.

Admittedly, there was a time when our exclusionary-rule cases were not nearly so discriminating in their approach to the doctrine. . . . In time, however, we came to acknowledge the exclusionary rule for what it undoubtedly is — a "judicially created remedy" of this Court's own making. We abandoned the old, "reflexive" application of the doctrine, and imposed a more rigorous weighing of its costs and deterrence benefits. In a line of cases beginning with United States v. Leon, 468 U.S. 897, we also recalibrated our cost-benefit analysis in exclusion cases to focus the inquiry on the "flagrancy of the police misconduct" at issue.

The basic insight of the *Leon* line of cases is that the deterrence benefits of exclusion "var[y] with the culpability of the law enforcement conduct" at issue. *Herring*, 555 U.S., at 143. When the police exhibit "deliberate," "reckless," or "grossly negligent" disregard for Fourth Amendment rights, the deterrent value of exclusion is strong and tends to outweigh the resulting costs. But when the police act with an objectively "reasonable good-faith belief" that their conduct is lawful, or when their conduct involves only simple, "isolated" negligence, the "'deterrence rationale loses much of its force,'" and exclusion cannot "pay its way." See *Leon*, supra, at 919, 908, n. 6 (quoting United States v. Peltier, 422 U.S. 531, 539 (1975)).

The Court has over time applied this "good-faith" exception across a range of cases. *Leon* itself, for example, held that the exclusionary rule does not apply when the police conduct a search in "objectively reasonable reliance" on a warrant later held invalid. The error in such a case rests with the issuing magistrate, not the police officer, and "punish[ing] the errors of judges" is not the office of the exclusionary rule.

Other good-faith cases have sounded a similar theme. Illinois v. Krull, 480 U.S. 340 (1987), extended the good-faith exception to searches conducted in reasonable reliance on subsequently invalidated statutes. In Arizona v. Evans, [514 U.S. 1 (1995)], the Court applied the good-faith exception in a case where the police reasonably relied on erroneous information concerning an arrest warrant in a database maintained by judicial employees. Most recently, in Herring v. United States, 555 U.S. 135 [2009], we extended *Evans* in a case where *police* employees erred in maintaining records in a warrant database. "[I]solated," "nonrecurring" police negligence, we determined, lacks the culpability required to justify the harsh sanction of exclusion. 555 U.S., at 137, 144.

III

The question in this case is whether to apply the exclusionary rule when the police conduct a search in objectively reasonable reliance on binding judicial precedent. At the time of the search at issue here, we had not yet decided Arizona v. Gant, and the Eleventh Circuit had interpreted our decision in New York v. Belton to establish a bright-line rule authorizing the search of a vehicle's passenger compartment incident to a recent occupant's arrest. The search incident to Davis's arrest in this case followed the Eleventh Circuit's . . . precedent to the letter. Although the search turned out to be unconstitutional under *Gant*, all agree that the officers' conduct was in strict compliance with then-binding Circuit law and was not culpable in any way.

Under our exclusionary-rule precedents, this acknowledged absence of police culpability dooms Davis's claim. Police practices trigger the harsh sanction of exclusion only when they are deliberate enough to yield "meaningfu[l]" deterrence, and culpable enough to be "worth the price paid by the justice system." *Herring*, 555 U.S., at 144. The conduct of the officers here was neither of these things. The officers who conducted the search did not violate Davis's Fourth Amendment rights deliberately, recklessly, or with gross negligence. Nor does this case involve any "recurring or systemic negligence" on the part of law enforcement. The police acted in strict compliance with binding precedent, and their behavior was not wrongful. Unless the exclusionary rule is to become a strict-liability regime, it can have no application in this case. . . .

About all that exclusion would deter in this case is conscientious police work. Responsible law-enforcement officers will take care to learn "what is required of them" under Fourth Amendment precedent and will conform their conduct to these rules. *Hudson*, 547 U.S., at 599. But by the same token, when binding appellate precedent specifically *authorizes* a particular police practice, well-trained officers will and should use that tool to fulfill their crime-detection and public-safety responsibilities. An officer who conducts a search in reliance on binding appellate precedent does no more than "'ac[t] as a reasonable officer would and should act'" under the circumstances. *Leon*, 468 U.S., at 920 (quoting *Stone*, 428 U.S., at 539-540 (White, J., dissenting)). The deterrent effect of exclusion in such a case can only be to discourage the officer from "'do[ing] his duty.'" 468 U.S., at 920.

That is not the kind of deterrence the exclusionary rule seeks to foster. We have stated before, and we reaffirm today, that the harsh sanction of exclusion "should not be applied to deter objectively reasonable law enforcement activity." Id., at 919. Evidence obtained during a search conducted in reasonable reliance on binding precedent is not subject to the exclusionary rule.

IV

. . . Davis . . . contends that applying the good-faith exception to searches conducted in reliance on binding precedent will stunt the development of Fourth Amendment law. With no possibility of suppression, criminal defendants will have no incentive, Davis maintains, to request that courts overrule precedent.[7]

This argument is difficult to reconcile with our modern understanding of the role of the exclusionary rule. We have never held that facilitating the overruling of precedent is a relevant consideration in an exclusionary-rule case. Rather, we have said time and again that the *sole* purpose of the exclusionary rule is to deter misconduct by law enforcement.

We have also repeatedly rejected efforts to expand the focus of the exclusionary rule beyond deterrence of culpable police conduct. In *Leon,* for example, we made clear that "the exclusionary rule is designed to deter police misconduct rather than to punish the errors of judges." 468 U.S., at 916. *Krull* too noted that "legislators, like judicial officers, are not the focus" of the exclusionary rule. 480 U.S., at 350. And in *Evans,* we said that the exclusionary rule was aimed at deterring "police misconduct, not mistakes by court employees." 514 U.S., at 14. These cases do not suggest that the exclusionary rule should be modified to serve a purpose other than deterrence of culpable law-enforcement conduct.

And in any event, applying the good-faith exception in this context will not prevent judicial reconsideration of prior Fourth Amendment precedents. In most instances, as in this case, the precedent sought to be challenged will be a decision of a Federal Court of Appeals or State Supreme Court. But a good-faith exception for objectively reasonable reliance on binding precedent will not prevent review and correction of such decisions. This Court reviews criminal convictions from 12 Federal Courts of Appeals, 50 state courts of last resort, and the District of

---

7. Davis also asserts that a good-faith rule would permit "new Fourth Amendment decisions to be applied only prospectively," thus amounting to "a regime of rule-creation by advisory opinion." Brief for Petitioner 23, 25. . . . [T]his argument conflates the question of retroactivity with the question of remedy.

Columbia Court of Appeals. If one or even many of these courts uphold a particular type of search or seizure, defendants in jurisdictions in which the question remains open will still have an undiminished incentive to litigate the issue. This Court can then grant certiorari, and the development of Fourth Amendment law will in no way be stunted.[8]

Davis argues that Fourth Amendment precedents of *this* Court will be effectively insulated from challenge under a good-faith exception for reliance on appellate precedent. But this argument is overblown. For one thing, it is important to keep in mind that this argument applies to an exceedingly small set of cases. Decisions overruling this Court's Fourth Amendment precedents are rare. Indeed, it has been more than 40 years since the Court last handed down a decision of the type to which Davis refers. . . . Moreover, as a practical matter, defense counsel in many cases will test this Court's Fourth Amendment precedents in the same way that *Belton* was tested in *Gant* — by arguing that the precedent is distinguishable.[9]

At most, Davis's argument might suggest that — to prevent Fourth Amendment law from becoming ossified — the petitioner in a case that results in the overruling of one of this Court's Fourth Amendment precedents should be given the benefit of the victory by permitting the suppression of evidence in that one case. Such a result would undoubtedly be a windfall to this one random litigant. But the exclusionary rule is "not a personal constitutional right." *Stone*, 428 U.S., at 486. It is a "judicially created" sanction, [United States v.] *Calandra*, 414 U.S. [338,] 348 [(1974)], specifically designed as a "windfall" remedy to deter future Fourth Amendment violations. The good-faith exception is a judicially created exception to this judicially created rule. Therefore, in a future case, we could, if necessary, recognize a limited exception to the good-faith exception for a defendant who obtains a judgment overruling one of our Fourth Amendment precedents. Cf. Friendly, The Bill of Rights as a Code of Criminal Procedure, 53 Cal. L. Rev. 929, 952-953 (1965) ("[T]he same authority that empowered the Court to supplement the amendment

8. The dissent does not dispute this point, but it claims that the good-faith exception will prevent us from "rely[ing] upon lower courts to work out Fourth Amendment differences among themselves." If that is correct, then today's holding may well lead to *more* circuit splits in Fourth Amendment cases and a *fuller* docket of Fourth Amendment cases in this Court. . . . Such a state of affairs is unlikely to result in ossification of Fourth Amendment doctrine.

9. Where the search at issue is conducted in accordance with a municipal "policy" or "custom," Fourth Amendment precedents may also be challenged, without the obstacle of the good-faith exception or qualified immunity, in civil suits against municipalities. See 42 U.S.C. § 1983. . . .

by the exclusionary rule a hundred and twenty-five years after its adoption, likewise allows it to modify that rule as the lessons of experience may teach" (internal quotation marks and footnotes omitted)).[10] . . .

But this is not such a case. Davis did not secure a decision overturning a Supreme Court precedent; the police in his case reasonably relied on binding Circuit precedent. That sort of blameless police conduct, we hold, comes within the good-faith exception and is not properly subject to the exclusionary rule.

* * *

It is one thing for the criminal "to go free because the constable has blundered." People v. Defore, 242 N.Y. 13, 21, (1926) (Cardozo, J.). It is quite another to set the criminal free because the constable has scrupulously adhered to governing law. Excluding evidence in such cases deters no police misconduct and imposes substantial social costs. We therefore hold that when the police conduct a search in objectively reasonable reliance on binding appellate precedent, the exclusionary rule does not apply. . . . Affirmed.

[JUSTICE SOTOMAYOR's opinion, concurring in the judgment, is omitted.]

JUSTICE BREYER, with whom JUSTICE GINSBURG joins, dissenting.
. . . [T]he Court's rationale for creating its new "good faith" exception threatens to undermine well-settled Fourth Amendment law. The Court correctly says that pre-*Gant* Eleventh Circuit precedent had held that a *Gant*-type search was constitutional; hence the police conduct in this case, consistent with that precedent, was "innocent." But the Court then finds this fact sufficient to create a new "good faith" exception to the exclusionary rule. It reasons that the "sole purpose" of the exclusionary rule "is

---

10. Davis contends that a criminal defendant will lack Article III standing to challenge an existing Fourth Amendment precedent if the good-faith exception to the exclusionary rule precludes the defendant from obtaining relief based on police conduct that conformed to that precedent. This argument confuses weakness on the merits with absence of Article III standing. . . . And as a practical matter, the argument is also overstated. In many instances, as in *Gant*, see 556 U.S., at ___, defendants will not simply concede that the police conduct conformed to the precedent; they will argue instead that the police conduct did not fall within the scope of the precedent.

In any event, even if some criminal defendants will be unable to challenge some precedents for the reason that Davis suggests, that provides no good reason for refusing to apply the good-faith exception. As noted, the exclusionary rule is not a personal right, see *Stone*, 428 U.S., at 486, 490, and therefore the rights of these defendants will not be impaired. And because (at least in almost all instances) the precedent can be challenged by others, Fourth Amendment case law will not be insulated from reconsideration.

to deter future Fourth Amendment violations." Those benefits are sufficient to justify exclusion where "police exhibit deliberate, reckless, or grossly negligent disregard for Fourth Amendment rights." But those benefits do not justify exclusion where, as here, the police act with "simple, isolated negligence" or an "objectively reasonable good-faith belief that their conduct is lawful."

If the Court means what it says, what will happen to the exclusionary rule, a rule that the Court adopted nearly a century ago for federal courts, and made applicable to state courts a half century ago through the Fourteenth Amendment? The Court has thought of that rule not as punishment for the individual officer or as reparation for the individual defendant but more generally as an effective way to secure enforcement of the Fourth Amendment's commands. This Court has deviated from the "suppression" norm in the name of "good faith" only a handful of times and in limited, atypical circumstances: where a magistrate has erroneously issued a warrant, where a database has erroneously informed police that they have a warrant, and where an unconstitutional statute purported to authorize the search.

The fact that such exceptions are few and far between is understandable. Defendants frequently move to suppress evidence on Fourth Amendment grounds. In many, perhaps most, of these instances the police, uncertain of how the Fourth Amendment applied to the particular factual circumstances they faced, will have acted in objective good faith. Yet, in a significant percentage of these instances, courts will find that the police were wrong. And, unless the police conduct falls into one of the exceptions previously noted, courts have required the suppression of the evidence seized.

But an officer who conducts a search that he believes complies with the Constitution but which, it ultimately turns out, falls just outside the Fourth Amendment's bounds is no more culpable than an officer who follows erroneous "binding precedent." Nor is an officer more culpable where circuit precedent is simply suggestive rather than "binding," where it only describes how to treat roughly analogous instances, or where it just does not exist. Thus, if the Court means what it now says, if it would place determinative weight upon the culpability of an individual officer's conduct, and if it would apply the exclusionary rule only where a Fourth Amendment violation was "deliberate, reckless, or grossly negligent," then the "good faith" exception will swallow the exclusionary rule. Indeed, our broad dicta in *Herring*—dicta the Court repeats and expands upon today—may already be leading lower courts in this direction. Today's decision will doubtless accelerate this trend.

Any such change (which may already be underway) would affect not "an exceedingly small set of cases," but a very large number of cases, potentially many thousands each year. And since the exclusionary rule is often the only sanction available for a Fourth Amendment violation, the Fourth Amendment would no longer protect ordinary Americans from "unreasonable searches and seizures." It would become a watered-down Fourth Amendment, offering its protection against only those searches and seizures that are *egregiously* unreasonable. . . .

NOTES AND QUESTIONS

1. Isn't this an easy case? Unlike *Herring*, where the negligent mistake, however isolated, took place within the police agency, the source of the error in *Davis* was squarely outside law enforcement; indeed, the responsible party was presumably the court that issued the binding precedent on which police relied. Why should the exclusionary rule apply in such circumstances? Why should we seek to deter officers from doing what a court has authorized them to do? In fact, don't we *want* officers to follow binding precedent without questioning its validity?

2. At the same time, doesn't *Davis* represent (at least potentially) a marked expansion in the reach of the good-faith exception? In Note 3 on page 666, we said that "[t]he good-faith exception has remained fairly cabined" in the years since *Leon*. Is this still the case? Justice Breyer, in dissent, says no: that the Court is now placing determinative weight on an officer's culpability, that there are many situations in which an officer might innocently and reasonably believe that less than binding precedent demonstrated the legality of his illegal conduct, and that the good-faith exception is therefore poised to "swallow the exclusionary rule." Do you agree with his reading of the majority opinion?

3. Let's assume Justice Breyer has read the majority opinion correctly. Aren't there circumstances in which an officer's conduct might well be characterized as "nonculpable" but excluding the evidence would still appreciably deter Fourth Amendment violations? If this is the case, is the majority's focus on culpability wise?

4. Whether Justice Breyer is right or not, it is surely correct to say that *Davis* has expanded the good-faith exception's potential application in the context of warrantless searches. Is that a good thing?

5. In a portion of his dissent that is not excerpted here, Justice Breyer argued that the majority's position violates basic principles of constitutional adjudication by treating the defendant in a case that announces a new rule one way "while treating similarly situated defendants whose

cases are pending on direct appeal in a different way." Since the Court's decision in Griffith v. Kentucky, 479 U.S. 314 (1987), Justice Breyer noted, new rules for the conduct of criminal prosecutions (such as the one announced in *Gant*) are supposed to apply retroactively to all cases, state or federal, pending on direct review or not yet final.

Justice Alito's majority opinion did not contest the latter point, but argued, in contrast, that *Davis* does not present a retroactivity issue (i.e., whether a new rule of substantive Fourth Amendment law is available to defendants whose cases are pending on direct review), but instead a remedy issue (i.e., whether exclusion is available as a remedy for violation of this substantive rule): "Remedy is a separate, analytically distinct issue. As a result, the retroactive application of a new rule of substantive Fourth Amendment law raises the question whether a suppression remedy applies; it does not answer the question."

Who do you think has the better of this argument, given what the Court has previously said about the exclusionary rule?

6. Relatedly, what should be made of Davis's argument that extending the good-faith exception will eliminate the incentive for litigants to challenge Fourth Amendment precedent (or even make it impossible for them to do so, as a consequence of Article III standing doctrine, because there isn't a "case or controversy" if a litigant can't possibly benefit from the Court's decision)? Won't this inevitably lead, as Davis suggests, to the "ossification" of Fourth Amendment law?

The majority basically pooh-poohed this argument. According to Justice Alito: (1) lower-court Fourth Amendment precedents can always be challenged (at least indirectly) by other litigants in other jurisdictions where the precedent in question isn't binding; (2) if a particular search or seizure was authorized by an official "policy," then it can always be challenged in a § 1983 lawsuit against the relevant municipality; (3) in any event, most litigants seek to distinguish binding precedent, not to have it overruled; (4) the Supreme Court hardly ever overrules a Fourth Amendment precedent anyway; and (5) in a jurisdictional pinch, the Court always has the power to grant a one-off exemption from the good-faith exception, granting relief to a single litigant if it proves necessary in order to be able to reconsider a Fourth Amendment precedent.

Are you convinced by these responses? Think about a relatively clear and binding Supreme Court precedent like, e.g., United States v. Greenwood, supra at page 385 (holding that trash searches are not "searches" within the meaning of the Fourth Amendment). Even if *Greenwood* is a bad decision, the police are completely protected when they rely on it—

they can't be sued (due to qualified immunity), and the resulting evidence can't be excluded (due to *Davis*).

If a litigant disagrees with *Greenwood*'s holding, and seeks to have it overruled (as opposed merely to distinguishing it), what exactly is she to do? She can't wait for another litigant to pursue the issue, because *Greenwood* is binding everywhere. She can file a § 1983 lawsuit against the municipality (presumably most municipalities have policies requiring their police to follow clear Fourth Amendment precedents like *Greenwood*), but does it seem plausible (as the majority seems to suggest in footnote 9) that such a lawsuit could succeed — even absent qualified immunity, which municipalities don't get — given that the police will merely have done something that the Court clearly said they could do?

Perhaps the only hope, in such a scenario, will be the one-off exemption — although, if that's the only hope, then (as *Davis* argues) most litigants surely will be discouraged from litigating their cases all the way to the Court.

7. In this regard, consider also the strange case of Camreta v. Greene, 131 S. Ct. 2020 (2011) (decided together with Alford v. Greene). Camreta was a state child protective service worker who was sued under § 1983 by the mother of a child whom Camreta had interviewed at school, without a warrant or parental consent, in connection with a sexual abuse allegation. (The child's father was put on trial for the sexual abuse, but the jury could not reach a verdict and the charges were later dismissed.) The Ninth Circuit found the interview to be a "seizure" in violation of the Fourth Amendment, but also held that Camreta was entitled to qualified immunity. Camreta petitioned for review in the Supreme Court, seeking to have the Ninth Circuit's Fourth Amendment holding (query: was it *really* a "holding"?) overturned; the mother did not cross-petition for review of the Ninth Circuit's qualified immunity holding.

The Court, per Justice Kagan, concluded as follows: (1) as a jurisdictional matter, the Court possesses the power to review a lower court's constitutional ruling, even when the certiorari petition is filed by a government actor who has actually prevailed below on grounds of qualified immunity; (2) no prudential rule prohibits the Court from reviewing such a case; (3) Article III's "case-or-controversy" requirement can be satisfied, in such a case, so long as *both* parties retain a "personal stake" in the Court's decision; (4) Camreta, who prevailed below, still retains a "personal stake" because the lower court's Fourth Amendment ruling, if left undisturbed, will bind Camreta's future behavior; (5) nevertheless, the case before the Court is moot, because the child in question has moved to Florida and is no longer subject to the Ninth Circuit's constitutional ruling, and thus lacks the required "personal stake" in the outcome; and (6) the appropriate remedy is to leave the judgment below (in Camreta's favor) intact, but vacate the portion of the Ninth Circuit's opinion announcing the Fourth Amendment rule.

Justice Kennedy, joined by Justice Thomas, dissented on the ground that the better solution would be to prohibit lower courts from creating "precedent" on constitutional issues in cases where the relevant government actor is then found to have qualified immunity. Justice Sotomayor, joined by Justice Breyer, concurred only in the judgment; she agreed with the majority that the case was moot and vacatur was the appropriate remedy, but would have stopped short of addressing the Article III jurisdiction question, finding it "a difficult one." Finally, Justice Scalia — the fifth vote for the majority opinion — concurred separately, stating: "The parties have not asked us to adopt [Justice Kennedy's] approach, but I would be willing to consider it in an appropriate case."

Does *Camreta* suggest that a majority of the Court (i.e., at least Justices Kennedy, Thomas, Sotomayor, Breyer, and Scalia) is about to become more strict in applying the Article III case-or-controversy requirement to cases where qualified immunity applies? If that's so, then shouldn't the same Article III requirement also be applied strictly to cases where the good-faith exception to the exclusionary rule applies? What might that mean for the future implications of *Davis*?

Chapter 6

The Fifth Amendment

D. Police Interrogation

2. The Scope of *Miranda*

a. *"Custody"*

Insert the following new case at the end of the subsection on page 799:

J.D.B. v. NORTH CAROLINA
Certiorari to the Supreme Court of North Carolina
131 S. Ct. 2394 (2011)

JUSTICE SOTOMAYOR delivered the opinion of the Court.

This case presents the question whether the age of a child subjected to police questioning is relevant to the custody analysis of Miranda v. Arizona, 384 U.S. 436 (1966). It is beyond dispute that children will often feel bound to submit to police questioning when an adult in the same circumstances would feel free to leave. Seeing no reason for police officers or courts to blind themselves to that commonsense reality, we hold that a child's age properly informs the *Miranda* custody analysis.

I

A

Petitioner J.D.B. was a 13-year-old, seventh-grade student attending class at Smith Middle School in Chapel Hill, North Carolina when he was removed from his classroom by a uniformed police officer, escorted to a closed-door conference room, and questioned by police for at least half an hour.

This was the second time that police questioned J.D.B. in the span of a week. Five days earlier, two home break-ins occurred, and various items were stolen. Police stopped and questioned J.D.B. after he was seen behind a residence in the neighborhood where the crimes occurred. That same day, police also spoke to J.D.B.'s grandmother — his legal guardian — as well as his aunt.

Police later learned that a digital camera matching the description of one of the stolen items had been found at J.D.B.'s middle school and seen in J.D.B.'s possession. Investigator DiCostanzo, the juvenile investigator with the local police force who had been assigned to the case, went to the school to question J.D.B. Upon arrival, DiCostanzo informed the uniformed police officer on detail to the school (a so-called school resource officer), the assistant principal, and an administrative intern that he was there to question J.D.B. about the break-ins. Although DiCostanzo asked the school administrators to verify J.D.B.'s date of birth, address, and parent contact information from school records, neither the police officers nor the school administrators contacted J.D.B.'s grandmother.

The uniformed officer interrupted J.D.B.'s afternoon social studies class, removed J.D.B. from the classroom, and escorted him to a school conference room. There, J.D.B. was met by DiCostanzo, the assistant principal, and the administrative intern. The door to the conference room was closed. With the two police officers and the two administrators present, J.D.B. was questioned for the next 30 to 45 minutes. Prior to the commencement of questioning, J.D.B. was given neither *Miranda* warnings nor the opportunity to speak to his grandmother. Nor was he informed that he was free to leave the room.

Questioning began with small talk — discussion of sports and J.D.B.'s family life. DiCostanzo asked, and J.D.B. agreed, to discuss the events of the prior weekend. Denying any wrongdoing, J.D.B. explained that he had been in the neighborhood where the crimes occurred because he was seeking work mowing lawns. DiCostanzo pressed J.D.B. for additional detail about his efforts to obtain work; asked J.D.B. to explain a prior incident, when one of the victims returned home to find J.D.B. behind her house; and confronted J.D.B. with the stolen camera. The assistant principal urged J.D.B. to "do the right thing," warning J.D.B. that "the truth always comes out in the end." App. 99a, 112a.

Eventually, J.D.B. asked whether he would "still be in trouble" if he returned the "stuff." Ibid. In response, DiCostanzo explained that return of the stolen items would be helpful, but "this thing is going to court" regardless. Id., at 112a; ibid. ("[W]hat's done is done[;] now you need to help yourself by making it right"); see also id., at 99a. DiCostanzo then warned that he may need to seek a secure custody order if he believed that J.D.B. would continue to break into other homes. When J.D.B. asked what a secure custody order was, DiCostanzo explained that "it's where you get sent to juvenile detention before court." Id., at 112a.

After learning of the prospect of juvenile detention, J.D.B. confessed that he and a friend were responsible for the break-ins. DiCostanzo only then informed J.D.B. that he could refuse to answer the investigator's questions and that he was free to leave. Asked whether he understood, J.D.B. nodded and provided further detail, including information about the location of the stolen items. Eventually J.D.B. wrote a statement, at DiCostanzo's request. When the bell rang indicating the end of the schoolday, J.D.B. was allowed to leave to catch the bus home.

Nonetheless, both parties' submissions to this Court suggest that the warnings came after DiCostanzo raised the possibility of a secure custody order but before J.D.B. confessed for the first time. See Brief for Petitioner 5; Brief for Respondent 5. Because we remand for a determination whether J.D.B. was in custody under the proper analysis, the state courts remain free to revisit whether the trial court made a conclusive finding of fact in this respect.

B

Two juvenile petitions were filed against J.D.B., each alleging one count of breaking and entering and one count of larceny. J.D.B.'s public defender moved to suppress his statements and the evidence derived therefrom, arguing that suppression was necessary because J.D.B. had been "interrogated by police in a custodial setting without being afforded *Miranda* warning[s]," App. 89a, and because his statements were involuntary under the totality of the circumstances test, id., at 142a; see Schneckloth v. Bustamonte, 412 U.S. 218, 226 (1973) (due process precludes admission of a confession where "a defendant's will was overborne" by the circumstances of the interrogation). After a suppression hearing at which DiCostanzo and J.D.B. testified, the trial court denied the motion, deciding that J.D.B. was not in custody at the time of the schoolhouse interrogation and that his statements were voluntary. As a result, J.D.B. entered a transcript of admission to all four counts, renewing his objection to the denial of his motion to suppress, and the court adjudicated J.D.B. delinquent.

A divided panel of the North Carolina Court of Appeals affirmed. In re J.D.B., 196 N.C. App. 234, 674 S.E.2d 795 (2009). The North Carolina Supreme Court held, over two dissents, that J.D.B. was not in custody when he confessed, "declin[ing] to extend the test for custody to include consideration of the age . . . of an individual subjected to questioning by police." In re J.D.B., 363 N.C. 664, 672, 686 S.E.2d 135, 140 (2009).[3]

We granted certiorari to determine whether the *Miranda* custody analysis includes consideration of a juvenile suspect's age. 562 U.S. __ (2010).

II

A

Any police interview of an individual suspected of a crime has "coercive aspects to it." Oregon v. Mathiason, 429 U.S. 492, 495 (1977) (per curiam). Only those interrogations that occur while a suspect is in police custody, however, "heighte[n] the risk" that statements obtained are not the product of the suspect's free choice. Dickerson v. United States, 530 U.S. 428, 435 (2000).

By its very nature, custodial police interrogation entails "inherently compelling pressures." *Miranda*, 384 U.S., at 467. Even for an adult, the physical and psychological isolation of custodial interrogation can "undermine the individual's will to resist and . . . compel him to speak where he would not otherwise do so freely." Ibid. Indeed, the pressure of custodial interrogation is so immense that it "can induce a frighteningly high percentage of people to confess to crimes they never committed." Corley v. United States, 556 U.S. 303, __ (2009) (citing Drizin & Leo, The Problem of False Confessions in the Post-DNA World, 82 N.C. L. Rev. 891, 906-907 (2004)); see also *Miranda*, 384 U.S., at 455, n. 23. That risk is all the more troubling — and recent studies suggest, all the more acute — when the subject of custodial interrogation is a juvenile. See Brief for Center on Wrongful Convictions of Youth et al. as Amici Curiae 21-22 (collecting empirical studies that "illustrate the heightened risk of false confessions from youth").

. . . As we have repeatedly emphasized, whether a suspect is "in custody" is an objective inquiry. . . . Rather than demarcate a limited set of relevant circumstances, we have required police officers and courts to "examine all of the circumstances surrounding the interrogation," Stansbury [v. California, 511 U.S. 318,] 322 [(1994) (per curiam)], including any circumstance that "would have affected how a reasonable person" in the suspect's position "would perceive his or her freedom to leave," id., at 325. On the other hand, the "subjective views harbored by either the

---

3. . . . The North Carolina Supreme Court did not address the trial court's holding that the statements were voluntary, and that question is not before us.

interrogating officers or the person being questioned" are irrelevant. Id., at 323. The test, in other words, involves no consideration of the "actual mindset" of the particular suspect subjected to police questioning. [Yarborough v.] Alvarado, [541 U.S. 652,] 667 [(2004)].

The benefit of the objective custody analysis is that it is "designed to give clear guidance to the police." *Alvarado*, 541 U.S., at 668. . . . By limiting analysis to the objective circumstances of the interrogation, and asking how a reasonable person in the suspect's position would under-stand his freedom to terminate questioning and leave, the objective test avoids burdening police with the task of anticipating the idiosyncrasies of every individual suspect and divining how those particular traits affect each person's subjective state of mind. . . .

B

The State and its amici contend that a child's age has no place in the custody analysis, no matter how young the child subjected to police questioning. We cannot agree. In some circumstances, a child's age "would have affected how a reasonable person" in the suspect's position "would perceive his or her freedom to leave." *Stansbury*, 511 U.S., at 325. That is, a reasonable child subjected to police questioning will sometimes feel pressured to submit when a reasonable adult would feel free to go. We think it clear that courts can account for that reality without doing any damage to the objective nature of the custody analysis.

A child's age is far "more than a chronological fact." Eddings v. Oklahoma, 455 U.S. 104, 115 (1982). . . . It is a fact that "generates commonsense conclusions about behavior and perception." *Alvarado*, 541 U.S., at 674 (Breyer, J., dissenting). Such conclusions apply broadly to children as a class. And, they are self-evident to anyone who was a child once himself, including any police officer or judge.

Time and again, this Court has drawn these commonsense conclusions for itself. . . . Addressing the specific context of police interrogation, we have observed that events that "would leave a man cold and unimpressed can overawe and overwhelm a lad in his early teens." Haley v. Ohio, 332 U.S. 596, 599 (1948) (plurality opinion); see also Gallegos v. Colorado, 370 U.S. 49, 54 (1962) ("[N]o matter how sophisticated," a juvenile subject of police interrogation "cannot be compared" to an adult subject). . . .[5]

---

5. Although citation to social science and cognitive science authorities is unnecessary to establish these commonsense propositions, the literature confirms what experience bears out. See, e.g., Graham v. Florida, 560 U.S. ___, ___ (2010) ("[D]evelopments in psychology and brain science continue to show fundamental differences between juvenile and adult minds").

Our various statements to this effect are far from unique. The law has historically reflected the same assumption that children characteristically lack the capacity to exercise mature judgment and possess only an incomplete ability to understand the world around them. See, e.g., 1 W. Blackstone, Commentaries on the Laws of England *464-*465 (explaining that limits on children's legal capacity under the common law "secure them from hurting themselves by their own improvident acts"). Like this Court's own generalizations, the legal disqualifications placed on children as a class—e.g., limitations on their ability to alienate property, enter a binding contract enforceable against them, and marry without parental consent—exhibit the settled understanding that the differentiating characteristics of youth are universal.

. . . We see no justification for taking a different course here. So long as the child's age was known to the officer at the time of the interview, or would have been objectively apparent to any reasonable officer, including age as part of the custody analysis requires officers neither to consider circumstances "unknowable" to them, Berkemer [v. McCarty, 468 U.S. 420,] 430 [(1984)], nor to "anticipat[e] the frailties or idiosyncrasies" of the particular suspect whom they question, Alvarado, 541 U.S., at 662 (internal quotation marks omitted). . . .

In other words, a child's age differs from other personal characteristics that, even when known to police, have no objectively discernible relationship to a reasonable person's understanding of his freedom of action. Alvarado holds, for instance, that a suspect's prior interrogation history with law enforcement has no role to play in the custody analysis because such experience could just as easily lead a reasonable person to feel free to walk away as to feel compelled to stay in place. 541 U.S., at 668. Because the effect in any given case would be "contingent [on the] psycholog[y]" of the individual suspect, the Court explained, such experience cannot be considered without compromising the objective nature of the custody analysis. Ibid. A child's age, however, is different. Precisely because childhood yields objective conclusions like those we have drawn ourselves—among others, that children are "most susceptible to influence," Eddings, 455 U.S., at 115, and "outside pressures," Roper [v. Simmons, 543 U.S. 551,] 569 [(2005)]—considering age in the custody analysis in no way involves a determination of how youth "subjectively affect[s] the mindset" of any particular child, Brief for Respondent 14.[7]

7. Thus, contrary to the dissent's protestations, today's holding neither invites consideration of whether a particular suspect is "unusually meek or compliant" (opinion of Alito, J.), nor "expan[ds]" the Miranda custody analysis into a test that requires officers to anticipate and account for a suspect's every personal characteristic.

In fact, in many cases involving juvenile suspects, the custody analysis would be nonsensical absent some consideration of the suspect's age. This case is a prime example. Were the court precluded from taking J.D.B.'s youth into account, it would be forced to evaluate the circumstances present here through the eyes of a reasonable person of average years. In other words, how would a reasonable adult understand his situation, after being removed from a seventh-grade social studies class by a uniformed school resource officer; being encouraged by his assistant principal to "do the right thing"; and being warned by a police investigator of the prospect of juvenile detention and separation from his guardian and primary caretaker? To describe such an inquiry is to demonstrate its absurdity. Neither officers nor courts can reasonably evaluate the effect of objective circumstances that, by their nature, are specific to children without accounting for the age of the child subjected to those circumstances.

Indeed, although the dissent suggests that concerns "regarding the application of the *Miranda* custody rule to minors can be accommodated by considering the unique circumstances present when minors are questioned in school" (opinion of Alito, J.), the effect of the schoolhouse setting cannot be disentangled from the identity of the person questioned. A student—whose presence at school is compulsory and whose disobedience at school is cause for disciplinary action—is in a far different position than, say, a parent volunteer on school grounds to chaperone an event, or an adult from the community on school grounds to attend a basketball game. Without asking whether the person "questioned in school" is a "minor," the coercive effect of the schoolhouse setting is unknowable.

Our prior decision in *Alvarado* in no way undermines these conclusions. In that case, we held that a state-court decision that failed to mention a 17-year-old's age as part of the *Miranda* custody analysis was not objectively unreasonable under the deferential standard of review [for habeas corpus cases] set forth by the Antiterrorism and Effective Death Penalty Act of 1996 (AEDPA), 110 Stat. 1214. . . . We said nothing, however, of whether such a view would be correct under the law. . . . To the contrary, Justice O'Connor's concurring opinion explained that a suspect's age may indeed "be relevant to the 'custody' inquiry." *Alvarado*, 541 U.S., at 669.

Reviewing the question de novo today, we hold that so long as the child's age was known to the officer at the time of police questioning, or would have been objectively apparent to a reasonable officer, its inclusion in the custody analysis is consistent with the objective nature of that test.

This is not to say that a child's age will be a determinative, or even a significant, factor in every case. . . . It is, however, a reality that courts cannot simply ignore. . . .[9]

. . . [T]he dissent insists that the clarity of the custody analysis will be destroyed unless a "one-size-fits-all reasonable-person test" applies. In reality, however, ignoring a juvenile defendant's age will often make the inquiry more artificial, and thus only add confusion. And in any event, a child's age, when known or apparent, is hardly an obscure factor to assess. Though the State and the dissent worry about gradations among children of different ages, that concern cannot justify ignoring a child's age altogether. Just as police officers are competent to account for other objective circumstances that are a matter of degree such as the length of questioning or the number of officers present, so too are they competent to evaluate the effect of relative age. Indeed, they are competent to do so even though an interrogation room lacks the "reflective atmosphere of a [jury] deliberation room." The same is true of judges, including those whose childhoods have long since passed. In short, officers and judges need no imaginative powers, knowledge of developmental psychology, training in cognitive science, or expertise in social and cultural anthropology to account for a child's age. They simply need the common sense to know that a 7-year-old is not a 13-year-old and neither is an adult.

There is, however, an even more fundamental flaw with the State's plea for clarity and the dissent's singular focus on simplifying the analysis: Not once have we excluded from the custody analysis a circumstance that we determined was relevant and objective, simply to make the fault line between custodial and noncustodial "brighter." Indeed, were the guiding concern clarity and nothing else, the custody test would presumably ask only whether the suspect had been placed under formal arrest. *Berkemer*, 468 U.S., at 441. . . . But we have rejected that "more easily administered line," recognizing that it would simply "enable the police to circumvent the constraints on custodial interrogations established by *Miranda*." Ibid.

Finally, the State and the dissent suggest that excluding age from the custody analysis comes at no cost to juveniles' constitutional rights because the due process voluntariness test independently accounts for a child's youth. To be sure, that test permits consideration of a child's age,

---

9. The State's purported distinction between blindness and age — that taking account of a suspect's youth requires a court "to get into the mind" of the child, whereas taking account of a suspect's blindness does not — is mistaken. In either case, the question becomes how a reasonable person would understand the circumstances, either from the perspective of a blind person or, as here, a 13-year-old child.

and it erects its own barrier to admission of a defendant's inculpatory statements at trial. See *Gallegos*, 370 U.S., at 53-55; *Haley*, 332 U.S., at 599-601. . . . But *Miranda*'s procedural safeguards exist precisely because the voluntariness test is an inadequate barrier when custodial interrogation is at stake. See 384 U.S., at 458 ("Unless adequate protective devices are employed to dispel the compulsion inherent in custodial surroundings, no statement obtained from the defendant can truly be the product of his free choice"); *Dickerson*, 530 U.S., at 442 ("[R]eliance on the traditional totality-of-the-circumstances test raise[s] a risk of overlooking an involuntary custodial confession"). To hold, as the State requests, that a child's age is never relevant to whether a suspect has been taken into custody — and thus to ignore the very real differences between children and adults — would be to deny children the full scope of the procedural safeguards that *Miranda* guarantees to adults.

* * *

The question remains whether J.D.B. was in custody when police interrogated him. We remand for the state courts to address that question, this time taking account of all of the relevant circumstances of the interrogation, including J.D.B.'s age at the time. The judgment of the North Carolina Supreme Court is reversed, and the case is remanded for proceedings not inconsistent with this opinion.

It is so ordered.

JUSTICE ALITO, with whom CHIEF JUSTICE ROBERTS, JUSTICE SCALIA, and JUSTICE THOMAS join, dissenting.

The Court's decision in this case may seem on first consideration to be modest and sensible, but in truth it is neither. It is fundamentally inconsistent with one of the main justifications for the *Miranda* rule: the perceived need for a clear rule that can be easily applied in all cases. And today's holding is not needed to protect the constitutional rights of minors who are questioned by the police.

Miranda's prophylactic regime places a high value on clarity and certainty. Dissatisfied with the highly fact-specific constitutional rule against the admission of involuntary confessions, the *Miranda* Court set down rigid standards that often require courts to ignore personal characteristics that may be highly relevant to a particular suspect's actual susceptibility to police pressure. This rigidity, however, has brought with it one of *Miranda*'s principal strengths — "the ease and clarity of its application" by law enforcement officials and courts. See Moran v. Burbine, 475 U.S. 412, 425-426 (1986). A key contributor to this clarity, at least up until now, has been *Miranda*'s objective reasonable-person test for determining custody.

Miranda's custody requirement is based on the proposition that the risk of unconstitutional coercion is heightened when a suspect is placed under formal arrest or is subjected to some functionally equivalent limitation on freedom of movement. When this custodial threshold is reached, *Miranda* warnings must precede police questioning. But in the interest of simplicity, the custody analysis considers only whether, under the circumstances, a hypothetical reasonable person would consider himself to be confined.

Many suspects, of course, will differ from this hypothetical reasonable person. Some, including those who have been hardened by past interrogations, may have no need for *Miranda* warnings at all. And for other suspects — those who are unusually sensitive to the pressures of police questioning — *Miranda* warnings may come too late to be of any use. That is a necessary consequence of *Miranda*'s rigid standards, but it does not mean that the constitutional rights of these especially sensitive suspects are left unprotected. A vulnerable defendant can still turn to the constitutional rule against *actual* coercion and contend that that his confession was extracted against his will.

Today's decision shifts the *Miranda* custody determination from a one-size-fits-all reasonable-person test into an inquiry that must account for at least one individualized characteristic — age — that is thought to correlate with susceptibility to coercive pressures. Age, however, is in no way the only personal characteristic that may correlate with pliability, and in future cases the Court will be forced to choose between two unpalatable alternatives. It may choose to limit today's decision by arbitrarily distinguishing a suspect's age from other personal characteristics — such as intelligence, education, occupation, or prior experience with law enforcement — that may also correlate with susceptibility to coercive pressures. Or, if the Court is unwilling to draw these arbitrary lines, it will be forced to effect a fundamental transformation of the *Miranda* custody test — from a clear, easily applied prophylactic rule into a highly fact-intensive standard resembling the voluntariness test that the *Miranda* Court found to be unsatisfactory.

For at least three reasons, there is no need to go down this road. First, many minors subjected to police interrogation are near the age of majority, and for these suspects the one-size-fits-all *Miranda* custody rule may not be a bad fit. Second, many of the difficulties in applying the *Miranda* custody rule to minors arise because of the unique circumstances present when the police conduct interrogations at school. The *Miranda* custody rule has always taken into account the setting in which questioning occurs, and accounting for the school setting in such cases will address many of these problems. Third, in cases like the one now before us, where the suspect is especially young, courts applying the constitutional voluntariness standard can take special care to ensure that incriminating statements were not obtained through coercion. . . .

I have little doubt that today's decision will soon be cited by defendants — and perhaps by prosecutors as well — for the proposition that all manner of other individual characteristics should be treated like age and taken into account in the *Miranda* custody calculus. Indeed, there are already lower court decisions that take this approach. See United States v. Beraun-Panez, 812 F.2d 578, 581, *modified* 830 F.2d 127 (CA9 1987) ("reasonable person who was an alien"); In re Jorge D., 202 Ariz. 277, 280, 43 P.3d 605, 608 (App. 2002) (age, maturity, and experience); State v. Doe, 130 Idaho 811, 818, 948 P.2d 166, 173 (1997) (same); In re Joshua David C., 116 Md. App. 580, 594, 698 A.2d 1155, 1162 (1997) ("education, age, and intelligence").

In time, the Court will have to confront these issues, and it will be faced with a difficult choice. It may choose to distinguish today's decision and adhere to the arbitrary proclamation that "age . . . is different." Or it may choose to extend today's holding and, in doing so, further undermine the very rationale for the *Miranda* regime. . . .

The Court holds that age must be taken into account when it "was known to the officer at the time of the interview," or when it "would have been objectively apparent" to a reasonable officer. . . . When, as here, the interrogation takes place in school, the [latter] inquiry may be relatively simple. But not all police questioning of minors takes place in schools. In many cases, courts will presumably have to make findings as to whether a particular suspect had a sufficiently youthful look to alert a reasonable officer to the possibility that the suspect was under 18, or whether a reasonable officer would have recognized that a suspect's I.D. was a fake. . . .

Even after courts clear this initial hurdle, further problems will likely emerge as judges attempt to put themselves in the shoes of the average 16-year-old, or 15-year-old, or 13-year-old, as the case may be. Consider, for example, a 60-year-old judge attempting to make a custody determination through the eyes of a hypothetical, average 15-year-old. Forty-five years of personal experience and societal change separate this judge from the days when he or she was 15 years old. And this judge may or may not have been an average 15-year-old. The Court's answer to these difficulties is to state that "no imaginative powers, knowledge of developmental psychology, [or] training in cognitive science" will be necessary. Judges "simply need the common sense," the Court assures, "to know that a 7-year-old is not a 13-year-old and neither is an adult." It is obvious, however, that application of the Court's new rule demands much more than this. . . .

. . . The *Miranda* custody determination . . . must be made in the first instance by police officers in the course of an investigation that may require quick decisionmaking. See *Alvarado*, 541 U.S., at 668, 669 ("[T]he custody inquiry states an objective rule designed to give clear guidance to the police"). . . . Today's decision . . . injects a new, complicating factor into what had been a clear, easily applied prophylactic rule. . . .[10]

The Court rests its decision to inject personal characteristics into the *Miranda* custody inquiry on the principle that judges applying *Miranda* cannot "blind themselves to . . . commonsense reality." But the Court's shift is fundamentally at odds with the clear prophylactic rules that *Miranda* has long enforced. *Miranda* frequently requires judges to blind themselves to the reality that many un-Mirandized custodial confessions are "by no means involuntary" or coerced. *Dickerson*, 530 U.S., at 444. It also requires police to provide a rote recitation of *Miranda* warnings that many suspects already know and could likely recite from memory.[13] Under today's new, "reality"-based approach to the doctrine, perhaps these and other principles of our *Miranda* jurisprudence will, like the custody standard, now be ripe for modification. Then, bit by bit, *Miranda* will lose the clarity and ease of application that has long been viewed as one of its chief justifications.

I respectfully dissent.

NOTES AND QUESTIONS

1. At first glance, *J.D.B.* seems pretty straightforward and pretty easy: Juveniles get special treatment throughout the vast universe of law. Why shouldn't they also get special treatment for purposes of determining

10. The Court also relies on North Carolina's concession at oral argument that a court could take into account a suspect's blindness as a factor relevant to the *Miranda* custody determination. This is a far-fetched hypothetical, and neither the parties nor their amici cite any case in which such a problem has actually arisen. . . .

13. Surveys have shown that "[l]arge majorities" of the public are aware that "individuals arrested for a crime" have a right to "remai[n] silent (81%)," a right to "a lawyer (95%)," and a right to have a lawyer "appointed" if the arrestee "cannot afford one (88%)." See Belden, Russonello & Stewart, Developing a National Message for Indigent Defense: Analysis of National Survey 4 (Oct. 2001), online at *http://www.nlada.org/DMS/Documents/1211996548.53/Polling%20results%20report.pdf*.

Miranda "custody"—especially given that *Miranda* is concerned primarily with the "coercive effect" of custodial interrogation, a problem that would seem especially acute in the context of juvenile suspects? Isn't Justice Sotomayor correct?

2. On the other hand, isn't *Miranda* designed to make things simple for police? It's supposed to be a clear set of rules: As soon as a suspect is in custody, then give the *Miranda* warnings, get the required waiver, and start questioning. But as long as the suspect isn't in custody, then no *Miranda* warnings are required. Once you've created an exception to the rules of *Miranda* "custody" for juveniles, then aren't you inevitably on a slippery slope? Isn't Justice Alito correct?

3. If clarity and certainty on the meaning of *Miranda* custody is the goal, consider Justice Alito's majority opinion in Howes v. Fields, 132 S. Ct. 1181 (2012), just one year after *J.D.B.* was handed down. A prison inmate was taken to a conference room where two police officers questioned him about a crime that had occurred before the inmate was sent to prison. The inmate made incriminating statements and later moved to suppress, arguing that he was in custody at the time of his interrogation but was not given his *Miranda* warnings. On federal habeas the court of appeals agreed, finding there was per se custody because the inmate was in prison and isolated from the rest of the inmate population during the interrogation.

The Supreme Court disagreed, concluding that the custody determination was not that simple. While incarceration, isolation during questioning, and the fact that the interrogation addressed matters that happened outside the prison walls were all relevant, they were not decisive. Instead, said the Court, "[w]hen a prisoner is questioned, the determination of custody should focus on all of the features of the interrogation," including "the language that is used in summoning the prisoner to the interview and the manner in which the interrogation is conducted." Here the fact that the door to the prison conference room was open during part of the questioning, that the inmate was not threatened or restrained, and most importantly, that he was told at the outset that he was free to leave and return to his cell, showed that there was no custody of the type contemplated by *Miranda*.

In a related case two years earlier (Maryland v. Shatzer, 130 S. Ct. 1213 (2010), discussed in the main volume at pages 826-828), the Court had observed that no one in that case had questioned the notion that a prison inmate is "in custody" for *Miranda* purposes, an observation that it distinguished in *Fields*. Why do you think the Court is working so hard to avoid creating a bright-line rule on the custody question?

d. Invocations

Insert the following note after Note 10 on page 828:

11. In the *Miranda* context of custodial interrogation, where coercion is inherent (or so says the Court), an invocation of rights produces at least temporary prophylactic protection against further police questioning pursuant to *Mosley, Edwards,* and *Shatzer*. But an invocation is not always necessary to enjoy the benefits of the Fifth Amendment right to be free from compelled self-incrimination. That is why the prosecution is barred from making any adverse comment about the defendant's decision not to testify at trial. Such adverse comment, by raising an inference of guilt with the jury, would penalize and therefore violate the defendant's absolute right not to testify but instead to remain silent. The same principle also prohibits instructing the jury that it can draw such an adverse inference, as well as forcing the defendant to take the witness stand and assert his Fifth Amendment privilege in front of the jury. See Griffin v. California, 380 U.S. 609 (1965), discussed supra at page 730. Nor may the prosecution comment adversely at trial on the silence of a suspect who has been arrested and given *Miranda* warnings; the Court has held that such a breach of the implied promise contained in the *Miranda* warnings would violate due process. See Doyle v. Ohio, 426 U.S. 610 (1976).

But what about a non-custodial suspect who voluntarily submits to police questioning? Should the same principle apply in such a context?

SALINAS v. TEXAS
Certiorari to the Court of Criminal Appeals of Texas
133 S. Ct. 2174 (2013)

JUSTICE ALITO announced the judgment of the Court and delivered an opinion in which CHIEF JUSTICE ROBERTS and JUSTICE KENNEDY join.

Without being placed in custody or receiving *Miranda* warnings, petitioner voluntarily answered the questions of a police officer who was investigating a murder. But petitioner balked when the officer asked whether a ballistics test would show that the shell casings found at the crime scene would match petitioner's shotgun. Petitioner was subsequently charged with murder, and at trial prosecutors argued that his reaction to the officer's question suggested that he was guilty. Petitioner claims that this argument violated the Fifth Amendment, which guarantees that "[n]o person . . . shall be compelled in any criminal case to be a witness against himself."

Petitioner's Fifth Amendment claim fails because he did not expressly invoke the privilege against self-incrimination in response to the officer's question. It has long been settled that the privilege "generally is not self-executing" and that a witness who desires its protection "'must claim it.'" Minnesota v. Murphy, 465 U.S. [420,] 425, 427 [(1984)]. Although "no ritualistic formula is necessary in order to invoke the privilege," Quinn v. United States, 349 U.S. 155, 164 (1955), a witness does not do so by simply standing mute. Because petitioner was required to assert the privilege in order to benefit from it, the judgment of the Texas Court of Criminal Appeals rejecting petitioner's Fifth Amendment claim is affirmed.

I

On the morning of December 18, 1992, two brothers were shot and killed in their Houston home. There were no witnesses to the murders, but a neighbor who heard gunshots saw someone run out of the house and speed away in a dark-colored car. Police recovered six shotgun shell casings at the scene. The investigation led police to petitioner, who had been a guest at a party the victims hosted the night before they were killed. Police visited petitioner at his home, where they saw a dark blue car in the driveway. He agreed to hand over his shotgun for ballistics testing and to accompany police to the station for questioning.

Petitioner's interview with the police lasted approximately one hour. All agree that the interview was noncustodial, and the parties litigated this case on the assumption that he was not read *Miranda* warnings. For most of the interview, petitioner answered the officer's questions. But when asked whether his shotgun "would match the shells recovered at the scene of the murder," petitioner declined to answer. Instead, petitioner "[l]ooked down at the floor, shuffled his feet, bit his bottom lip, cl[e]nched his hands in his lap, [and] began to tighten up." After a few moments of silence, the officer asked additional questions, which petitioner answered. . . .

Petitioner did not testify at trial. Over his objection, prosecutors used his reaction to the officer's question during the 1993 interview as evidence of his guilt. The jury found petitioner guilty, and he received a 20-year sentence. . . .

We granted certiorari to resolve a division of authority in the lower courts over whether the prosecution may use a defendant's assertion of the privilege against self-incrimination during a noncustodial police interview as part of its case in chief. But because petitioner did not invoke the privilege during his interview, we find it unnecessary to reach that question.

II

A

The privilege against self-incrimination "is an exception to the general principle that the Government has the right to everyone's testimony." Garner v. United States, 424 U.S. 648, 658, n. 11 (1976). To prevent the privilege from shielding information not properly within its scope, we have long held that a witness who "'desires the protection of the privilege . . . must claim it'" at the time he relies on it. *Murphy*, 465 U.S., at 427.

That requirement ensures that the Government is put on notice when a witness intends to rely on the privilege so that it may either argue that the testimony sought could not be self-incriminating, or cure any potential self-incrimination through a grant of immunity. The express invocation requirement also gives courts tasked with evaluating a Fifth Amendment claim a contemporaneous record establishing the witness' reasons for refusing to answer. In these ways, insisting that witnesses expressly invoke the privilege assures that the Government obtains all the information to which it is entitled.

We have previously recognized two exceptions to the requirement that witnesses invoke the privilege, but neither applies here. First, we held in Griffin v. California, 380 U.S. 609, 613-615 (1965), that a criminal defendant need not take the stand and assert the privilege at his own trial. That exception reflects the fact that a criminal defendant has an "absolute right not to testify. Since a defendant's reasons for remaining silent at trial are irrelevant to his constitutional right to do so, requiring that he expressly invoke the privilege would serve no purpose; neither a showing that his testimony would not be self-incriminating nor a grant of immunity could force him to speak. Because petitioner had no comparable unqualified right during his interview with police, his silence falls outside the *Griffin* exception.

Second, we have held that a witness' failure to invoke the privilege must be excused where governmental coercion makes his forfeiture of the privilege involuntary. Thus, in *Miranda*, we said that a suspect who is subjected to the "inherently compelling pressures" of an unwarned custodial interrogation need not invoke the privilege. Due to the uniquely coercive nature of custodial interrogation, a suspect in custody cannot be said to have voluntarily forgone the privilege "unless [he] fails to claim [it] after being suitably warned."

For similar reasons, we have held that threats to withdraw a governmental benefit such as public employment sometimes make exercise of the privilege so costly that it need not be affirmatively asserted. And where assertion of the privilege would itself tend to incriminate, we have allowed witnesses to exercise the privilege through silence. See, e. g., Leary v. United States, 395 U.S. 6, 28-29 (1969) (no requirement that taxpayer complete tax form where doing so would have revealed income from illegal activities); Albertson v. Subversive Activities Control Bd., 382 U.S. 70, 77-79 (1965) (members of the Communist Party not required to complete registration form "where response to any of the form's questions . . . might involve [them] in the admission of a crucial element of a crime"). The principle that unites all of those cases is that a witness need not expressly invoke the privilege where some form of official compulsion denies him "a 'free choice to admit, to deny, or to refuse to answer.'"

Petitioner cannot benefit from that principle because it is undisputed that his interview with police was voluntary. As petitioner himself acknowledges, he agreed to accompany the officers to the station and "was free to leave at any time during the interview. That places petitioner's situation outside the scope of *Miranda* and other cases in which we have held that various forms of governmental coercion prevented defendants from voluntarily invoking the privilege. The dissent elides this point when it cites our precedents in this area for the proposition that "[c]ircumstances, rather than explicit invocation, trigger the protection of the Fifth Amendment." The critical question is whether, under the "circumstances" of this case, petitioner was deprived of the ability to voluntarily invoke the Fifth Amendment. He was not. We have before us no allegation that petitioner's failure to assert the privilege was involuntary, and it would have been a simple matter for him to say that he was not answering the officer's question on Fifth Amendment grounds. Because he failed to do so, the prosecution's use of his noncustodial silence did not violate the Fifth Amendment.

B

Petitioner urges us to adopt a third exception to the invocation requirement for cases in which a witness stands mute and thereby declines to give an answer that officials suspect would be incriminating. Our cases all but foreclose such an exception, which would needlessly burden the

Government's interests in obtaining testimony and prosecuting criminal activity. We therefore decline petitioner's invitation to craft a new exception to the "general rule" that a witness must assert the privilege to subsequently benefit from it.

Our cases establish that a defendant normally does not invoke the privilege by remaining silent. In Roberts v. United States, 445 U.S. 552 [(1980)], for example, we rejected the Fifth Amendment claim of a defendant who remained silent throughout a police investigation and received a harsher sentence for his failure to cooperate. In so ruling, we explained that "if [the defendant] believed that his failure to cooperate was privileged, he should have said so at a time when the sentencing court could have determined whether his claim was legitimate."

We have also repeatedly held that the express invocation requirement applies even when an official has reason to suspect that the answer to his question would incriminate the witness. Thus, in *Murphy* we held that the defendant's self-incriminating answers to his probation officer were properly admitted at trial because he failed to invoke the privilege. In reaching that conclusion, we rejected the notion "that a witness must 'put the Government on notice by formally availing himself of the privilege' only when he alone 'is reasonably aware of the incriminating tendency of the questions.'"

Petitioner does not dispute the vitality of either of those lines of precedent but instead argues that we should adopt an exception for cases at their intersection. Thus, petitioner would have us hold that although neither a witness' silence nor official suspicions are enough to excuse the express invocation requirement, the invocation requirement does not apply where a witness is silent in the face of official suspicions. For the same reasons that neither of those factors is sufficient by itself to relieve a witness of the obligation to expressly invoke the privilege, we conclude that they do not do so together. A contrary result would do little to protect those genuinely relying on the Fifth Amendment privilege while placing a needless new burden on society's interest in the admission of evidence that is probative of a criminal defendant's guilt.

Petitioner's proposed exception would also be very difficult to reconcile with Berghuis v. Thompkins, 560 U.S. 370 (2010). There, we held in the closely related context of post-*Miranda* silence that a defendant failed to invoke the privilege when he refused to respond to police questioning for 2 hours and 45 minutes. If the extended custodial silence in that case did not invoke the privilege, then surely the momentary silence in this case did not do so either.

Petitioner and the dissent attempt to distinguish *Berghuis* by observing that it did not concern the admissibility of the defendant's silence but instead involved the admissibility of his subsequent statements. But regardless of whether prosecutors seek to use silence or a confession that follows, the logic of *Berghuis* applies with equal force: A suspect who stands mute has not done enough to put police on notice that he is relying on his Fifth Amendment privilege.

In support of their proposed exception to the invocation requirement, petitioner and the dissent argue that reliance on the Fifth Amendment privilege is the most likely explanation for silence in a case such as this one. But whatever the most probable explanation, such silence is "insolubly ambiguous." To be sure, someone might decline to answer a police officer's question in reliance on his constitutional privilege. But he also might do so because he is trying to think of a good lie, because he is embarrassed, or because he is protecting someone else. Not every such possible explanation for silence is probative of guilt, but neither is every possible explanation protected by the Fifth Amendment. Petitioner alone knew why he did not answer the officer's question, and it was therefore his "burden . . . to make a timely assertion of the privilege."

At oral argument, counsel for petitioner suggested that it would be unfair to require a suspect unschooled in the particulars of legal doctrine to do anything more than remain silent in order to invoke his "right to remain silent." But popular misconceptions notwithstanding, the Fifth Amendment guarantees that no one may be "compelled in any criminal case to be a witness against himself"; it does not establish an unqualified "right to remain silent." A witness' constitutional right to refuse to answer questions depends on his reasons for doing so, and courts need to know those reasons to evaluate the merits of a Fifth Amendment claim.

In any event, it is settled that forfeiture of the privilege against self-incrimination need not be knowing. Statements against interest are regularly admitted into evidence at criminal trials, see Fed. Rule of Evid. 804(b)(3), and there is no good reason to approach a defendant's silence any differently.

c

Finally, we are not persuaded by petitioner's arguments that applying the usual express invocation requirement where a witness is silent during a noncustodial police interview will prove unworkable in practice. Petitioner and the dissent suggest that our approach will "unleash complicated and persistent litigation" over what a suspect must say to invoke the privilege, but our cases have long required that a witness assert the privilege to subsequently benefit from it. That rule has not proved difficult to apply. Nor did the potential for close cases dissuade us from adopting similar invocation requirements for suspects who wish to assert their rights and cut off police questioning during custodial interviews.

Notably, petitioner's approach would produce its own line-drawing problems, as this case vividly illustrates. When the interviewing officer asked petitioner if his shotgun would match the shell casings found at the crime scene, petitioner did not merely remain silent; he made movements that suggested surprise and anxiety. At precisely what point such reactions transform "silence" into expressive conduct would be a difficult and recurring question that our decision allows us to avoid.

We also reject petitioner's argument that an express invocation requirement will encourage police officers to "'unfairly "tric[k]"'" suspects into cooperating. Petitioner worries that officers could unduly pressure suspects into talking by telling them that their silence could be used in a future prosecution. But as petitioner himself concedes, police officers "have done nothing wrong" when they "accurately stat[e] the law." We found no constitutional infirmity in government officials telling the defendant in *Murphy* that he was required to speak truthfully to his parole officer and we see no greater danger in the interview tactics petitioner identifies. So long as police do not deprive a witness of the ability to voluntarily invoke the privilege, there is no Fifth Amendment violation.

* * *

Before petitioner could rely on the privilege against self-incrimination, he was required to invoke it. Because he failed to do so, the judgment of the Texas Court of Criminal Appeals is affirmed.

JUSTICE THOMAS, with whom JUSTICE SCALIA joins, concurring in the judgment.

. . . In Griffin v. California, this Court held that the Fifth Amendment prohibits a prosecutor or judge from commenting on a defendant's failure to testify. The Court reasoned that such comments, and any adverse inferences drawn from them, are a "penalty" imposed on the defendant's exercise of his Fifth Amendment privilege. Salinas argues that we should extend *Griffin*'s no-adverse-inference rule to a defendant's silence during a precustodial interview. I have previously explained that the Court's decision in *Griffin* "lacks foundation in the Constitution's text, history, or logic" and should not be extended. I adhere to that view today.

Griffin is impossible to square with the text of the Fifth Amendment, which provides that "[n]o person . . . shall be compelled in any criminal case to be a witness against himself." A defendant is not "compelled . . . to be a witness against himself" simply because a jury has been told that it may draw an adverse inference from his silence.

Nor does the history of the Fifth Amendment support *Griffin*. At the time of the founding, English and American courts strongly encouraged defendants to give unsworn statements and drew adverse inferences when they failed to do so.

JUSTICE BREYER, with whom JUSTICE GINSBURG, JUSTICE SOTOMAYOR, and JUSTICE KAGAN join, dissenting.

In my view the Fifth Amendment here prohibits the prosecution from commenting on the petitioner's silence in response to police questioning. And I dissent from the Court's contrary conclusion.

II . . .

A

The Fifth Amendment prohibits prosecutors from commenting on an individual's silence where that silence amounts to an effort to avoid becoming "a witness against himself." This Court has specified that "a rule of evidence" permitting "commen[t] . . . by counsel" in a criminal case upon a defendant's failure to testify "violates the Fifth Amendment." Griffin v. California. And, since "it is impermissible to penalize an individual for exercising his Fifth Amendment privilege when he is under police custodial interrogation," the "prosecution may not . . . use at trial the fact that he stood mute or claimed his privilege in the face of accusation." Miranda v. Arizona, 384 U.S. 436, 468, n. 37.

Particularly in the context of police interrogation, a contrary rule would undermine the basic protection that the Fifth Amendment provides. To permit a prosecutor to comment on a defendant's constitutionally protected silence would put that defendant in an impossible predicament. He must either answer the question or remain silent. If he answers the question, he may well reveal, for example, prejudicial facts, disreputable associates, or suspicious circumstances — even if he is innocent. If he remains silent, the prosecutor may well use that silence to suggest a consciousness of guilt. And if the defendant then takes the witness stand in order to explain either his speech or his silence, the prosecution may introduce, say for impeachment purposes, a prior conviction that the law would otherwise make inadmissible. Thus, where the Fifth Amendment is at issue, to allow comment on silence directly or

indirectly can compel an individual to act as "a witness against himself" —
very much what the Fifth Amendment forbids. And that is similarly so
whether the questioned individual, as part of his decision to remain
silent, invokes the Fifth Amendment explicitly or implicitly, through
words, through deeds, or through reference to surrounding circumstances.

B

It is consequently not surprising that this Court, more than half a
century ago, explained that "no ritualistic formula is necessary in order
to invoke the privilege." . . .

The cases in which this Court has insisted that a defendant expressly
mention the Fifth Amendment by name in order to rely on its privilege
to protect silence are cases where (1) the circumstances surrounding the
silence (unlike the present case) did not give rise to an inference that the
defendant intended, by his silence, to exercise his Fifth Amendment
rights; and (2) the questioner greeted by the silence (again unlike the
present case) had a special need to know whether the defendant sought
to rely on the protections of the Fifth Amendment.

Thus, we have two sets of cases: One where express invocation of the
Fifth Amendment was not required to tie one's silence to its protections,
and another where something like express invocation was required, because circumstances demanded some explanation for the silence (or the
statements) in order to indicate that the Fifth Amendment was at
issue. . . .

The plurality refers to one additional case, namely Berghuis v.
Thompkins, But that case is here beside the point. In *Berghuis*, the
defendant was in custody, he had been informed of his *Miranda* rights,
and he was subsequently silent in the face of 2 hours and 45 minutes of
questioning before he offered any substantive answers. The Court held
that he had waived his Fifth Amendment rights in respect to his later
speech. The Court said nothing at all about a prosecutor's right to
comment on his preceding silence and no prosecutor sought to do so.
Indeed, how could a prosecutor lawfully have tried to do so, given this
Court's statement in *Miranda* itself that a prosecutor cannot comment on
the fact that, after receiving *Miranda* warnings, the suspect "stood mute"?

We end where we began. "[N]o ritualistic formula is necessary in order
to invoke the privilege." Much depends on the circumstances of the
particular case, the most important circumstances being: (1) whether
one can fairly infer that the individual being questioned is invoking the

Amendment's protection; (2) if that is unclear, whether it is particularly important for the questioner to know whether the individual is doing so; and (3) even if it is, whether, in any event, there is a good reason for excusing the individual from referring to the Fifth Amendment, such as inherent penalization simply by answering.

c

Applying these principles to the present case, I would hold that Salinas need not have expressly invoked the Fifth Amendment. The context was that of a criminal investigation. Police told Salinas that and made clear that he was a suspect. His interrogation took place at the police station. Salinas was not represented by counsel. The relevant question — about whether the shotgun from Salinas' home would incriminate him — amounted to a switch in subject matter. And it was obvious that the new question sought to ferret out whether Salinas was guilty of murder.

These circumstances give rise to a reasonable inference that Salinas' silence derived from an exercise of his Fifth Amendment rights. This Court has recognized repeatedly that many, indeed most, Americans are aware that they have a constitutional right not to incriminate themselves by answering questions posed by the police during an interrogation conducted in order to figure out the perpetrator of a crime. The nature of the surroundings, the switch of topic, the particular question — all suggested that the right we have and generally know we have was at issue at the critical moment here. Salinas, not being represented by counsel, would not likely have used the precise words "Fifth Amendment" to invoke his rights because he would not likely have been aware of technical legal requirements, such as a need to identify the Fifth Amendment by name.

At the same time, the need to categorize Salinas' silence as based on the Fifth Amendment is supported here by the presence, in full force, of the predicament I discussed earlier, namely that of not forcing Salinas to choose between incrimination through speech and incrimination through silence. That need is also supported by the absence of any special reason that the police had to know, with certainty, whether Salinas was, in fact, relying on the Fifth Amendment — such as whether to doubt that there really was a risk of self-incrimination, or whether to grant immunity. Given these circumstances, Salinas' silence was "sufficient to put the [government] on notice of an apparent claim of the privilege." That being so, for reasons similar to those given in *Griffin*, the Fifth

Amendment bars the evidence of silence admitted against Salinas and mentioned by the prosecutor.

D

I recognize that other cases may arise where facts and circumstances surrounding an individual's silence present a closer question. The critical question—whether those circumstances give rise to a fair inference that the silence rests on the Fifth Amendment—will not always prove easy to administer. But that consideration does not support the plurality's rule-based approach here, for the administrative problems accompanying the plurality's approach are even worse.

The plurality says that a suspect must "expressly invoke the privilege against self-incrimination." But does it really mean that the suspect must use the exact words "Fifth Amendment"? How can an individual who is not a lawyer know that these particular words are legally magic? Nor does the Solicitor General help when he adds that the suspect may "mak[e] the claim 'in any language that [the questioner] may reasonably be expected to understand as an attempt to invoke the privilege.'" What counts as "making the claim"? Suppose the individual says, "Let's discuss something else," or "I'm not sure I want to answer that"; or suppose he just gets up and leaves the room. . . .

The basic problem for the plurality is that an effort to have a simple, clear "explicit statement" rule poses a serious obstacle to those who, like Salinas, seek to assert their basic Fifth Amendment right to remain silent, for they are likely unaware of any such linguistic detail. At the same time, acknowledging that our case law does not require use of specific words, leaves the plurality without the administrative benefits it might hope to find in requiring that detail.

Far better, in my view, to pose the relevant question directly: Can one fairly infer from an individual's silence and surrounding circumstances an exercise of the Fifth Amendment's privilege? The need for simplicity, the constitutional importance of applying the Fifth Amendment to those who seek its protection, and this Court's case law all suggest that this is the right question to ask here. And the answer to that question in the circumstances of today's case is clearly: yes.

NOTES AND QUESTIONS

1. Isn't *Salinas* an easy case? He was not compelled to attend a meeting; he was not compelled to stay; and he was not compelled to say

anything or remain silent. If there is no compulsion of any sort, how can he be said to have been compelled to be a witness against himself?

2. Of course, the plurality did not exactly address that question. It addressed a different question, to-wit whether there was anything about the circumstances of this case that excused the normal requirement of invoking the Fifth Amendment right to be free from compelled self-incrimination in order to benefit from its protection. And both the plurality and the concurrence concluded that the answer was no.

3. What if Salinas *had* invoked the Fifth Amendment? Would that make a difference in the outcome? What compulsion would he be trying to fend off? If there really is none, there is no Fifth Amendment right to invoke. Thus, what the plurality is saying is not, as the dissent seems to imply, that the problem here is just the failure of invocation. The plurality is saying that the Court needed not address the substantive question because of the procedural failure. The plurality is most definitely not saying that, had he invoked, his body language could not have been used against him if it met the normal evidentiary requirements for admissibility.

The issue of Fifth Amendment compulsion (outside the special context of custodial police interrogation) can be a confusing one. Part of the confusion may stem from the fact that some of the Court's "compulsion" cases involve allegations of government compulsion, e.g., to appear, to produce evidence, or to answer questions; while other "compulsion" cases (and perhaps this was really the underlying complaint, albeit not very well articulated, in *Salinas*) involve allegations of compulsion not to invoke one's Fifth Amendment privilege (i.e., by means of imposing a "penalty," see Griffin v. California and other so-called "penalty" cases discussed supra at pages 730-735).

4. These questions point out the subtle but important difference between a right to remain silent, which the dissent seems to think exists, and the right to be free from compulsion. If there is no right to remain silent, and there is no compulsion, there is no "right" to invoke, and thus Salinas's mouthing of the words "I invoke some right or other" would be completely beside the point. Its evidentiary implications would then be determined by the law of evidence, not the U.S. Constitution.

5. How far would the dissent go? Suppose a burglary alarm goes off. The police arrive at the scene and see someone, who also spots the police. Suppose the person shouts: "I'm invoking my Fifth Amendment right not to incriminate myself," and runs from the scene but is later caught. Flight from a crime scene is usually admissible as evidence of consciousness of guilt. Would it be in this case? If not, under the dissent's view, what difference does the articulation make? Shouldn't the same outcome

obtain if the person just flees? But isn't that perfectly ridiculous? Has the dissent confused compulsion with causation? Merely because a state actor is in the causal chain leading to the creation of some evidence hardly means the state has "compelled" the creation of that evidence, does it? And if a person truly has a right to remain silent, another possible confusion in the dissent, wouldn't it equally apply to the putative burglary suspect running away from the scene? Indeed, the communication in *Salinas* itself was largely body language.

e. Waivers

Replace the first two sentences of Note 3 on page 838 with the following:

The relationship between police deception, due process, and *Miranda* waivers is complex. Consider Miller v. Fenton, 796 F.2d 598 (3d Cir. 1986), in which a divided Court of Appeals panel found that the police interrogation described below did not violate the Fifth Amendment:

Chapter 7

Complex Investigations in the Fourth Amendment's Shadow

A. Electronic Surveillance and the Search of Electronic Files

2. The Search of Electronic Files

Replace the second paragraph of Note 3 on page 912 with the following material:

In Warshak v. United States, 490 F.3d 455 (6th Cir. 2007) (*"Warshak I"*), a panel of the Sixth Circuit determined that an individual does, indeed, have a privacy interest in the content of his emails. The decision, however, was later vacated on ripeness grounds by the en banc court. See Warshak v. United States, 532 F.3d 521 (6th Cir. 2008) (en banc) (*"Warshak II"*). The case subsequently returned to the Sixth Circuit on appeal from the criminal convictions of Warshak and his co-defendants. The court determined that the issues whether Warshak had a privacy interest in the content of his emails and whether his Fourth Amendment rights were violated when government agents accessed those emails were now ripe for decision.

UNITED STATES v. WARSHAK
Appeal to the United States Court of Appeals for the Sixth Circuit
631 F.3d 266 (2010)

BOGGS, CIRCUIT JUDGE.
Berkeley Premium Nutraceuticals, Inc., was an incredibly profitable company that served as the distributor of Enzyte, an herbal supplement purported to enhance male sexual performance. In this appeal, defendants Steven Warshak ("Warshak"), Harriet Warshak ("Harriet"), and TCI Media, Inc. ("TCI"), challenge their convictions stemming from a massive scheme to defraud Berkeley's customers. . . .

[W]e provide the following summary of our holding[:] Warshak enjoyed a reasonable expectation of privacy in his emails vis-à-vis NuVox, his Internet Service Provider. See Katz v. United States, 389 U.S. 347 (1967). Thus, government agents violated his Fourth Amendment rights by compelling NuVox to turn over the emails without first obtaining a warrant based on probable cause. However, because the agents relied in good faith on provisions of the Stored Communications Act, the exclusionary rule does not apply in this instance. . . .

I. STATEMENT OF THE FACTS

A. FACTUAL BACKGROUND

In 2001, Steven Warshak ("Warshak") owned and operated a number of small businesses in the Cincinnati area. One of his businesses was TCI Media, Inc. ("TCI"), which sold advertisements in sporting venues. Warshak also owned a handful of companies that offered a modest line of so-called "nutraceuticals," or herbal supplements. While the companies bore different names and sold different products, they appear to have been run as a single business, and they were later aggregated to form Berkeley Premium Nutraceuticals, Inc. ("Berkeley"). In Berkeley's early days, the company's workforce was relatively minute; the company employed approximately 12 to 15 people, nearly all of whom were Warshak's friends and family. Among them was his mother, Harriet Warshak ("Harriet"), who processed credit-card payments.

As the company grew, Warshak brought on additional employees to facilitate expansion, but he remained extremely "hands-on" with respect to the company's operations. In 2001, he hired James Teegarden, who eventually became Berkeley's Chief Operating Officer. . . .

To sell its products, Berkeley took orders over the phone, but it also made sales through the mail and over the Internet. Customers purchased products with their credit cards, and their credit-card numbers were entered into a database along with other information. During sales calls, representatives would read from sales scripts, which listed the major points to cover during the transaction. . . .

In the latter half of 2001, Berkeley launched Enzyte, its flagship product. At the time of its launch, Enzyte was purported to increase the size of a man's erection. The product proved tremendously popular, and business rose sharply. By 2004, demand for Berkeley's products had grown so dramatically that the company employed 1500 people, and the call center remained open throughout the night, taking orders at breakneck speed. . . .

1. Advertising

The popularity of Enzyte appears to have been due in large part to Berkeley's aggressive advertising campaigns. The vast majority of the advertising — approximately 98% — was conducted through television spots. Around 2004, network television was saturated with Enzyte advertisements featuring a character called "Smilin' Bob," whose trademark exaggerated smile was presumably the result of Enzyte's efficacy. . . .

In addition to the television commercials, however, there were also advertisements in other media, such as print and radio. In 2001, just after Enzyte's premiere, advertisements appeared in a number of men's interest magazines. At Warshak's direction, those advertisements cited a 2001 independent customer study, which purported to show that, over a three-month period, 100 English-speaking men who took Enzyte experienced a 12 to 31% increase in the size of their penises. The 2001 study was also referenced in radio advertisements and appeared on the company's website, as well as in brochures and sales calls. James Teegarden later testified that the survey was bogus. He stated that, prior to the appearance of the advertisements, Warshak instructed him to create a spreadsheet and to fill it with fabricated data. Teegarden testified that he plucked the numbers out of the air and generated the spreadsheet over a twenty-four hour period.

A number of advertisements also indicated that Enzyte boasted a 96% customer satisfaction rating. Teegarden testified that that statistic, too, was totally spurious. . . .

Finally, numerous print and radio advertisements boasted that Enzyte was the brainchild of reputable doctors with impressive educational pedigrees. According to the ads, "Enzyte was developed by Dr. Fredrick Thomkins, a physician with a biology degree from Stanford and Dr. Michael Moore, a leading urologist from Harvard." The ads also stated that the doctors had collaborated for thirteen years in developing a supplement designed to "stretch and elongate." In reality, the doctors were just as fictitious as "Smilin' Bob." . . .

2. The Auto-Ship Program

The "life blood" of the business was its auto-ship program, which was instituted in 2001, shortly before Enzyte hit the market. The auto-ship program was a continuity or negative-option program, in which a customer would order a free trial of a product and then continue to receive additional shipments of that product until he opted out. . . .

In the early days of the auto-ship program, customers who ordered products over the phone were not told that they were being enrolled. . . . According to Teegarden, Warshak explained that the auto-ship program was never mentioned because "nobody would sign up." If nobody signed up, "you couldn't make revenue."

This policy resulted in a substantial volume of complaints. . . . In October 2002, the Better Business Bureau ("BBB") contacted Berkeley and indicated that more than 1,500 customers had called to voice their consternation. Because of the complaints, Berkeley's sales scripts and website began to include some language disclosing the auto-ship program. A number of internal emails indicate that sales representatives were required to read the disclosure language and faced punishment if they failed to do so. . . .

However, as a number of Berkeley insiders testified, the compulsory disclosure language was not always read, and it was designed not to work. [One witness] testified that the disclosure of the continuity shipments was only made *after* the customer had placed his order. . . . Also, the disclosures were deliberately made with haste, and they were placed after unrelated language that was intended to divert or deaden the customer's attention. . . .

Moreover, disclosure of the auto-ship program was sometimes irrelevant. For example, in November 2003, Berkeley hired a company called West to handle "sales calls that were from . . . Avlimil or Enzyte advertisements." During the calls, West's representatives asked customers if they wanted to be enrolled in the auto-ship program, and over 80% of customers declined. When Warshak learned what was happening, he issued instructions to "take those customers, even if they decline[d], even if they said no to the Auto-Ship program, go ahead and put them on the Auto-Ship program." . . .

By July 2004, the complaints arising from Berkeley's auto-ship program had not slowed, so the President of the BBB reached out to Berkeley, sending a letter directly to Warshak. The purpose of the letter was to express "serious concerns about the number of complaints that [the BBB] had received." . . .

3. The Merchant Banks

In order for Berkeley's business to operate, it was essential that the company be able to accept credit cards as a form of payment. To process credit-card transactions, Berkeley obtained lines of credit from several merchant banks. The relationships between Berkeley and the merchant banks involved intermediaries known as credit-card processors. . . . [E]ither the banks or the processors could terminate Berkeley's merchant accounts.

In early 2002, Warshak's merchant account at the Bank of Kentucky was terminated for excessive "chargebacks." A chargeback occurs when a customer calls the credit card company directly and contests or disputes a charge. Merchant banks — and credit-card processors — will generally not do business with merchants that experience high volumes of chargebacks, as those merchants present a greater financial risk. In determining whether a merchant is experiencing excessive chargebacks, the banks refer to a figure known as the chargeback ratio, which is simply the percentage of transactions in a given 30-day period that result in a chargeback. . . . Typically, if a merchant experiences more than one chargeback per hundred transactions, its chargeback ratio is deemed too high, resulting in fines and, eventually, termination of its accounts, either by the merchant bank or the credit-card processor.

Following the termination of the merchant account at the Bank of Kentucky, the company applied for merchant accounts with a number of other banks. In some instances, the applications, which often bore Harriet's signature, falsely listed her as the CEO and 100% owner of the company. In other instances, Warshak would complete the applications in his own name but falsely claim that he had never had a merchant account terminated. These prevarications were included in the applications because the prior termination would likely diminish Berkeley's chances of securing the services of other processors.

Despite its history with the Bank of Kentucky, Berkeley was able to land (or retain) merchant accounts with several processors. However, due to the auto-ship program and an extremely onerous refund policy, Berkeley was repeatedly at risk of crossing the critical 1% chargeback threshold. At company meetings, the chargeback ratio was a frequent topic of discussion, as was the possibility that Berkeley's accounts would be terminated. To prevent that from happening, a number of strategies were devised to artificially inflate the number of sales transactions and thus the denominator of the chargeback ratio, reducing that crucial ratio. One strategy was called "double-dinging." That practice involved splitting a single transaction into two, thereby driving up the number of transactions and diminishing the chargeback ratio. A double-ding might entail carving a $59.95 charge into a $54.95 charge for the product itself and a $5.00 charge for shipping. Warshak directed that virtually all sales be double-dinged, and by 2003, triple-dinging was initiated.

Another way the company depressed the chargeback ratio was to make numerous charges to Warshak's personal credit cards. At Warshak's behest, Berkeley employees would ring up $1.00 charges on each of his credit cards until their limits were reached. Apparently, the thinking was that this torrent of additional transactions would dilute the number of chargebacks and keep the ratio under 1%. The same thinking led the company to charge and then refund the credit cards of randomly selected customers. The charges were made without authorization, and if anyone complained about the odd activity on his card, he was told that it was the result of a computer glitch. Through the use of these techniques and others, the company was able to stave off termination of its merchant-bank accounts.

B.   PROCEDURAL HISTORY

In September 2006, a grand jury sitting in the Southern District of Ohio returned a 112-count indictment charging Warshak, Harriet, TCI, and several others with various crimes related to Berkeley's business. . . .

. . . Warshak moved to exclude thousands of emails that the government obtained from his Internet Service Providers. That motion was denied. . . . Over fifteen months later, in January 2008, the case proceeded to trial. Approximately six weeks later, the trial ended and the defendants were convicted of the majority of the charges. . . .

Following a series of unsuccessful post-trial motions, the defendants timely appealed.

II.   ANALYSIS

A.   THE SEARCH AND SEIZURE OF WARSHAK'S EMAILS

Warshak argues that the government's warrantless, ex parte seizure of approximately 27,000 of his private emails constituted a violation of the Fourth Amendment's prohibition on unreasonable searches and seizures. The government counters that, even if government agents violated the Fourth Amendment in obtaining the emails, they relied in good faith on the Stored Communications Act ("SCA"), 18 U.S.C. §§ 2701 et seq., a statute that allows the government to obtain certain electronic communications without procuring a warrant. . . . We find that the government *did* violate Warshak's Fourth Amendment rights by compelling his Internet Service Provider ("ISP") to turn over the contents of his emails. However, we agree that agents relied on the SCA in good faith, and therefore hold that reversal is unwarranted.

1. The Stored Communications Act

The Stored Communications Act ("SCA"), 18 U.S.C. §§ 2701 et seq., "permits a 'governmental entity' to compel a service provider to disclose the contents of [electronic] communications in certain circumstances." Warshak [v. United States], 532 F.3d [521, 523 (6th Cir. 2008) (en banc) ("*Warshak II*")]. As this court explained in *Warshak II*:

> Three relevant definitions bear on the meaning of the compelled-disclosure provisions of the Act. "[E]lectronic communication service[s]" permit "users . . . to send or receive wire or electronic communications," [18 U.S.C.] § 2510(15), a definition that covers basic e-mail services, *see* Patricia L. Bellia et al., Cyberlaw: Problems of Policy and Jurisprudence in the Information Age 584 (2d ed. 2004). "[E]lectronic storage" is "any temporary, intermediate storage of a wire or electronic communication . . . and . . . any storage of such communication by an electronic communication service for purposes of backup protection of such communication." 18 U.S.C. § 2510(17). "[R]emote computing service[s]" provide "computer storage or processing services" to customers, *id.* § 2711(2), and are designed for longer-term storage, *see* Orin S. Kerr, A User's Guide to the Stored Communications Act, and a Legislator's Guide to Amending It, 72 Geo. Wash. L. Rev. 1208, 1216 (2004).
>
> The compelled-disclosure provisions give different levels of privacy protection based on whether the e-mail is held with an electronic communication service or a remote computing service and based on how long the e-mail has been in electronic storage. The government may obtain the contents of e-mails that are "in electronic storage" with an electronic communication service for 180 days or less "only pursuant to a warrant." 18 U.S.C. § 2703(a). The government has three options for obtaining communications stored with a remote computing service and communications that have been in electronic storage with an electronic service provider for more than 180 days: (1) obtain a warrant; (2) use an administrative subpoena; or (3) obtain a court order under § 2703(d). *Id.* § 2703(a), (b).

532 F.3d at 523-24 (some alterations in original).

2. Factual Background

Email was a critical form of communication among Berkeley personnel. As a consequence, Warshak had a number of email accounts with various ISPs, including an account with NuVox Communications. In October 2004, the government formally requested that NuVox prospectively preserve the contents of any emails to or from Warshak's email account. The request was made pursuant to 18 U.S.C. § 2703(f) and it instructed NuVox to preserve all future messages. NuVox acceded to the government's request and began preserving copies of Warshak's incoming and outgoing emails — copies that would not have existed absent the prospective preservation request. Per the government's instructions, Warshak was not informed that his messages were being archived.

In January 2005, the government obtained a subpoena under § 2703(b) and compelled NuVox to turn over the emails that it had begun preserving the previous year. In May 2005, the government served NuVox with an ex parte court order under § 2703(d) that required NuVox to surrender any additional email messages in Warshak's account. In all, the government compelled NuVox to reveal the contents of approximately 27,000 emails. Warshak did not receive notice of either the subpoena or the order until May 2006.

3. The Fourth Amendment

The Fourth Amendment provides that "[t]he right of the people to be secure in their persons, houses, papers, and effects, against unreasonable searches and seizures, shall not be violated, and no Warrants shall issue, but upon probable cause. . . ." U.S. Const. amend. IV. The fundamental purpose of the Fourth Amendment "is to safeguard the privacy and security of individuals against arbitrary invasions by government officials." Camara v. Mun. Ct., 387 U.S. 523, 528 (1967); see Skinner v. Ry. Labor Execs.' Ass'n, 489 U.S. 602, 613-14 (1989) ("The [Fourth] Amendment guarantees the privacy, dignity, and security of persons against certain arbitrary and invasive acts by officers of the Government or those acting at their direction.").

Not all government actions are invasive enough to implicate the Fourth Amendment. "The Fourth Amendment's protections hinge on the occurrence of a 'search,' a legal term of art whose history is riddled with complexity." Widgren v. Maple Grove Twp., 429 F.3d 575, 578 (6th Cir. 2005). A "search" occurs when the government infringes upon "an expectation of privacy that society is prepared to consider reasonable." United States v. Jacobsen, 466 U.S. 109, 113 (1984). This standard breaks down into two discrete inquiries: "first, has the [target of the investigation] manifested a subjective expectation of privacy in the object of the challenged search? Second, is society willing to recognize that expectation as reasonable?" California v. Ciraolo, 476 U.S. 207, 211 (1986) (citing Smith v. Maryland, 442 U.S. 735, 740 (1979)).

Turning first to the subjective component of the test, we find that Warshak plainly manifested an expectation that his emails would be shielded from outside scrutiny. As he notes in his brief, his "entire business and personal life was contained within the . . . emails seized." Appellant's Br. at 39-40. Given the often sensitive and sometimes damning substance of his emails, we think it highly unlikely that Warshak expected them to be made public, for people seldom unfurl their dirty laundry in plain view. See, e.g., United States v. Maxwell, 45 M.J. 406, 417 (C.A.A.F.1996) ("[T]he tenor and content of e-mail conversations between appellant and his correspondent, 'Launchboy,' reveal a[n] . . . expectation that the conversations were private."). Therefore, we conclude that Warshak had a subjective expectation of privacy in the contents of his emails.

The next question is whether society is prepared to recognize that expectation as reasonable. See *Smith,* 442 U.S. at 740. This question is one of grave import and enduring consequence, given the prominent role that email has assumed in modern communication. Cf. *Katz,* 389 U.S. at 352 (suggesting that the Constitution must be read to account for "the vital role that the public telephone has come to play in private communication"). Since the advent of email, the telephone call and the letter have waned in importance, and an explosion of Internet-based communication has taken place. People are now able to send sensitive and intimate information, instantaneously, to friends, family, and colleagues half a world away. Lovers exchange sweet nothings, and businessmen swap ambitious plans, all with the click of a mouse button. Commerce has also taken hold in email. Online purchases are often documented in email accounts, and email is frequently used to remind patients and clients of imminent appointments. In short, "account" is an apt word for the conglomeration of stored messages that comprises an email account, as it provides an account of its owner's life. By obtaining access to someone's email, government agents gain the ability to peer deeply into his activities. Much hinges, therefore, on whether the government is permitted to request that a commercial ISP turn over the contents of a subscriber's emails without triggering the machinery of the Fourth Amendment.

In confronting this question, we take note of two bedrock principles. First, the very fact that information is being passed through a communications network is a paramount Fourth Amendment consideration. See ibid.; United States v. U.S. Dist. Court, 407 U.S. 297, 313 (1972) ("[T]he broad and unsuspected governmental incursions into conversational privacy which electronic surveillance entails necessitate the application of Fourth Amendment safeguards."). Second, the Fourth Amendment must keep pace with the inexorable march of technological progress, or its guarantees will wither and perish. See Kyllo v. United States, 533 U.S.

27, 34 (2001) (noting that evolving technology must not be permitted to "erode the privacy guaranteed by the Fourth Amendment"); see also Orin S. Kerr, Applying the Fourth Amendment to the Internet: A General Approach, 62 Stan. L. Rev. 1005, 1007 (2010) (arguing that "the differences between the facts of physical space and the facts of the Internet require courts to identify new Fourth Amendment distinctions to maintain the function of Fourth Amendment rules in an online environment").

With those principles in mind, we begin our analysis by considering the manner in which the Fourth Amendment protects traditional forms of communication. In *Katz*, the Supreme Court was asked to determine how the Fourth Amendment applied in the context of the telephone. There, government agents had affixed an electronic listening device to the exterior of a public phone booth, and had used the device to intercept and record several phone conversations. See 389 U.S. at 348. The Supreme Court held that this constituted a search under the Fourth Amendment, see id. at 353, notwithstanding the fact that the telephone company had the capacity to monitor and record the calls, see *Smith*, 442 U.S. at 746-47 (Stewart, J., dissenting). In the eyes of the Court, the caller was "surely entitled to assume that the words he utter[ed] into the mouthpiece w[ould] not be broadcast to the world." *Katz*, 389 U.S. at 352. The Court's holding in *Katz* has since come to stand for the broad proposition that, in many contexts, the government infringes a reasonable expectation of privacy when it surreptitiously intercepts a telephone call through electronic means. *Smith*, 442 U.S. at 746 (Stewart, J., dissenting) ("[S]ince *Katz*, it has been abundantly clear that telephone conversations are fully protected by the Fourth and Fourteenth Amendments.").

Letters receive similar protection. See *Jacobsen*, 466 U.S. at 114 ("Letters and other sealed packages are in the general class of effects in which the public at large has a legitimate expectation of privacy[.]"); Ex Parte Jackson, 96 U.S. 727, 733 (1877). While a letter is in the mail, the police may not intercept it and examine its contents unless they first obtain a warrant based on probable cause. Ibid. This is true despite the fact that sealed letters are handed over to perhaps dozens of mail carriers, any one of whom could tear open the thin paper envelopes that separate the private words from the world outside. Put another way, trusting a letter to an intermediary does not necessarily defeat a reasonable expectation that the letter will remain private. See *Katz*, 389 U.S. at 351 ("[W]hat [a person] seeks to preserve as private, even in an area accessible to the public, may be constitutionally protected.").

Given the fundamental similarities between email and traditional forms of communication, it would defy common sense to afford emails lesser Fourth Amendment protection. See Patricia L. Bellia & Susan Freiwald, Fourth Amendment Protection for Stored E-Mail, 2008 U. Chi. Legal F. 121, 135 (2008) (recognizing the need to "eliminate the strangely disparate treatment of mailed and telephonic communications on the one hand and electronic communications on the other"); City of Ontario v. Quon, ___ U.S. ___, 130 S. Ct. 2619, 2631 (2010) (implying that "a search of [an individual's] personal e-mail account" would be just as intrusive as "a wiretap on his home phone line"); United States v. Forrester, 512 F.3d 500, 511 (9th Cir. 2008) (holding that "[t]he privacy interests in [mail and email] are identical"). Email is the technological scion of tangible mail, and it plays an indispensable part in the Information Age. Over the last decade, email has become "so pervasive that some persons may consider [it] to be [an] essential means or necessary instrument[ ] for self-expression, even self-identification." *Quon*, 130 S. Ct. at 2630. It follows that email requires strong protection under the Fourth Amendment; otherwise, the Fourth Amendment would prove an ineffective guardian of private communication, an essential purpose it has long been recognized to serve. See *U.S. Dist. Court*, 407 U.S. at 313. As some forms of communication begin to diminish, the Fourth Amendment must recognize and protect nascent ones that arise.

If we accept that an email is analogous to a letter or a phone call, it is manifest that agents of the government cannot compel a commercial ISP to turn over the contents of an email without triggering the Fourth Amendment. An ISP is the intermediary that makes email communication possible. Emails must pass through an ISP's servers to reach their intended recipient. Thus, the ISP is the functional equivalent of a post office or a telephone company. As we have discussed above, the police may not storm the post office and intercept a letter, and they are likewise forbidden from using the phone system to make a clandestine recording of a telephone call—unless they get a warrant, that is. See *Jacobsen*, 466 U.S. at 114. It only stands to reason that, if government agents compel an ISP to surrender the contents of a subscriber's emails, those agents have thereby conducted a Fourth Amendment search, which necessitates compliance with the warrant requirement absent some exception.

In *Warshak I*, [490 F.3d 455 (6th Cir. 2007)], the government argued that this conclusion was improper, pointing to the fact that NuVox contractually reserved the right to access Warshak's emails for certain purposes. While we acknowledge that a subscriber agreement might, in some cases, be sweeping enough to defeat a reasonable expectation of privacy in the contents of an email account, we doubt that will be the case in most situations, and it is certainly not the case here.

As an initial matter, it must be observed that the mere *ability* of a third-party intermediary to access the contents of a communication cannot be sufficient to extinguish a reasonable expectation of privacy. In *Katz*, the Supreme Court found it reasonable to expect privacy during a telephone call despite the ability of an operator to listen in. See *Smith*, 442 U.S. at 746-47 (Stewart, J., dissenting). Similarly, the ability of a rogue mail handler to rip open a letter does not make it unreasonable to assume that sealed mail will remain private on its journey across the country. Therefore, the threat or possibility of access is not decisive when it comes to the reasonableness of an expectation of privacy.

Nor is the *right* of access. As the Electronic Frontier Foundation points out in its amicus brief, at the time *Katz* was decided, telephone companies had a right to monitor calls in certain situations. Specifically, telephone companies could listen in when reasonably necessary to "protect themselves and their properties against the improper and illegal use of their facilities." Bubis v. United States, 384 F.2d 643, 648 (9th Cir.1967). In this case, the NuVox subscriber agreement tracks that language, indicating that "NuVox *may* access and use individual Subscriber information in the operation of the Service and as necessary to protect the Service." Acceptable Use Policy, *available at* http://business.windstream.com/Legal/acceptableUse.htm (last visited Aug. 12, 2010). Thus, under *Katz*, the degree of access granted to NuVox does not diminish the reasonableness of Warshak's trust in the privacy of his emails.

Our conclusion finds additional support in the application of Fourth Amendment doctrine to rented space. Hotel guests, for example, have a reasonable expectation of privacy in their rooms. See United States v. Allen, 106 F.3d 695, 699 (6th Cir. 1997). This is so even though maids routinely enter hotel rooms to replace the towels and tidy the furniture. Similarly, tenants have a legitimate expectation of privacy in their apartments. See United States v. Washington, 573 F.3d 279, 284 (6th Cir. 2009). That expectation persists, regardless of the incursions of handymen to fix leaky faucets. Consequently, we are convinced that some degree of routine access is hardly dispositive with respect to the privacy question.

Again, however, we are unwilling to hold that a subscriber agreement will *never* be broad enough to snuff out a reasonable expectation of privacy. As the panel noted in *Warshak I*, if the ISP expresses an intention to "audit, inspect, and monitor" its subscriber's emails, that might be enough to render an expectation of privacy unreasonable. See 490 F.3d at 472-73 (quoting United States v. Simons, 206 F.3d 392, 398 (4th Cir. 2000)). But where, as here, there is no such statement, the ISP's "control over the [emails] and ability to access them under certain limited circumstances will not be enough to overcome an expectation of privacy." Id. at 473.

We recognize that our conclusion may be attacked in light of the Supreme Court's decision in United States v. Miller, 425 U.S. 435 (1976). In *Miller,* the Supreme Court held that a bank depositor does not have a reasonable expectation of privacy in the contents of bank records, checks, and deposit slips. The Court's holding in *Miller* was based on the fact that bank documents, "including financial statements and deposit slips, contain only information voluntarily conveyed to the banks and exposed to their employees in the ordinary course of business." The Court noted,

> The depositor takes the risk, in revealing his affairs to another, that the information will be conveyed by that person to the Government. . . . [T]he Fourth Amendment does not prohibit the obtaining of information revealed to a third party and conveyed by him to Government authorities, even if the information is revealed on the assumption that it will be used only for a limited purpose and the confidence placed in the third party will not be betrayed.

Id. at 443 (citations omitted).

But *Miller* is distinguishable. First, *Miller* involved simple business records, as opposed to the potentially unlimited variety of "confidential communications" at issue here. Second, the bank depositor in *Miller* conveyed information to the bank so that the bank could put the information to use "in the ordinary course of business." By contrast, Warshak received his emails through NuVox. NuVox was an *intermediary,* not the intended recipient of the emails. See Bellia & Freiwald, Stored E-Mail, 2008 U. Chi. Legal F. at 165 ("[W]e view the best analogy for this scenario as the cases in which a third party carries, transports, or stores property for another. In these cases, as in the stored e-mail case, the customer grants access to the ISP because it is essential to the customer's interests."). Thus, *Miller* is not controlling.

Accordingly, we hold that a subscriber enjoys a reasonable expectation of privacy in the contents of emails "that are stored with, or sent or received through, a commercial ISP." *Warshak I,* 490 F.3d at 473; see *Forrester,* 512 F.3d at 511 (suggesting that "[t]he contents [of email messages] may deserve Fourth Amendment protection"). The government may not compel a commercial ISP to turn over the contents of a subscriber's emails without first obtaining a warrant based on probable cause. Therefore, because they did not obtain a warrant, the government agents violated the Fourth Amendment when they obtained the contents of Warshak's emails. Moreover, to the extent that the SCA purports to permit the government to obtain such emails warrantlessly, the SCA is unconstitutional.

4. Good-Faith Reliance

Even though the government's search of Warshak's emails violated the Fourth Amendment, the emails are not subject to the exclusionary remedy if the officers relied in good faith on the SCA to obtain them. See [Illinois v.] Krull, 480 U.S. [340, 349-50 (1987)], at 349-50, In *Krull*, the Supreme Court noted that the exclusionary rule's purpose of deterring law enforcement officers from engaging in unconstitutional conduct would not be furthered by holding officers accountable for mistakes of the legislature. Thus, even if a statute is later found to be unconstitutional, an officer "cannot be expected to question the judgment of the legislature." Ibid. However, an officer cannot "be said to have acted in good-faith reliance upon a statute if its provisions are such that a reasonable officer should have known that the statute was unconstitutional." Id. at 355.

Naturally, Warshak argues that the provisions of the SCA at issue in this case were plainly unconstitutional. He argues that any reasonable law enforcement officer would have understood that a warrant based on probable cause would be required to compel the production of private emails. In making this argument, he leans heavily on *Warshak I*, which opined that the SCA permits agents to engage in searches "that clearly do not comport with the Fourth Amendment." 490 F.3d at 477.

However, we disagree that the SCA is so conspicuously unconstitutional as to preclude good-faith reliance. As we noted in *Warshak II*, "[t]he Stored Communications Act has been in existence since 1986 and to our knowledge has not been the subject of any successful Fourth Amendment challenges, in any context, whether to §2703(d) or to any other provision." 532 F.3d at 531. Furthermore, given the complicated thicket of issues that we were required to navigate when passing on the constitutionality of the SCA, it was not plain or obvious that the SCA was unconstitutional, and it was therefore reasonable for the government to rely upon the SCA in seeking to obtain the contents of Warshak's emails.

But the good-faith reliance inquiry does not end with the facial validity of the statute at issue. In *Krull*, the Supreme Court hinted that the good-faith exception does not apply if the government acted "outside the scope of the statute" on which it purported to rely. 480 U.S. at 360 n. 17. It should be noted that this portion of the *Krull* Court's opinion was merely dicta, and it appears that we have yet to pass on the question. However, it seems evident that an officer's failure to adhere to the boundaries of a given statute should preclude him from relying upon it in the face of a constitutional challenge. Once the officer steps outside the scope of an unconstitutional statute, the mistake is no longer the legislature's, but the officer's. Therefore, use of the exclusionary rule is once again efficacious in deterring officers from engaging in conduct that violates the Constitution.

Warshak argues that the government violated several provisions of the SCA and should therefore be precluded from arguing good-faith reliance. First, Warshak argues that the government violated the SCA's notice provisions. Under § 2703(b)(1)(B), the government must provide notice to an account holder if it seeks to compel the disclosure of his emails through either a § 2703(b) subpoena or a § 2703(d) order. However, § 2705 permits the government to delay notification in certain situations. The initial period of delay is 90 days, but the government may seek to extend that period in 90-day increments. In this case, the government issued both a § 2703(b) subpoena and a § 2703(d) order to NuVox, seeking disclosure of Warshak's emails. At the time, the government made the requisite showing that notice should be delayed. However, the government did not seek to renew the period of delay. In all, the government failed to inform Warshak of either the subpoena or the order for over a year.

Conceding that it violated the notice provisions, the government argues that such violations are irrelevant to the issue of whether it reasonably relied on the SCA in *obtaining* the contents of Warshak's emails. We agree. As the government notes, the violations occurred *after* the emails had been obtained. Thus, the mistakes at issue had no bearing on the constitutional violations. Because the exclusionary rule was designed to deter constitutional violations, we decline to invoke it in this situation.

But Warshak does not hang his hat exclusively on the government's violations of the SCA's notice provisions. He also argues that the government exceeded its authority under another SCA provision— § 2703(f)— by requesting NuVox to engage in *prospective* preservation of his future emails. Under § 2703(f), "[a] provider of wire or electronic communication services or a remote computing service, upon the request of a governmental entity, shall take all necessary steps to *preserve* records and other evidence *in its possession* pending the issuance of a court order or other process." 18 U.S.C. § 2703(f) (emphasis added). Warshak argues that this statute permits only *retrospective* preservation—in other words, preservation of emails already in existence. He notes that the

Department of Justice ("DOJ") generally agrees with his construction of the statute, pointing to the DOJ's own computer-surveillance manual, which states: "[Section] 2703(f) letters should not be used prospectively to order providers to preserve records not yet created. If agents want providers to record information about future electronic communications, they should comply with the [Wiretap Act and the Pen/Trap statute]."

Ultimately, however, this statutory violation, whether it occurred or not, is irrelevant to the issue of good-faith reliance. The question here is whether the government relied in good faith on § 2703(b) and § 2703(d) to *obtain* copies of Warshak's emails. True, the government might not have been able to gain access to the emails without the prospective preservation request, as it was NuVox's practice to delete all emails once they were downloaded to the account holder's computer. Thus, in a sense, the government's use of § 2703(f) was a but-for cause of the constitutional violation. But the actual violation at issue was obtaining the emails, and the government did not rely on § 2703(f) specifically to do that. Instead, the government relied on § 2703(b) and § 2703(d). The proper inquiry, therefore, is whether the government violated either of *those* provisions, and the preservation request is of no consequence to that inquiry.

Warshak's next argument is that the government violated § 2703(d) by failing to provide any particularized factual basis when seeking an order for disclosure. Under § 2703(d), such an order "shall issue only if the governmental entity offers specific and articulable facts showing that there are reasonable grounds to believe that the contents of a wire or electronic communication . . . are relevant and material to an ongoing criminal investigation."

To the extent that he is arguing that the government's application was insufficient, Warshak is wrong. The government's application indicated that it was "investigating a complex, large-scale mail and wire fraud operation based in Cincinnati, Ohio." The application also indicated that "interviews of current and former employees of the target company suggest that electronic mail is a vital communication tool that has been used to perpetuate the fraudulent conduct." Additionally, the application observed that "various sources [have verified] that NuVox provides electronic communications services to certain individual(s) [under] investigation." In light of these statements, it is clear that the application was, in fact, supported by specific and articulable facts, especially given the diminished standard that applies to § 2703(d) applications. See United States v. Perrine, 518 F.3d 1196, 1202 (10th Cir. 2008) (noting that "the 'specific and articulable facts' standard derives from the Supreme Court's decision in *Terry*"); *Warshak I*, 490 F.3d at 463 ("The parties agree that the standard of proof for a court order — 'specific and articulable facts showing that there are reasonable grounds to believe that the contents . . . or records . . . are relevant and material to an ongoing criminal investigation' — falls short of probable cause.").

Finally, Warshak argues that a finding of good-faith reliance is improper because the government presented the magistrate with an erroneous definition of the term "electronic storage." As noted above, if an email is in electronic storage for less than 180 days, the government may not compel its disclosure without a warrant. 18 U.S.C. § 2703(a). In applying for the subpoena and the order that eventually resulted in the disclosure of Warshak's NuVox emails, the government suggested to the magistrate that an email is not in electronic storage if it has already been "accessed, viewed, or downloaded." Warshak argues that this definition of electronic storage does not comport with the Ninth Circuit's decision in Theofel v. Farey-Jones, 359 F.3d 1066, 1071 (9th Cir. 2004), which held that "prior access is irrelevant to whether the [emails] at issue were in electronic storage." Warshak further argues that, because the government failed to mention the Ninth Circuit's definition, it "usurped the court's function to determine whether an email . . . [is] in 'electronic storage[.]'" Appellant's Br. at 38.

As an initial matter, it is manifest that the decisions of the Ninth Circuit are not binding on courts in this circuit. It therefore cannot be said that the government somehow violated § 2703 by failing to cite an out-of-circuit decision that it thought to be wrongly decided. Incidentally, the government is not alone in thinking that the Ninth Circuit's definition of electronic storage is incorrect. One commentator has noted that "*Theofel* is quite implausible and hard to square with the statutory test." Kerr, A User's Guide to the Stored Communications Act, 72 Geo. Wash. L. Rev. at 1217; see also United States v. Weaver, 636 F. Supp. 2d 769, 773 (C.D. Ill. 2009) ("Previously opened emails stored by Microsoft for Hotmail users are not in electronic storage, and the Government can obtain copies of such emails using a trial subpoena.").

Furthermore, it does a disservice to the magistrate judge to suggest that the government usurped the role of the court. The government's application did include a proposed definition of the term "electronic storage." That does not mean, however, that the magistrate judge unhesitatingly received that definition, and, as the government notes, the magistrate "presumably [had] the opportunity to consider and review relevant precedent." Appellee's Br. at 117.

Consequently, we find that, although the government violated the Fourth Amendment, the exclusionary rule does not apply, as the government relied in good faith on § 2703(b) and § 2703(d) to access the contents of Warshak's emails. . . .

[JUDGE KEITH's concurring opinion is omitted.]

NOTES AND QUESTIONS

1. Is *Warshak*'s Fourth Amendment analysis as obvious as the panel seems to think? Remember that as a statutory matter, real-time interception of an individual's email traffic by the government requires compliance with Title III, so that a warrant must generally be obtained, and on multiple probable cause showings. Is it so clear that the Fourth Amendment imposes similar demands for the retrieval of emails that have sat in a user's account for a lengthy period — including years — of time? Such emails are patently not like telephone calls — which are not (generally) intended to be preserved — but rather more like retained (or perhaps discarded) documents. Suppose a traveling friend entrusts you with her clothing and a laptop for temporary storage and you produce those items to the government pursuant to a subpoena. Without more, can the government review the laptop? Test the clothing for DNA?

2. As the court states, the Department of Justice's manual on Searching and Seizing Computers and Obtaining Electronic Evidence in Criminal Investigations (2009), currently available at http://www.justice.gov/criminal/cybercrime/ssmanual/index.html, takes the position that preservation requests under the SCA cannot apply prospectively — instead, prospective preservation by the service provider requires compliance with the laws governing real-time electronic surveillance. Must the statute be interpreted in that manner? Would a prospective interpretation run afoul of the Fourth Amendment?

3. The Sixth Circuit rejects application of the Ninth Circuit's decision that accessing, viewing, or downloading an email is irrelevant to whether the email remains in electronic storage. Suppose that NuVox was located in California and the emails were preserved and disclosed from that location to an agent working on the Southern District of Ohio's Warshak investigation. What law should the agent have looked to in assessing whether the emails were in "storage" — the law of the Sixth Circuit or that of the Ninth Circuit? And how might this have affected the question whether the good-faith exception applies? Does this question suggest yet additional complexities in applying this exception? Review Davis v. United States, 131 S. Ct. 2419 (2011), included in the Fourth Amendment chapter of this Supplement, and consider what you might have advised the agent about the "then-binding circuit law."

PART FOUR

THE ADJUDICATION PROCESS

Chapter 11

The Scope of the Prosecution

A. The Right to a Speedy Trial

Insert the following note after Note 4 on page 1065:

4a. The goal of the Speedy Trial Act was to provide certainty to parties and judges about when trials were supposed to begin. But like any piece of legislation that regulates tens of thousands of cases each year, the text of the statute can't always be taken at face value. Consider United States v. Tinklenberg, 131 S. Ct. 2007 (2011). Defendant's trial was to begin long after the 70-day period had run, so he moved to dismiss the indictment. The district court concluded that once certain days were properly excluded, the trial began on day 69. On appeal, the dispute centered on the propriety of excluding nine days during which the court had considered and resolved three pretrial motions. Defendant argued that these nine days should not be excluded from the Speedy Trial calculations, because under § 3161(h)(1)(D), days are only excluded if they constitute *"delay resulting from* any pretrial motion, from the filing of the motion through the conclusion of the hearing, or other prompt disposition of such motion" (emphasis added). Defendant argued that the nine days that it took the court to resolve the three motions did not cause any delay, and thus should not be excluded, and the Court of Appeals agreed.

Although the defendant's argument seemed to be supported by the text of the Speedy Trial Act — indeed, the Supreme Court found it "linguistically reasonable" — not a single Justice agreed with this reading. Instead, said the Court, when the party files a pretrial motion, the time it takes the judge to consider and resolve a motion is automatically excluded from the Act's 70-day period, regardless whether the motion causes any delay in the pretrial process. While Justice Breyer's opinion found this to be the better reading of the statutory language (and one that had been adopted by every other appellate court to consider the questions), he also noted how administratively difficult it would be to figure out the extent to which any particular motion "caused" delay.

Given the frequency with which at least some pretrial motions are filed, this was an additional burden that the Court was unwilling to impose on the district courts.

One ironic result of the Court's reading of the Act was that the three days it took the district court to consider and deny Mr. Tinklenberg's motion to dismiss the indictment because the Speedy Trial Act was violated were now excluded from the Speedy Trial Act calculation.

Chapter 12

Discovery and Disclosure

B. Disclosure by the Government

2. The Prosecutor's Constitutional Disclosure Obligations

Insert the following notes before Note 4 on page 1157:

3a. Suppose the prosecutor has evidence that might confirm the defendant's guilt but also might exonerate the accused. Does *Brady* require the prosecutor to test the evidence? To turn the evidence over to the accused and let him test it? Or can the prosecutor refuse to disclose the evidence, on the theory that the government has no idea whether the information is favorable or unfavorable, and thus *Brady* does not come into play?

This was the situation in Connick v. Thompson, 131 S. Ct. 1350 (2011). The police recovered a blood sample at the scene of an armed robbery, and it was undisputed that the blood came from the perpetrator. But rather than test the sample against the defendant's blood, the prosecutor simply went ahead with the prosecution and obtained a conviction, never disclosing the sample to the defense, and not telling the defense that it knew the perpetrator's blood type (the prosecution claimed that it did not knew Thompson's blood type). Years later the defense found the report that revealed the perpetrator's blood type, which proved the defendant's innocence. The prosecutor conceded the *Brady* violation, and defendant successfully sued under § 1983. A divided Supreme Court ruled, however, that the defendant could not sustain a § 1983 claim against the District Attorney under a "failure to train" theory.

Because the District Attorney had conceded the *Brady* violation, the majority opinion did not analyze whether the prosecution's ignorance about the character of the blood evidence (was it favorable or unfavorable to the accused?) was in fact a *Brady* violation. But in his concurring opinion, Justice Scalia was not so reticent — he concluded "[t]here was probably no *Brady* violation at all" in the case, and certainly not one that the Supreme Court had ever recognized.

Can this be right? Can the prosecutor really just sit on evidence that might prove the defendant's innocence, not testing it, and not even telling the defense of its existence? If the prosecutor is so sure that defendant is guilty, what is she afraid of? On the other hand, is there anything in *Brady* that covers this case, assuming that the prosecutor is truly ignorant of what the evidence would show, if tested? How would you articulate what a prosecutor is obligated to do in a case like *Thompson*?

3b. Although prosecutors make the threshold decision whether evidence constitutes *Brady* material, the Court recently reaffirmed that the State must be fair-minded about how it evaluates conflicting evidence. In Smith v. Cain, 132 S. Ct. 627 (2012), the lone witness to a multiple murder told the police both at the scene and several days later that he could not identify the shooter. The witness subsequently changed his story and positively identified Smith as the killer, and testified to that effect at trial. The prosecutor did not, however, disclose the witness's earlier, inconsistent statements. Noting that the eyewitness testimony "was the *only* evidence linking Smith to the crime," the Supreme Court, 8-1, found a *Brady* violation in the withholding of the earlier statements and reversed the convictions. Chief Justice Roberts's majority opinion acknowledged that the witness's reluctance to identify the shooter right away *might* have been caused by a fear of retaliation by the shooter, as the State claimed, but found the State's argument on this point irrelevant. The proper course, the Court said, was for the government to disclose the conflicting information, let each side argue about the reason for the inconsistency, and let the jury sort things out.

Smith looks like an easy case, and the Court certainly treated it as such — the entire majority opinion is fewer than 1,000 words, and during the oral argument, the State's arguments for non-disclosure were so strained that Justice Kagan asked the Assistant District Attorney "did your office ever consider just confessing error in this case?" Given this, and given that the Court's opinion broke no new legal ground, why do you think the Court agreed to hear this case? Was it simply a belief that Mr. Smith was wrongly convicted? If so, consider Justice Scalia's dissent in Kyles v. Whitley, the case in the main volume at page 1141. In a part of the dissent not reproduced there, Scalia writes:

> The greatest puzzle of [the *Kyles*] decision is what could have caused *this* capital case to be singled out for favored treatment [by receiving Supreme Court review]. Perhaps it has been randomly selected as a symbol, to reassure America that the United States Supreme Court is reviewing capital convictions to make sure no factual error has been made. If so, it is a false symbol, for we assuredly do not do that. . . . The reality is that responsibility for

factual accuracy, in capital cases as in other cases, rests elsewhere — with trial judges and juries, state appellate courts, and the lower federal courts; we do nothing but encourage foolish reliance to pretend otherwise.

Although *Smith* was not a capital case, does Justice Scalia's observation explain the Court's interest in the case? Or is there something else at work? Note that the District Attorney's Office that prosecuted Smith is the same one that violated *Brady* in Kyles v. Whitley, and committed the *Brady* violations that led to the civil suit in Connick v. Thompson, supra. Should the Supreme Court scrutinize cases more closely that come from State prosecutor's offices that have committed multiple violations? Can the Court realistically do this?

Chapter 13

Guilty Pleas and Plea Bargaining

A. Guilty Pleas as a Substitute for Trials

1. The Plea Process

Replace the word "admissible" on the fourth-to-last line of page 1169 with the word "inadmissible".

C. The Role of Defense Counsel

SPECIAL EDITOR'S NOTE: The issue of ineffective assistance of counsel in the context of guilty pleas and plea bargaining has taken on much greater significance because of the Supreme Court's 2012 decisions in Missouri v. Frye and Lafler v. Cooper. For this reason, we assume that many teachers will want to cover this material, either as part of Chapter 3 (Right to Counsel), or as part of Chapter 13 (Guilty Pleas and Plea Bargaining). In this Supplement, we have included Missouri v. Frye and Lafler v. Cooper as main cases in Chapter 3. Teachers who want to cover the new cases as part of Chapter 3 may also want to incorporate the main case of Hill v. Lockhart, which now appears in Chapter 13, at pages 1251-1254. The following alternative instructions are meant for teachers who want to cover the new cases as part of Chapter 13.

Delete Note 4 at page 1256, and the main case of Williams v. Jones at pages 1256-1264. Delete the first sentence of Note 1 at page 1264, and renumber Notes 1-3 at pages 1264-1266 as Notes 4-6. After the end of the newly renumbered Note 6 at page 1266, insert the new material that appears in this Supplement in Chapter 3 at pages 8-38, including the new main cases of Missouri v. Frye and Lafler v. Cooper.

Chapter 14

The Jury and the Criminal Trial

C. The Defendant's Rights to Be Present, to Testify, to Obtain Evidence, to Confront His Accusers, and to Present a Defense at Trial

NOTES ON THE CONFRONTATION CLAUSE

Insert the following parenthetical phrase at the end of the first paragraph after this heading on page 1339, just before Note 1:

(this third possibility is discussed beginning at page 1369, Note 12).

Add the following material to the end of Note 7 on page 1364:

In Bullcoming v. New Mexico, 131 S. Ct. 2705 (2011), the Court took up the following issue: "[W]hether the Confrontation Clause permits the prosecution to introduce a forensic laboratory report containing a testimonial certification — made for the purpose of proving a particular fact — through the in-court testimony of a scientist who did not sign the certification or perform or observe the test reported in the certification." In a 5-4 decision, the Court held that the answer is "emphatically 'no'": "The accused's right is to be confronted with the analyst who made the certification, unless that analyst is unavailable at trial, and the accused had an opportunity, pretrial, to cross-examine that particular scientist." Id. at ___.

Justice Ginsburg, joined in full by Justice Scalia and in large part by Justices Thomas, Sotomayor, and Kagan, explained for the majority why the appearance in court of forensic scientist Gerasimos Razatos could not substitute for the appearance of Curtis Caylor, the analyst who had actually conducted the blood-alcohol test (BAC) in question (and who happened to be on unpaid leave at the time of Bullcoming's trial):

[T]he New Mexico Supreme Court believed that Razatos could substitute for Caylor because Razatos "qualified as an expert witness with respect to the gas chromatograph machine and the SLD's laboratory procedures." But surrogate testimony of the kind Razatos was equipped to give could not convey what Caylor knew or observed about the events his certification concerned, i.e., the particular test and testing process he employed. Nor could such surrogate testimony expose any lapses or lies on the certifying analyst's part. Significant here, Razatos had no knowledge of the reason why Caylor had been placed on unpaid leave. With Caylor on the stand, Bullcoming's counsel could have asked questions designed to reveal whether incompetence, evasiveness, or dishonesty accounted for Caylor's removal from his work station. Notable in this regard, the State never asserted that Caylor was "unavailable"; the prosecution conveyed only that Caylor was on uncompensated leave. Nor did the State assert that Razatos had any "independent opinion" concerning Bullcoming's BAC. See Brief for Respondent 58, n. 15. In this light, Caylor's live testimony could hardly be typed "a hollow formality."

More fundamentally, as this Court stressed in *Crawford*, "[t]he text of the Sixth Amendment does not suggest any open-ended exceptions from the confrontation requirement to be developed by the courts." 541 U.S., at 54. Nor is it "the role of courts to extrapolate from the words of the [Confrontation Clause] to the values behind it, and then to enforce its guarantees only to the extent they serve (in the courts' views) those underlying values." Giles v. California, 554 U.S. 353, 375 (2008). Accordingly, the Clause does not tolerate dispensing with confrontation simply because the court believes that questioning one witness about another's testimonial statements provides a fair enough opportunity for cross-examination. . . .

In short, when the State elected to introduce Caylor's certification, Caylor became a witness Bullcoming had the right to confront. Our precedent cannot sensibly be read any other way. See *Melendez-Diaz*, 557 U.S., at __ (Kennedy, J., dissenting) (Court's holding means "the . . . analyst who must testify is the person who signed the certificate").

Bullcoming, 131 S. Ct., at __. Another portion of Justice Ginsburg's majority opinion concluded that the lab report in question was "testimonial":

> In all material respects, the laboratory report in this case resembles those in *Melendez-Diaz*. Here, as in *Melendez-Diaz*, a law-enforcement officer provided seized evidence to a state laboratory required by law to assist in police investigations, N.M. Stat. Ann. § 29-3-4 (2004). Like the analysts in *Melendez-Diaz*, analyst Caylor tested the evidence and prepared a certificate concerning the result of his analysis. Like the *Melendez-Diaz* certificates, Caylor's certificate is "formalized" in a signed document, *Davis*, 547 U.S., at 837, n. 2 (opinion of Thomas, J.), headed a "report." Noteworthy as well, the [Scientific Laboratory Division] report form contains a legend referring to municipal and magistrate courts' rules that provide for the admission of certified blood-alcohol analyses.

In sum, the formalities attending the "report of blood alcohol analysis" are more than adequate to qualify Caylor's assertions as testimonial. The absence of notarization does not remove his certification from Confrontation Clause governance. . . .

Bullcoming, 131 S. Ct., at ___.

In a separate concurring opinion, Justice Sotomayor identified four issues *not* addressed or resolved in *Bullcoming*:

First, this is not a case in which the State suggested an alternate purpose, much less an alternate *primary* purpose, for the BAC report. For example, the State has not claimed that the report was necessary to provide Bullcoming with medical treatment. . . .

Second, this is not a case in which the person testifying is a supervisor, reviewer, or someone else with a personal, albeit limited, connection to the scientific test at issue. Razatos conceded on cross-examination that he played no role in producing the BAC report and did not observe any portion of Curtis Caylor's conduct of the testing. The court below also recognized Razatos' total lack of connection to the test at issue. 226 P.3d, at 6. It would be a different case if, for example, a supervisor who observed an analyst conducting a test testified about the results or a report about such results. We need not address what degree of involvement is sufficient because here Razatos had no involvement whatsoever in the relevant test and report.

Third, this is not a case in which an expert witness was asked for his independent opinion about underlying testimonial reports that were not themselves admitted into evidence. . . . We would face a different question if asked to determine the constitutionality of allowing an expert witness to discuss others' testimonial statements if the testimonial statements were not themselves admitted as evidence.

Finally, this is not a case in which the State introduced only machine-generated results, such as a printout from a gas chromatograph. . . . Thus, we do not decide whether, as the New Mexico Supreme Court suggests, 226 P.3d, at 10, a State could introduce (assuming an adequate chain of custody foundation) raw data generated by a machine in conjunction with the testimony of an expert witness.

This case does not present, and thus the Court's opinion does not address, any of these factual scenarios.

Bullcoming, 131 S. Ct., ___ (Sotomayor, J., concurring).

In dissent, Justice Kennedy, joined by Chief Justice Roberts, Justice Breyer, and Justice Alito, bemoaned the Court's decision:

Whether or not one agrees with the reasoning and the result in *Melendez-Diaz*, the Court today takes the new and serious misstep of extending that holding to instances like this one. . . .

. . . From 2008 to 2010, subpoenas requiring New Mexico analysts to testify in impaired-driving cases rose 71%, to 1,600 — or 8 or 9 every workday. In a State that is the Nation's fifth largest by area and that employs just 10 total analysts, each analyst in blood alcohol cases recently received 200 subpoenas per year. The analysts now must travel great distances on most working days. The result has been, in the laboratory's words, "chaotic." And if the defense raises an objection and the analyst is tied up in another court proceeding; or on leave; or absent; or delayed in transit; or no longer employed; or ill; or no longer living, the defense gets a windfall. As a result, good defense attorneys will object in ever-greater numbers to a prosecution failure or inability to produce laboratory analysts at trial. The concomitant increases in subpoenas will further impede the state laboratory's ability to keep pace with its obligations. Scarce state resources could be committed to other urgent needs in the criminal justice system.

Seven years after its initiation, it bears remembering that the *Crawford* approach was not preordained. This Court's missteps have produced an interpretation of the word "witness" at odds with its meaning elsewhere in the Constitution, including elsewhere in the Sixth Amendment, see Amar, Sixth Amendment First Principles, 84 Geo. L. J. 641, 647, 691-696 (1996), and at odds with the sound administration of justice. It is time to return to solid ground. A proper place to begin that return is to decline to extend *Melendez-Diaz* to bar the reliable, commonsense evidentiary framework the State sought to follow in this case.

Bullcoming, 131 S. Ct., at ___ (Kennedy, J., dissenting).

Insert the following note after Note 9 on page 1365; renumber Notes 10, 11, and 12 on pages 1365-1369 as Notes 2, 3, and 4, respectively, following the new main case of Michigan v. Bryant:

10. Or maybe we have already fallen into the abyss. As if *Crawford*, *Davis*, *Hammon*, and *Melendez-Diaz* weren't quite enough to addle the minds of lower-court judges and litigants across the land, the Supreme Court made matters even worse when it reviewed a Michigan case involving a classic "dying declaration" by a murder victim identifying his killer. Recall that, in footnote 6 of *Crawford*, the Court suggested that "dying declarations" might be a "sui generis" exception from the new regime altogether, on purely historical grounds, see *Crawford*, supra at page 1344. But the Michigan murder case couldn't be resolved by means of the "dying declaration" exception because the state courts had failed to make a finding that the relevant victim statement really *was* a "dying declaration," and the prosecution had failed to preserve the issue. That led to the following tortured decision.

MICHIGAN v. BRYANT
Certiorari to the Supreme Court of Michigan
131 S. Ct. 1143 (2011)

JUSTICE SOTOMAYOR delivered the opinion of the Court.

At respondent Richard Bryant's trial, the court admitted statements that the victim, Anthony Covington, made to police officers who discovered him mortally wounded in a gas station parking lot. A jury convicted Bryant of, inter alia, second-degree murder. 483 Mich. 132, 137, 768 N.W.2d 65, 67-68 (2009). On appeal, the Supreme Court of Michigan held that the Sixth Amendment's Confrontation Clause, as explained in our decisions in Crawford v. Washington, 541 U.S. 36 (2004), and Davis v. Washington, 547 U.S. 813 (2006), rendered Covington's statements inadmissible testimonial hearsay, and the court reversed Bryant's conviction. 483 Mich., at 157, 768 N.W.2d, at 79. We granted the State's petition for a writ of certiorari to consider whether the Confrontation Clause barred the admission at trial of Covington's statements to the police. We hold that the circumstances of the interaction between Covington and the police objectively indicate that the "primary purpose of the interrogation" was "to enable police assistance to meet an ongoing emergency." Davis, 547 U.S., at 822. Therefore, Covington's identification and description of the shooter and the location of the shooting were not testimonial statements, and their admission at Bryant's trial did not violate the Confrontation Clause. We vacate the judgment of the Supreme Court of Michigan and remand.

I

Around 3:25 a.m. on April 29, 2001, Detroit, Michigan police officers responded to a radio dispatch indicating that a man had been shot. At the scene, they found the victim, Anthony Covington, lying on the ground next to his car in a gas station parking lot. Covington had a gunshot wound to his abdomen, appeared to be in great pain, and spoke with difficulty.

The police asked him "what had happened, who had shot him, and where the shooting had occurred." Covington stated that "Rick" shot him at around 3 a.m. He also indicated that he had a conversation with Bryant, whom he recognized based on his voice, through the back door of Bryant's house. Covington explained that when he turned to leave, he was shot through the door and then drove to the gas station, where police found him.

Covington's conversation with the police ended within 5 to 10 minutes when emergency medical services arrived. Covington was transported to a hospital and died within hours. The police left the gas station after speaking with Covington, called for backup, and traveled to Bryant's house. They did not find Bryant there but did find blood and a bullet on the back porch and an apparent bullet hole in the back door. Police also found Covington's wallet and identification outside the house.

At trial, which occurred prior to our decisions in *Crawford*, 541 U.S. 36, and *Davis*, 547 U.S. 813, the police officers who spoke with Covington at the gas station testified about what Covington had told them. The jury returned a guilty verdict on charges of second-degree murder, being a felon in possession of a firearm, and possession of a firearm during the commission of a felony.

Bryant appealed, and the Michigan Court of Appeals affirmed his conviction. No. 247039 (Aug. 24, 2004) (per curiam). Bryant then appealed to the Supreme Court of Michigan, arguing that the trial court erred in admitting Covington's statements to the police. The Supreme Court of Michigan eventually remanded the case to the Court of Appeals for reconsideration in light of our 2006 decision in *Davis*. 477 Mich. 902, 722 N.W.2d 797 (2006). On remand, the Court of Appeals again affirmed, holding that Covington's statements were properly admitted because they were not testimonial. No. 247039 (Mar. 6, 2007) (per curiam). Bryant again appealed to the Supreme Court of Michigan, which reversed his conviction. 483 Mich. 132, 768 N.W.2d 65.

Before the Supreme Court of Michigan, Bryant argued that Covington's statements to the police were testimonial under *Crawford* and *Davis* and were therefore inadmissible. The State, on the other hand, argued that the statements were admissible as "excited utterances" under the Michigan Rules of Evidence. There was no dispute that Covington was unavailable at trial and Bryant had no prior opportunity to cross-examine him. The court therefore assessed whether Covington's statements to the police identifying and describing the shooter and the time and location of the shooting were testimonial hearsay for purposes of the Confrontation Clause. The court concluded that the circumstances "clearly indicate that the 'primary purpose' of the questioning was to establish the facts of an event that had *already* occurred; the 'primary purpose' was not to enable police assistance to meet an ongoing emergency." Id., at 143, 768 N.W.2d, at 71. ... Noting that the officers' actions did not suggest that they perceived an ongoing emergency at the gas station, the court held that there was in fact no ongoing emergency. ... Based on this analysis, the Supreme Court of Michigan held that the admission of Covington's statements constituted prejudicial plain error warranting reversal and ordered a new trial. The court did not address whether, absent a Confrontation Clause bar, the statements' admission would have been otherwise consistent with Michigan's hearsay rules or due process.[1]

. . . We granted certiorari to determine whether the Confrontation Clause barred admission of Covington's statements. 559 U.S. ___ (2010).

II

. . . *Crawford* examined the common-law history of the confrontation right. . . . In light of this history, we emphasized the word "witnesses" in the Sixth Amendment, defining it as "those who 'bear testimony.'" Id., at 51 (quoting 2 N. Webster, An American Dictionary of the English Language (1828)). . . . We noted that "[a]n accuser who makes a formal statement to government officers bears testimony in a sense that a person who makes a casual remark to an acquaintance does not." We therefore limited the Confrontation Clause's reach to testimonial statements. . . .

In 2006, the Court in Davis v. Washington and Hammon v. Indiana, 547 U.S. 813, . . . explained that when *Crawford* said that

> "'interrogations by law enforcement officers fall squarely within [the] class' of testimonial hearsay, we had immediately in mind (for that was the case before us) interrogations solely directed at establishing the facts of a past crime, in order to identify (or provide evidence to convict) the perpetrator. The product of such interrogation, whether reduced to a writing signed by the declarant or embedded in the memory (and perhaps notes) of the interrogating officer, is testimonial." *Davis*, 547 U.S., at 826.

We thus made clear in *Davis* that not all those questioned by the police are witnesses and not all "interrogations by law enforcement officers," *Crawford*, 541 U.S., at 53, are subject to the Confrontation Clause.

Davis and *Hammon* were both domestic violence cases. . . . To address the facts of both cases, we expanded upon the meaning of "testimonial" that we first employed in *Crawford* and discussed the concept of an ongoing emergency. We explained:

---

1. The Supreme Court of Michigan held that the question whether the victim's statements would have been admissible as "dying declarations" was not properly before it because at the preliminary examination, the prosecution, after first invoking both the dying declaration and excited utterance hearsay exceptions, established the factual foundation only for admission of the statements as excited utterances. The trial court ruled that the statements were admissible as excited utterances and did not address their admissibility as dying declarations. . . . We noted in *Crawford* that we "need not decide in this case whether the Sixth Amendment incorporates an exception for testimonial dying declarations." 541 U.S., at 56, n. 6. Because of the State's failure to preserve its argument with regard to dying declarations, we similarly need not decide that question here.

"Statements are nontestimonial when made in the course of police interrogation under circumstances objectively indicating that the primary purpose of
the interrogation is to enable police assistance to meet an ongoing emergency. They are testimonial when the circumstances objectively indicate that
there is no such ongoing emergency, and that the primary purpose of the
interrogation is to establish or prove past events potentially relevant to later
criminal prosecution." *Davis*, 547 U.S., at 822.

Examining the *Davis* and *Hammon* statements in light of those definitions, we held that the statements at issue in *Davis* were nontestimonial
and the statements in *Hammon* were testimonial. We distinguished the
statements in *Davis* from the testimonial statements in *Crawford* on several
grounds, including that the victim in *Davis* was "speaking about events *as
they were actually happening*, rather than 'describ[ing] past events,'" that
there was an ongoing emergency, that the "elicited statements were necessary to be able to *resolve* the present emergency," and that the statements
were not formal. 547 U.S., at 827. In *Hammon*, on the other hand, we held
that, "[i]t is entirely clear from the circumstances that the interrogation
was part of an investigation into possibly criminal past conduct." Id., at
829. There was "no emergency in progress." Ibid. . . .
    . . . The basic purpose of the Confrontation Clause was to "targe[t]" the
sort of "abuses" exemplified at the notorious treason trial of Sir Walter
Raleigh. *Crawford*, 541 U.S., at 51. Thus, the most important instances in
which the Clause restricts the introduction of out-of-court statements are
those in which state actors are involved in a formal, out-of-court interrogation of a witness to obtain evidence for trial. . . . When, as in *Davis*,
the primary purpose of an interrogation is to respond to an "ongoing
emergency," its purpose is not to create a record for trial and thus is not
within the scope of the Clause. But there may be *other* circumstances,
aside from ongoing emergencies, when a statement is not procured with
a primary purpose of creating an out-of-court substitute for trial testimony. In making the primary purpose determination, standard rules of
hearsay, designed to identify some statements as reliable, will be relevant.
Where no such primary purpose exists, the admissibility of a statement is
the concern of state and federal rules of evidence, not the Confrontation
Clause.
    Deciding this case also requires further explanation of the "ongoing
emergency" circumstance addressed in *Davis*. Because *Davis* and *Hammon*
arose in the domestic violence context, that was the situation "we had
immediately in mind (for that was the case before us)." 547 U.S., at 826.
We now face a new context: a nondomestic dispute, involving a victim
found in a public location, suffering from a fatal gunshot wound, and a

perpetrator whose location was unknown at the time the police located the victim. Thus, we confront for the first time circumstances in which the "ongoing emergency" discussed in *Davis* extends beyond an initial victim to a potential threat to the responding police and the public at large. This new context requires us to provide additional clarification with regard to what *Davis* meant by "the primary purpose of the interrogation is to enable police assistance to meet an ongoing emergency." Id., at 822.

III

To determine whether the "primary purpose" of an interrogation is "to enable police assistance to meet an ongoing emergency," *Davis*, 547 U.S., at 822, which would render the resulting statements nontestimonial, we objectively evaluate the circumstances in which the encounter occurs and the statements and actions of the parties.

A

The Michigan Supreme Court correctly understood that this inquiry is objective. 483 Mich., at 142, 768 N.W.2d, at 70. *Davis* uses the word "objective" or "objectively" no fewer than eight times in describing the relevant inquiry. See 547 U.S., at 822, 826-828, 830-831, and n. 5. . . .

An objective analysis of the circumstances of an encounter and the statements and actions of the parties to it provides the most accurate assessment of the "primary purpose of the interrogation." The circumstances in which an encounter occurs — e.g., at or near the scene of the crime versus at a police station, during an ongoing emergency or afterwards — are clearly matters of objective fact. The statements and actions of the parties must also be objectively evaluated. That is, the relevant inquiry is not the subjective or actual purpose of the individuals involved in a particular encounter, but rather the purpose that reasonable participants would have had, as ascertained from the individuals' statements and actions and the circumstances in which the encounter occurred.[7]

7. This approach is consistent with our rejection of subjective inquiries in other areas of criminal law. See, e.g., Whren v. United States, 517 U.S. 806, 813 (1996) (refusing to evaluate Fourth Amendment reasonableness subjectively in light of the officers' actual motivations); New York v. Quarles, 467 U.S. 649, 655-656, and n. 6 (1984) (holding that an officer's subjective motivation is irrelevant to determining the applicability of the public safety exception to Miranda v. Arizona, 384 U.S. 436 (1966)); Rhode Island v. Innis, 446 U.S. 291, 301-302 (1980) (holding that a police officer's subjective intent to obtain incriminatory statements is not relevant to determining whether an interrogation has occurred).

B

As our recent Confrontation Clause cases have explained, the existence of an "ongoing emergency" at the time of an encounter between an
individual and the police is among the most important circumstances
informing the "primary purpose" of an interrogation. See *Davis*, 547
U.S., at 828-830; *Crawford*, 541 U.S., at 65. The existence of an ongoing emergency is relevant to determining the primary purpose of the
interrogation because an emergency focuses the participants on something other than "prov[ing] past events potentially relevant to later
criminal prosecution."[8] *Davis*, 547 U.S., at 822. Rather, it focuses them on
"end[ing] a threatening situation." Id., at 832. Implicit in *Davis* is the idea
that because the prospect of fabrication in statements given for the
primary purpose of resolving that emergency is presumably significantly
diminished, the Confrontation Clause does not require such statements
to be subject to the crucible of cross-examination.

This logic is not unlike that justifying the excited utterance exception in
hearsay law. Statements "relating to a startling event or condition made
while the declarant was under the stress of excitement caused by the event
or condition," Fed. Rule Evid. 803(2); see also Mich. Rule Evid. 803(2)
(2010), are considered reliable because the declarant, in the excitement,
presumably cannot form a falsehood. See Idaho v. Wright, 497 U.S. 805,
820 (1990) ("The basis for the 'excited utterance' exception . . . is that
such statements are given under circumstances that eliminate the possibility of fabrication, coaching, or confabulation . . ."); 5 J. Weinstein &
M. Berger, Weinstein's Federal Evidence § 803.04[1] (J. McLaughlin ed.,
2d ed. 2010) (same); Advisory Committee's Notes on Fed. Rule Evid. 803(2),
28 U.S.C. App., p. 371 (same). An ongoing emergency has a similar effect of
focusing an individual's attention on responding to the emergency.[9]

---

8. The existence of an ongoing emergency must be objectively assessed from the perspective of the parties to the interrogation at the time, not with the benefit of hindsight. If the
information the parties knew at the time of the encounter would lead a reasonable person to
believe that there was an emergency, even if that belief was later proved incorrect, that is
sufficient for purposes of the Confrontation Clause. The emergency is relevant to the "primary purpose of the interrogation" because of the effect it has on the parties' purpose, not
because of its actual existence.

9. Many other exceptions to the hearsay rules similarly rest on the belief that certain
statements are, by their nature, made for a purpose other than use in a prosecution
and therefore should not be barred by hearsay prohibitions. See, e.g., Fed. Rule Evid.
801(d)(2)(E) (statement by a co-conspirator during and in furtherance of the conspiracy);
803(4) (Statements for Purposes of Medical Diagnosis or Treatment); 803(6) (Records of
Regularly Conducted Activity); 803(8) (Public Records and Reports); 803(9) (Records of
Vital Statistics); 803(11) (Records of Religious Organizations); 803(12) (Marriage, Baptismal,
and Similar Certificates); 803(13) (Family Records); 804(b)(3) (Statement Against Interest);
see also Melendez-Diaz v. Massachusetts, 557 U.S. ___, ___ (2009) ("Business and public

Following our precedents, the court below correctly began its analysis with the circumstances in which Covington interacted with the police. 483 Mich., at 143, 768 N.W.2d, at 71. But in doing so, the court construed *Davis* to have decided more than it did and thus employed an unduly narrow understanding of "ongoing emergency" that *Davis* does not require.

First, the Michigan Supreme Court repeatedly and incorrectly asserted that *Davis* "defined" "'ongoing emergency.'" 483 Mich., at 147, 768 N.W.2d, at 73; see also id., at 144, 768 N.W.2d, at 71-72. In fact, *Davis* did not even define the extent of the emergency in that case. The Michigan Supreme Court erroneously read *Davis* as deciding that "the statements made after the defendant stopped assaulting the victim and left the premises did *not* occur during an 'ongoing emergency.'" 483 Mich., at 150, n. 15, 768 N.W.2d, at 75, n. 15. We explicitly explained in *Davis*, however, that we were asked to review only the testimonial nature of Michelle McCottry's initial statements during the 911 call; we therefore merely *assumed* the correctness of the Washington Supreme Court's holding that admission of her other statements was harmless, without deciding whether those subsequent statements were also made for the primary purpose of resolving an ongoing emergency. 547 U.S., at 829.

Second, by assuming that *Davis* defined the outer bounds of "ongoing emergency," the Michigan Supreme Court failed to appreciate that whether an emergency exists and is ongoing is a highly context-dependent inquiry. See Brief for United States as Amicus Curiae 20. *Davis* and *Hammon* involved domestic violence, a known and identified perpetrator, and, in *Hammon*, a neutralized threat. Because *Davis* and *Hammon* were domestic violence cases, we focused only on the threat to the victims and assessed the ongoing emergency from the perspective of whether there was a continuing threat *to them.* 547 U.S., at 827, 829-830.

Domestic violence cases like *Davis* and *Hammon* often have a narrower zone of potential victims than cases involving threats to public safety. An assessment of whether an emergency that threatens the police and public is ongoing cannot narrowly focus on whether the threat solely to the first victim has been neutralized because the threat to the first responders and public may continue. See 483 Mich., at 164, 768 N.W.2d, at 82 (Corrigan, J.,

---

records are generally admissible absent confrontation not because they qualify under an exception to the hearsay rules, but because — having been created for the administration of an entity's affairs and not for the purpose of establishing or proving some fact at trial — they are not testimonial"); Giles v. California, 554 U.S., at 376 (noting in the context of domestic violence that "[s]tatements to friends and neighbors about abuse and intimidation and statements to physicians in the course of receiving treatment would be excluded, if at all, only by hearsay rules"); *Crawford*, 541 U.S., at 56 ("Most of the hearsay exceptions covered statements that by their nature were not testimonial — for example, business records or statements in furtherance of a conspiracy").

dissenting) (examining the threat to the victim, police, and the public); Brief for United States as Amicus Curiae 19-20 ("An emergency posed by an unknown shooter who remains at large does not automatically abate just because the police can provide security to his first victim.").

The Michigan Supreme Court also did not appreciate that the duration and scope of an emergency may depend in part on the type of weapon employed. The court relied on *Davis* and *Hammon*, in which the assailants used their fists, as controlling the scope of the emergency here, which involved the use of a gun. The problem with that reasoning is clear when considered in light of the assault on Amy Hammon. Hershel Hammon was armed only with his fists when he attacked his wife, so removing Amy to a separate room was sufficient to end the emergency. 547 U.S., at 830-832. If Hershel had been reported to be armed with a gun, however, separation by a single household wall might not have been sufficient to end the emergency. Id., at 819.

The Michigan Supreme Court's failure to focus on the context-dependent nature of our *Davis* decision also led it to conclude that the medical condition of a declarant is irrelevant. 483 Mich., at 149, 768 N.W.2d, at 74. . . . But *Davis* and *Hammon* did not present medical emergencies, despite some injuries to the victims. 547 U.S., at 818, 820. Thus, we have not previously considered, much less ruled out, the relevance of a victim's severe injuries to the primary purpose inquiry.

. . . The medical condition of the victim is important to the primary purpose inquiry to the extent that it sheds light on the ability of the victim to have any purpose at all in responding to police questions and on the likelihood that any purpose formed would necessarily be a testimonial one. The victim's medical state also provides important context for first responders to judge the existence and magnitude of a continuing threat to the victim, themselves, and the public.

As the Solicitor General's brief observes, Brief for United States as Amicus Curiae 20, . . . none of this suggests that an emergency is ongoing in every place or even just surrounding the victim for the entire time that the perpetrator of a violent crime is on the loose. As we recognized in *Davis*, "a conversation which begins as an interrogation to determine the need for emergency assistance" can "evolve into testimonial statements." 547 U.S., at 828 (internal quotation marks omitted). This evolution may occur if, for example, a declarant provides police with information that makes clear that what appeared to be an emergency is not or is no longer an emergency or that what appeared to be a public threat is actually a private dispute. It could also occur if a perpetrator is disarmed, surrenders, is apprehended, or, as in *Davis*, flees with little prospect of posing a threat to the public. Trial courts can determine in the first instance when any transition from nontestimonial to testimonial occurs, and exclude "the portions of any statement that have become testimonial, as they do, for example, with unduly prejudicial portions of otherwise admissible evidence." Id., at 829.

Finally, our discussion of the Michigan Supreme Court's misunderstanding of what *Davis* meant by "ongoing emergency" should not be taken to imply that the existence vel non of an ongoing emergency is dispositive of the testimonial inquiry. As *Davis* made clear, whether an ongoing emergency exists is simply one factor — albeit an important factor — that informs the ultimate inquiry regarding the "primary purpose" of an interrogation. Another factor the Michigan Supreme Court did not sufficiently account for is the importance of *informality* in an encounter between a victim and police. Formality is not the sole touchstone of our primary purpose inquiry because, although formality suggests the absence of an emergency and therefore an increased likelihood that the purpose of the interrogation is to "establish or prove past events potentially relevant to later criminal prosecution," id., at 822, informality does not necessarily indicate the presence of an emergency or the lack of testimonial intent. Cf. id., at 826 (explaining that Confrontation Clause requirements cannot "readily be evaded" by the parties deliberately keeping the written product of an interrogation informal "instead of having the declarant sign a deposition"). The court below, however, too readily dismissed the informality of the circumstances in this case in a single brief footnote and in fact seems to have suggested that the encounter in this case was formal. 483 Mich., at 150, n. 16, 768 N.W.2d, at 75, n. 16. As we explain further below, the questioning in this case occurred in an exposed, public area, prior to the arrival of emergency medical services, and in a disorganized fashion. All of those facts make this case distinguishable from the formal station-house interrogation in *Crawford*. . . .

C

In addition to the circumstances in which an encounter occurs, the statements and actions of both the declarant and interrogators provide objective evidence of the primary purpose of the interrogation. See, e.g., *Davis*, 547 U.S., at 827 ("[T]he nature of what was *asked and answered* in *Davis*, again viewed objectively, was such that the elicited statements were necessary to be able to *resolve* the present emergency, rather than simply to learn (as in *Crawford*) what had happened in the past" (first emphasis added)). . . .

... *Davis* requires a combined inquiry that accounts for both the declarant and the interrogator.[11] In many instances, the primary purpose of the interrogation will be most accurately ascertained by looking to the contents of both the questions and the answers. To give an extreme example, if the police say to a victim, "Tell us who did this to you so that we can arrest and prosecute them," the victim's response that "Rick did it," appears purely accusatory because by virtue of the phrasing of the question, the victim necessarily has prosecution in mind when she answers.

The combined approach also ameliorates problems that could arise from looking solely to one participant. Predominant among these is the problem of mixed motives on the part of both interrogators and declarants. Police officers in our society function as both first responders and criminal investigators. Their dual responsibilities may mean that they act with different motives simultaneously or in quick succession. See New York v. Quarles, 467 U.S. 649, 656 (1984) ("Undoubtedly most police officers [deciding] whether to give *Miranda* warnings in a possible emergency situation] would act out of a host of different, instinctive, and largely unverifiable motives — their own safety, the safety of others, and perhaps as well the desire to obtain incriminating evidence from the suspect"); see also *Davis*, 547 U.S., at 839 (Thomas, J., concurring in judgment in part and dissenting in part) ("In many, if not most, cases where police respond to a report of a crime, whether pursuant to a 911 call from the victim or otherwise, the purposes of an interrogation, viewed from the perspective of the police, are *both* to respond to the emergency situation *and* to gather evidence").

Victims are also likely to have mixed motives when they make statements to the police. During an ongoing emergency, a victim is most likely to want the threat to her and to other potential victims to end, but that does not necessarily mean that the victim wants or envisions prosecution of the assailant. A victim may want the attacker to be incapacitated

11. Some portions of *Davis*, however, have caused confusion about whether the inquiry prescribes examination of one participant to the exclusion of the other. *Davis'* language indicating that a statement's testimonial or nontestimonial nature derives from "the primary purpose *of the interrogation*," 547 U.S., at 822 (emphasis added), could be read to suggest that the relevant purpose is that of the interrogator. In contrast, footnote 1 in *Davis* explains, "it is in the final analysis the declarant's statements, not the interrogator's questions, that the Confrontation Clause requires us to evaluate." Id., at 822-823, n. 1. . . . But this statement in footnote 1 of *Davis* merely acknowledges that the Confrontation Clause is not implicated when statements are offered "for purposes other than establishing the truth of the matter asserted." *Crawford*, 541 U.S., at 60, n. 9. An interrogator's questions, unlike a declarant's answers, do not assert the truth of any matter. The language in the footnote was not meant to determine *how* the courts are to assess the nature of the declarant's purpose, but merely to remind readers that it is the statements, and not the questions, that must be evaluated under the Sixth Amendment.

temporarily or rehabilitated. Alternatively, a severely injured victim may have no purpose at all in answering questions posed; the answers may be simply reflexive. The victim's injuries could be so debilitating as to prevent her from thinking sufficiently clearly to understand whether her statements are for the purpose of addressing an ongoing emergency or for the purpose of future prosecution.[12] Taking into account a victim's injuries does not transform this objective inquiry into a subjective one. The inquiry is still objective because it focuses on the understanding and purpose of a reasonable victim in the circumstances of the actual victim — circumstances that prominently include the victim's physical state.

The dissent suggests that we intend to give controlling weight to the "intentions of the police". . . . That is a misreading of our opinion. At trial, the declarant's statements, not the interrogator's questions, will be introduced to "establis[h] the truth of the matter asserted," *Crawford*, 541 U.S., at 60, n. 9, and must therefore pass the Sixth Amendment test. See n. 11, supra. In determining whether a declarant's statements are testimonial, courts should look to all of the relevant circumstances. Even Justice Scalia concedes that the interrogator is relevant to this evaluation, and we agree that "[t]he identity of an interrogator, and the content and tenor of his questions," can illuminate the "primary purpose of the interrogation." The dissent criticizes the complexity of our approach, but we, at least, are unwilling to sacrifice accuracy for simplicity. Simpler is not always better, and courts making a "primary purpose" assessment should not be unjustifiably restrained from consulting all relevant information, including the statements and actions of interrogators.

Objectively ascertaining the primary purpose of the interrogation by examining the statements and actions of all participants is also the approach most consistent with our past holdings. E.g., *Davis*, 547 U.S., at 822-823, n. 1 (noting that "volunteered testimony" is still testimony and remains subject to the requirements of the Confrontation Clause).

IV

As we suggested in *Davis*, when a court must determine whether the Confrontation Clause bars the admission of a statement at trial, it should determine the "primary purpose of the interrogation" by objectively evaluating the statements and actions of the parties to the encounter, in light of the circumstances in which the interrogation occurs. The exis-

---

12. In such a situation, the severe injuries of the victim would undoubtedly also weigh on the credibility and reliability that the trier of fact would afford to the statements. . . .

tence of an emergency or the parties' perception that an emergency is ongoing is among the most important circumstances that courts must take into account in determining whether an interrogation is testimonial because statements made to assist police in addressing an ongoing emergency presumably lack the testimonial purpose that would subject them to the requirement of confrontation.[13] As the context of this case brings into sharp relief, the existence and duration of an emergency depend on the type and scope of danger posed to the victim, the police, and the public.

Applying this analysis to the facts of this case is more difficult than in *Davis* because we do not have the luxury of reviewing a transcript of the conversation between the victim and the police officers. Further complicating our task is the fact that the trial in this case occurred before our decisions in *Crawford* and *Davis*. We therefore review a record that was not developed to ascertain the "primary purpose of the interrogation."

We first examine the circumstances in which the interrogation occurred. The parties disagree over whether there was an emergency when the police arrived at the gas station. Bryant argues, and the Michigan Supreme Court accepted, 483 Mich., at 147, 768 N.W.2d, at 73, that there was no ongoing emergency because "there . . . was no criminal conduct occurring. No shots were being fired, no one was seen in possession of a firearm, nor were any witnesses seen cowering in fear or running from the scene." Brief for Respondent 27. Bryant, while conceding that "a serious or life-threatening injury creates a medical emergency for a victim," id., at 30, further argues that a declarant's medical emergency is not relevant to the ongoing emergency determination.

In contrast, Michigan and the Solicitor General explain that when the police responded to the call that a man had been shot and found Covington bleeding on the gas station parking lot, "they did not know who Covington was, whether the shooting had occurred at the gas station or at a different location, who the assailant was, or whether the assailant posed a continuing threat to Covington or others." Brief for United States as Amicus Curiae 15; Brief for Petitioner 16; see also id., at 15 ("[W]hen an officer arrives on the scene and does not know where the perpetrator is, whether he is armed, whether he might have other targets, and whether the violence might continue at the scene or elsewhere, interrogation that

---

13. Of course the Confrontation Clause is not the only bar to admissibility of hearsay statements at trial. State and federal rules of evidence prohibit the introduction of hearsay, subject to exceptions. Consistent with those rules, the Due Process Clauses of the Fifth and Fourteenth Amendments may constitute a further bar to admission of, for example, unreliable evidence. . . .

has the primary purpose of establishing those facts to assess the situation is designed to meet the ongoing emergency and is nontestimonial").

The Michigan Supreme Court stated that the police asked Covington, "what had happened, who had shot him, and where the shooting had occurred." 483 Mich., at 143, 768 N.W.2d, at 71. The joint appendix contains the transcripts of the preliminary examination, suppression hearing, and trial testimony of five officers who responded to the scene and found Covington. The officers' testimony is essentially consistent but, at the same time, not specific. The officers basically agree on what information they learned from Covington, but not on the order in which they learned it or on whether Covington's statements were in response to general or detailed questions. They all agree that the first question was "what happened?" The answer was either "I was shot" or "Rick shot me."

As explained above, the scope of an emergency in terms of its threat to individuals other than the initial assailant and victim will often depend on the type of dispute involved. Nothing Covington said to the police indicated that the cause of the shooting was a purely private dispute or that the threat from the shooter had ended. The record reveals little about the motive for the shooting. The police officers who spoke with Covington at the gas station testified that Covington did not tell them what words Covington and Rick had exchanged prior to the shooting. What Covington did tell the officers was that he fled Bryant's back porch, indicating that he perceived an ongoing threat.[16] The police did not know, and Covington did not tell them, whether the threat was limited to him. The potential scope of the dispute and therefore the emergency in this case thus stretches more broadly than those at issue in *Davis* and *Hammon* and encompasses a threat potentially to the police and the public.

This is also the first of our post-*Crawford* Confrontation Clause cases to involve a gun. The physical separation that was sufficient to end the emergency in *Hammon* was not necessarily sufficient to end the threat

---

16. See id., at 127-128 ("A: He said he'd went up, he went up to the back door of a house; that a person he said he knew, and he was knocking and he was knocking on the door he said he'd talked to somebody through the door. He said he recognized the voice. Q: Did he say who it was that he recognized the voice of? A: That's when he told me it was, he said it was Rick a/k/a Buster. Q: And did he say what the conversation was about at the door? A: I don't, I don't believe so. Q: All right. And did he say what happened there, whether or not they had a conversation or not, did he say what ended up happening? A: He said what happened was that he heard a shot and then he started to turn to get off the porch and then another one and then that's when he was hit by a gunshot" (testimony of Officer Stuglin) (paragraph breaks omitted)). Unlike the dissent's apparent ability to read Covington's mind, we rely on the available evidence, which suggests that Covington perceived an ongoing threat.

in this case; Covington was shot through the back door of Bryant's house. Bryant's argument that there was no ongoing emergency because "[n]o shots were being fired," Brief for Respondent 27, surely construes ongoing emergency too narrowly. An emergency does not last only for the time between when the assailant pulls the trigger and the bullet hits the victim. If an out-of-sight sniper pauses between shots, no one would say that the emergency ceases during the pause. That is an extreme example and not the situation here, but it serves to highlight the implausibility, at least as to certain weapons, of construing the emergency to last only precisely as long as the violent act itself, as some have construed our opinion in *Davis*.

At no point during the questioning did either Covington or the police know the location of the shooter. In fact, Bryant was not at home by the time the police searched his house at approximately 5:30 a.m. 483 Mich., at 136, 768 N.W.2d, at 67. At some point between 3 a.m. and 5:30 a.m., Bryant left his house. At bottom, there was an ongoing emergency here where an armed shooter, whose motive for and location after the shooting were unknown, had mortally wounded Covington within a few blocks and a few minutes of the location where the police found Covington.

This is not to suggest that the emergency continued until Bryant was arrested in California a year after the shooting. Id., at 137, 768 N.W.2d, at 67. We need not decide precisely when the emergency ended because Covington's encounter with the police and all of the statements he made during that interaction occurred within the first few minutes of the police officers' arrival and well before they secured the scene of the shooting — the shooter's last known location.

We reiterate, moreover, that the existence vel non of an ongoing emergency is not the touchstone of the testimonial inquiry; rather, the ultimate inquiry is whether the "primary purpose of the interrogation [was] to enable police assistance to meet [the] ongoing emergency." *Davis*, 547 U.S., at 822. We turn now to that inquiry, as informed by the circumstances of the ongoing emergency just described. The circumstances of the encounter provide important context for understanding Covington's statements to the police. When the police arrived at Covington's side, their first question to him was "What happened?"[18] Covington's response was either "Rick shot me" or "I was shot," followed

---

18. Although the dissent claims otherwise, at least one officer asked Covington something akin to "how was he doing." App. 131 (testimony of Officer Stuglin) ("A: I approached the subject, the victim, Mr. Covington, on the ground and had asked something like what happened or are you okay, something to that line. . . . Q: So you asked this man how are you, how are you doing? A: Well, basically it's, you know, what's wrong, you know" (paragraph breaks omitted)). . . .

very quickly by an identification of "Rick" as the shooter. In response to further questions, Covington explained that the shooting occurred through the back door of Bryant's house and provided a physical description of the shooter. When he made the statements, Covington was lying in a gas station parking lot bleeding from a mortal gunshot wound to his abdomen. His answers to the police officers' questions were punctuated with questions about when emergency medical services would arrive. He was obviously in considerable pain and had difficulty breathing and talking. From this description of his condition and report of his statements, we cannot say that a person in Covington's situation would have had a "primary purpose" "to establish or prove past events potentially relevant to later criminal prosecution." *Davis*, 547 U.S., at 822.

For their part, the police responded to a call that a man had been shot. As discussed above, they did not know why, where, or when the shooting had occurred. Nor did they know the location of the shooter or anything else about the circumstances in which the crime occurred.[19] The questions they asked . . . were the exact type of questions necessary to allow the police to "'assess the situation, the threat to their own safety, and possible danger to the potential victim'" and to the public, *Davis*, 547 U.S., at 832 (quoting Hiibel v. Sixth Judicial Dist. Court of Nev., Humboldt Cty., 542 U.S. 177, 186 (2004)), including to allow them to ascertain "whether they would be encountering a violent felon,"[20] *Davis*, 547 U.S., at 827. In other words, they solicited the information necessary to enable them "to meet an ongoing emergency." Id., at 822.

Nothing in Covington's responses indicated to the police that, contrary to their expectation upon responding to a call reporting a shooting, there was no emergency or that a prior emergency had ended. Covington

---

19. Contrary to the dissent's suggestion, and despite the fact that the record was developed prior to *Davis*' focus on the existence of an "ongoing emergency," the record contains some testimony to support the idea that the police officers were concerned about the location of the shooter when they arrived on the scene and thus to suggest that the purpose of the questioning of Covington was to determine the shooter's location. See App. 136 (testimony of Officer Stuglin) (stating that upon arrival officers questioned the gas station clerk about whether the shooting occurred in the gas station parking lot and about concern for safety); see also ibid. (testimony of Officer Stuglin) ("Q: . . . So you have some concern, there may be a person with a gun or somebody, a shooter right there in the immediate area? A: Sure, yes. Q: And you want to see that that area gets secured? A: Correct. Q: For your safety as well as everyone else? A: Correct" (paragraph breaks omitted)); id., at 82 (testimony of Officer McCallister). But see id., at 83 (cross-examination of Officer McAllister) ("Q: You didn't, you didn't look around and say, gee, there might be a shooter around here, I better keep an eye open? A: I did not, no. That could have been my partner I don't know" (paragraph breaks omitted)).

20. *Hiibel*, like our post-*Crawford* Confrontation Clause cases, involved domestic violence, which explains the Court's focus on the security of the victim and the police: they were the only parties potentially threatened by the assailant. 542 U.S., at 186 (noting that the case involved a "domestic assault").

did indicate that he had been shot at another location about 25 minutes earlier, but he did not know the location of the shooter at the time the police arrived and, as far as we can tell from the record, he gave no indication that the shooter, having shot at him twice, would be satisfied that Covington was only wounded. In fact, Covington did not indicate any possible motive for the shooting, and thereby gave no reason to think that the shooter would not shoot again if he arrived on the scene. As we noted in *Davis*, "initial inquiries" may "*often* . . . produce nontestimonial statements." Id., at 832. The initial inquiries in this case resulted in the type of nontestimonial statements we contemplated in *Davis*.

Finally, we consider the informality of the situation and the interrogation. This situation is more similar, though not identical, to the informal, harried 911 call in *Davis* than to the structured, station-house interview in *Crawford*. As the officers' trial testimony reflects, the situation was fluid and somewhat confused: the officers arrived at different times; apparently each, upon arrival, asked Covington "what happened?"; and, contrary to the dissent's portrayal, post, at 7-9 (opinion of Scalia, J.), they did not conduct a structured interrogation. App. 84 (testimony of Officer McCallister) (explaining duplicate questioning, especially as to "what happened?"); id., at 101-102 (testimony of Sgt. Wenturine) (same); id., at 126-127 (testimony of Officer Stuglin) (same). The informality suggests that the interrogators' primary purpose was simply to address what they perceived to be an ongoing emergency, and the circumstances lacked any formality that would have alerted Covington to or focused him on the possible future prosecutorial use of his statements.

Because the circumstances of the encounter as well as the statements and actions of Covington and the police objectively indicate that the "primary purpose of the interrogation" was "to enable police assistance to meet an ongoing emergency," *Davis*, 547 U.S., at 822, Covington's identification and description of the shooter and the location of the shooting were not testimonial hearsay. The Confrontation Clause did not bar their admission at Bryant's trial.

* * *

For the foregoing reasons, we hold that Covington's statements were not testimonial and that their admission at Bryant's trial did not violate the Confrontation Clause. We leave for the Michigan courts to decide on remand whether the statements' admission was otherwise permitted by state hearsay rules. The judgment of the Supreme Court of Michigan is vacated, and the case is remanded for further proceedings not inconsistent with this opinion.

It is so ordered.

JUSTICE KAGAN took no part in the consideration or decision of this case.

JUSTICE THOMAS, concurring in the judgment.

I agree with the Court that the admission of Covington's out-of-court statements did not violate the Confrontation Clause, but I reach this conclusion because Covington's questioning by police lacked sufficient formality and solemnity for his statements to be considered "testimonial." See Crawford v. Washington, 541 U.S. 36 (2004). . . .

JUSTICE SCALIA, dissenting.

Today's tale — a story of five officers conducting successive examinations of a dying man with the primary purpose, not of obtaining and preserving his testimony regarding his killer, but of protecting him, them, and others from a murderer somewhere on the loose — is so transparently false that professing to believe it demeans this institution. But reaching a patently incorrect conclusion on the facts is a relatively benign judicial mischief; it affects, after all, only the case at hand. In its vain attempt to make the incredible plausible, however — or perhaps as an intended second goal — today's opinion distorts our Confrontation Clause jurisprudence and leaves it in a shambles. Instead of clarifying the law, the Court makes itself the obfuscator of last resort. Because I continue to adhere to the Confrontation Clause that the People adopted, as described in Crawford v. Washington, 541 U.S. 36 (2004), I dissent.

I

A

. . . *Crawford* and *Davis* did not address whose perspective matters — the declarant's, the interrogator's, or both — when assessing "the primary purpose of [an] interrogation." In those cases the statements were testimonial from any perspective. I think the same is true here, but because the Court picks a perspective so will I: The declarant's intent is what counts. In-court testimony is more than a narrative of past events; it is a solemn declaration made in the course of a criminal trial. For an out-of-court statement to qualify as testimonial, the declarant must intend the statement to be a solemn declaration rather than an unconsidered or offhand remark; and he must make the statement with the understanding that it may be used to invoke the coercive machinery of the State against the accused.[1] See

---

1. I remain agnostic about whether and when statements to nonstate actors are testimonial. See Davis v. Washington, 547 U.S. 813, 823, n. 2 (2006).

Friedman, Grappling with the Meaning of "Testimonial," 71 Brooklyn L. Rev. 241, 259 (2005). That is what distinguishes a narrative told to a friend over dinner from a statement to the police. See *Crawford*, supra, at 51. The hidden purpose of an interrogator cannot substitute for the declarant's intentional solemnity or his understanding of how his words may be used.

A declarant-focused inquiry is also the only inquiry that would work in every fact pattern implicating the Confrontation Clause. The Clause applies to volunteered testimony as well as statements solicited through police interrogation. See *Davis*, supra, at 822-823, n. 1. An inquiry into an officer's purposes would make no sense when a declarant blurts out "Rick shot me" as soon as the officer arrives on the scene. I see no reason to adopt a different test—one that accounts for an officer's intent—when the officer asks "what happened" before the declarant makes his accusation. (This does not mean the interrogator is irrelevant. The identity of an interrogator, and the content and tenor of his questions, can bear upon whether a declarant intends to make a solemn statement, and envisions its use at a criminal trial. But none of this means that the interrogator's purpose matters.)

In an unsuccessful attempt to make its finding of emergency plausible, the Court instead adopts a test that looks to the purposes of both the police and the declarant. It claims that this is demanded by necessity, fretting that a domestic-violence victim may want her abuser briefly arrested—presumably to teach him a lesson—but not desire prosecution. See ante, at 22. I do not need to probe the purposes of the police to solve that problem. Even if a victim speaks to the police "to establish or prove past events" solely for the purpose of getting her abuser arrested, she surely knows her account is "potentially relevant to later criminal prosecution" should one ensue. *Davis*, supra, at 822.

The Court also wrings its hands over the possibility that "a severely injured victim" may lack the capacity to form a purpose, and instead answer questions "reflexive[ly]." Ante, at 22. How to assess whether a declarant with diminished capacity bore testimony is a difficult question, and one I do not need to answer today. But the Court's proposed answer—to substitute the intentions of the police for the missing intentions of the declarant—cannot be the correct one. When the declarant has diminished capacity, focusing on the interrogators make less sense, not more. The inquiry under *Crawford* turns in part on the actions and statements of a declarant's audience only because they shape the declarant's perception of why his audience is listening and therefore influence *his purpose* in making the declaration. See 541 U.S., at 51. But a person who cannot perceive his own purposes certainly cannot perceive why a listener might be interested in what he has to say. . . .

The only virtue of the Court's approach (if it can be misnamed a virtue) is that it leaves judges free to reach the "fairest" result under the totality of the circumstances. If the dastardly police trick a declarant into giving an incriminating statement against a sympathetic defendant, a court can focus on the police's intent and declare the statement testimonial. If the defendant "deserves" to go to jail, then a court can focus on whatever perspective is necessary to declare damning hearsay nontestimonial. And when all else fails, a court can mix-and-match perspectives to reach its desired outcome. Unfortunately, under this malleable approach "the guarantee of confrontation is no guarantee at all." Giles v. California, 554 U.S. 353, 375 (2008) (plurality).

B

Looking to the declarant's purpose (as we should), this is an absurdly easy case. Roughly 25 minutes after Anthony Covington had been shot, Detroit police responded to a 911 call reporting that a gunshot victim had appeared at a neighborhood gas station. They quickly arrived at the scene, and in less than 10 minutes five different Detroit police officers questioned Covington about the shooting. Each asked him a similar battery of questions: "what happened" and when, App. 39, 126, "who shot" the victim, id., at 22, and "where" did the shooting take place, id., at 132. See also id., at 113. After Covington would answer, they would ask follow-up questions, such as "how tall is" the shooter, id., at 134, "[h]ow much does he weigh," ibid. what is the exact address or physical description of the house where the shooting took place, and what chain of events led to the shooting. The battery relented when the paramedics arrived and began tending to Covington's wounds.

From Covington's perspective, his statements had little value except to ensure the arrest and eventual prosecution of Richard Bryant. He knew the "threatening situation," Davis, 547 U.S., at 832, had ended six blocks away and 25 minutes earlier when he fled from Bryant's back porch. See 483 Mich. 132, 135-136, 768 N.W.2d 65, 67 (2009); App. 105. Bryant had not confronted him face-to-face before he was mortally wounded, instead shooting him through a door. See 483 Mich., at 136-137, 768 N.W.2d, at 67. Even if Bryant had pursued him (unlikely), and after seeing that Covington had ended up at the gas station was unable to confront him there before the police arrived (doubly unlikely), it was entirely beyond imagination that Bryant would again open fire while Covington was surrounded by five armed police officers. And Covington knew the shooting was the work of a drug dealer, not a spree killer who might randomly threaten others. Id., at 135, 137, 768 N.W.2d, at 67. . . .

Covington's pressing medical needs do not suggest that he was responding to an emergency, but to the contrary reinforce the testimonial character of his statements. He understood the police were focused on investigating a past crime, not his medical needs. None of the officers asked Covington how he was doing, attempted more than superficially to assess the severity of his wounds, or attempted to administer first aid.[2] They instead primarily asked questions with little, if any, relevance to Covington's dire situation. Police, paramedics, and doctors do not need to know the address where a shooting took place, the name of the shooter, or the shooter's height and weight to provide proper medical care. Underscoring that Covington understood the officers' investigative role, he interrupted their interrogation to ask "when is EMS coming?" App. 57. When, in other words, would the focus shift to his medical needs rather than Bryant's crime?

Neither Covington's statements nor the colloquy between him and the officers would have been out of place at a trial; it would have been a routine direct examination. See *Davis*, 547 U.S., at 830. Like a witness, Covington recounted in detail how a past criminal event began and progressed, and like a prosecutor, the police elicited that account through structured questioning. . . . Ex parte examinations raise the same constitutional concerns whether they take place in a gas-station parking lot or in a police interrogation room.

C

Worse still for the repute of today's opinion, this is an absurdly easy case even if one (erroneously) takes the interrogating officers' purpose into account. The five officers interrogated Covington primarily to investigate past criminal events. . . .

D

A final word about the Court's active imagination. The Court invents a world where an ongoing emergency exists whenever "an armed shooter, whose motive for and location after the shooting [are] unknown, . . .

---

2. Officer Stuglin's testimony does not undermine my assessment of the officers' behavior, although the Court suggests otherwise. Officer Stuglin first testified that he "asked something like what happened or are you okay, something to that line." App., 131. When pressed on whether he asked "how are you doing?," he responded, "Well, basically . . . what's wrong." Ibid. Other officers were not so equivocal: They admitted they had no need to "ask him how he was doing. . . . It was very obvious how he was doing." Id., at 110; see also id., at 19.

mortally wound[s]" one individual "within a few blocks and [25] minutes of the location where the police" ultimately find that victim. Breathlessly, it worries that a shooter could leave the scene armed and ready to pull the trigger again. Nothing suggests the five officers in this case shared the Court's dystopian[4] view of Detroit, where drug dealers hunt their shooting victim down and fire into a crowd of police officers to finish him off, or where spree killers shoot through a door and then roam the streets leaving a trail of bodies behind. Because almost 90 percent of murders involve a single victim,[5] it is much more likely—indeed, I think it certain—that the officers viewed their encounter with Covington for what it was: an investigation into a past crime with no ongoing or immediate consequences.

The Court's distorted view creates an expansive exception to the Confrontation Clause for violent crimes. Because Bryant posed a continuing threat to public safety in the Court's imagination, the emergency persisted for confrontation purposes at least until the police learned his "motive for and location after the shooting." . . . This is a dangerous definition of emergency. Many individuals who testify against a defendant at trial first offer their accounts to police in the hours after a violent act. If the police can plausibly claim that a "potential threat to . . . the public" persisted through those first few hours, . . . a defendant will have no constitutionally protected right to exclude the uncross-examined testimony of such witnesses. His conviction could rest (as perhaps it did here) solely on the officers' recollection at trial of the witnesses' accusations. . . .

II

A

But today's decision is not only a gross distortion of the facts. It is a gross distortion of the law—a revisionist narrative in which reliability continues to guide our Confrontation Clause jurisprudence, at least where emergencies and faux emergencies are concerned. . . .

---

4. The opposite of utopian. The word was coined by John Stuart Mill as a caustic description of British policy. See 190 Hansard's Parliamentary Debates, Third Series 1517 (3d Ser. 1868); 5 Oxford English Dictionary 13 (2d ed. 1989).

5. See Federal Bureau of Investigation, Crime in the United States, 2009: Expanded Homicide Data Table 4, Murder by Victim/Offender Situations, 2009 (Sept. 2010), online at *http://www2.fbi.gov/ucr/cius2009/offenses/expandedinformation/data/shrtable04.html* (as visited Feb. 25, 2011, and available in Clerk of Court's case file).

The Court announces that in future cases it will look to "standard rules of hearsay, designed to identify some statements as reliable," when deciding whether a statement is testimonial. Ohio v. Roberts, 448 U.S. 56 (1980) said something remarkably similar: An out-of-court statement is admissible if it "falls within a firmly rooted hearsay exception" or otherwise "bears adequate 'indicia of reliability.'" Id., at 66. We tried that approach to the Confrontation Clause for nearly 25 years before *Crawford* *rejected* it as an unworkable standard unmoored from the text and the historical roots of the Confrontation Clause. . . .

The Court attempts to fit its resurrected interest in reliability into the *Crawford* framework, but the result is incoherent. Reliability, the Court tells us, is a good indicator of whether "a statement is . . . an out-of-court substitute for trial testimony." That is patently false. Reliability tells us *nothing* about whether a statement is testimonial. Testimonial and non-testimonial statements alike come in varying degrees of reliability. An eyewitness's statements to the police after a fender-bender, for example, are both reliable and testimonial. Statements to the police from one driver attempting to blame the other would be similarly testimonial but rarely reliable.

The Court suggests otherwise because it "misunderstands the relationship" between qualification for one of the standard hearsay exceptions and exemption from the confrontation requirement. Melendez-Diaz v. Massachusetts, 557 U.S. __, __ (2009). That relationship is not a causal one. Hearsay law exempts business records, for example, because businesses have a financial incentive to keep reliable records. See Fed. Rule Evid. 803(6). The Sixth Amendment also generally admits business records into evidence, but not because the records are reliable or because hearsay law says so. It admits them "because—having been created for the administration of an entity's affairs and not for the purpose of establishing or proving some fact at trial—they are not" weaker substitutes for live testimony. *Melendez-Diaz*, 557 U.S., at __. . . .

Is it possible that the Court does not recognize the contradiction between its focus on reliable statements and *Crawford*'s focus on testimonial ones? Does it not realize that the two cannot coexist? Or does it intend, by following today's illogical roadmap, to resurrect *Roberts* by a thousand unprincipled distinctions without ever explicitly overruling *Crawford*? After all, honestly overruling *Crawford* would destroy the illusion of judicial minimalism and restraint. And it would force the Court to explain how the Justices' preference comports with the meaning of the Confrontation Clause that the People adopted—or to confess that only the Justices' preference really matters.

B

The Court recedes from *Crawford* in a second significant way. It requires judges to conduct "open-ended balancing tests" and "amorphous, if not entirely subjective," inquiries into the totality of the circumstances bearing upon reliability. 541 U.S., at 63, 68. Where the prosecution cries "emergency," the admissibility of a statement now turns on "a highly context-dependent inquiry," into the type of weapon the defendant wielded; the type of crime the defendant committed; the medical condition of the declarant; if the declarant is injured, whether paramedics have arrived on the scene; whether the encounter takes place in an "exposed public area"; whether the encounter appears disorganized; whether the declarant is capable of forming a purpose; whether the police have secured the scene of the crime; the formality of the statement; and finally, whether the statement strikes us as reliable. This is no better than the nine-factor balancing test we rejected in *Crawford*, 541 U.S., at 63. I do not look forward to resolving conflicts in the future over whether knives and poison are more like guns or fists for Confrontation Clause purposes, or whether rape and armed robbery are more like murder or domestic violence.

It can be said, of course, that under *Crawford* analysis of whether a statement is testimonial requires consideration of all the circumstances, and so is also something of a multifactor balancing test. But the "reliability" test does not replace that analysis; it supplements it. As I understand the Court's opinion, even when it is determined that no emergency exists (or perhaps before that determination is made) the statement would be found admissible as far as the Confrontation Clause is concerned if it is not testimonial.

In any case, we did not disavow multifactor balancing for reliability in *Crawford* out of a preference for rules over standards. We did so because it "d[id] violence to" the Framers' design. . . .

* * *

Judicial decisions, like the Constitution itself, are nothing more than "parchment barriers," 5 Writings of James Madison 269, 272 (G. Hunt ed. 1901). Both depend on a judicial culture that understands its constitutionally assigned role, has the courage to persist in that role when it means announcing unpopular decisions, and has the modesty to persist when it produces results that go against the judges' policy preferences. Today's opinion falls far short of living up to that obligation — short on the facts, and short on the law.

For all I know, Bryant has received his just deserts. But he surely has not received them pursuant to the procedures that our Constitution requires. And what has been taken away from him has been taken away from us all.

JUSTICE GINSBURG, dissenting.

I agree with Justice Scalia that Covington's statements were testimonial and that "[t]he declarant's intent is what counts." . . . I would add, however, this observation. In Crawford v. Washington, 541 U.S. 36, 56, n. 6 (2004), this Court noted that, in the law we inherited from England, there was a well-established exception to the confrontation requirement: The cloak protecting the accused against admission of out-of-court testimonial statements was removed for dying declarations. . . . Were the issue properly tendered here, I would take up the question whether the exception for dying declarations survives our recent Confrontation Clause decisions. The Michigan Supreme Court, however, held, as a matter of state law, that the prosecutor had abandoned the issue. The matter, therefore, is not one the Court can address in this case.

NOTES AND QUESTIONS

1. OMG! What's going on in *Bryant*? How can we possibly make sense of *Bryant*, given the prior decisions in *Crawford*, *Davis*, *Hammon*, and *Melendez-Diaz*, and especially given the *subsequent* decision — rendered less than four months after *Bryant* — in *Bullcoming*?

Perhaps it might help to think about *Crawford* doctrine in terms of the evolving views of the individual Justices. Although Justice Scalia enjoyed strong majorities in *Crawford* (seven Justices) and *Davis/Hammon* (eight Justices), he lost a couple of votes when Justice Stevens and Justice Souter left the Court. And *Melendez-Diaz* marked a key turning point; as a result of that case, four of the other Justices who had supported Justice Scalia in *Davis/Hammon* suddenly woke up and realized the absurd lengths to which *Crawford* doctrine eventually might go.

At this point, it seems that there are only two "true believers" in the hard-core revolutionary vision of the Confrontation Clause represented by *Crawford*, *Davis/Hammon*, and *Melendez-Diaz*: Justice Scalia (the author of the majority opinion in each of those cases) and Justice Ginsburg. Justice Thomas was never entirely on board; he joined *Crawford*, but his unique emphasis on "formality" as the key to the Confrontation Clause means that he has always held a much narrower view of that decision than Justice Scalia. Then there were the four "rebels," who turned sharply against Justice Scalia's view in *Melendez-Diaz*, and who were now committed to limiting *Crawford* as much as humanly possible: Chief Justice Roberts, Justice Kennedy, Justice Breyer, and Justice Alito. Finally, the two "new" Justices — Justice Sotomayor and (as far as we can tell, on limited data) Justice Kagan — seemed to prefer a pragmatic case-by-case and issue-by-issue approach to one based on abstract principles. In fact, Justice Sotomayor — at least in light of her majority opinion in *Bryant* — seemed to long for a return to the fact-specific, contextual doctrine of Ohio v. Roberts. Given this line-up, there was little hope for coherence in the Court's Confrontation Clause decisions.

1a. OMG! PART II! Although any sane observer (like your editors) might very well have thought that the *Crawford*-inspired jurisprudence could not possibly get any more ridiculous, this was proved wrong in the Court's very next term, by its decision in Williams v. Illinois, 132 S. Ct. 2221 (2012). The facts, according to the Court, were:

> At petitioner's bench trial for rape, Sandra Lambatos, a forensic specialist at the Illinois State Police lab, testified that she matched a DNA profile produced by an outside laboratory, Cellmark, to a profile the state lab produced using a sample of petitioner's blood. She testified that Cellmark was an accredited laboratory and that business records showed that vaginal swabs taken from the victim, L.J., were sent to Cellmark and returned. She offered no other statement for the purpose of identifying the sample used for Cellmark's profile or establishing how Cellmark handled or tested the sample. Nor did she vouch for the accuracy of Cellmark's profile. The defense moved to exclude, on Confrontation Clause grounds, Lambatos' testimony insofar as it implicated events at Cellmark, but the prosecution said that petitioner's confrontation rights were satisfied because he had the opportunity to cross-examine the expert who had testified as to the match. The prosecutor argued that Illinois Rule of Evidence 703 permitted an expert to disclose facts on which the expert's opinion is based even if the expert is not competent to testify to those underlying facts, and that any deficiency went to the weight of the evidence, not its admissibility.

The hypothetical sane observer obviously would have concluded that this was an easy case, given *Bullcoming*'s "emphatic no," as the answer to whether a lab report may be admitted if the person signing it is not produced for cross-examination. The sane observer would notice that a *certified* lab report is most likely more reliable than an *uncertified*, more or less anonymous, report from a faceless organization. In any sane world, there is greater reason to insist on cross-examination in *Williams* than *Bullcoming*.

But, confirming that the legal world is on occasion a wondrous sight to behold, the Court upheld the admission of the lab report in a 4-1-4 split that will surely go down in history as one of the most peculiar decisions of all time. A four-person plurality, authored by Justice Alito and joined by Chief Justice Roberts and Justices Kennedy and Breyer, issued a tortured opinion focusing on why the report was not being admitted for its truth, and therefore there was no constitutional problem. Justice Thomas concurred in the result on the (now-familiar, for him) ground that the Confrontation Clause is limited to formal, affidavit-like documents ("a narrow class of statements bearing indicia of solemnity"), which excluded this unsworn document from its coverage. In passing, Thomas rejected every proposition uttered by the plurality and the dissent. A four-person dissent, authored by Justice Kagan, and joined by Justices Scalia, Ginsburg, and Sotomayor, expressed a continued willingness to make it cost-prohibitive to enforce much of the criminal law, and in passing rejected every proposition offered in both the plurality and the concurrence. As anyone who can count can immediately see, five of the Justices rejected the plurality's arguments, five of the Justices rejected the dissent's arguments, and eight of the Justices rejected the concurrence's arguments, yet future cases now will be decided largely by Justice Thomas's view as to the formalities of the evidentiary proffer.

Although it is a parlous enterprise to divine the actual states of mind of Supreme Court Justices, the plurality opinion in *Williams* is so strained that the obvious inference is that those Justices in the plurality were looking for any way to cut back on the destructive effect of the *Crawford* line of cases. The first argument, as noted above, involved whether the lab report was being offered for its truth. In an opinion that would make the old masters of the common law of evidence proud, the plurality said "no." The witness was only asked whether there was a match between the Cellmark report and a separate DNA analysis done by the state from a sample taken from Williams. She was not asked if the Cellmark report was based on a sample that came from defendant. Thus, she was not relying on the Cellmark report to show that it was reporting tests of a sample from Williams. Other evidence made it clear that this sample had come from Williams and had been reliably done. There was conventional chain-of-custody evidence, and the match itself was "circumstantial evidence" that the sample came from Williams. "In contrast, Cellmark's report was considered for the limited purpose of seeing whether it matched something else, and the relevance of that match was established by independent circumstantial evidence showing that the report was based on a sample from the crime scene." The trouble with this entire line of reasoning is that, without the actual findings in the report, there is nothing to match, and thus there is no relevance to Lambatos' testimony.

There is nothing but the report that details the DNA profile in the sample tested by Cellmark. For a discussion of this problem, and its contemporary manifestations in the law, see Ronald J. Allen, et al., Evidence: Text, Problems, and Cases 686-693 (5th ed. 2011). It should also be noted that standard hearsay evidence can always be classified as non-hearsay because of a circumstantial-evidence argument. Were the Court to adopt the more general theory, the Confrontation Clause would go away to the extent it depends upon the admission of hearsay.

Perhaps not content with its own reasoning about the hearsay rule, the plurality went on to make a second argument that there was not a Confrontation Clause violation in any event:

> In *Melendez-Diaz* and *Bullcoming*, the Court held that the particular forensic reports at issue qualified as testimonial statements, but the Court did not hold that all forensic reports fall into the same category. Introduction of the reports in those cases ran afoul of the Confrontation Clause because they were the equivalent of affidavits made for the purpose of proving the guilt of a particular criminal defendant at trial. There was nothing resembling an ongoing emergency, as the suspects in both cases had already been captured, and the tests in question were relatively simple and can generally be performed by a single analyst. In addition, the technicians who prepared the reports must have realized that their contents (which reported an elevated blood-alcohol level and the presence of an illegal drug) would be incriminating. . . .
>
> The Cellmark report is very different. It plainly was not prepared for the primary purpose of accusing a targeted individual. In identifying the primary purpose of an out-of-court statement, we apply an objective test. We look for the primary purpose that a reasonable person would have ascribed to the statement, taking into account all of the surrounding circumstances.
>
> Here, the primary purpose of the Cellmark report, viewed objectively, was not to accuse petitioner or to create evidence for use at trial. When the ISP lab sent the sample to Cellmark, its primary purpose was to catch a dangerous rapist who was still at large, not to obtain evidence for use against petitioner, who was neither in custody nor under suspicion at that time. Similarly, no one at Cellmark could have possibly known that the profile that it produced would turn out to inculpate petitioner — or for that matter, anyone else whose DNA profile was in a law enforcement database. Under these circumstances, there was no "prospect of fabrication" and no incentive to produce anything other than a scientifically sound and reliable profile.

Given Justice Thomas's concurrence, the lesson to the states seems to be that by eliminating any formal certification process, and by keeping lab technicians in the dark as to what they are doing (which actually would be a good thing in any event, to avoid various biases), the states may be able to avoid the exclusionary effect on lab reports of the *Crawford* line of cases.

PART FIVE

POSTTRIAL PROCEEDINGS

Chapter 15

Sentencing

A. Introduction to Sentencing

3. Substantive Limits on Sentencing — Eighth Amendment Proportionality

Add the following note at the end of Note 4 on page 1439:

5. In Miller v. Alabama, 132 S. Ct. 2455 (2012) (decided together with the companion case of Jackson v. Hobbs), a narrowly divided 5-4 Court — relying heavily on the same social-science evidence as in *Graham* — held that juveniles who commit homicides may not be sentenced to life imprisonment without possibility of parole *under mandatory sentencing schemes* (i.e., under sentencing statutes that require the imposition of an LWOP sentence without allowing the sentencer to consider possible mitigating or extenuating circumstances). Mass media accounts of the *Miller* decision, unfortunately, were largely inaccurate. Despite the facial similarity to *Graham*, *Miller* is *not* a proportionality case, and the Court did *not* rule in *Miller* that juveniles cannot receive LWOP sentences. Instead, *Miller* is a case about the *procedure* that a jurisdiction must follow, before it can sentence a juvenile defendant to life without parole. At the same time, the Court in *Miller* clearly signalled its discomfort with such sentences:

> [W]e do not consider Jackson's and Miller's alternative argument that the Eighth Amendment requires a categorical bar on life without parole for juveniles, or at least for those 14 and younger. But given all we have said in *Roper*, *Graham*, and this decision about children's diminished culpability and heightened capacity for change, we think appropriate occasions for sentencing juveniles to this harshest possible penalty will be uncommon. . . . Although we do not foreclose a sentencer's ability to make that judgment in homicide cases, we require it to take into account how children are different, and how those differences counsel against irrevocably sentencing them to a lifetime in prison.

Will *Miller* lead, eventually, to an Eighth Amendment proportionality decision barring life without parole for all juveniles? We'll have to wait and see.

C. Do the Rules of Constitutional Criminal Procedure Apply to Sentencing?

Delete everything in Note 5 after the second paragraph on page 1453. Proceed directly to Note 6 on page 1454.

Add the following note at the end of Note 4 on page 1489:

5. If Justice Scalia was upset by the Court's decision in *Ice*, he may have gained a measure of solace — and seems to have gained a couple of new allies — in the 2012 case of Southern Union Co. v. United States, 132 S. Ct. 2344 (2012). *Southern Union Co.* presented the issue whether *Apprendi* doctrine applies to the imposition of criminal fines. In a (remarkably historically detailed) majority opinion by Justice Sotomayor, joined by Chief Justice Roberts and Justices Scalia, Thomas, Ginsburg, and Kagan, the Court held that the answer is yes — so long as the criminal fine in question is substantial enough to render the relevant criminal case "non-petty," and thereby trigger the Sixth Amendment's right to jury trial, on which *Apprendi* is largely based. [A quick editorial aside: Does the due process component of *Apprendi* doctrine, which requires all facts that determine the defendant's maximum sentence to be found "beyond a reasonable doubt," apply even to those "non-petty" criminal cases to which the Sixth Amendment's right to jury trial is inapplicable? That's a pretty interesting question, and one about which the Court does not yet seem to have carefully thought.] In *Southern Union Co.*, the Court explicitly rejected the argument of the dissenters — Justice Breyer, joined by Justices Kennedy and Alito — that *Ice* was good precedent for refusing to extend *Apprendi* to contexts beyond the "central sphere of [its] concern." According to the majority: "While the punishments at stake in [prior] cases were imprisonment or a death sentence, we see no principled basis under *Apprendi* for treating criminal fines differently. . . . In stating *Apprendi*'s rule, we have never distinguished one form of punishment from another. Instead, our decisions broadly prohibit judicial factfinding that increases maximum criminal 'sentence[s],' 'penalties,' or 'punishment[s]' — terms that each undeniably embrace fines."

6. In Peugh v. United States, 133 S. Ct. 1310 (2013), the Court ruled by 5-4 that the Federal Sentencing Guidelines — notwithstanding their "advisory" nature, ever since *Booker* — carry sufficiently persuasive force with sentencing judges to trigger the protection of the Ex Post Facto Clause. Thus, when an applicable sentencing guideline was increased after the defendant's commission of the crime, but before his sentencing, the defendant was entitled to be sentenced under the prior version. Justice Sotomayor's lead opinion was joined by Justices Ginsburg, Breyer, and Kagan in full, and by Justice Kennedy with the exception of a section that discussed broadly the "animating principles" of "fundamental justice" that underlie the Ex Post Facto Clause.

7.And what about McMillan v. Pennsylvania, the 1986 case that upheld the constitutionality of allowing judges to make the factual findings upon which "mandatory minimum" sentences were based? Did *McMillan* survive *Apprendi*?

In Harris v. United States, 536 U.S. 545 (2002), the Court — by 5-4, and without a complete majority opinion — initially reaffirmed the post-*Apprendi* validity of *McMillan*. But barely more than a decade later, the Court reversed course, in yet another fractured decision that reflects the continuing controversy over *Apprendi*.

ALLEYNE v. UNITED STATES
Certiorari to the U.S. Court of Appeals for the Fourth Circuit
133 S. Ct. 2151 (2013)

JUSTICE THOMAS announced the judgment of the Court and delivered the opinion of the Court with respect to Parts I, III-B, III-C, and IV, and an opinion with respect to Parts II and III-A, in which JUSTICE GINSBURG, JUSTICE SOTOMAYOR, and JUSTICE KAGAN join.

In Harris v. United States, 536 U.S. 545 (2002), this Court held that judicial factfinding that increases the mandatory minimum sentence for a crime is permissible under the Sixth Amendment. We granted certiorari to consider whether that decision should be overruled.

Harris drew a distinction between facts that increase the statutory maximum and facts that increase only the mandatory minimum. We conclude that this distinction is inconsistent with our decision in Apprendi v. New Jersey, 530 U.S. 466 (2000), and with the original meaning of the Sixth Amendment. Any fact that, by law, increases the penalty for a crime is an "element" that must be submitted to the jury and found beyond a reasonable doubt. See Id., at 483, n. 10. Mandatory minimum sentences increase the penalty for a crime. It follows, then, that any fact that increases the mandatory minimum is an "element" that must be submitted to the jury. Accordingly, *Harris* is overruled.

I

Petitioner Allen Ryan Alleyne and an accomplice devised a plan to rob a store manager as he drove the store's daily deposits to a local bank. By feigning car trouble, they tricked the manager to stop. Alleyne's accomplice approached the manager with a gun and demanded the store's deposits, which the manager surrendered. Alleyne was later charged with multiple federal offenses, including robbery affecting interstate commerce, 18 U.S.C. § 1951(a), and using or carrying a firearm in relation to a crime of violence, § 924(c)(1)(A). Section 924(c)(1)(A) provides, in relevant part, that anyone who "uses or carries a firearm" in relation to a "crime of violence" shall:

> "(i) be sentenced to a term of imprisonment of not less than 5 years;
> "(ii) if the firearm is brandished, be sentenced to a term of imprisonment of not less than 7 years; and
> "(iii) if the firearm is discharged, be sentenced to a term of imprisonment of not less than 10 years."

The jury convicted Alleyne. The jury indicated on the verdict form that Alleyne had "[u]sed or carried a firearm during and in relation to a crime of violence," but did not indicate a finding that the firearm was "[b]randished." App. 40.

The presentence report recommended a 7-year sentence on the § 924(c) count, which reflected the mandatory minimum sentence for cases in which a firearm has been "brandished," § 924(c)(1)(A)(ii). Alleyne objected to this recommendation. He argued that it was clear from the verdict form that the jury did not find brandishing beyond a reasonable doubt and that he was subject only to the 5-year minimum for "us[ing] or carr[ying] a firearm." Alleyne contended that raising his mandatory minimum sentence based on a sentencing judge's finding that he brandished a firearm would violate his Sixth Amendment right to a jury trial.

The District Court overruled Alleyne's objection. It explained that, under *Harris*, brandishing was a sentencing factor that the court could find by a preponderance of evidence without running afoul of the Constitution. It found that the evidence supported a finding of brandishing, and sentenced Alleyne to seven years' imprisonment on the § 924(c) count. The Court of Appeals affirmed. . . .

II

The Sixth Amendment provides that those "accused" of a "crime" have the right to a trial "by an impartial jury." This right, in conjunction with the Due Process Clause, requires that each element of a crime be proved to the jury beyond a reasonable doubt. United States v. Gaudin, 515 U.S. 506, 510 (1995); In re Winship, 397 U.S. 358, 364 (1970). The substance and scope of this right depend upon the proper designation of the facts that are elements of the crime.

A

The question of how to define a "crime" — and, thus, how to determine what facts must be submitted to the jury — has generated a number of divided opinions from this Court. The principal source of disagreement is the constitutional status of a special sort of fact known as a "sentencing factor." This term was first used in McMillan v. Pennsylvania, 477 U.S. 79, 86 (1986), to refer to facts that are not found by a jury but that can still increase the defendant's punishment. Following *McMillan*'s introduction of this term, this Court has made a number of efforts to delimit its boundaries.

McMillan initially invoked the distinction between "elements" and "sentencing factors" to reject a constitutional challenge to Pennsylvania's Mandatory Minimum Sentencing Act, 42 Pa. Cons. Stat. § 9712 (1982). . . .

McMillan did not address whether legislatures' freedom to define facts as sentencing factors extended to findings that increased the maximum term of imprisonment for an offense. We foreshadowed an answer to this question in Jones v. United States, 526 U.S. 227, 243, n. 6 (1999), but did not resolve the issue until *Apprendi*. There, we identified a concrete limit on the types of facts that legislatures may designate as sentencing factors.

In *Apprendi*, . . . [w]e explained that there was no "principled basis for treating" a fact increasing the maximum term of imprisonment differently than the facts constituting the base offense. 530 U.S., at 476. The historic link between crime and punishment, instead, led us to conclude that any fact that increased the prescribed statutory maximum sentence must be an "element" of the offense to be found by the jury. Id., at 483, n. 10. . . .

B

While *Apprendi* only concerned a judicial finding that increased the statutory maximum, the logic of *Apprendi* prompted questions about the continuing vitality, if not validity, of McMillan's holding that facts found to increase the mandatory minimum sentence are sentencing factors and not elements of the crime. We responded two years later in Harris v. United States, 536 U.S. 545, where we considered the same statutory provision and the same question before us today. . . .

The Court declined to apply *Apprendi* to facts that increased the mandatory minimum sentence but not the maximum sentence. 536 U.S., at 557. In the Court's view, judicial factfinding that increased the mandatory minimum did not implicate the Sixth Amendment. Because the jury's verdict "authorized the judge to impose the minimum with or without the finding," ibid., the Court was of the view that the factual basis for increasing the minimum sentence was not "'essential'" to the defendant's punishment. Id., at 560-561 (plurality opinion). Instead, it merely limited the judge's "choices within the authorized range." Id., at 567. From this, the Court drew a distinction between "facts increasing the defendant's minimum sentence and facts extending the sentence beyond the statutory maximum," Id., at 566. The Court limited *Apprendi*'s holding to instances where the factual finding increases the statutory maximum sentence.

III

Alleyne contends that *Harris* was wrongly decided and that it cannot be reconciled with our reasoning in *Apprendi*. We agree.

A

The touchstone for determining whether a fact must be found by a jury beyond a reasonable doubt is whether the fact constitutes an "element" or "ingredient" of the charged offense. United States v. O'Brien, 560 U.S. 218, ___ (2010) (slip op., at 5); *Apprendi*, supra, at 483, n. 10; J. Archbold, Pleading and Evidence in Criminal Cases 52 (5th Am. ed. 1846) (hereinafter Archbold). In *Apprendi*, we held that a fact is by definition an element of the offense and must be submitted to the jury if it increases the punishment above what is otherwise legally prescribed. 530 U.S., at 483, n. 10. While *Harris* declined to extend this principle to facts increasing mandatory minimum sentences, *Apprendi*'s definition of "elements" necessarily includes not only facts that increase the ceiling, but also those that increase the floor. Both kinds of facts alter the pre-scribed range of sentences to which a defendant is exposed and do so in a manner that aggravates the punishment. 530 U.S., at 483, n. 10; *Harris,* supra, at 579 (Thomas, J., dissenting). Facts that increase the mandatory minimum sentence are therefore elements and must be submitted to the jury and found beyond a reasonable doubt.

[In the rest of this section, Justice Thomas reviewed a wide range of historical evidence in support of the close link between "crimes" and "punishments" at common law. — EDS.]

B

Consistent with common-law and early American practice, *Apprendi* concluded that any "facts that increase the prescribed range of penalties to which a criminal defendant is exposed" are elements of the crime. Id., at 490 (internal quotation marks omitted); Id., at 483, n. 10 ("[F]acts that expose a defendant to a punishment greater than that otherwise legally prescribed were by definition 'elements' of a separate legal offense").[1] We held that the Sixth Amendment provides defendants with the right to have a jury find those facts beyond a reasonable doubt. Id., at 484. While *Harris* limited *Apprendi* to facts increasing the statutory maximum, the principle applied in *Apprendi* applies with equal force to facts increasing the mandatory minimum.

It is indisputable that a fact triggering a mandatory minimum alters the prescribed range of sentences to which a criminal defendant is exposed. *Apprendi,* supra, at 490; *Harris,* 536 U.S., at 575, 582 (Thomas, J., dissenting). But for a finding of brandishing, the penalty is five years to life in prison; with a finding of brandishing, the penalty becomes seven years to life. Just as the maximum of life marks the outer boundary of the range, so seven years marks its floor. And because the legally prescribed range is the penalty affixed to the crime, infra, this page, it follows that a fact increasing either end of the range produces a new penalty and constitutes an ingredient of the offense. *Apprendi,* supra, at 501 (Thomas, J., concurring). . . .

It is impossible to dissociate the floor of a sentencing range from the penalty affixed to the crime. See *Harris,* supra, at 569 (Breyer, J., con-curring in part and concurring in judgment) (facts increasing the

1. In Almendarez-Torres v. United States, 523 U.S. 224 (1998), we recognized a narrow exception to this general rule for the fact of a prior conviction. Because the parties do not contest that decision's vitality, we do not revisit it for purposes of our decision today.

minimum and facts increasing the maximum cannot be distinguished "in terms of logic"). Indeed, criminal statutes have long specified both the floor and ceiling of sentence ranges, which is evidence that both define the legally prescribed penalty. See, e.g., supra, at 7-8; N.Y. Penal Code §§ 231-232, p. 70 (1882) (punishment for first-degree robbery was 10 to 20 years' imprisonment; second-degree robbery was 5 to 15 years); Va. Code ch. 192, §§ 1-2, p. 787 (2d ed. 1860) (arson committed at night was punishable by 5 to 10 years; arson committed during the day was 3 to 10 years). This historical practice allowed those who violated the law to know, ex ante, the contours of the penalty that the legislature affixed to the crime — and comports with the obvious truth that the floor of a mandatory range is as relevant to wrongdoers as the ceiling. A fact that increases a sentencing floor, thus, forms an essential ingredient of the offense.

Moreover, it is impossible to dispute that facts increasing the legally prescribed floor aggravate the punishment. *Harris*, supra, at 579 (Thomas, J., dissenting); *O'Brien*, 560 U.S., at ___ (Thomas, J., concurring in judgment) (slip op., at 2). Elevating the low-end of a sentencing range heightens the loss of liberty associated with the crime: the defendant's "expected punishment has increased as a result of the narrowed range" and "the prosecution is empowered, by invoking the mandatory minimum, to require the judge to impose a higher punishment than he might wish." *Apprendi*, supra, at 522 (Thomas, J., concurring). Why else would Congress link an increased mandatory minimum to a particular aggravating fact other than to heighten the consequences for that behavior? See *McMillan*, 477 U.S., at 88, 89 (twice noting that a mandatory minimum "'ups the ante'" for a criminal defendant); *Harris*, supra, at 580 (Thomas, J., dissenting). This reality demonstrates that the core crime and the fact triggering the mandatory minimum sentence together constitute a new, aggravated crime, each element of which must be submitted to the jury.[2]

Defining facts that increase a mandatory statutory minimum to be part of the substantive offense enables the defendant to predict the legally applicable penalty from the face of the indictment. See *Apprendi*, 530

---

2. Juries must find any facts that increase either the statutory maximum or minimum because the Sixth Amendment applies where a finding of fact both alters the legally prescribed range and does so in a way that aggravates the penalty. Importantly, this is distinct from factfinding used to guide judicial discretion in selecting a punishment "within limits fixed by law." Williams v. New York, 337 U.S. 241, 246 (1949). While such findings of fact may lead judges to select sentences that are more severe than the ones they would have selected without those facts, the Sixth Amendment does not govern that element of sentencing. Infra, at 15-17, and n. 6.

U.S., at 478-479. It also preserves the historic role of the jury as an intermediary between the State and criminal defendants. See United States v. Gaudin, 515 U.S., at 510-511 ("This right was designed 'to guard against a spirit of oppression and tyranny on the part of rulers,' and 'was from very early times insisted on by our ancestors in the parent country, as the great bulwark of their civil and political liberties'" (quoting 2 J. Story, Commentaries on the Constitution of the United States §§ 1779, 1780, pp. 540-541 (4th ed. 1873))); Williams v. Florida, 399 U.S. 78, 100 (1970) ("[T]he essential feature of a jury obviously lies in [its] interposition between the accused and his accuser"); Duncan v. Louisiana, 391 U.S. 145, 155 (1968) ("A right to jury trial is granted to criminal defendants in order to prevent oppression by the Government").

In adopting a contrary conclusion, *Harris* relied on the fact that the 7-year minimum sentence could have been imposed with or without a judicial finding of brandishing, because the jury's finding already authorized a sentence of five years to life. 536 U.S., at 561. The dissent repeats this argument today. See post, at 5 (opinion of Roberts, C.J.) ("The jury's verdict authorized the judge to impose the precise sentence he imposed for the precise factual reason he imposed it"). While undoubtedly true, this fact is beside the point.

As noted, the essential Sixth Amendment inquiry is whether a fact is an element of the crime. When a finding of fact alters the legally prescribed punishment so as to aggravate it, the fact necessarily forms a constituent part of a new offense and must be submitted to the jury. It is no answer to say that the defendant could have received the same sentence with or without that fact. It is obvious, for example, that a defendant could not be convicted and sentenced for assault, if the jury only finds the facts for larceny, even if the punishments prescribed for each crime are identical. One reason is that each crime has different elements and a defendant can be convicted only if the jury has found each element of the crime of conviction.

Similarly, because the fact of brandishing aggravates the legally prescribed range of allowable sentences, it constitutes an element of a separate, aggravated offense that must be found by the jury, regardless of what sentence the defendant might have received if a different range had been applicable. Indeed, if a judge were to find a fact that increased the statutory maximum sentence, such a finding would violate the Sixth Amendment, even if the defendant ultimately received a sentence falling within the original sentencing range (i.e., the range applicable without that aggravating fact). Cf. Hobbs v. State, 44 Tex. 353 (1875) (reversing conviction where the defendant was indicted for a crime punishable by 2 to 5 years and sentenced to 3 years because the trial court improperly instructed the jury to sentence the defendant between 2 to 10 years if it found a particular aggravating fact); State v. Callahan, 109 La. 946, 33 So. 931 (1903) (finding ex post facto violation where a newly enacted law increased the range of punishment, even though defendant was sentenced within the range established by the prior law). The essential point is that the aggravating fact produced a higher range, which, in turn, conclusively indicates that the fact is an element of a distinct and aggravated crime. It must, therefore, be submitted to the jury and found beyond a reasonable doubt.

Because there is no basis in principle or logic to distinguish facts that raise the maximum from those that increase the minimum, *Harris* was inconsistent with *Apprendi*. It is, accordingly, overruled.[5]

C

In holding that facts that increase mandatory minimum sentences must be submitted to the jury, we take care to note what our holding does not entail. Our ruling today does not mean that any fact that influences judicial discretion must be found by a jury. We have long recognized that broad sentencing discretion, informed by judicial fact-finding, does not violate the Sixth Amendment. See, e.g., Dillon v. United States, 560 U.S. ___, ___ (2010) ("[W]ithin established limits[,] . . . the exercise of [sentencing] discretion does not contravene the Sixth Amendment even if it is informed by judge-found facts" (emphasis deleted and internal quotation marks omitted)); *Apprendi*, 530 U.S., at 481 ("[N]othing in this history suggests that it is impermissible for judges to exercise discretion — taking into consideration various factors relating both to offense and offender — in imposing a judgment within the range prescribed by statute"). This position has firm historical roots as well. As Bishop explained:

> "[W]ithin the limits of any discretion as to the punishment which the law may have allowed, the judge, when he pronounces sentence, may suffer his discretion to be influenced by matter shown in aggravation or mitigation, not covered by the allegations of the indictment." Bishop § 85, at 54.

---

5. The force of stare decisis is at its nadir in cases concerning procedural rules that implicate fundamental constitutional protections. Because *Harris* is irreconcilable with the reasoning of *Apprendi* and the original meaning of the Sixth Amendment, we follow the latter.

"[E]stablishing what punishment is available by law and setting a specific punishment within the bounds that the law has prescribed are two different things." *Apprendi*, supra, at 519 (Thomas, J., concurring). Our decision today is wholly consistent with the broad discretion of judges to select a sentence within the range authorized by law.

IV

Here, the sentencing range supported by the jury's verdict was five years' imprisonment to life. The District Court imposed the 7-year mandatory minimum sentence based on its finding by a preponderance of evidence that the firearm was "brandished." Because the finding of brandishing increased the penalty to which the defendant was subjected, it was an element, which had to be found by the jury beyond a reasonable doubt. The judge, rather than the jury, found brandishing, thus violating petitioner's Sixth Amendment rights.

Accordingly, we vacate the Fourth Circuit's judgment with respect to Alleyne's sentence on the § 924(c)(1)(A) conviction and remand the case for resentencing consistent with the jury's verdict.

JUSTICE SOTOMAYOR, with whom JUSTICE GINSBURG and JUSTICE KAGAN join, concurring.

I join the opinion of the Court, which persuasively explains why Harris v. United States, 536 U.S. 545 (2002), and McMillan v. Pennsylvania, 477 U.S. 79 (1986), were wrongly decided. . . .

. . . Justice Alito exaggerates when he suggests that this case creates an important "precedent about precedent." Rarely will a claim for stare decisis be as weak as it is here, where a constitutional rule of criminal procedure is at issue that a majority of the Court has previously recognized is incompatible with our broader jurisprudence. And . . . Justice Alito's contention that *Apprendi* and *Harris* stand on equal footing for stare decisis purposes, post, at n.*, is simply inconsistent with our last decade of Sixth Amendment jurisprudence.

JUSTICE BREYER, concurring in part and concurring in the judgment.

Eleven years ago, in Harris v. United States, 536 U.S. 545 (2002), I wrote that "I cannot easily distinguish Apprendi v. New Jersey, 530 U.S. 466 (2000), from this case in terms of logic." Id., at 569 (opinion concurring in part and concurring in judgment). I nonetheless accepted *Harris'* holding because I could "[n]ot yet accept [*Apprendi's*] rule." 536 U.S., at 569. I continue to disagree with *Apprendi*. See 536 U.S., at

569-570; United States v. Booker, 543 U.S. 220, 326 (2005) (opinion dissenting in part); Blakely v. Washington, 542 U.S. 296, 328 (2004) (dissenting opinion); *Apprendi*, supra, at 555 (same). But *Apprendi* has now defined the relevant legal regime for an additional decade. And, in my view, the law should no longer tolerate the anomaly that the *Apprendi/ Harris* distinction creates. . . .

. . . I cannot accept the dissent's characterization of the Sixth Amendment as simply seeking to prevent "judicial overreaching" when sentencing facts are at issue. At the very least, the Amendment seeks to protect defendants against "the wishes and opinions of the government" as well. And, that being so, it seems to me highly anomalous to read *Apprendi* as insisting that juries find sentencing facts that permit a judge to impose a higher sentence while not insisting that juries find sentencing facts that require a judge to impose a higher sentence. See *Harris*, supra, at 569-570 (opinion of Breyer, J.).

To overrule *Harris* and to apply *Apprendi*'s basic jury-determination rule to mandatory minimum sentences would erase that anomaly. Where a maximum sentence is at issue, *Apprendi* means that a judge who wishes to impose a higher sentence cannot do so unless a jury finds the requisite statutory factual predicate. Where a mandatory minimum sentence is at issue, application of *Apprendi* would mean that the government cannot force a judge who does not wish to impose a higher sentence to do so unless a jury finds the requisite statutory factual predicate. In both instances the matter concerns higher sentences; in both instances factfinding must trigger the increase; in both instances jury-based factfinding would act as a check: in the first instance, against a sentencing judge wrongly imposing the higher sentence that the judge believes is appropriate, and in the second instance, against a sentencing judge wrongly being required to impose the higher sentence that the judge believes is inappropriate.

While *Harris* has been the law for 11 years, *Apprendi* has been the law for even longer; and I think the time has come to end this anomaly in *Apprendi*'s application. Consequently, I vote to overrule *Harris*. I join Parts I, III-B, III-C, and IV of the Court's opinion and concur in its judgment.

CHIEF JUSTICE ROBERTS, with whom JUSTICE SCALIA and JUSTICE KENNEDY join, dissenting.

Suppose a jury convicts a defendant of a crime carrying a sentence of five to ten years. And suppose the judge says he would sentence the defendant to five years, but because he finds that the defendant used a gun during the crime, he is going to add two years and sentence him to seven. No one thinks that this violates the defendant's right to a jury trial in any way.

Now suppose the legislature says that two years should be added to the five year minimum, if the judge finds that the defendant used a gun during the crime. Such a provision affects the role of the judge—limiting his discretion—but has no effect on the role of the jury. And because it does not affect the jury's role, it does not violate the jury trial guarantee of the Sixth Amendment.

The Framers envisioned the Sixth Amendment as a protection for defendants from the power of the Government. The Court transforms it into a protection for judges from the power of the legislature. For that reason, I respectfully dissent.

I

In a steady stream of cases decided over the last 15 years, this Court has sought to identify the historical understanding of the Sixth Amendment jury trial right and determine how that understanding applies to modern sentencing practice. Our key sources in this task have been 19th-century treatises and common law cases identifying which facts qualified as "elements" of a crime, and therefore had to be alleged in the indictment and proved to a jury beyond a reasonable doubt. See, e.g., Apprendi v. New Jersey, 530 U.S. 466, 476-483, 489-490, n. 15 (2000) (collecting sources); Id., at 501-518 (Thomas, J., concurring) (same). With remarkable uniformity, those authorities provided that an element was "whatever is in law essential to the punishment sought to be inflicted." 1 J. Bishop, Criminal Procedure 50 (2d ed. 1872); see also Apprendi, supra, at 489, n. 15 ("'[T]he indictment must contain an allegation of every fact which is legally essential to the punishment to be inflicted'" (quoting United States v. Reese, 92 U.S. 214, 232 (1876) (Clifford, J., dissenting))); 1 Bishop, supra, § 87, at 55 (an indictment must include "any particular fact which the law makes essential to the punishment").

Judging that this common law rule best reflects what the Framers understood the Sixth Amendment jury right to protect, we have struck down sentencing schemes that were inconsistent with the rule. . . .

We have embraced this 19th-century common law rule based not only on a judgment that it reflects the understanding in place when the Sixth Amendment was ratified, but also on the "need to give intelligible content to the right of jury trial." Blakely, supra, at 305. As Justice Scalia wrote in Apprendi, it is unclear "what the right to trial by jury does guarantee if . . . it does not guarantee . . . the right to have a jury deter-

mine those facts that determine the maximum sentence the law allows."
530 U.S., at 498-499 (concurring opinion).

After all, if a judge's factfinding could authorize a sentence beyond
that allowed by the jury's verdict alone, the jury trial would be "a mere
preliminary to a judicial inquisition into the facts of the crime the State
actually seeks to punish." *Blakely*, supra, at 306-307. The Framers clearly
envisioned a more robust role for the jury. . . . The Sixth Amendment
therefore provided for trial by jury as a "double security, against the
prejudices of judges, who may partake of the wishes and opinions of
the government, and against the passions of the multitude, who may
demand their victim with a clamorous precipitancy." J. Story, Commentaries on the Constitution of the United States § 924, p. 657 (Abr. 1833);
see also The Federalist No. 83, p. 499 (C. Rossiter ed. 1961) (A. Hamilton) (discussing criminal jury trial as a protection against "judicial
despotism"). Our holdings that a judge may not sentence a defendant
to more than the jury has authorized properly preserve the jury right as a
guard against judicial overreaching.

II

There is no such risk of judicial overreaching here. Under 18 U.S.C.
§ 924(c)(1)(A)(i), the jury's verdict fully authorized the judge to impose a
sentence of anywhere from five years to life in prison. No additional
finding of fact was "essential" to any punishment within the range.
After rendering the verdict, the jury's role was completed, it was discharged, and the judge began the process of determining where within
that range to set Alleyne's sentence.

Everyone agrees that in making that determination, the judge was free
to consider any relevant facts about the offense and offender, including
facts not found by the jury beyond a reasonable doubt. . . .

In my view, that is enough to resolve this case. The jury's verdict
authorized the judge to impose the precise sentence he imposed for
the precise factual reason he imposed it. As we have recognized twice
before, the Sixth Amendment demands nothing more. See Harris v.
United States, 536 U.S. 545, 568-569 (2002); McMillan v. Pennsylvania,
477 U.S. 79, 93 (1986).

III

This approach is entirely consistent with *Apprendi*. As I have explained,
Apprendi's constraint on the normal legislative control of criminal proce-

dure draws its legitimacy from two primary principles: (1) common law understandings of the "elements" of a crime, and (2) the need to preserve the jury as a "strong barrier" between defendants and the State. Neither of those principles supports the rule the majority adopts today.

First, there is no body of historical evidence supporting today's new rule. . . .

Nor does the majority's extension of *Apprendi* do anything to preserve the role of the jury as a safeguard between the defendant and the State. That is because even if a jury does not find that the firearm was brandished, a judge can do so and impose a harsher sentence because of his finding, so long as that sentence remains under the statutory maximum. The question here is about the power of judges, not juries. . . .

I find this new rule impossible to square with the historical understanding of the jury right as a defense from judges, not a defense of judges. See *Apprendi*, supra, at 498 (Scalia, J., concurring) ("Judges, it is sometimes necessary to remind ourselves, are part of the State"). Just as the Sixth Amendment "limits judicial power only to the extent that the claimed judicial power infringes on the province of the jury," *Blakely*, 542 U.S. at 308, so too it limits legislative power only to the extent that power infringes on the province of the jury. Because the claimed infringement here is on the province of the judge, not the jury, the jury right has no work to do.

IV

. . . I will not quibble with the majority's application of our stare decisis precedents. But because I believe the majority's new rule — safeguarding the power of judges, not juries — finds no support in the history or purpose of the Sixth Amendment, I respectfully dissent.

JUSTICE ALITO, dissenting.

. . . If the Court is of a mind to reconsider existing precedent, a prime candidate should be Apprendi v. New Jersey, 530 U.S. 466 (2000). . . .

The Court's decision creates a precedent about precedent that may have greater precedential effect than the dubious decisions on which it relies.*

---

* . . . [O]ther than the fact that there are currently five Justices willing to vote to overrule *Harris*, and not five Justices willing to overrule *Apprendi*, there is no compelling reason why the Court overrules the former rather than the latter. If the opportunity arises in the future to overrule *Apprendi* or the present case . . . the precedent the Court sets today will be relevant to the issue of stare decisis.

Chapter 16

Double Jeopardy

A. "Twice Put in Jeopardy"

1. Acquittals

Add the following paragraph at the bottom of page 1495, just after the discussion of Sanabria:

The Court has recently reaffirmed that an acquittal is the end of the case, even if it was entered by a judge who made a legal error. In Evans v. Michigan, 133 S. Ct. 1069 (2013), the trial judge mistakenly thought that the crime charged required proof a certain element, and since the prosecutor had not proven that element, granted a directed verdict for defendant. The state court of appeals agreed with the government that the trial judge has misinterpreted the statute, and remanded for further prosecution. The U.S. Supreme Court, with only one dissent, said that double jeopardy should have barred the State's appeal and now barred a retrial. Cases such as *Fong Foo* and *Sanabria*, said the Court, firmly established that an acquittal, even one that was based on a judicial misinterpretation of the criminal statute, was entitled to the full measure of Double Jeopardy protection.

Add the following paragraph at the end of the second full paragraph on page 1502, just before the paragraph labelled "Protecting Acquittals":

In Blueford v. Arkansas, 132 S. Ct. 2044 (2012), the Court refused to apply *Green* to a case involving lesser-included offenses in which a mistrial was declared because the jury was deadlocked. Blueford was charged in the alternative with capital murder, first-degree murder, manslaughter, and negligent homicide. The trial judge instructed the jury to consider the charges by starting with the most serious (i.e., capital murder), and then progressing to a less serious charge only if they found reasonable doubt on the more serious charge. The verdict forms allowed the jury either to acquit on all charges, or to convict on any one charge, but did not allow for any combination of acquittals and convictions. After a few hours of deliberation, the jury reported that it was deadlocked. In response to an inquiry from the trial judge, the foreperson explained that the jury was unanimous in agreeing that the defendant should be acquitted of capital murder and first-degree murder, was deadlocked on the manslaughter charge, and had not yet voted on the negligent homicide charge. The judge instructed the jury to continue deliberating, but declined a defense request to give the jury an additional verdict form that would have allowed for an acquittal on some but not all of the charges. After another half-hour of deliberation, the jury remained deadlocked, and the judge declared a mistrial. The Court held that Blueford could be retried on all of the charges:

> The foreperson's report was not a final resolution of anything. When the foreperson told the court how the jury had voted on each offense, the jury's deliberations had not yet concluded. The jurors in fact went back to the jury room to deliberate further, even after the foreperson had delivered her report. When they emerged a half hour later, the foreperson stated only that they were unable to reach a verdict. She gave no indication whether it was still the case that all 12 jurors believed Blueford was not guilty of capital or first-degree murder, that 9 of them believed he was guilty of manslaughter, or that a vote had not been taken on negligent homicide. The fact that deliberations continued after the report deprives that report of the finality necessary to constitute an acquittal on the murder offenses.

The Court also rejected Blueford's alternative argument that, before declaring a mistrial, the trial judge should have been required — as a matter of double jeopardy law — to give the jury the requested additional verdict form. Justices Sotomayor, Ginsburg, and Kagan dissented.

Chapter 17

Appellate and Collateral Review

B. Collateral Review

3. Procedural Issues in Federal Habeas

c. Procedural Default

Add the following paragraph at the end of Note 4 on page 1607:

In Martinez v. Ryan, 132 S. Ct. 1309 (2012), the Court addressed the issue of failure to pursue a claim in state collateral proceedings and its impact on federal habeas review. The habeas petitioner, Martinez, was convicted in Arizona, where — as in many states — claims of ineffective assistance of counsel at trial must be raised in a collateral proceeding, so that (if necessary) additional facts relevant to the claim can be developed at an evidentiary hearing. Although defendants have a constitutional right to counsel on their first direct appeal as of right, see Douglas v. California, 372 U.S. 353 (1963), they do not enjoy such a constitutional right in federal or state collateral proceedings, see Ross v. Moffitt, 417 U.S. 600 (1974) (these cases are discussed in Chapter 3, supra, at pages 172-195). After Martinez's conviction was affirmed on direct appeal, his appellate counsel filed a "notice of post-conviction relief" on his behalf, but did not include a claim of ineffectiveness of trial counsel, and then essentially declined to continue representing Martinez. Later, in a second state collateral proceeding, Martinez (now represented by new counsel) tried to raise the trial ineffectiveness claim, but it was denied on grounds of procedural default because it had not been raised in the first state collateral proceeding. The Supreme Court ultimately held that Martinez should be allowed to raise his ineffectiveness claim in federal habeas — notwithstanding the state procedural default — because the lack of effective assistance of counsel in the first state collateral proceeding constituted "cause" for Martinez's failure to raise the trial ineffectiveness claim in that proceeding. The Court stressed (confusingly!) that it was *not* holding that there is a constitutional right to counsel in state collateral proceedings — only that a lack of effective counsel in such a proceeding can, under certain circumstances (such as where, as in *Martinez*, a particular claim *must* be raised in such a proceeding), excuse a procedural default and allow a federal habeas court to reach the merits of the claim.

d. Evidentiary Hearings

Insert the following new paragraph at the end of this section on page 1609:

In Cullen v. Pinholster, 131 S. Ct. 1388 (2011), the Court — in a majority opinion by Justice Thomas that was joined, in this particular aspect, by a total of seven Justices — held that federal habeas courts are generally required to apply the § 2254(d)(1) review standard on the basis of the record as it existed at the time that the relevant state court made its decision on the merits. According to the *Pinholster* Court, any other interpretation would be incompatible with AEDPA's view that the purpose of habeas review is to ensure that state courts comply with federal law; if the state court made a decision that was "reasonable" in light of the record available to it at the time, then there is no lack of compliance for the habeas court to deter. Even though § 2254(e)(2) clearly contemplates that the habeas court may hold an evidentiary hearing under certain circumstances, that provision — as construed by Michael Williams v. Taylor — is limited to situations where the state court did *not* make a decision on the merits.

Add the following new paragraph after the first full paragraph on page 1631, and before the discussion of the Troy Anthony Davis litigation:

The Supreme Court may finally be starting to acknowledge the special status of innocence claims in federal habeas, and the corresponding need for special procedural rules to deal with such claims. In McQuiggin v. Perkins, 133 S. Ct. 1924 (2013), the Court held (by 5-4 per Justice Ginsburg, joined by Justices Kennedy, Breyer, Sotomayor, and Kagan in the majority) that "actual innocence, if proved, serves as a gateway through which a petitioner may pass whether the impediment is a procedural bar, as it was in *Schlup* and *House*, or, as in this case, expiration of the statute of limitations." The Court described this rule as an "equitable exception" to the normal one-year statute of limitations for federal habeas petitions, and held that even a petitioner's failure to engage in "due diligence" to find evidence of his innocence would not preclude him from claiming the exception (although it might undermine the reliability of any "new evidence" offered in support of his innocence claim).

Selected Rules and Statutes

Federal Rules of Criminal Procedure

Rule 1. Scope; Definitions

(a) Scope.

(1) In General. These rules govern the procedure in all criminal proceedings in the United States district courts, the United States courts of appeals, and the Supreme Court of the United States.

(2) State or Local Judicial Officer. When a rule so states, it applies to a proceeding before a state or local judicial officer.

(3) Territorial Courts. These rules also govern the procedure in all criminal proceedings in the following courts:

(A) the district court of Guam;

(B) the district court for the Northern Mariana Islands, except as otherwise provided by law; and

(C) the district court of the Virgin Islands, except that the prosecution of offenses in that court must be by indictment or information as otherwise provided by law.

(4) Removed Proceedings. Although these rules govern all proceedings after removal from a state court, state law governs a dismissal by the prosecution.

(5) Excluded Proceedings. Proceedings not governed by these rules include:

(A) the extradition and rendition of a fugitive;

(B) a civil property forfeiture for violating a federal statute;

(C) the collection of a fine or penalty;

(D) a proceeding under a statute governing juvenile delinquency to the extent the procedure is inconsistent with the statute, unless Rule 20(d) provides otherwise;

(E) a dispute between seamen under 22 U.S.C. §§ 256-258; and

(F) a proceeding against a witness in a foreign country under 28 U.S.C. § 1784.

(b) Definitions. The following definitions apply to these rules:

(1) "Attorney for the government" means:

(A) the Attorney General or an authorized assistant;

(B) a United States attorney or an authorized assistant;

(C) when applicable to cases arising under Guam law, the Guam Attorney General or other person whom Guam law authorizes to act in the matter; and

(D) any other attorney authorized by law to conduct proceedings under these rules as a prosecutor.

(2) "Court" means a federal judge performing functions authorized by law.

(3) "Federal judge" means:

(A) a justice or judge of the United States as these terms are defined in 28 U.S.C. § 451;

(B) a magistrate judge; and

(C) a judge confirmed by the United States Senate and empowered by statute in any commonwealth, territory, or possession to perform a function to which a particular rule relates.

(4) "Judge" means a federal judge or a state or local judicial officer.

(5) "Magistrate judge" means a United States magistrate judge as defined in 28 U.S.C. §§ 631-639.

(6) "Oath" includes an affirmation.

(7) "Organization" is defined in 18 U.S.C. § 18.

(8) "Petty offense" is defined in 18 U.S.C. § 19.

(9) "State" includes the District of Columbia, and any commonwealth, territory, or possession of the United States.

(10) "State or local judicial officer" means:

(A) a state or local officer authorized to act under 18 U.S.C. § 3041; and

(B) a judicial officer empowered by statute in the District of Columbia or in any commonwealth, territory, or possession to perform a function to which a particular rule relates.

(11) "Telephone" means any technology for transmitting live electronic voice communication.

(12) "Victim" means a "crime victim" as defined in 18 U.S.C. § 3771(e).

(c) Authority of a Justice or Judge of the United States. When these rules authorize a magistrate judge to act, any other federal judge may also act.

Rule 3. The Complaint

The complaint is a written statement of the essential facts constituting the offense charged. Except as provided in Rule 4.1, it must be made under oath before a magistrate judge or, if none is reasonably available, before a state or local judicial officer.

Rule 4. Arrest Warrant or Summons on a Complaint

(a) **Issuance.** If the complaint or one or more affidavits filed with the complaint establish probable cause to believe that an offense has been committed and that the defendant committed it, the judge must issue an arrest warrant to an officer authorized to execute it. At the request of an attorney for the government, the judge must issue a summons, instead of a warrant, to a person authorized to serve it. A judge may issue more than one warrant or summons on the same complaint. If a defendant fails to appear in response to a summons, a judge may, and upon request of an attorney for the government must, issue a warrant.

(b) **Form.**

(1) Warrant. A warrant must:

(A) contain the defendant's name or, if it is unknown, a name or description by which the defendant can be identified with reasonable certainty;

(B) describe the offense charged in the complaint;

(C) command that the defendant be arrested and brought without unnecessary delay before a magistrate judge or, if none is reasonably available, before a state or local judicial officer; and

(D) be signed by a judge.

(2) Summons. A summons must be in the same form as a warrant except that it must require the defendant to appear before a magistrate judge at a stated time and place.

(c) **Execution or Service, and Return.**

(1) By Whom. Only a marshal or other authorized officer may execute a warrant. Any person authorized to serve a summons in a federal civil action may serve a summons.

(2) Location. A warrant may be executed, or a summons served, within the jurisdiction of the United States or anywhere else a federal statute authorizes an arrest.

(3) Manner.

(A) A warrant is executed by arresting the defendant. Upon arrest, an officer possessing the original or a duplicate original warrant must show it to the defendant. If the officer does not possess the warrant, the officer must inform the defendant of the warrant's existence and of the offense charged and, at the defendant's request, must show the original or a duplicate original warrant to the defendant as soon as possible.

(B) A summons is served on an individual defendant:

(i) by delivering a copy to the defendant personally; or

(ii) by leaving a copy at the defendant's residence or usual place of abode with a person of suitable age and discretion residing at that location and by mailing a copy to the defendant's last known address.

(C) A summons is served on an organization by delivering a copy to an officer, to a managing or general agent, or to another agent appointed or legally authorized to receive service of process. A copy must also be mailed to the organization's last known address within the district or to its principal place of business elsewhere in the United States.

(4) Return.

(A) After executing a warrant, the officer must return it to the judge before whom the defendant is brought in accordance with Rule 5. The officer may do so by reliable electronic means. At the request of an attorney for the government, an unexecuted warrant must be brought back to and canceled by a magistrate judge or, if none is reasonably available, by a state or local judicial officer.

(B) The person to whom a summons was delivered for service must return it on or before the return day.

(C) At the request of an attorney for the government, a judge may deliver an unexecuted warrant, an unserved summons, or a copy of the warrant or summons to the marshal or other authorized person for execution or service.

(d) Warrant by Telephone or Other Reliable Electronic Means. In accordance with Rule 4.1, a magistrate judge may issue a warrant or summons based on information communicated by telephone or other reliable electronic means.

Rule 4.1. Complaint, Warrant, or Summons by Telephone or Other Reliable Electronic Means

(a) In General. A magistrate judge may consider information communicated by telephone or other reliable electronic means when reviewing a complaint or deciding whether to issue a warrant or summons.

(b) Procedures. If a magistrate judge decides to proceed under this rule, the following procedures apply:

(1) *Taking Testimony Under Oath.* The judge must place under oath — and may examine — the applicant and any person on whose testimony the application is based.

(2) *Creating a Record of the Testimony and Exhibits.*

(A) *Testimony Limited to Attestation.* If the applicant does no more than attest to the contents of a written affidavit submitted by reliable electronic means, the judge must acknowledge the attestation in writing on the affidavit.

(B) *Additional Testimony or Exhibits.* If the judge considers additional testimony or exhibits, the judge must:

(i) have the testimony recorded verbatim by an electronic recording device, by a court reporter, or in writing;

(ii) have any recording or reporter's notes transcribed, have the transcription certified as accurate, and file it;

(iii) sign any other written record, certify its accuracy, and file it; and

(iv) make sure that the exhibits are filed.

(3) *Preparing a Proposed Duplicate Original of a Complaint, Warrant, or Summons.* The applicant must prepare a proposed duplicate original of a complaint, warrant, or summons, and must read or otherwise transmit its contents verbatim to the judge.

(4) *Preparing an Original Complaint, Warrant, or Summons.* If the applicant reads the contents of the proposed duplicate original, the judge must enter those contents into an original complaint, warrant, or summons. If the applicant transmits the contents by reliable electronic means, the transmission received by the judge may serve as the original.

(5) *Modification.* The judge may modify the complaint, warrant, or summons. The judge must then:

(A) transmit the modified version to the applicant by reliable electronic means; or

(B) file the modified original and direct the applicant to modify the proposed duplicate original accordingly.

(6) *Issuance.* To issue the warrant or summons, the judge must:

(A) sign the original documents;

(B) enter the date and time of issuance on the warrant or summons; and

(C) transmit the warrant or summons by reliable electronic means to the applicant or direct the applicant to sign the judge's name and enter the date and time on the duplicate original.

(c) Suppression Limited. Absent a finding of bad faith, evidence obtained from a warrant issued under this rule is not subject to suppression on the ground that issuing the warrant in this manner was unreasonable under the circumstances.

Rule 5. Initial Appearance

(a) In General.

(1) Appearance Upon an Arrest.

(A) A person making an arrest within the United States must take the defendant without unnecessary delay before a magistrate judge, or before a state or local judicial officer as Rule 5(c) provides, unless a statute provides otherwise.

(B) A person making an arrest outside the United States must take the defendant without unnecessary delay before a magistrate judge, unless a statute provides otherwise.

(2) Exceptions.

(A) An officer making an arrest under a warrant issued upon a complaint charging solely a violation of 18 U.S.C. § 1073 need not comply with this rule if:

(i) the person arrested is transferred without unnecessary delay to the custody of appropriate state or local authorities in the district of arrest; and

(ii) an attorney for the government moves promptly, in the district where the warrant was issued, to dismiss the complaint.

(B) If a defendant is arrested for violating probation or supervised release, Rule 32.1 applies.

(C) If a defendant is arrested for failing to appear in another district, Rule 40 applies.

(3) Appearance Upon a Summons. When a defendant appears in response to a summons under Rule 4, a magistrate judge must proceed under Rule 5(d) or (e), as applicable.

(b) Arrest Without a Warrant. If a defendant is arrested without a warrant, a complaint meeting Rule 4(a)'s requirement of probable cause must be promptly filed in the district where the offense was allegedly committed.

(c) Place of Initial Appearance; Transfer to Another District.

(1) Arrest in the District Where the Offense Was Allegedly Committed. If the defendant is arrested in the district where the offense was allegedly committed:

    (A) the initial appearance must be in that district; and

    (B) if a magistrate judge is not reasonably available, the initial appearance may be before a state or local judicial officer.

    (2) *Arrest in a District Other Than Where the Offense Was Allegedly Committed.* If the defendant was arrested in a district other than where the offense was allegedly committed, the initial appearance must be:

    (A) in the district of arrest; or

    (B) in an adjacent district if:

        (i) the appearance can occur more promptly there; or

        (ii) the offense was allegedly committed there and the initial appearance will occur on the day of arrest.

    (3) *Procedures in a District Other Than Where the Offense Was Allegedly Committed.* If the initial appearance occurs in a district other than where the offense was allegedly committed, the following procedures apply:

    (A) the magistrate judge must inform the defendant about the provisions of Rule 20;

    (B) if the defendant was arrested without a warrant, the district court where the offense was allegedly committed must first issue a warrant before the magistrate judge transfers the defendant to that district;

    (C) the magistrate judge must conduct a preliminary hearing if required by Rule 5.1;

    (D) the magistrate judge must transfer the defendant to the district where the offense was allegedly committed if:

        (i) the government produces the warrant, a certified copy of the warrant, or a reliable electronic form of either; and

        (ii) the judge finds that the defendant is the same person named in the indictment, information, or warrant; and

    (E) when a defendant is transferred and discharged, the clerk must promptly transmit the papers and any bail to the clerk in the district where the offense was allegedly committed.

    (4) *Procedure for Persons Extradited to the United States.* If the defendant is surrendered to the United States in accordance with a request for the defendant's extradition, the initial appearance must be in the district (or one of the districts) where the offense is charged.

    (d) **Procedure in a Felony Case.**

    (1) *Advice.* If the defendant is charged with a felony, the judge must inform the defendant of the following:

(A) the complaint against the defendant, and any affidavit filed with it;

(B) the defendant's right to retain counsel or to request that counsel be appointed if the defendant cannot obtain counsel;

(C) the circumstances, if any, under which the defendant may secure pretrial release;

(D) any right to a preliminary hearing; and

(E) the defendant's right not to make a statement, and that any statement made may be used against the defendant.

(2) Consulting with Counsel. The judge must allow the defendant reasonable opportunity to consult with counsel.

(3) Detention or Release. The judge must detain or release the defendant as provided by statute or these rules.

(4) Plea. A defendant may be asked to plead only under Rule 10.

(e) Procedure in a Misdemeanor Case. If the defendant is charged with a misdemeanor only, the judge must inform the defendant in accordance with Rule 58(b)(2).

(f) Video Teleconferencing. Video teleconferencing may be used to conduct an appearance under this rule if the defendant consents.

Rule 5.1. Preliminary Hearing

(a) In General. If a defendant is charged with an offense other than a petty offense, a magistrate judge must conduct a preliminary hearing unless:

(1) the defendant waives the hearing;

(2) the defendant is indicted;

(3) the government files an information under Rule 7(b) charging the defendant with a felony;

(4) the government files an information charging the defendant with a misdemeanor; or

(5) the defendant is charged with a misdemeanor and consents to trial before a magistrate judge.

(b) Selecting a District. A defendant arrested in a district other than where the offense was allegedly committed may elect to have the preliminary hearing conducted in the district where the prosecution is pending.

(c) Scheduling. The magistrate judge must hold the preliminary hearing within a reasonable time, but no later than 14 days after the initial appearance if the defendant is in custody and no later than 21 days if not in custody.

(d) Extending the Time. With the defendant's consent and upon a showing of good cause — taking into account the public interest in the prompt disposition of criminal cases — a magistrate judge may extend the time limits in Rule 5.1(c) one or more times. If the defendant does not consent, the magistrate judge may extend the time limits only on a showing that extraordinary circumstances exist and justice requires the delay.

(e) Hearing and Finding. At the preliminary hearing, the defendant may cross-examine adverse witnesses and may introduce evidence but may not object to evidence on the ground that it was unlawfully acquired. If the magistrate judge finds probable cause to believe an offense has been committed and the defendant committed it, the magistrate judge must promptly require the defendant to appear for further proceedings.

(f) Discharging the Defendant. If the magistrate judge finds no probable cause to believe an offense has been committed or the defendant committed it, the magistrate judge must dismiss the complaint and discharge the defendant. A discharge does not preclude the government from later prosecuting the defendant for the same offense.

(g) Recording the Proceedings. The preliminary hearing must be recorded by a court reporter or by a suitable recording device. A recording of the proceeding may be made available to any party upon request. A copy of the recording and a transcript may be provided to any party upon request and upon any payment required by applicable Judicial Conference regulations.

(h) Producing a Statement.

(1) In General. Rule 26.2(a)-(d) and (f) applies at any hearing under this rule, unless the magistrate judge for good cause rules otherwise in a particular case.

(2) Sanctions for Not Producing a Statement. If a party disobeys a Rule 26.2 order to deliver a statement to the moving party, the magistrate judge must not consider the testimony of a witness whose statement is withheld.

Rule 6. The Grand Jury

(a) Summoning a Grand Jury.

(1) In General. When the public interest so requires, the court must order that one or more grand juries be summoned. A grand

jury must have 16 to 23 members, and the court must order that enough legally qualified persons be summoned to meet this requirement.

(2) Alternate Jurors. When a grand jury is selected, the court may also select alternate jurors. Alternate jurors must have the same qualifications and be selected in the same manner as any other juror. Alternate jurors replace jurors in the same sequence in which the alternates were selected. An alternate juror who replaces a juror is subject to the same challenges, takes the same oath, and has the same authority as the other jurors.

(b) Objection to the Grand Jury or to a Grand Juror.

(1) Challenges. Either the government or a defendant may challenge the grand jury on the ground that it was not lawfully drawn, summoned, or selected, and may challenge an individual juror on the ground that the juror is not legally qualified.

(2) Motion to Dismiss an Indictment. A party may move to dismiss the indictment based on an objection to the grand jury or on an individual juror's lack of legal qualification, unless the court has previously ruled on the same objection under Rule 6(b)(1). The motion to dismiss is governed by 28 U.S.C. § 1867(e). The court must not dismiss the indictment on the ground that a grand juror was not legally qualified if the record shows that at least 12 qualified jurors concurred in the indictment.

(c) Foreperson and Deputy Foreperson. The court will appoint one juror as the foreperson and another as the deputy foreperson. In the foreperson's absence, the deputy foreperson will act as the foreperson. The foreperson may administer oaths and affirmations and will sign all indictments. The foreperson — or another juror designated by the foreperson — will record the number of jurors concurring in every indictment and will file the record with the clerk, but the record may not be made public unless the court so orders.

(d) Who May Be Present.

(1) While the Grand Jury Is in Session. The following persons may be present while the grand jury is in session: attorneys for the government, the witness being questioned, interpreters when needed, and a court reporter or an operator of a recording device.

(2) During Deliberations and Voting. No person other than the jurors, and any interpreter needed to assist a hearing-impaired or speech-impaired juror, may be present while the grand jury is deliberating or voting.

(e) Recording and Disclosing the Proceedings.

(1) Recording the Proceedings. Except while the grand jury is deliberating or voting, all proceedings must be recorded by a court reporter or by a suitable recording device. But the validity of a prosecution is not affected by the unintentional failure to make a recording. Unless the court orders otherwise, an attorney for the government will retain control of the recording, the reporter's notes, and any transcript prepared from those notes.

(2) Secrecy.

(A) No obligation of secrecy may be imposed on any person except in accordance with Rule 6(e)(2)(B).

(B) Unless these rules provide otherwise, the following persons must not disclose a matter occurring before the grand jury:

(i) a grand juror;

(ii) an interpreter;

(iii) a court reporter;

(iv) an operator of a recording device;

(v) a person who transcribes recorded testimony;

(vi) an attorney for the government; or

(vii) a person to whom disclosure is made under Rule 6(e)(3)(A)(ii) or (iii).

(3) Exceptions.

(A) Disclosure of a grand-jury matter — other than the grand jury's deliberations or any grand juror's vote — may be made to:

(i) an attorney for the government for use in performing that attorney's duty;

(ii) any government personnel — including those of a state, state subdivision, Indian tribe, or foreign government — that an attorney for the government considers necessary to assist in performing that attorney's duty to enforce federal criminal law; or

(iii) a person authorized by 18 U.S.C. § 3322.

(B) A person to whom information is disclosed under Rule 6(e)(3)(A)(ii) may use that information only to assist an attorney for the government in performing that attorney's duty to enforce federal criminal law. An attorney for the government must promptly provide the court that impaneled the grand jury with the names of all persons to whom a disclosure has been made, and must certify that the attorney has advised those persons of their obligation of secrecy under this rule.

(C) An attorney for the government may disclose any grand-jury matter to another federal grand jury.

(D) An attorney for the government may disclose any grand-jury matter involving foreign intelligence, counterintelligence (as defined in 50 U.S.C. § 401a), or foreign intelligence information (as defined in Rule 6(e)(3)(D)(iii)) to any federal law enforcement, intelligence, protective, immigration, national defense, or national security official to assist the official receiving the information in the performance of that official's duties. An attorney for the government may also disclose any grand-jury matter involving, within the United States or elsewhere, a threat of attack or other grave hostile acts of a foreign power or its agent, a threat of domestic or international sabotage or terrorism, or clandestine intelligence gathering activities by an intelligence service or network of a foreign power or by its agent, to any appropriate federal, state, state subdivision, Indian tribal, or foreign government official, for the purpose of preventing or responding to such threat or activities.

(i) Any official who receives information under Rule 6(e)(3)(D) may use the information only as necessary in the conduct of that person's official duties subject to any limitations on the unauthorized disclosure of such information. Any state, state subdivision, Indian tribal, or foreign government official who receives information under Rule 6(e)(3)(D) may use the information only in a manner consistent with any guidelines issued by the Attorney General and the Director of National Intelligence.

(ii) Within a reasonable time after disclosure is made under Rule 6(e)(3)(D), an attorney for the government must file, under seal, a notice with the court in the district where the grand jury convened stating that such information was disclosed and the departments, agencies, or entities to which the disclosure was made.

(iii) As used in Rule 6(e)(3)(D), the term "foreign intelligence information" means:

(a) information, whether or not it concerns a United States person, that relates to the ability of the United States to protect against—

- actual or potential attack or other grave hostile acts of a foreign power or its agent;
- sabotage or international terrorism by a foreign power or its agent; or
- clandestine intelligence activities by an intelligence service or network of a foreign power or by its agent; or

(b) information, whether or not it concerns a United States person, with respect to a foreign power or foreign territory that relates to —

- the national defense or the security of the United States; or
- the conduct of the foreign affairs of the United States.

(E) The court may authorize disclosure — at a time, in a manner, and subject to any other conditions that it directs — of a grand-jury matter:

(i) preliminarily to or in connection with a judicial proceeding;

(ii) at the request of a defendant who shows that a ground may exist to dismiss the indictment because of a matter that occurred before the grand jury;

(iii) at the request of the government, when sought by a foreign court or prosecutor for use in an official criminal investigation;

(iv) at the request of the government if it shows that the matter may disclose a violation of State, Indian tribal, or foreign criminal law, as long as the disclosure is to an appropriate state, state-subdivision, Indian tribal, or foreign government official for the purpose of enforcing that law; or

(v) at the request of the government if it shows that the matter may disclose a violation of military criminal law under the Uniform Code of Military Justice, as long as the disclosure is to an appropriate military official for the purpose of enforcing that law.

(F) A petition to disclose a grand-jury matter under Rule 6(e)(3)(E)(i) must be filed in the district where the grand jury convened. Unless the hearing is ex parte — as it may be when the government is the petitioner — the petitioner must serve the petition on, and the court must afford a reasonable opportunity to appear and be heard to:

(i) an attorney for the government;

(ii) the parties to the judicial proceeding; and

(iii) any other person whom the court may designate.

(G) If the petition to disclose arises out of a judicial proceeding in another district, the petitioned court must transfer the petition to the other court unless the petitioned court can reasonably determine whether disclosure is proper. If the petitioned court decides to transfer, it must send to the transferee court the material sought to be disclosed, if feasible, and a written evaluation of the need for continued grand-jury secrecy. The transferee court must afford those persons identified in Rule 6(e)(3)(F) a reasonable opportunity to appear and be heard.

(4) Sealed Indictment. The magistrate judge to whom an indictment is returned may direct that the indictment be kept secret until the defendant is in custody or has been released pending trial. The clerk must then seal the indictment, and no person may disclose the indictment's existence except as necessary to issue or execute a warrant or summons.

(5) Closed Hearing. Subject to any right to an open hearing in a contempt proceeding, the court must close any hearing to the extent necessary to prevent disclosure of a matter occurring before a grand jury.

(6) Sealed Records. Records, orders, and subpoenas relating to grand-jury proceedings must be kept under seal to the extent and as long as necessary to prevent the unauthorized disclosure of a matter occurring before a grand jury.

(7) Contempt. A knowing violation of Rule 6, or of any guidelines jointly issued by the Attorney General and the Director of National Intelligence under Rule 6, may be punished as a contempt of court.

(f) Indictment and Return. A grand jury may indict only if at least 12 jurors concur. The grand jury — or its foreperson or deputy foreperson — must return the indictment to a magistrate judge in open court. To avoid unnecessary cost or delay, the magistrate judge may take the return by video teleconference from the court where the grand jury sits. If a complaint or information is pending against the defendant and 12 jurors do not concur in the indictment, the foreperson must promptly and in writing report the lack of concurrence to the magistrate judge.

(g) Discharging the Grand Jury. A grand jury must serve until the court discharges it, but it may serve more than 18 months only if the court, having determined that an extension is in the public interest, extends the grand jury's service. An extension may be granted for no more than 6 months, except as otherwise provided by statute.

(h) Excusing a Juror. At any time, for good cause, the court may excuse a juror either temporarily or permanently, and if permanently, the court may impanel an alternate juror in place of the excused juror.

(i) "Indian Tribe" Defined. "Indian tribe" means an Indian tribe recognized by the Secretary of the Interior on a list published in the Federal Register under 25 U.S.C. § 479a-1.

Rule 7. The Indictment and the Information

(a) When Used.

(1) Felony. An offense (other than criminal contempt) must be prosecuted by an indictment if it is punishable:

(A) by death; or

(B) by imprisonment for more than one year.

(2) Misdemeanor. An offense punishable by imprisonment for one year or less may be prosecuted in accordance with Rule 58(b)(1).

(b) Waiving Indictment. An offense punishable by imprisonment for more than one year may be prosecuted by information if the defendant — in open court and after being advised of the nature of the charge and of the defendant's rights — waives prosecution by indictment.

(c) Nature and Contents.

(1) In General. The indictment or information must be a plain, concise, and definite written statement of the essential facts constituting the offense charged and must be signed by an attorney for the government. It need not contain a formal introduction or conclusion. A count may incorporate by reference an allegation made in another count. A count may allege that the means by which the defendant committed the offense are unknown or that the defendant committed it by one or more specified means. For each count, the indictment or information must give the official or customary citation of the statute, rule, regulation, or other provision of law that the defendant is alleged to have violated. For purposes of an indictment referred to in section 3282 of title 18, United States Code, for which the identity of the defendant is unknown, it shall be sufficient for the indictment to describe the defendant as an individual whose name is unknown, but who has a particular DNA profile, as that term is defined in section 3282.

(2) Citation Error. Unless the defendant was misled and thereby prejudiced, neither an error in a citation nor a citation's omission is a ground to dismiss the indictment or information or to reverse a conviction.

(d) Surplusage. Upon the defendant's motion, the court may strike surplusage from the indictment or information.

(e) Amending an Information. Unless an additional or different offense is charged or a substantial right of the defendant is prejudiced, the court may permit an information to be amended at any time before the verdict or finding.

(f) Bill of Particulars. The court may direct the government to file a bill of particulars. The defendant may move for a bill of particulars before or within 14 days after arraignment or at a later time if the court permits. The government may amend a bill of particulars subject to such conditions as justice requires.

Rule 8. Joinder of Offenses or Defendants

(a) Joinder of Offenses. The indictment or information may charge a defendant in separate counts with two or more offenses if the offenses charged—whether felonies or misdemeanors or both— are of the same or similar character, or are based on the same act or transaction, or are connected with or constitute parts of a common scheme or plan.

(b) Joinder of Defendants. The indictment or information may charge two or more defendants if they are alleged to have participated in the same act or transaction, or in the same series of acts or transactions, constituting an offense or offenses. The defendants may be charged in one or more counts together or separately. All defendants need not be charged in each count.

Rule 9. Arrest Warrant or Summons on an Indictment or Information

(a) Issuance. The court must issue a warrant—or at the government's request, a summons—for each defendant named in an indictment or named in an information if one or more affidavits accompanying the information establish probable cause to believe that an offense has been committed and that the defendant committed it. The court may issue more than one warrant or summons for the same defendant. If a defendant fails to appear in response to a summons, the court may, and upon request of an attorney for the government must, issue a warrant. The court must issue the arrest warrant to an officer authorized to execute it or the summons to a person authorized to serve it.

(b) Form.

(1) Warrant. The warrant must conform to Rule 4(b)(1) except that it must be signed by the clerk and must describe the offense charged in the indictment or information.

(2) Summons. The summons must be in the same form as a warrant except that it must require the defendant to appear before the court at a stated time and place.

(c) Execution or Service; Return; Initial Appearance.

(1) Execution or Service.

(A) The warrant must be executed or the summons served as provided in Rule 4(c)(1), (2), and (3).

(B) The officer executing the warrant must proceed in accordance with Rule 5(a)(1).

(2) Return. A warrant or summons must be returned in accordance with Rule 4(c)(4).

(3) Initial Appearance. When an arrested or summoned defendant first appears before the court, the judge must proceed under Rule 5.

Rule 10. Arraignment

(a) In General. An arraignment must be conducted in open court and must consist of:

(1) ensuring that the defendant has a copy of the indictment or information;

(2) reading the indictment or information to the defendant or stating to the defendant the substance of the charge; and then

(3) asking the defendant to plead to the indictment or information.

(b) Waiving Appearance. A defendant need not be present for the arraignment if:

(1) the defendant has been charged by indictment or misdemeanor information;

(2) the defendant, in a written waiver signed by both the defendant and defense counsel, has waived appearance and has affirmed that the defendant received a copy of the indictment or information and that the plea is not guilty; and

(3) the court accepts the waiver.

(c) Video Teleconferencing. Video teleconferencing may be used to arraign a defendant if the defendant consents.

Rule 11. Pleas

(a) Entering a Plea.

(1) In General. A defendant may plead not guilty, guilty, or (with the court's consent) nolo contendere.

(2) Conditional Plea. With the consent of the court and the government, a defendant may enter a conditional plea of guilty or nolo contendere, reserving in writing the right to have an appellate court review an adverse determination of a specified pretrial motion. A defendant who prevails on appeal may then withdraw the plea.

(3) Nolo Contendere Plea. Before accepting a plea of nolo contendere, the court must consider the parties' views and the public interest in the effective administration of justice.

(4) Failure to Enter a Plea. If a defendant refuses to enter a plea or if a defendant organization fails to appear, the court must enter a plea of not guilty.

(b) Considering and Accepting a Guilty or Nolo Contendere Plea.

(1) Advising and Questioning the Defendant. Before the court accepts a plea of guilty or nolo contendere, the defendant may be placed under oath and the court must address the defendant personally in open court. During this address, the court must inform the defendant of, and determine that the defendant understands, the following:

(A) the government's right, in a prosecution for perjury or false statement, to use against the defendant any statement that the defendant gives under oath;

(B) the right to plead not guilty, or having already so pleaded, to persist in that plea;

(C) the right to a jury trial;

(D) the right to be represented by counsel—and, if necessary, have the court appoint counsel—at trial and at every other stage of the proceeding;

(E) the right at trial to confront and cross-examine adverse witnesses, to be protected from compelled self-incrimination, to testify and present evidence, and to compel the attendance of witnesses;

(F) the defendant's waiver of these trial rights if the court accepts a plea of guilty or nolo contendere;

(G) the nature of each charge to which the defendant is pleading;

(H) any maximum possible penalty, including imprisonment, fine, and term of supervised release;

(I) any mandatory minimum penalty;

(J) any applicable forfeiture;

(K) the court's authority to order restitution;

(L) the court's obligation to impose a special assessment;

(M) in determining a sentence, the court's obligation to calculate the applicable sentencing-guideline range and to consider that range, possible departures under the Sentencing Guidelines, and other sentencing factors under 18 U.S.C. § 3553(a);

(N) the terms of any plea-agreement provision waiving the right to appeal or to collaterally attack the sentence; and

(O) that, if convicted, a defendant who is not a United States citizen may be removed from the United States, denied citizenship, and denied admission to the United States in the future.

(2) Ensuring That a Plea Is Voluntary. Before accepting a plea of guilty or nolo contendere, the court must address the defendant personally in open court and determine that the plea is voluntary and did not result from force, threats, or promises (other than promises in a plea agreement).

(3) Determining the Factual Basis for a Plea. Before entering judgment on a guilty plea, the court must determine that there is a factual basis for the plea.

(c) Plea Agreement Procedure.

(1) In General. An attorney for the government and the defendant's attorney, or the defendant when proceeding pro se, may discuss and reach a plea agreement. The court must not participate in these discussions. If the defendant pleads guilty or nolo contendere to either a charged offense or a lesser or related offense, the plea agreement may specify that an attorney for the government will:

(A) not bring, or will move to dismiss, other charges;

(B) recommend, or agree not to oppose the defendant's request, that a particular sentence or sentencing range is appropriate or that a particular provision of the Sentencing Guidelines, or policy statement, or sentencing factor does or does not apply (such a recommendation or request does not bind the court); or

(C) agree that a specific sentence or sentencing range is the appropriate disposition of the case, or that a particular provision of the Sentencing Guidelines, policy statement, or sentencing factor does or does not apply (such a recommendation or request binds the court once the court accepts the plea agreement).

(2) Disclosing a Plea Agreement. The parties must disclose the plea agreement in open court when the plea is offered, unless the court for good cause allows the parties to disclose the plea agreement in camera.

(3) Judicial Consideration of a Plea Agreement.

(A) To the extent the plea agreement is of the type specified in Rule 11(c)(l)(A) or (C), the court may accept the agreement, reject it, or defer a decision until the court has reviewed the presentence report.

(B) To the extent the plea agreement is of the type specified in Rule 11(c)(l)(B), the court must advise the defendant that the defendant has no right to withdraw the plea if the court does not follow the recommendation or request.

(4) Accepting a Plea Agreement. If the court accepts the plea agreement, it must inform the defendant that to the extent the plea agreement is of the type specified in Rule 11(c)(1)(A) or (C), the agreed disposition will be included in the judgment.

(5) Rejecting a Plea Agreement. If the court rejects a plea agreement containing provisions of the type specified in Rule 11(c)(1)(A) or (C), the court must do the following on the record and in open court (or, for good cause, in camera):

(A) inform the parties that the court rejects the plea agreement;

(B) advise the defendant personally that the court is not required to follow the plea agreement and give the defendant an opportunity to withdraw the plea; and

(C) advise the defendant personally that if the plea is not withdrawn, the court may dispose of the case less favorably toward the defendant than the plea agreement contemplated.

(d) Withdrawing a Guilty or Nolo Contendere Plea. A defendant may withdraw a plea of guilty or nolo contendere:

(1) before the court accepts the plea, for any reason or no reason; or

(2) after the court accepts the plea but before it imposes sentence if:

(A) the court rejects a plea agreement under Rule 11(c)(5); or

(B) the defendant can show a fair and just reason for requesting the withdrawal.

(e) Finality of a Guilty or Nolo Contendere Plea. After the court imposes sentence, the defendant may not withdraw a plea of guilty or nolo contendere, and the plea may be set aside only on direct appeal or collateral attack.

(f) Admissibility or Inadmissibility of a Plea, Plea Discussions, and Related Statements. The admissibility or inadmissibility of a plea, a plea discussion, and any related statement is governed by Federal Rule of Evidence 410.

(g) Recording the Proceedings. The proceedings during which the defendant enters a plea must be recorded by a court reporter or by a suitable recording device. If there is a guilty plea or a nolo contendere plea, the record must include the inquiries and advice to the defendant required under Rule 11(b) and (c).

(h) Harmless Error. A variance from the requirements of this rule is harmless error if it does not affect substantial rights.

Rule 12.1. Notice of an Alibi Defense

(a) Government's Request for Notice and Defendant's Response.

(1) Government's Request. An attorney for the government may request in writing that the defendant notify an attorney for the government of any intended alibi defense. The request must state the time, date, and place of the alleged offense.

(2) Defendant's Response. Within 14 days after the request, or at some other time the court sets, the defendant must serve written notice on an attorney for the government of any intended alibi defense. The defendant's notice must state:

(A) each specific place where the defendant claims to have been at the time of the alleged offense; and

(B) the name, address, and telephone number of each alibi witness on whom the defendant intends to rely.

(b) Disclosing Government Witnesses.

(1) Disclosure.

(A) In general. If the defendant serves a Rule 12.1(a)(2) notice, an attorney for the government must disclose in writing to the defendant or the defendant's attorney:

(i) the name, address, and telephone number of each witness the government intends to rely on to establish the defendant's presence at the scene of the alleged offense; and

(ii) each government rebuttal witness to the defendant's alibi defense.

(B) Victim's Address and Telephone Number. If the government intends to rely on a victim's testimony to establish that the defendant was present at the scene of the alleged offense and the defendant establishes a need for the victim's address and telephone number, the court may:

(i) order the government to provide the information in writing to the defendant or the defendant's attorney; or

(ii) fashion a reasonable procedure that allows preparation of the defense and also protects the victim's interests.

(2) Time to Disclose. Unless the court directs otherwise, an attorney for the government must give its Rule 12.1(b)(1) disclosure within 14 days after the defendant serves notice of an intended alibi defense under Rule 12.1(a)(2), but no later than 14 days before trial.

(c) Continuing Duty to Disclose.

(1) In General. Both an attorney for the government and the defendant must promptly disclose in writing to the other party the name of each additional witness — and the address and telephone number of each additional witness other than a victim — if:

(A) the disclosing party learns of the witness before or during trial; and

(B) the witness should have been disclosed under Rule 12.1(a) or (b) if the disclosing party had known of the witness earlier.

(2) Address and Telephone Number of an Additional Victim Witness. The address and telephone number of an additional victim witness must not be disclosed except as provided in Rule 12.1(b)(1)(B).

(d) Exceptions. For good cause, the court may grant an exception to any requirement of Rule 12.1(a)-(c).

(e) Failure to Comply. If a party fails to comply with this rule, the court may exclude the testimony of any undisclosed witness regarding the defendant's alibi. This rule does not limit the defendant's right to testify.

(f) Inadmissibility of Withdrawn Intention. Evidence of an intention to rely on an alibi defense, later withdrawn, or of a statement made in connection with that intention, is not, in any civil or criminal proceeding, admissible against the person who gave notice of the intention.

Rule 13. Joint Trial of Separate Cases

The court may order that separate cases be tried together as though brought in a single indictment or information if all offenses and all defendants could have been joined in a single indictment or information.

Rule 14. Relief from Prejudicial Joinder

(a) Relief. If the joinder of offenses or defendants in an indictment, an information, or a consolidation for trial appears to prejudice a defendant or the government, the court may order separate trials of counts, sever the defendants' trials, or provide any other relief that justice requires.

(b) Defendant's Statements. Before ruling on a defendant's motion to sever, the court may order an attorney for the government to deliver to the court for in camera inspection any defendant's statement that the government intends to use as evidence.

Rule 16. Discovery and Inspection

(a) Government's Disclosure.

(1) Information Subject to Disclosure.

(A) Defendant's Oral Statement. Upon a defendant's request, the government must disclose to the defendant the substance of any relevant oral statement made by the defendant, before or after arrest, in response to interrogation by a person the defendant knew was a government agent if the government intends to use the statement at trial.

(B) Defendant's Written or Recorded Statement. Upon a defendant's request, the government must disclose to the defendant, and make available for inspection, copying, or photographing, all of the following:

(i) any relevant written or recorded statement by the defendant if:

- the statement is within the government's possession, custody, or control; and
- the attorney for the government knows — or through due diligence could know — that the statement exists;

(ii) the portion of any written record containing the substance of any relevant oral statement made before or after arrest if the defendant made the statement in response to interrogation by a person the defendant knew was a government agent; and

(iii) the defendant's recorded testimony before a grand jury relating to the charged offense.

(C) Organizational Defendant. Upon a defendant's request, if the defendant is an organization, the government must disclose to the defendant any statement described in Rule 16(a)(l)(A) and (B) if the government contends that the person making the statement:

(i) was legally able to bind the defendant regarding the subject of the statement because of that person's position as the defendant's director, officer, employee, or agent; or

(ii) was personally involved in the alleged conduct constituting the offense and was legally able to bind the defendant regarding that conduct because of that person's position as the defendant's director, officer, employee, or agent.

(D) Defendant's Prior Record. Upon a defendant's request, the government must furnish the defendant with a copy of the defendant's prior criminal record that is within the government's possession, custody, or control if the attorney for the government knows — or through due diligence could know — that the record exists.

(E) Documents and Objects. Upon a defendant's request, the government must permit the defendant to inspect and to copy or photograph books, papers, documents, data, photographs, tangible objects, buildings or places, or copies or portions of any of these items, if the item is within the government's possession, custody, or control and:

(i) the item is material to preparing the defense;

(ii) the government intends to use the item in its case-in-chief at trial; or

(iii) the item was obtained from or belongs to the defendant.

(F) Reports of Examinations and Tests. Upon a defendant's request, the government must permit a defendant to inspect and to copy or photograph the results or reports of any physical or mental examination and of any scientific test or experiment if:

(i) the item is within the government's possession, custody, or control;

(ii) the attorney for the government knows — or through due diligence could know — that the item exists; and

(iii) the item is material to preparing the defense or the government intends to use the item in its case-in-chief at trial.

(G) Expert Witnesses. At the defendant's request, the government must give to the defendant a written summary of any testimony that the government intends to use under Rules 702, 703, or 705 of the Federal Rules of Evidence during its case-in-chief at trial. If the government requests discovery under subdivision (b)(1)(C)(ii) and the defendant complies, the government must, at the defendant's request, give to the defendant a written summary of testimony that the government intends to use under Rules 702, 703, or 705 of the Federal Rules of Evidence as evidence at trial on the issue of the defendant's mental condition. The summary provided under this subparagraph must describe the witness's opinions, the bases and reasons for those opinions, and the witness's qualifications.

(2) Information Not Subject to Disclosure. Except as permitted by Rule 16(a)(1)(A)-(D), (F), and (G), this rule does not authorize the discovery or inspection of reports, memoranda, or other internal government documents made by an attorney for the government or other government agent in connection with investigating or prosecuting the case. Nor does this rule authorize the discovery or inspection of statements made by prospective government witnesses except as provided in 18 U.S.C. § 3500.

(3) Grand Jury Transcripts. This rule does not apply to the discovery or inspection of a grand jury's recorded proceedings, except as provided in Rules 6, 12(h), 16(a)(l), and 26.2.

(b) Defendant's Disclosure.

(1) Information Subject to Disclosure.

(A) Documents and Objects. If a defendant requests disclosure under Rule 16(a)(1)(E) and the government complies, then the defendant must permit the government, upon request, to inspect and to copy or photograph books, papers, documents, data, photographs, tangible objects, buildings or places, or copies or portions of any of these items if:

(i) the item is within the defendant's possession, custody, or control; and

(ii) the defendant intends to use the item in the defendant's case-in-chief at trial.

(B) Reports of Examinations and Tests. If a defendant requests disclosure under Rule 16(a)(1)(F) and the government complies, the defendant must permit the government, upon request, to inspect and to copy or photograph the results or reports of any physical or mental examination and of any scientific test or experiment if:

(i) the item is within the defendant's possession, custody, or control; and

(ii) the defendant intends to use the item in the defendant's case-in-chief at trial, or intends to call the witness who prepared the report and the report relates to the witness's testimony.

(C) Expert Witnesses. The defendant must, at the government's request, give to the government a written summary of any testimony that the defendant intends to use under Rules 702, 703, or 705 of the Federal Rules of Evidence as evidence at trial, if —

(i) the defendant requests disclosure under subdivision (a)(1)(G) and the government complies; or

(ii) the defendant has given notice under Rule 12.2(b) of an intent to present expert testimony on the defendant's mental condition.

This summary must describe the witness's opinions, the bases and reasons for those opinions, and the witness's qualifications[.]

(2) Information Not Subject to Disclosure. Except for scientific or medical reports, Rule 16(b)(1) does not authorize discovery or inspection of:

(A) reports, memoranda, or other documents made by the defendant, or the defendant's attorney or agent, during the case's investigation or defense; or

(B) a statement made to the defendant, or the defendant's attorney or agent, by:

(i) the defendant;

(ii) a government or defense witness; or

(iii) a prospective government or defense witness.

(c) Continuing Duty to Disclose. A party who discovers additional evidence or material before or during trial must promptly disclose its existence to the other party or the court if:

(1) the evidence or material is subject to discovery or inspection under this rule; and

(2) the other party previously requested, or the court ordered, its production.

(d) Regulating Discovery.

(1) Protective and Modifying Orders. At any time the court may, for good cause, deny, restrict, or defer discovery or inspection, or grant other appropriate relief. The court may permit a party to show good cause by a written statement that the court will inspect ex parte. If relief is granted, the court must preserve the entire text of the party's statement under seal.

(2) Failure to Comply. If a party fails to comply with this rule, the court may:

(A) order that party to permit the discovery or inspection; specify its time, place, and manner; and prescribe other just terms and conditions;

(B) grant a continuance;

(C) prohibit that party from introducing the undisclosed evidence; or

(D) enter any other order that is just under the circumstances.

Rule 17. Subpoena

(a) Content. A subpoena must state the court's name and the title of the proceeding, include the seal of the court, and command the witness to attend and testify at the time and place the subpoena specifies. The clerk must issue a blank subpoena—signed and sealed—to the party requesting it, and that party must fill in the blanks before the subpoena is served.

(b) Defendant Unable to Pay. Upon a defendant's ex parte application, the court must order that a subpoena be issued for a named witness if the defendant shows an inability to pay the witness's fees and the necessity of the witness's presence for an adequate defense. If the court orders a subpoena to be issued, the process costs and witness fees will be paid in the same manner as those paid for witnesses the government subpoenas.

(c) Producing Documents and Objects.

(1) In General. A subpoena may order the witness to produce any books, papers, documents, data, or other objects the subpoena

designates. The court may direct the witness to produce the designated items in court before trial or before they are to be offered in evidence. When the items arrive, the court may permit the parties and their attorneys to inspect all or part of them.

(2) Quashing or Modifying the Subpoena. On motion made promptly, the court may quash or modify the subpoena if compliance would be unreasonable or oppressive.

(3) Subpoena for Personal or Confidential Information About a Victim. After a complaint, indictment, or information is filed, a subpoena requiring the production of personal or confidential information about a victim may be served on a third party only by court order. Before entering the order and unless there are exceptional circumstances, the court must require giving notice to the victim so that the victim can move to quash or modify the subpoena or otherwise object.

(d) Service. A marshal, a deputy marshal, or any nonparty who is at least 18 years old may serve a subpoena. The server must deliver a copy of the subpoena to the witness and must tender to the witness one day's witness-attendance fee and the legal mileage allowance. The server need not tender the attendance fee or mileage allowance when the United States, a federal officer, or a federal agency has requested the subpoena.

(e) Place of Service.

(1) In the United States. A subpoena requiring a witness to attend a hearing or trial may be served at any place within the United States.

(2) In a Foreign Country. If the witness is in a foreign country, 28 U.S.C. § 1783 governs the subpoena's service.

(f) Issuing a Deposition Subpoena.

(1) Issuance. A court order to take a deposition authorizes the clerk in the district where the deposition is to be taken to issue a subpoena for any witness named or described in the order.

(2) Place. After considering the convenience of the witness and the parties, the court may order — and the subpoena may require — the witness to appear anywhere the court designates.

(g) Contempt. The court (other than a magistrate judge) may hold in contempt a witness who, without adequate excuse, disobeys a subpoena issued by a federal court in that district. A magistrate judge may hold in contempt a witness who, without adequate excuse, disobeys a subpoena issued by that magistrate judge as provided in 28 U.S.C. § 636(e).

(h) Information Not Subject to a Subpoena. No party may subpoena a statement of a witness or of a prospective witness under this rule. Rule 26.2 governs the production of the statement.

Rule 18.   Place of Prosecution and Trial

Unless a statute or these rules permit otherwise, the government must prosecute an offense in a district where the offense was committed. The court must set the place of trial within the district with due regard for the convenience of the defendant, any victim, and the witnesses, and the prompt administration of justice.

Rule 21.   Transfer for Trial

(a) For Prejudice. Upon the defendant's motion, the court must transfer the proceeding against that defendant to another district if the court is satisfied that so great a prejudice against the defendant exists in the transferring district that the defendant cannot obtain a fair and impartial trial there.

(b) For Convenience. Upon the defendant's motion, the court may transfer the proceeding, or one or more counts, against that defendant to another district for the convenience of the parties, any victim, and the witnesses, and in the interest of justice.

(c) Proceedings on Transfer. When the court orders a transfer, the clerk must send to the transferee district the file, or a certified copy, and any bail taken. The prosecution will then continue in the transferee district.

(d) Time to File a Motion to Transfer. A motion to transfer may be made at or before arraignment or at any other time the court or these rules prescribe.

Rule 23.   Jury or Nonjury Trial

(a) Jury Trial. If the defendant is entitled to a jury trial, the trial must be by jury unless:

(1) the defendant waives a jury trial in writing;

(2) the government consents; and

(3) the court approves.

(b) Jury Size.

(1) In General. A jury consists of 12 persons unless this rule provides otherwise.

(2) Stipulation for a Smaller Jury. At any time before the verdict, the parties may, with the court's approval, stipulate in writing that:

(A) the jury may consist of fewer than 12 persons; or

(B) a jury of fewer than 12 persons may return a verdict if the court finds it necessary to excuse a juror for good cause after the trial begins.

(3) Court Order for a Jury of 11. After the jury has retired to deliberate, the court may permit a jury of 11 persons to return a verdict, even without a stipulation by the parties, if the court finds good cause to excuse a juror.

(c) Nonjury Trial. In a case tried without a jury, the court must find the defendant guilty or not guilty. If a party requests before the finding of guilty or not guilty, the court must state its specific findings of fact in open court or in a written decision or opinion.

Rule 24.   Trial Jurors

(a) Examination.

(1) In General. The court may examine prospective jurors or may permit the attorneys for the parties to do so.

(2) Court Examination. If the court examines the jurors, it must permit the attorneys for the parties to:

(A) ask further questions that the court considers proper; or

(B) submit further questions that the court may ask if it considers them proper.

(b) Peremptory Challenges. Each side is entitled to the number of peremptory challenges to prospective jurors specified below. The court may allow additional peremptory challenges to multiple defendants, and may allow the defendants to exercise those challenges separately or jointly.

(1) Capital Case. Each side has 20 peremptory challenges when the government seeks the death penalty.

(2) Other Felony Case. The government has 6 peremptory challenges and the defendant or defendants jointly have 10

peremptory challenges when the defendant is charged with a crime punishable by imprisonment of more than one year.

(3) Misdemeanor Case. Each side has 3 peremptory challenges when the defendant is charged with a crime punishable by fine, imprisonment of one year or less, or both.

(c) Alternate Jurors.

(1) In General. The court may impanel up to 6 alternate jurors to replace any jurors who are unable to perform or who are disqualified from performing their duties.

(2) Procedure.

(A) Alternate jurors must have the same qualifications and be selected and sworn in the same manner as any other juror.

(B) Alternate jurors replace jurors in the same sequence in which the alternates were selected. An alternate juror who replaces a juror has the same authority as the other jurors.

(3) Retaining Alternate Jurors. The court may retain alternate jurors after the jury retires to deliberate. The court must ensure that a retained alternate does not discuss the case with anyone until that alternate replaces a juror or is discharged. If an alternate replaces a juror after deliberations have begun, the court must instruct the jury to begin its deliberations anew.

(4) Peremptory Challenges. Each side is entitled to the number of additional peremptory challenges to prospective alternate jurors specified below. These additional challenges may be used only to remove alternate jurors.

(A) One or Two Alternates. One additional peremptory challenge is permitted when one or two alternates are impaneled.

(B) Three or Four Alternates. Two additional peremptory challenges are permitted when three or four alternates are impaneled.

(C) Five or Six Alternates. Three additional peremptory challenges are permitted when five or six alternates are impaneled.

Rule 26.2. Producing a Witness's Statement

(a) Motion to Produce. After a witness other than the defendant has testified on direct examination, the court, on motion of a party who did not call the witness, must order an attorney for the government or the defendant and the defendant's attorney to produce, for the examination and use of the moving party, any statement of the witness that is in their possession and that relates to the subject matter of the witness's testimony.

(b) Producing the Entire Statement. If the entire statement relates to the subject matter of the witness's testimony, the court must order that the statement be delivered to the moving party.

(c) Producing a Redacted Statement. If the party who called the witness claims that the statement contains information that is privileged or does not relate to the subject matter of the witness's testimony, the court must inspect the statement in camera. After excising any privileged or unrelated portions, the court must order delivery of the redacted statement to the moving party. If the defendant objects to an excision, the court must preserve the entire statement with the excised portion indicated, under seal, as part of the record.

(d) Recess to Examine a Statement. The court may recess the proceedings to allow time for a party to examine the statement and prepare for its use.

(e) Sanction for Failure to Produce or Deliver a Statement. If the party who called the witness disobeys an order to produce or deliver a statement, the court must strike the witness's testimony from the record. If an attorney for the government disobeys the order, the court must declare a mistrial if justice so requires.

(f) "Statement" Defined. As used in this rule, a witness's "statement" means:

(1) a written statement that the witness makes and signs, or otherwise adopts or approves;

(2) a substantially verbatim, contemporaneously recorded recital of the witness's oral statement that is contained in any recording or any transcription of a recording; or

(3) the witness's statement to a grand jury, however taken or recorded, or a transcription of such a statement.

(g) Scope. This rule applies at trial, at a suppression hearing under Rule 12, and to the extent specified in the following rules:

(1) Rule 5.1(h) (preliminary hearing);

(2) Rule 32(i)(2) (sentencing);

(3) Rule 32.1(e) (hearing to revoke or modify probation or supervised release);

(4) Rule 46(j) (detention hearing); and

(5) Rule 8 of the Rules Governing Proceedings under 28 U.S.C. § 2255.

Rule 29.   Motion for a Judgment of Acquittal

(a) Before Submission to the Jury. After the government closes its evidence or after the close of all the evidence, the court on the defendant's motion must enter a judgment of acquittal of any offense for which the evidence is insufficient to sustain a conviction. The court may on its own consider whether the evidence is insufficient to sustain a conviction. If the court denies a motion for a judgment of acquittal at the close of the government's evidence, the defendant may offer evidence without having reserved the right to do so.

(b) Reserving Decision. The court may reserve decision on the motion, proceed with the trial (where the motion is made before the close of all the evidence), submit the case to the jury, and decide the motion either before the jury returns a verdict or after it returns a verdict of guilty or is discharged without having returned a verdict. If the court reserves decision, it must decide the motion on the basis of the evidence at the time the ruling was reserved.

(c) After Jury Verdict or Discharge.

(1) Time for a Motion. A defendant may move for a judgment of acquittal, or renew such a motion, within 14 days after a guilty verdict or after the court discharges the jury, whichever is later.

(2) Ruling on the Motion. If the jury has returned a guilty verdict, the court may set aside the verdict and enter an acquittal. If the jury has failed to return a verdict, the court may enter a judgment of acquittal.

(3) No Prior Motion Required. A defendant is not required to move for a judgment of acquittal before the court submits the case to the jury as a prerequisite for making such a motion after jury discharge.

(d) Conditional Ruling on a Motion for a New Trial.

(1) Motion for a New Trial. If the court enters a judgment of acquittal after a guilty verdict, the court must also conditionally determine whether any motion for a new trial should be granted if the judgment of acquittal is later vacated or reversed. The court must specify the reasons for that determination.

(2) Finality. The court's order conditionally granting a motion for a new trial does not affect the finality of the judgment of acquittal.

(3) Appeal.

(A) Grant of a Motion for a New Trial. If the court conditionally grants a motion for a new trial and an appellate court later reverses the judgment of acquittal, the trial court must proceed with the new trial unless the appellate court orders otherwise.

(B) Denial of a Motion for a New Trial. If the court conditionally denies a motion for a new trial, an appellee may assert that the denial was erroneous. If the appellate court later reverses the judgment of acquittal, the trial court must proceed as the appellate court directs.

Rule 29.1. Closing Argument

Closing arguments proceed in the following order:
    (a) the government argues;
    (b) the defense argues; and
    (c) the government rebuts.

Rule 31. Jury Verdict

(a) Return. The jury must return its verdict to a judge in open court. The verdict must be unanimous.

(b) Partial Verdicts, Mistrial, and Retrial.

(1) Multiple Defendants. If there are multiple defendants, the jury may return a verdict at any time during its deliberations as to any defendant about whom it has agreed.

(2) Multiple Counts. If the jury cannot agree on all counts as to any defendant, the jury may return a verdict on those counts on which it has agreed.

(3) Mistrial and Retrial. If the jury cannot agree on a verdict on one or more counts, the court may declare a mistrial on those counts. The government may retry any defendant on any count on which the jury could not agree.

(c) Lesser Offense or Attempt. A defendant may be found guilty of any of the following:

(1) an offense necessarily included in the offense charged;

(2) an attempt to commit the offense charged; or

(3) an attempt to commit an offense necessarily included in the offense charged, if the attempt is an offense in its own right.

(d) Jury Poll. After a verdict is returned but before the jury is discharged, the court must on a party's request, or may on its own, poll the jurors individually. If the poll reveals a lack of unanimity, the court may direct the jury to deliberate further or may declare a mistrial and discharge the jury.

Rule 32.   Sentencing and Judgment

(a) [Reserved.]

(b) Time of Sentencing.

(1) In General. The court must impose sentence without unnecessary delay.

(2) Changing Time Limits. The court may, for good cause, change any time limits prescribed in this rule.

(c) Presentence Investigation.

(1) Required Investigation.

(A) In General. The probation officer must conduct a presentence investigation and submit a report to the court before it imposes sentence unless:

(i) 18 U.S.C. § 3593(c) or another statute requires otherwise; or

(ii) the court finds that the information in the record enables it to meaningfully exercise its sentencing authority under 18 U.S.C. § 3553, and the court explains its finding on the record.

(B) Restitution. If the law permits restitution, the probation officer must conduct an investigation and submit a report that contains sufficient information for the court to order restitution.

(2) Interviewing the Defendant. The probation officer who interviews a defendant as part of a presentence investigation must, on request, give the defendant's attorney notice and a reasonable opportunity to attend the interview.

(d) Presentence Report.

(1) Applying the Advisory Sentencing Guidelines. The presentence report must:

(A) identify all applicable guidelines and policy statements of the Sentencing Commission;

(B) calculate the defendant's offense level and criminal history category;

(C) state the resulting sentencing range and kinds of sentences available;

(D) identify any factor relevant to:

(i) the appropriate kind of sentence, or

(ii) the appropriate sentence within the applicable sentencing range; and

(E) identify any basis for departing from the applicable sentencing range.

(2) Additional Information. The presentence report must also contain the following:

(A) the defendant's history and characteristics, including:

(i) any prior criminal record;

(ii) the defendant's financial condition; and

(iii) any circumstances affecting the defendant's behavior that may be helpful in imposing sentence or in correctional treatment;

(B) information that assesses any financial, social, psychological, and medical impact on any victim;

(C) when appropriate, the nature and extent of nonprison programs and resources available to the defendant;

(D) when the law provides for restitution, information sufficient for a restitution order;

(E) if the court orders a study under 18 U.S.C. § 3552(b), any resulting report and recommendation;

(F) a statement of whether the government seeks forfeiture under Rule 32.2 and any other law; and

(G) any other information that the court requires, including information relevant to the factors under 18 U.S.C. § 3553(a).

(3) Exclusions. The presentence report must exclude the following:

(A) any diagnoses that, if disclosed, might seriously disrupt a rehabilitation program;

(B) any sources of information obtained upon a promise of confidentiality; and

(C) any other information that, if disclosed, might result in physical or other harm to the defendant or others.

(e) Disclosing the Report and Recommendation.

(1) Time to Disclose. Unless the defendant has consented in writing, the probation officer must not submit a presentence report to the court or disclose its contents to anyone until the defendant has pleaded guilty or nolo contendere, or has been found guilty.

(2) Minimum Required Notice. The probation officer must give the presentence report to the defendant, the defendant's attorney, and an attorney for the government at least 35 days before sentencing unless the defendant waives this minimum period.

(3) Sentence Recommendation. By local rule or by order in a case, the court may direct the probation officer not to disclose to anyone other than the court the officer's recommendation on the sentence.

(f) Objecting to the Report.

(1) Time to Object. Within 14 days after receiving the presentence report, the parties must state in writing any objections, including objections to material information, sentencing guideline ranges, and policy statements contained in or omitted from the report.

(2) Serving Objections. An objecting party must provide a copy of its objections to the opposing party and to the probation officer.

(3) Action on Objections. After receiving objections, the probation officer may meet with the parties to discuss the objections. The probation officer may then investigate further and revise the presentence report as appropriate.

(g) Submitting the Report. At least 14 days before sentencing, the probation officer must submit to the court and to the parties the presentence report and an addendum containing any unresolved objections, the grounds for those objections, and the probation officer's comments on them.

(h) Notice of Possible Departure from Sentencing Guidelines. Before the court may depart from the applicable sentencing range on a ground not identified for departure either in the presentence report or in a party's prehearing submission, the court must give the parties reasonable notice that it is contemplating such a departure. The notice must specify any ground on which the court is contemplating a departure.

(i) Sentencing.

(1) In General. At sentencing, the court:

(A) must verify that the defendant and the defendant's attorney have read and discussed the presentence report and any addendum to the report;

(B) must give to the defendant and an attorney for the government a written summary of—or summarize in camera—any information excluded from the presentence report under Rule 32(d)(3) on which the court will rely in sentencing, and give them a reasonable opportunity to comment on that information;

(C) must allow the parties' attorneys to comment on the probation officer's determinations and other matters relating to an appropriate sentence; and

(D) may, for good cause, allow a party to make a new objection at any time before sentence is imposed.

(2) Introducing Evidence; Producing a Statement. The court may permit the parties to introduce evidence on the objections. If a witness testifies at sentencing, Rule 26.2(a)-(d) and (f) applies. If a party fails to comply with a Rule 26.2 order to produce a witness's statement, the court must not consider that witness's testimony.

(3) Court Determinations. At sentencing, the court:

(A) may accept any undisputed portion of the presentence report as a finding of fact;

(B) must — for any disputed portion of the presentence report or other controverted matter — rule on the dispute or determine that a ruling is unnecessary either because the matter will not affect sentencing, or because the court will not consider the matter in sentencing; and

(C) must append a copy of the court's determinations under this rule to any copy of the presentence report made available to the Bureau of Prisons.

(4) Opportunity to Speak.

(A) By a Party. Before imposing sentence, the court must:

(i) provide the defendant's attorney an opportunity to speak on the defendant's behalf;

(ii) address the defendant personally in order to permit the defendant to speak or present any information to mitigate the sentence; and

(iii) provide an attorney for the government an opportunity to speak equivalent to that of the defendant's attorney.

(B) By a Victim. Before imposing sentence, the court must address any victim of the crime who is present at sentencing and must permit the victim to be reasonably heard.

(C) By a Victim of a Felony Offense. Before imposing sentence, the court must address any victim of a felony offense, not involving violence or sexual abuse, who is present at sentencing and must permit the victim to speak or submit any information about the sentence. If the felony offense involved multiple victims, the court may limit the number of victims who will address the court.

(D) In Camera Proceedings. Upon a party's motion and for good cause, the court may hear in camera any statement made under Rule 32(i)(4).

(j) Defendant's Right to Appeal.

(1) Advice of a Right to Appeal.

(A) Appealing a Conviction. If the defendant pleaded not guilty and was convicted, after sentencing the court must advise the defendant of the right to appeal the conviction.

(B) Appealing a Sentence. After sentencing — regardless of the defendant's plea — the court must advise the defendant of any right to appeal the sentence.

(C) Appeal Costs. The court must advise a defendant who is unable to pay appeal costs of the right to ask for permission to appeal in forma pauperis.

(2) Clerk's Filing of Notice. If the defendant so requests, the clerk must immediately prepare and file a notice of appeal on the defendant's behalf.

(k) Judgment.

(1) In General. In the judgment of conviction, the court must set forth the plea, the jury verdict or the court's findings, the adjudication, and the sentence. If the defendant is found not guilty or is otherwise entitled to be discharged, the court must so order. The judge must sign the judgment, and the clerk must enter it.

(2) Criminal Forfeiture. Forfeiture procedures are governed by Rule 32.2.

Rule 33. New Trial

(a) Defendant's Motion. Upon the defendant's motion, the court may vacate any judgment and grant a new trial if the interest of justice so requires. If the case was tried without a jury, the court may take additional testimony and enter a new judgment.

(b) Time to File.

(1) Newly Discovered Evidence. Any motion for a new trial grounded on newly discovered evidence must be filed within 3 years after the verdict or finding of guilty. If an appeal is pending, the court may not grant a motion for a new trial until the appellate court remands the case.

(2) Other Grounds. Any motion for a new trial grounded on any reason other than newly discovered evidence must be filed within 14 days after the verdict or finding of guilty.

Rule 41. Search and Seizure

(a) Scope and Definitions.

(1) Scope. This rule does not modify any statute regulating search or seizure, or the issuance and execution of a search warrant in special circumstances.

(2) Definitions. The following definitions apply under this rule:

(A) "Property" includes documents, books, papers, any other tangible objects, and information.

(B) "Daytime" means the hours between 6:00 a.m. and 10:00 p.m. according to local time.

(C) "Federal law enforcement officer" means a government agent (other than an attorney for the government) who is engaged in enforcing the criminal laws and is within any category of officers authorized by the Attorney General to request a search warrant.

(D) "Domestic terrorism" and "international terrorism" have the meanings set out in 18 U.S.C. § 2331.

(E) "Tracking device" has the meaning set out in 18 U.S.C. § 3117(b).

(b) Authority to Issue a Warrant. At the request of a federal law enforcement officer or an attorney for the government:

(1) a magistrate judge with authority in the district — or if none is reasonably available, a judge of a state court of record in the district — has authority to issue a warrant to search for and seize a person or property located within the district;

(2) a magistrate judge with authority in the district has authority to issue a warrant for a person or property outside the district if the person or property is located within the district when the warrant is issued but might move or be moved outside the district before the warrant is executed;

(3) a magistrate judge — in an investigation of domestic terrorism or international terrorism — with authority in any district in which activities related to the terrorism may have occurred has authority to issue a warrant for a person or property within or outside that district;

(4) a magistrate judge with authority in the district has authority to issue a warrant to install within the district a tracking device; the warrant may authorize use of the device to track the movement of a person or property located within the district, outside the district, or both; and

(5) a magistrate judge having authority in any district where activities related to the crime may have occurred, or in the District of Columbia, may issue a warrant for property that is located outside the jurisdiction of any state or district, but within any of the following:

(A) a United States territory, possession, or commonwealth;

(B) the premises — no matter who owns them — of a United States diplomatic or consular mission in a foreign state, including any appurtenant building, part of a building, or land used for the mission's purposes; or

(C) a residence and any appurtenant land owned or leased by the United States and used by United States personnel assigned to a United States diplomatic or consular mission in a foreign state.

(c) Persons or Property Subject to Search or Seizure. A warrant may be issued for any of the following:

(1) evidence of a crime;

(2) contraband, fruits of crime, or other items illegally possessed;

(3) property designed for use, intended for use, or used in committing a crime; or

(4) a person to be arrested or a person who is unlawfully restrained.

(d) Obtaining a Warrant.

(1) In General. After receiving an affidavit or other information, a magistrate judge — or if authorized by Rule 41(b), a judge of a state court of record — must issue the warrant if there is probable cause to search for and seize a person or property or to install and use a tracking device.

(2) Requesting a Warrant in the Presence of a Judge.

(A) Warrant on an Affidavit. When a federal law enforcement officer or an attorney for the government presents an affidavit in support of a warrant, the judge may require the affiant to appear personally and may examine under oath the affiant and any witness the affiant produces.

(B) Warrant on Sworn Testimony. The judge may wholly or partially dispense with a written affidavit and base a warrant on sworn testimony if doing so is reasonable under the circumstances.

(C) Recording Testimony. Testimony taken in support of a warrant must be recorded by a court reporter or by a suitable recording device, and the judge must file the transcript or recording with the clerk, along with any affidavit.

(3) Requesting a Warrant by Telephonic or Other Reliable Electronic Means. In accordance with Rule 4.1, a magistrate judge may issue a warrant based on information communicated by telephone or other reliable electronic means.

(e) Issuing the Warrant.

(1) In General. The magistrate judge or a judge of a state court of record must issue the warrant to an officer authorized to execute it.

(2) Contents of the Warrant.

(A) Warrant to Search for and Seize a Person or Property. Except for a tracking-device warrant, the warrant must identify the person or property to be searched, identify any person or property to be seized, and designate the magistrate judge to whom it must be returned. The warrant must command the officer to:

(i) execute the warrant within a specified time no longer than 14 days;

(ii) execute the warrant during the daytime, unless the judge for good cause expressly authorizes execution at another time; and

(iii) return the warrant to the magistrate judge designated in the warrant.

(B) Warrant Seeking Electronically Stored Information. A warrant under Rule 41(e)(2)(A) may authorize the seizure of electronic storage media or the seizure or copying of electronically stored information. Unless otherwise specified, the warrant authorizes a later review of the media or information consistent with the warrant. The time for executing the warrant in Rule 41(e)(2)(A) and (f)(1)(A) refers to the seizure or on-site copying of the media or information, and not to any later off-site copying or review.

(C) Warrant for a Tracking Device. A tracking-device warrant must identify the person or property to be tracked, designate the magistrate judge to whom it must be returned, and specify a reasonable length of time that the device may be used. The time must not exceed 45 days from the date the warrant was issued. The court may, for good cause, grant one or more extensions for a reasonable period not to exceed 45 days each. The warrant must command the officer to:

(i) complete any installation authorized by the warrant within a specified time no longer than 10 days;

(ii) perform any installation authorized by the warrant during the daytime, unless the judge for good cause expressly authorizes installation at another time; and

(iii) return the warrant to the judge designated in the warrant.

(f) Executing and Returning the Warrant.

(1) Warrant to Search for and Seize a Person or Property.

(A) Noting the Time. The officer executing the warrant must enter on it the exact date and time it was executed.

(B) Inventory. An officer present during the execution of the warrant must prepare and verify an inventory of any property seized. The officer must do so in the presence of another officer and the person from whom, or from whose premises, the property was taken. If either one is not present, the officer must prepare and verify the inventory in the presence of at least one other credible person. In a case involving the seizure of electronic storage media or the seizure or copying of electronically stored information, the inventory may be limited to describing the physical storage media that were seized or copied. The officer may retain a copy of the electronically stored information that was seized or copied.

(C) Receipt. The officer executing the warrant must give a copy of the warrant and a receipt for the property taken to the person from whom, or from whose premises, the property was taken or leave a copy of the warrant and receipt at the place where the officer took the property.

(D) Return. The officer executing the warrant must promptly return it — together with a copy of the inventory — to the magistrate judge designated on the warrant. The officer may do so by reliable electronic means. The judge must, on request, give a copy of the inventory to the person from whom, or from whose premises, the property was taken and to the applicant for the warrant.

(2) Warrant for a Tracking Device.

(A) Noting the Time. The officer executing a tracking-device warrant must enter on it the exact date and time the device was installed and the period during which it was used.

(B) Return. Within 10 days after the use of the tracking device has ended, the officer executing the warrant must return it to the judge designated in the warrant. The officer may do so by reliable electronic means.

(C) Service. Within 10 days after the use of the tracking device has ended, the officer executing a tracking-device warrant must serve a copy of the warrant on the person who was tracked or whose property was tracked. Service may be accomplished by delivering a copy to the person who, or whose property, was tracked; or by leaving a copy at the person's residence or usual place of abode with an individual of suitable age and discretion who resides at that location and by mailing a copy to the person's last known address. Upon request of the government, the judge may delay notice as provided in Rule 41(f)(3).

(3) Delayed Notice. Upon the government's request, a magistrate judge — or if authorized by Rule 41(b), a judge of a state court of record — may delay any notice required by this rule if the delay is authorized by statute.

(g) Motion to Return Property. A person aggrieved by an unlawful search and seizure of property or by the deprivation of property may move for the property's return. The motion must be filed in the district where the property was seized. The court must receive evidence on any factual issue necessary to decide the motion. If it grants the motion, the court must return the property to the movant, but may impose reasonable conditions to protect access to the property and its use in later proceedings.

(h) Motion to Suppress. A defendant may move to suppress evidence in the court where the trial will occur, as Rule 12 provides.

(i) Forwarding Papers to the Clerk. The magistrate judge to whom the warrant is returned must attach to the warrant a copy of the return, of the inventory, and of all other related papers and must deliver them to the clerk in the district where the property was seized.

Rule 44.   Right to and Appointment of Counsel

(a) Right to Appointed Counsel. A defendant who is unable to obtain counsel is entitled to have counsel appointed to represent the defendant at every stage of the proceeding from initial appearance through appeal, unless the defendant waives this right.

(b) Appointment Procedure. Federal law and local court rules govern the procedure for implementing the right to counsel.

(c) Inquiry into Joint Representation.

(1) Joint Representation. Joint representation occurs when:

(A) two or more defendants have been charged jointly under Rule 8(b) or have been joined for trial under Rule 13; and

(B) the defendants are represented by the same counsel or counsel who are associated in law practice.

(2) Court's Responsibilities in Cases of Joint Representation. The court must promptly inquire about the propriety of joint representation and must personally advise each defendant of the right to the effective assistance of counsel, including separate representation. Unless there is good cause to believe that no conflict of interest is likely to arise, the court must take appropriate measures to protect each defendant's right to counsel.

Rule 46. Release from Custody; Supervising Detention

(a) Before Trial. The provisions of 18 U.S.C. §§ 3142 and 3144 govern pretrial release.

(b) During Trial. A person released before trial continues on release during trial under the same terms and conditions. But the court may order different terms and conditions or terminate the release if necessary to ensure that the person will be present during trial or that the person's conduct will not obstruct the orderly and expeditious progress of the trial.

(c) Pending Sentencing or Appeal. The provisions of 18 U.S.C. § 3143 govern release pending sentencing or appeal. The burden of establishing that the defendant will not flee or pose a danger to any other person or to the community rests with the defendant.

(d) Pending Hearing on a Violation of Probation or Supervised Release. Rule 32.1(a)(6) governs release pending a hearing on a violation of probation or supervised release.

(e) Surety. The court must not approve a bond unless any surety appears to be qualified. Every surety, except a legally approved corporate surety, must demonstrate by affidavit that its assets are adequate. The court may require the affidavit to describe the following:

(1) the property that the surety proposes to use as security;

(2) any encumbrance on that property;

(3) the number and amount of any other undischarged bonds and bail undertakings the surety has issued; and

(4) any other liability of the surety.

(f) Bail Forfeiture.

(1) Declaration. The court must declare the bail forfeited if a condition of the bond is breached.

(2) Setting Aside. The court may set aside in whole or in part a bail forfeiture upon any condition the court may impose if:

(A) the surety later surrenders into custody the person released on the surety's appearance bond; or

(B) it appears that justice does not require bail forfeiture.

(3) Enforcement.

(A) Default Judgment and Execution. If it does not set aside a bail forfeiture, the court must, upon the government's motion, enter a default judgment.

(B) Jurisdiction and Service. By entering into a bond, each surety submits to the district court's jurisdiction and irrevocably appoints the district clerk as its agent to receive service of any filings affecting its liability.

(C) Motion to Enforce. The court may, upon the government's motion, enforce the surety's liability without an independent action. The government must serve any motion, and notice as the court prescribes, on the district clerk. If so served, the clerk must promptly mail a copy to the surety at its last known address.

(4) Remission. After entering a judgment under Rule 46(f)(3), the court may remit in whole or in part the judgment under the same conditions specified in Rule 46(f)(2).

(g) Exoneration. The court must exonerate the surety and release any bail when a bond condition has been satisfied or when the court has set aside or remitted the forfeiture. The court must exonerate a surety who deposits cash in the amount of the bond or timely surrenders the defendant into custody.

(h) Supervising Detention Pending Trial.

(1) In General. To eliminate unnecessary detention, the court must supervise the detention within the district of any defendants awaiting trial and of any persons held as material witnesses.

(2) Reports. An attorney for the government must report biweekly to the court, listing each material witness held in custody for more than 10 days pending indictment, arraignment, or trial. For each material witness listed in the report, an attorney for the government must state why the witness should not be released with or without a deposition being taken under Rule 15(a).

(i) Forfeiture of Property. The court may dispose of a charged offense by ordering the forfeiture of 18 U.S.C. § 3142(c)(1)(B)(xi) property under 18 U.S.C. § 3146(d), if a fine in the amount of the property's value would be an appropriate sentence for the charged offense.

(j) Producing a Statement.

(1) In General. Rule 26.2(a)-(d) and (f) applies at a detention hearing under 18 U.S.C. § 3142, unless the court for good cause rules otherwise.

(2) Sanctions for Not Producing a Statement. If a party disobeys a Rule 26.2 order to produce a witness's statement, the court must not consider that witness's testimony at the detention hearing.

Rule 52. Harmless and Plain Error

(a) Harmless Error. Any error, defect, irregularity, or variance that does not affect substantial rights must be disregarded.

(b) Plain Error. A plain error that affects substantial rights may be considered even though it was not brought to the court's attention.

Wire and Electronic Communications Interception and Interception of Oral Communications Act

18 U.S.C. §2510. Definitions

As used in this chapter —

(1) "wire communication" means any aural transfer made in whole or in part through the use of facilities for the transmission of communications by the aid of wire, cable, or other like connection between the point of origin and the point of reception (including the use of such connection in a switching station) furnished or operated by any person engaged in providing or operating such facilities for the transmission of interstate or foreign communications or communications affecting interstate or foreign commerce;

(2) "oral communication" means any oral communication uttered by a person exhibiting an expectation that such communication is not subject to interception under circumstances justifying such expectation, but such term does not include any electronic communication;

(3) "State" means any State of the United States, the District of Columbia, the Commonwealth of Puerto Rico, and any territory or possession of the United States;

(4) "intercept" means the aural or other acquisition of the contents of any wire, electronic, or oral communication through the use of any electronic, mechanical, or other device.

(5) "electronic, mechanical, or other device" means any device or apparatus which can be used to intercept a wire, oral, or electronic communication other than—

(a) any telephone or telegraph instrument, equipment or facility, or any component thereof,

(i) furnished to the subscriber or user by a provider of wire or electronic communication service in the ordinary course of its business and being used by the subscriber or user in the ordinary course of its business or furnished by such subscriber or user for connection to the facilities of such service and used in the ordinary course of its business; or

(ii) being used by a provider of wire or electronic communication service in the ordinary course of its business, or by an investigative or law enforcement officer in the ordinary course of his duties;

(b) a hearing aid or similar device being used to correct subnormal hearing to not better than normal;

(6) "person" means any employee, or agent of the United States or any State or political subdivision thereof, and any individual, partnership, association, joint stock company, trust, or corporation;

(7) "Investigative or law enforcement officer" means any officer of the United States or of a State or political subdivision thereof, who is empowered by law to conduct investigations of or to make arrests for offenses enumerated in this chapter, and any attorney authorized by law to prosecute or participate in the prosecution of such offenses;

(8) "contents", when used with respect to any wire, oral, or electronic communication, includes any information concerning the substance, purport, or meaning of that communication;

(9) "Judge of competent jurisdiction" means—

(a) a judge of a United States district court or a United States court of appeals; and

(b) a judge of any court of general criminal jurisdiction of a State who is authorized by a statute of that State to enter orders authorizing interceptions of wire, oral, or electronic communications;

(10) "communication common carrier" has the meaning given that term in section 3 of the Communications Act of 1934;

(11) "aggrieved person" means a person who was a party to any intercepted wire, oral, or electronic communication or a person against whom the interception was directed;

(12) "electronic communication" means any transfer of signs, signals, writing, images, sounds, data, or intelligence of any nature transmitted in whole or in part by a wire, radio, electromagnetic, photoelectronic or photooptical system that affects interstate or foreign commerce, but does not include —

(A) any wire or oral communication;

(B) any communication made through a tone-only paging device;

(C) any communication from a tracking device (as defined in section 3117 of this title); or

(D) electronic funds transfer information stored by a financial institution in a communications system used for the electronic storage and transfer of funds;

(13) "user" means any person or entity who —

(A) uses an electronic communication service; and

(B) is duly authorized by the provider of such service to engage in such use;

(14) "electronic communications system" means any wire, radio, electromagnetic, photooptical or photoelectronic facilities for the transmission of wire or electronic communications, and any computer facilities or related electronic equipment for the electronic storage of such communications;

(15) "electronic communication service" means any service which provides to users thereof the ability to send or receive wire or electronic communications;

(16) "readily accessible to the general public" means, with respect to a radio communication, that such communication is not —

(A) scrambled or encrypted;

(B) transmitted using modulation techniques whose essential parameters have been withheld from the public with the intention of preserving the privacy of such communication;

(C) carried on a subcarrier or other signal subsidiary to a radio transmission;

(D) transmitted over a communication system provided by a common carrier, unless the communication is a tone only paging system communication; or

(E) transmitted on frequencies allocated under part 25, subpart D, E, or F of part 74, or part 94 of the Rules of the Federal Communications Commission, unless, in the case of a communication transmitted on a frequency allocated under part 74 that is not exclusively allocated to broadcast auxiliary services, the communication is a two-way voice communication by radio;

(17) "electronic storage" means —

(A) any temporary, intermediate storage of a wire or electronic communication incidental to the electronic transmission thereof; and

(B) any storage of such communication by an electronic communication service for purposes of backup protection of such communication;

(18) "aural transfer" means a transfer containing the human voice at any point between and including the point of origin and the point of reception;

(19) "foreign intelligence information," for purposes of section 2517(6) of this title, means —

(A) information, whether or not concerning a United States person, that relates to the ability of the United States to protect against —

(i) actual or potential attack or other grave hostile acts of a foreign power or an agent of a foreign power;

(ii) sabotage or international terrorism by a foreign power or an agent of a foreign power; or

(iii) clandestine intelligence activities by an intelligence service or network of a foreign power or by an agent of a foreign power; or

(B) information, whether or not concerning a United States person, with respect to a foreign power or foreign territory that relates to —

(i) the national defense or the security of the United States; or

(ii) the conduct of the foreign affairs of the United States;

(20) "protected computer" has the meaning set forth in section 1030; and

(21) "computer trespasser" —

(A) means a person who accesses a protected computer without authorization and thus has no reasonable expectation of privacy in any communication transmitted to, through, or from the protected computer; and

(B) does not include a person known by the owner or operator of the protected computer to have an existing contractual relationship with the owner or operator of the protected computer for access to all or part of the protected computer.

18 U.S.C. §2511. Interception and disclosure of wire, oral, or electronic communications prohibited

(1) Except as otherwise specifically provided in this chapter any person who —

(a) intentionally intercepts, endeavors to intercept, or procures any other person to intercept or endeavor to intercept, any wire, oral, or electronic communication;

(b) intentionally uses, endeavors to use, or procures any other person to use or endeavor to use any electronic, mechanical, or other device to intercept any oral communication when —

(i) such device is affixed to, or otherwise transmits a signal through, a wire, cable, or other like connection used in wire communication; or

(ii) such device transmits communications by radio, or interferes with the transmission of such communication; or

(iii) such person knows, or has reason to know, that such device or any component thereof has been sent through the mail or transported in interstate or foreign commerce; or

(iv) such use or endeavor to use (A) takes place on the premises of any business or other commercial establishment the operations of which affect interstate or foreign commerce; or (B) obtains or is for the purpose of obtaining information relating to the operations of any business or other commercial establishment the operations of which affect interstate or foreign commerce; or

(v) such person acts in the District of Columbia, the Commonwealth of Puerto Rico, or any territory or possession of the United States;

(c) intentionally discloses, or endeavors to disclose, to any other person the contents of any wire, oral, or electronic communication, knowing or having reason to know that the information was obtained through the interception of a wire, oral, or electronic communication in violation of this subsection;

(d) intentionally uses, or endeavors to use, the contents of any wire, oral, or electronic communication, knowing or having reason to know that the information was obtained through the interception of a wire, oral, or electronic communication in violation of this subsection; or (e)(i) intentionally discloses, or endeavors to disclose, to any other person the contents of any wire, oral, or electronic communication, intercepted by means authorized by sections 2511(2)(a)(ii), 2511(2)(b)-(c), 2511(2)(e), 2516, and 2518 of this chapter,

(ii) knowing or having reason to know that the information was obtained through the interception of such a communication in connection with a criminal investigation,

(iii) having obtained or received the information in connection with a criminal investigation, and

(iv) with intent to improperly obstruct, impede, or interfere with a duly authorized criminal investigation, shall be punished as provided in subsection (4) or shall be subject to suit as provided in subsection (5).

(2)(a)(i) It shall not be unlawful under this chapter for an operator of a switchboard, or an officer, employee, or agent of a provider of wire or electronic communication service, whose facilities are used in the transmission of a wire or electronic communication, to intercept, disclose, or use that communication in the normal course of his employment while engaged in any activity which is a necessary incident to the rendition of his service or to the protection of the rights or property of the provider of that service, except that a provider of wire communication service to the public shall not utilize service observing or random monitoring except for mechanical or service quality control checks.

(ii) Notwithstanding any other law, providers of wire or electronic communication service, their officers, employees, and agents, landlords, custodians, or other persons, are authorized to provide information, facilities, or technical assistance to persons authorized by law to intercept wire, oral, or electronic communications or to conduct electronic surveillance, as defined in section 101 of the Foreign Intelligence Surveillance Act of 1978, if such provider, its officers, employees, or agents, landlord, custodian, or other specified person, has been provided with—

(A) a court order directing such assistance or a court order pursuant to section 704 of the Foreign Intelligence Surveillance Act of 1978 signed by the authorizing judge, or

(B) a certification in writing by a person specified in section 2518(7) of this title or the Attorney General of the United States that no warrant or court order is required by law, that all statutory requirements have been met, and that the specified assistance is required, setting forth the period of time during which the provision of the information, facilities, or technical assistance is authorized and specifying the information, facilities, or technical assistance required. No provider of wire or electronic communication service, officer, employee, or agent thereof, or landlord, custodian, or other specified person shall disclose the existence of any interception or surveillance or the device used to accomplish the interception or surveillance with respect to which the person has been furnished a court order or certification under this chapter, except as may otherwise be required by legal process and then only after prior notification to the Attorney General or to the principal prosecuting attorney of a State or any political subdivision of a State, as may be appropriate. Any such disclosure, shall render such person liable for the civil damages provided for in section 2520. No cause of action shall lie in any court against any provider of wire or electronic communication service, its officers, employees, or agents, landlord, custodian, or other specified person for providing information, facilities, or assistance in accordance with the terms of a court order, statutory authorization, or certification under this chapter.

(iii) If a certification under subparagraph (ii)(B) for assistance to obtain foreign intelligence information is based on statutory authority, the certification shall identify the specific statutory provision and shall certify that the statutory requirements have been met.

(b) It shall not be unlawful under this chapter for an officer, employee, or agent of the Federal Communications Commission, in the normal course of his employment and in discharge of the monitoring responsibilities exercised by the Commission in the enforcement of chapter 5 of title 47 of the United States Code, to intercept a wire or electronic communication, or oral communication transmitted by radio, or to disclose or use the information thereby obtained.

(c) It shall not be unlawful under this chapter for a person acting under color of law to intercept a wire, oral, or electronic communication, where such person is a party to the communication or one of the parties to the communication has given prior consent to such interception.

(d) It shall not be unlawful under this chapter for a person not acting under color of law to intercept a wire, oral, or electronic communication where such person is a party to the communication or where one of the parties to the communication has given prior consent to such interception unless such communication is intercepted for the purpose of committing any criminal or tortious act in violation of the Constitution or laws of the United States or of any State.

(e) Notwithstanding any other provision of this title or section 705 or 706 of the Communications Act of 1934, it shall not be unlawful for an officer, employee, or agent of the United States in the normal course of his official duty to conduct electronic surveillance, as defined in section 101 of the Foreign Intelligence Surveillance Act of 1978, as authorized by that Act.

(f) Nothing contained in this chapter or chapter 121 or 206 of this title, or section 705 of the Communications Act of 1934, shall be deemed to affect the acquisition by the United States Government of foreign intelligence information from international or foreign communications, or foreign intelligence activities conducted in accordance with otherwise applicable Federal law involving a foreign electronic communications system, utilizing a means other than electronic surveillance as defined in section 101 of the Foreign Intelligence Surveillance Act of 1978, and procedures in this chapter or chapter 121 and the Foreign Intelligence Surveillance Act of 1978 shall be the exclusive means by which electronic surveillance, as defined in section 101 of such Act, and the interception of domestic wire, oral, and electronic communications may be conducted.

(g) It shall not be unlawful under this chapter or chapter 121 of this title for any person —

(i) to intercept or access an electronic communication made through an electronic communication system that is configured so that such electronic communication is readily accessible to the general public;

(ii) to intercept any radio communication which is transmitted —

(I) by any station for the use of the general public, or that relates to ships, aircraft, vehicles, or persons in distress;

(II) by any governmental, law enforcement, civil defense, private land mobile, or public safety communications system, including police and fire, readily accessible to the general public;

(III) by a station operating on an authorized frequency within the bands allocated to the amateur, citizens band, or general mobile radio services; or

(IV) by any marine or aeronautical communications system;

(iii) to engage in any conduct which —

(I) is prohibited by section 633 of the Communications Act of 1934; or

(II) is excepted from the application of section 705(a) of the Communications Act of 1934 by section 705(b) of that Act;

(iv) to intercept any wire or electronic communication the transmission of which is causing harmful interference to any lawfully operating station or consumer electronic equipment, to the extent necessary to identify the source of such interference; or

(v) for other users of the same frequency to intercept any radio communication made through a system that utilizes frequencies monitored by individuals engaged in the provision or the use of such system, if such communication is not scrambled or encrypted.

(h) It shall not be unlawful under this chapter —

(i) to use a pen register or a trap and trace device (as those terms are defined for the purposes of chapter 206 (relating to pen registers and trap and trace devices) of this title); or

(ii) for a provider of electronic communication service to record the fact that a wire or electronic communication was initiated or completed in order to protect such provider, another provider furnishing service toward the completion of the wire or electronic communication, or a user of that service, from fraudulent, unlawful or abusive use of such service.

(i) It shall not be unlawful under this chapter for a person acting under color of law to intercept the wire or electronic communications of a computer trespasser transmitted to, through, or from the protected computer, if—

(I) the owner or operator of the protected computer authorizes the interception of the computer trespasser's communications on the protected computer;

(II) the person acting under color of law is lawfully engaged in an investigation;

(III) the person acting under color of law has reasonable grounds to believe that the contents of the computer trespasser's communications will be relevant to the investigation; and

(IV) such interception does not acquire communications other than those transmitted to or from the computer trespasser.

(3)(a) Except as provided in paragraph (b) of this subsection, a person or entity providing an electronic communication service to the public shall not intentionally divulge the contents of any communication (other than one to such person or entity, or an agent thereof) while in transmission on that service to any person or entity other than an addressee or intended recipient of such communication or an agent of such addressee or intended recipient.

(b) A person or entity providing electronic communication service to the public may divulge the contents of any such communication—

(i) as otherwise authorized in section 2511(2)(a) or 2517 of this title;

(ii) with the lawful consent of the originator or any addressee or intended recipient of such communication;

(iii) to a person employed or authorized, or whose facilities are used, to forward such communication to its destination; or

(iv) which were inadvertently obtained by the service provider and which appear to pertain to the commission of a crime, if such divulgence is made to a law enforcement agency.

(4)(a) Except as provided in paragraph (b) of this subsection or in subsection (5), whoever violates subsection (1) of this section shall be fined under this title or imprisoned not more than five years, or both.

(b) Conduct otherwise an offense under this subsection that consists of or relates to the interception of a satellite transmission that is not encrypted or scrambled and that is transmitted—

(i) to a broadcasting station for purposes of retransmission to the general public; or

(ii) as an audio subcarrier intended for redistribution to facilities open to the public, but not including data transmissions or telephone calls, is not an offense under this subsection unless the conduct is for the purposes of direct or indirect commercial advantage or private financial gain.

(5)(a)(i) If the communication is—

(A) a private satellite video communication that is not scrambled or encrypted and the conduct in violation of this chapter is the private viewing of that communication and is not for a tortious or illegal purpose or for purposes of direct or indirect commercial advantage or private commercial gain; or

(B) a radio communication that is transmitted on frequencies allocated under subpart D of part 74 of the rules of the Federal Communications Commission that is not scrambled or encrypted and the conduct in violation of this chapter is not for a tortious or illegal purpose or for purposes of direct or indirect commercial advantage or private commercial gain, then the person who engages in such conduct shall be subject to suit by the Federal Government in a court of competent jurisdiction.

(ii) In an action under this subsection —

(A) if the violation of this chapter is a first offense for the person under paragraph (a) of subsection (4) and such person has not been found liable in a civil action under section 2520 of this title, the Federal Government shall be entitled to appropriate injunctive relief; and

(B) if the violation of this chapter is a second or subsequent offense under paragraph (a) of subsection (4) or such person has been found liable in any prior civil action under section 2520, the person shall be subject to a mandatory $500 civil fine.

(b) The court may use any means within its authority to enforce an injunction issued under paragraph (ii)(A), and shall impose a civil fine of not less than $500 for each violation of such an injunction.

18 U.S.C. §2515. Prohibition of use as evidence of intercepted wire or oral communications

Whenever any wire or oral communication has been intercepted, no part of the contents of such communication and no evidence derived therefrom may be received in evidence in any trial, hearing, or other proceeding in or before any court, grand jury, department, officer, agency, regulatory body, legislative committee, or other authority of the United States, a State, or a political subdivision thereof if the disclosure of that information would be in violation of this chapter.

Bail Reform Act of 1984 (as amended)

18 U.S.C. §3141. Release and Detention Authority Generally

(a) Pending trial. A judicial officer authorized to order the arrest of a person under section 3041 of this title before whom an arrested person is brought shall order that such person be released or detained, pending judicial proceedings, under this chapter [18 U.S.C. §§ 3141 et seq.].

(b) Pending sentence or appeal. A judicial officer of a court of original jurisdiction over an offense, or a judicial officer of a Federal appellate court, shall order that, pending imposition or execution of sentence, or pending appeal of conviction or sentence, a person be released or detained under this chapter [18 U.S.C. §§ 3141 et seq.].

18 U.S.C. §3142. Release or Detention of a Defendant Pending Trial

(a) In general. Upon the appearance before a judicial officer of a person charged with an offense, the judicial officer shall issue an order that, pending trial, the person be —

(1) Released on personal recognizance or upon execution of an unsecured appearance bond, under subsection (b) of this section;

(2) released on a condition or combination of conditions under subsection (c) of this section;

(3) temporarily detained to permit revocation of conditional release, deportation, or exclusion under subsection (d) of this section; or

(4) detained under subsection (e) of this section.

(b) Release on personal recognizance or unsecured appearance bond. The judicial officer shall order the pretrial release of the person on personal recognizance, or upon execution of an unsecured appearance bond in an amount specified by the court, subject to the condition that the person not commit a Federal, State, or local crime during the period of release, unless the judicial officer determines that such release will not reasonably assure the appearance of the person as required or will endanger the safety of any other person or the community.

(c) Release on conditions.

(1) If the judicial officer determines that the release described in subsection (b) of this section will not reasonably assure the appearance of the person as required or will endanger the safety of any other person or the community, such judicial officer shall order the pretrial release of the person —

(A) subject to the condition that the person not commit a Federal, State, or local crime during the period of release; and

(B) subject to the least restrictive further condition, or combination of conditions, that such judicial officer determines will reasonably assure the appearance of the person as required and the safety of any other person and the community, which may include the condition that the person —

(i) remain in the custody of a designated person, who agrees to assume supervision and to report any violation of a release condition to the court, if the designated person is able reasonably to assure the judicial officer that the person will appear as required and will not pose a danger to the safety of any other person or the community;

(ii) maintain employment, or, if unemployed, actively seek employment;

(iii) maintain or commence an educational program;

(iv) abide by specified restrictions on personal associations, place of abode, or travel;

(v) avoid all contact with an alleged victim of the crime and with a potential witness who may testify concerning the offense;

(vi) report on a regular basis to a designated law enforcement agency, pretrial services agency, or other agency;

(vii) comply with a specified curfew;

(viii) refrain from possessing a firearm, destructive device, or other dangerous weapon;

(ix) refrain from excessive use of alcohol, or any use of a narcotic drug or other controlled substance, as defined in section 102 of the Controlled Substances Act (21 U.S.C. § 802), without a prescription by a licensed medical practitioner;

(x) undergo available medical, psychological, or psychiatric treatment, including treatment for drug or alcohol dependency, and remain in a specified institution if required for that purpose;

(xi) execute an agreement to forfeit, upon failing to appear as required, property of a sufficient unencumbered value, including money, as is reasonably necessary to assure the appearance of the person as required, and shall provide the court with proof of ownership and the value of the property along with information regarding existing encumbrances as the judicial office may require;

(xii) execute a bail bond with solvent sureties; who will execute an agreement to forfeit in such amount as is reasonably necessary to assure appearance of the person as required and shall provide the court with information regarding the value of the assets and liabilities of the surety if other than an approved surety and the nature and extent of encumbrances against the surety's property; such surety shall have a net worth which shall have sufficient unencumbered value to pay the amount of the bail bond;

(xiii) return to custody for specified hours following release for employment, schooling, or other limited purposes; and

(xiv) satisfy any other condition that is reasonably necessary to assure the appearance of the person as required and to assure the safety of any other person and the community.

(2) The judicial officer may not impose a financial condition that results in the pretrial detention of the person.

(3) The judicial officer may at any time amend the order to impose additional or different conditions of release.

(d) Temporary detention to permit revocation of conditional release, deportation, or exclusion. If the judicial officer determines that —

(1) such person —

(A) is, and was at the time the offense was committed, on —

(i) release pending trial for a felony under Federal, State, or local law;

(ii) release pending imposition or execution of sentence, appeal of sentence or conviction, or completion of sentence, for any offense under Federal, State, or local law; or

(iii) probation or parole for any offense under Federal, State, or local law; or

(B) is not a citizen of the United States or lawfully admitted for permanent residence, as defined in section 101(a)(20) of the Immigration and Nationality Act (8 U.S.C. § 1101(a)(20)); and

(2) the person may flee or pose a danger to any other person or the community; such judicial officer shall order the detention of the person, for a period of not more than ten days, excluding Saturdays, Sundays, and holidays, and direct the attorney for the Government to notify the appropriate court, probation or parole official, or State or local law enforcement official, or the appropriate official of the Immigration and Naturalization Service. If the official fails or declines to take the person into custody during that period, the person shall be treated in accordance with the other provisions of this section, notwithstanding the applicability of other provisions of law governing release pending trial or deportation or exclusion proceedings. If temporary detention is sought under paragraph (1)(B) of this subsection, the person has the burden of proving to

the court such person's United States citizenship or lawful admission for permanent residence.

(e) Detention.

(1) If, after a hearing pursuant to the provisions of subsection (f) of this section, the judicial officer finds that no condition or combination of conditions will reasonably assure the appearance of the person as required and the safety of any other person and the community, such judicial officer shall order the detention of the person before trial.

(2) In a case described in subsection (f)(l) of this section, a rebuttable presumption arises that no condition or combination of conditions will reasonably assure the safety of any other person and the community if such judicial officer finds that —

(A) the person has been convicted of a Federal offense that is described in subsection (f)(l) of this section, or of a State or local offense that would have been an offense described in subsection (f)(l) of this section if a circumstance giving rise to Federal jurisdiction had existed;

(B) the offense described in paragraph (A) of this subsection was committed while the person was on release pending trial for a Federal, State, or local offense; and

(C) a period of not more than five years has elapsed since the date of conviction, or the release of the person from imprisonment, for the offense described in paragraph (A) of this subsection, whichever is later.

(3) Subject to rebuttal by the person, it shall be presumed that no condition or combination of conditions will reasonably assure the appearance of the person as required and the safety of the community if the judicial officer finds that there is probable cause to believe that the person committed —

(A) an offense for which a maximum term of imprisonment of ten years or more is prescribed in the Controlled Substances Act (21 U.S.C. §§ 801 et seq.), the Controlled Substances Import and Export Act (21 U.S.C. §§ 951 et seq.), or chapter 705 of title 46;

(B) an offense under section 924(c), 956(a), or 2332b of this title;

(C) an offense listed in section 2332b(g)(5)(B) of title 18, United States Code, for which a maximum term of imprisonment of 10 years or more is prescribed;

(D) an offense under chapter 77 of this title for which a maximum term of imprisonment of 20 years or more is prescribed; or

(E) an offense involving a minor victim under section 1201, 1591, 2241, 2242, 2244(a)(1), 2245, 2251, 2251A, 2252(a)(1), 2252(a)(2), 2252(a)(3), 2252A(a)(1), 2252A(a)(2), 2252A(a)(3), 2252A(a)(4), 2260, 2421, 2422, 2423, or 2425 of this title.

(f) Detention hearing. The judicial officer shall hold a hearing to determine whether any condition or combination of conditions set forth in subsection (c) of this section will reasonably assure the appearance of the person as required and the safety of any other person and the community —

(1) upon motion of the attorney for the Government, in a case that involves —

(A) a crime of violence;

(B) an offense for which the maximum sentence is life imprisonment or death;

(C) an offense for which a maximum term of imprisonment often years or more is prescribed in the Controlled Substances Act (21 U.S.C. §§ 801 et seq.), the Controlled Substances Import and Export Act (21 U.S.C. §§ 951 et seq.), or the Maritime Drug Law Enforcement Act (46 U.S.C. App. §§ 1901 et seq.); or

(D) any felony if the person has been convicted of two or more offenses described in subparagraphs (A) through (C) of this paragraph, or two or more State or local offenses that would have been offenses described in subparagraphs (A) through (C) of this paragraph if a circumstance giving rise to Federal jurisdiction had existed, or a combination of such offenses; or

(2) upon motion of the attorney for the Government or upon the judicial officer's own motion, in a case that involves —

(A) a serious risk that such person will flee; or

(B) a serious risk that the person will obstruct or attempt to obstruct justice, or threaten, injure, or intimidate, or attempt to threaten, injure, or intimidate, a prospective witness or juror.

The hearing shall be held immediately upon the person's first appearance before the judicial officer unless that person, or the attorney for the Government, seeks a continuance. Except for good cause, a continuance on motion of the person may not exceed five days (not including any intermediate Saturday, Sunday, or legal holiday), and a continuance on motion of the attorney for the Government may not exceed three days (not including any intermediate Saturday, Sunday, or legal holiday). During a continuance, the person shall be detained and the judicial officer, on motion of the attorney for the Government or sua sponte, may order that, while in custody, a person who appears to be a narcotics addict receive a medical examination to determine whether such person is an addict. At the hearing, the person has the right to be represented by counsel and, if financially unable to obtain adequate representation, to have counsel appointed. The person shall be afforded an opportunity to testify, to present witnesses, to cross-examine witnesses who appear at the hearing, and to present information by proffer or otherwise. The rules concerning admissibility of evidence in criminal trials do not apply to the presentation and consideration of information at the hearing. The facts the judicial officer uses to support a finding pursuant to subsection (e) that no condition or combination of conditions will reasonably assure the safety of any other person and the community shall be supported by clear and convincing evidence. The person may be detained pending completion of the hearing. The hearing may be reopened, before or after a determination by the judicial officer, at any time before trial if the judicial officer finds that information exists that was not known to the movant at the time of the hearing and that has a material bearing on the issue whether there are conditions of release that will reasonably assure the appearance of the person as required and the safety of any other person and the community.

(g) Factors to be considered. The judicial officer shall, in determining whether there are conditions of release that will reasonably assure the appearance of the person as required and the safety of any other person and the community, take into account the available information concerning —

(1) the nature and circumstances of the offense charged, including whether the offense is a crime of violence or involves a narcotic drug;

(2) the weight of the evidence against the person;

(3) the history and characteristics of the person, including —

(A) the person's character, physical and mental condition, family ties, employment, financial resources, length of residence in the community, community ties, past conduct, history relating to drug or alcohol abuse, criminal history, and record concerning appearance at court proceedings; and

(B) whether, at the time of the current offense or arrest, the person was on probation, on parole, or on other release pending trial, sentencing, appeal, or completion of sentence for an offense under Federal, State, or local law; and

(4) the nature and seriousness of the danger to any person or the community that would be posed by the person's release. In

considering the conditions of release described in subsection (c)(1)(B)(xi) or (c)(1)(B)(xii) of this section, the judicial officer may, upon his own motion, or shall, upon the motion of the Government, conduct an inquiry into the source of the property to be designated for potential forfeiture or offered as collateral to secure a bond, and shall decline to accept the designation, or the use as collateral, of property that, because of its source, will not reasonably assure the appearance of the person as required.

(h) Contents of release order. In a release order issued under subsection (b) or (c) of this section, the judicial officer shall —

(1) include a written statement that sets forth all the conditions to which the release is subject, in a manner sufficiently clear and specific to serve as a guide for the person's conduct; and

(2) advise the person of —

(A) the penalties for violating a condition of release, including the penalties for committing an offense while on pretrial release;

(B) the consequences of violating a condition of release, including the immediate issuance of a warrant for the person's arrest; and

(C) sections 1503 of this title (relating to intimidation of witnesses, jurors, and officers of the court), 1510 (relating to obstruction of criminal investigations), 1512 (tampering with a witness, victim, or an informant), and 1513 (retaliating against a witness, victim, or an informant).

(i) Contents of detention order. In a detention order issued under subsection (e) of this section, the judicial officer shall —

(1) include written findings of fact and a written statement of the reasons for the detention;

(2) direct that the person be committed to the custody of the Attorney General for confinement in a corrections facility separate, to the extent practicable, from persons awaiting or serving sentences or being held in custody pending appeal;

(3) direct that the person be afforded reasonable opportunity for private consultation with counsel; and

(4) direct that, on order of a court of the United States or on request of an attorney for the Government, the person in charge of the corrections facility in which the person is confined deliver the person to a United States marshal for the purpose of an appearance in connection with a court proceeding.

The judicial officer may, by subsequent order, permit the temporary release of the person, in the custody of a United States marshal or another appropriate person, to the extent that the judicial officer determines such release to be necessary for preparation of the person's defense or for another compelling reason.

(j) Presumption of innocence. Nothing in this section shall be construed as modifying or limiting the presumption of innocence.

18 U.S.C. §3143. Release or Detention of a Defendant Pending Sentence or Appeal

(a) Release or detention pending sentence.

(1) Except as provided in paragraph (2), the judicial officer shall order that a person who has been found guilty of an offense and who is awaiting imposition or execution of sentence, other than a person for whom the applicable guideline promulgated pursuant to 28 U.S.C. § 994 does not recommend a term of imprisonment, be detained, unless the judicial officer finds by clear and convincing evidence that the person is not likely to flee or pose a danger to the safety of any other person or the community if released under section 3142(b) or (c). If the judicial officer makes such a finding, such judicial officer shall order the release of the person in accordance with section 3142(b) or (c).

(2) The judicial officer shall order that a person who has been found guilty of an offense in a case described in subparagraph (A), (B), or (C) of subsection (f)(1) of section 3142 and is awaiting imposition or execution of sentence be detained unless —

(A) (i) the judicial officer finds there is a substantial likelihood that a motion for acquittal or new trial will be granted; or

(ii) an attorney for the Government has recommended that no sentence of imprisonment be imposed on the person; and

(B) the judicial officer finds by clear and convincing evidence that the person is not likely to flee or pose a danger to any other person or the community.

(b) Release or detention pending appeal by the defendant.

(1) Except as provided in paragraph (2), the judicial officer shall order that a person who has been found guilty of an offense and sentenced to a term of imprisonment, and who has filed an appeal or a petition for a writ of certiorari, be detained, unless the judicial officer finds —

(A) by clear and convincing evidence that the person is not likely to flee or pose a danger to the safety of any other person or the community if released under section 3142(b) or (c) of this title; and

(B) that the appeal is not for the purpose of delay and raises a substantial question of law or fact likely to result in —

(i) reversal

(ii) an order for a new trial,

(iii) a sentence that does not include a term of imprisonment, or

(iv) a reduced sentence to a term of imprisonment less than the total of the time already served plus the expected duration of the appeal process.

If the judicial officer makes such findings, such judicial officer shall order the release of the person in accordance with section 3142(b) or (c) of this title, except that in the circumstance described in subparagraph (B)(iv) of this paragraph, the judicial officer shall order the detention terminated at the expiration of the likely reduced sentence.

(2) The judicial officer shall order that a person who has been found guilty of an offense in a case described in subparagraph (A), (B), or (C) of subsection (f)(1) of section 3142 and sentenced to a term of imprisonment, and who has filed an appeal or a petition for a writ of certiorari, be detained.

(c) Release or detention pending appeal by the government. The judicial officer shall treat a defendant in a case in which an appeal has been taken by the United States under section 3731 of this title, in accordance with section 3142 of this title, unless the defendant is otherwise subject to a release or detention order. Except as provided in subsection (b) of this section, the judicial officer, in a case in which an appeal has been taken by the United States under section 3742, shall —

(1) if the person has been sentenced to a term of imprisonment, order that person detained; and

(2) in any other circumstance, release or detain the person under section 3142.

18 U.S.C. §3144. Release or Detention of a Material Witness

If it appears from an affidavit filed by a party that the testimony of a person is material in a criminal proceeding, and if it is shown that it may become impracticable to secure the presence of the person by subpoena, a judicial officer may order the arrest of the person and treat the person in accordance with the provisions of section 3142 of this title. No material witness may be detained because of inability to comply with any condition of release if the testimony of such witness can adequately be secured by deposition, and if further detention is not necessary to prevent a failure of justice. Release of a material witness may be delayed for a reasonable period of time until the deposition of the witness can be taken pursuant to the Federal Rules of Criminal Procedure.

18 U.S.C. §3145. Review and Appeal of a Release or Detention Order

(a) Review of a release order. If a person is ordered released by a magistrate [United States magistrate judge], or by a person other than a judge of a court having original jurisdiction over the offense and other than a Federal appellate court —

(1) the attorney for the Government may file, with the court having original jurisdiction over the offense, a motion for revocation of the order or amendment of the conditions of release; and

(2) the person may file, with the court having original jurisdiction over the offense, a motion for amendment of the conditions of release. The motion shall be determined promptly.

(b) Review of a detention order. If a person is ordered detained by a magistrate [United States magistrate judge], or by a person other than a judge of a court having original jurisdiction over the offense and other than a Federal appellate court, the person may file, with the court having original jurisdiction over the offense, a motion for revocation or amendment of the order. The motion shall be determined promptly.

(c) Appeal from a release or detention order. An appeal from a release or detention order, or from a decision denying revocation or amendment of such an order, is governed by the provisions of section 1291 of title 28 and section 3731 of this title. The appeal shall be determined promptly. A person subject to detention pursuant to section 3143(a)(2) or (b)(2), and who meets the conditions of release set forth in section 3143(a)(1) or (b)(1), may be ordered released, under appropriate conditions, by the judicial officer if it is clearly shown that there are exceptional reasons why such person's detention would not be appropriate.

18 U.S.C. §3146. Penalty for Failure to Appear

(a) Offense. Whoever, having been released under this chapter [18 U.S.C. §§ 3141 et seq.] knowingly —

(1) fails to appear before a court as required by the conditions of release; or

(2) fails to surrender for service of sentence pursuant to a court order; shall be punished as provided in subsection (b) of this section.

(b) Punishment.

(1) The punishment for an offense under this section is —

(A) if the person was released in connection with a charge of, or while awaiting sentence, surrender for service of sentence, or appeal or certiorari after conviction for —

(i) an offense punishable by death, life imprisonment, or imprisonment for a term of 15 years or more, a fine under this title or imprisonment for not more than ten years, or both;

(ii) an offense punishable by imprisonment for a term of five years or more, a fine under this title or imprisonment for not more than five years, or both;

(iii) any other felony, a fine under this title or imprisonment for not more than two years, or both; or

(iv) a misdemeanor, a fine under this title or imprisonment for not more than one year, or both; and

(B) if the person was released for appearance as a material witness, a fine under this chapter [18 U.S.C. §§ 3141 et seq.] or imprisonment for not more than one year, or both.

(2) A term of imprisonment imposed under this section shall be consecutive to the sentence of imprisonment for any other offense.

(c) Affirmative defense. It is an affirmative defense to a prosecution under this section that uncontrollable circumstances prevented the person from appearing or surrendering, and that the person did not contribute to the creation of such circumstances in reckless disregard of the requirement to appear or surrender, and that the person appeared or surrendered as soon as such circumstances ceased to exist.

(d) Declaration of forfeiture. If a person fails to appear before a court as required, and the person executed an appearance bond pursuant to section 3142(b) of this title or is subject to the release condition set forth in clause (xi) or (xii) of section 3142(c)(1)(B) of this title, the judicial officer may, regardless of whether the person has been charged with an offense under this section, declare any property designated pursuant to that section to be forfeited to the United States.

18 U.S.C. §3147. Penalty for an Offense Committed While on Release

A person convicted of an offense committed while released under this chapter [18 U.S.C. §§ 3141 et seq.] shall be sentenced, in addition to the sentence prescribed for the offense, to —

(1) a term of imprisonment of not more than ten years if the offense is a felony; or

(2) a term of imprisonment of not more than one year if the offense is a misdemeanor.

A term of imprisonment imposed under this section shall be consecutive to any other sentence of imprisonment.

18 U.S.C. §3148. Sanctions for Violation of a Release Condition

(a) Available sanctions. A person who has been released pursuant to the provisions of section 3142 of this title, and who has violated a condition of his release, is subject to a revocation of release, an order of detention, and a prosecution for contempt of court.

(b) Revocation of release. The attorney for the Government may initiate a proceeding for revocation of an order of release by filing a motion with the district court. A judicial officer may issue a warrant for the arrest of a person charged with violating a condition of release, and the person shall be brought before a judicial officer in the district in which such person's arrest was ordered for a proceeding in accordance with this section. To the extent practicable, a person charged with violating the condition of release that such person not commit a Federal, State, or local crime during the period of release, shall be brought before the judicial officer who ordered the release and whose order is alleged to have been violated. The judicial officer shall enter an order of revocation and detention if, after a hearing, the judicial officer —

(1) finds that there is —

(A) probable cause to believe that the person has committed a Federal, State, or local crime while on release; or

(B) clear and convincing evidence that the person has violated any other condition of release; and

(2) finds that —

(A) based on the factors set forth in section 3142(g) of this title, there is no condition or combination of conditions of release that will assure that the person will not flee or pose a danger to the safety of any other person or the community; or

(B) the person is unlikely to abide by any condition or combination of conditions of release.

If there is probable cause to believe that, while on release, the person committed a Federal, State, or local felony, a rebuttable presumption arises that no condition or combination of conditions will assure that the person will not pose a danger to the safety of any other person or the community. If the judicial officer finds that there are conditions of release that will assure that the person will not flee or pose a danger to the safety of any other person or the community, and that the person will abide by such conditions, the judicial officer shall treat the person in accordance with the provisions of section 3142 of this title and may amend the conditions of release accordingly.

(c) Prosecution for contempt. The judicial officer may commence a prosecution for contempt, under section 401 of this title, if the person has violated a condition of release.

18 U.S.C. §3149. Surrender of an Offender by a Surety

A person charged with an offense, who is released upon the execution of an appearance bond with a surety, may be arrested by the surety, and if so arrested, shall be delivered promptly to a United States marshal and brought before a judicial officer. The judicial officer shall determine in accordance with the provisions of section 3148(b) whether to revoke the release of the person, and may absolve the surety of responsibility to pay all or part of the bond in accordance with the provisions of Rule 46 of the Federal Rules of Criminal Procedure. The person so committed shall be held in official detention until released pursuant to this chapter [18 U.S.C. §§ 3141 et seq.] or another provision of law.

18 U.S.C. §3150. Applicability to a Case Removed from a State Court

The provisions of this chapter [18 U.S.C. §§ 3141 et seq.] apply to a criminal case removed to a Federal court from a State court.

Speedy Trial Act of 1974 (as amended)

18 U.S.C. §3161. Time Limits and Exclusions

(a) In any case involving a defendant charged with an offense, the appropriate judicial officer, at the earliest practicable time, shall, after consultation with the counsel for the defendant and the attorney for the Government, set the case for trial on a day certain, or list it for trial on a weekly or other short-term trial calendar at a place within the judicial district, so as to assure a speedy trial.

(b) Any information or indictment charging an individual with the commission of an offense shall be filed within thirty days from the date on which such individual was arrested or served with a summons in connection with such charges. If an individual has been charged with a felony in a district in which no grand jury has been in session during such thirty-day period, the period of time for filing of the indictment shall be extended an additional thirty days.

(c)(1) In any case in which a plea of not guilty is entered, the trial of a defendant charged in an information or indictment with the commission of an offense shall commence within seventy days from the filing date (and making public) of the information or indictment, or from the date the defendant has appeared before a judicial officer of the court in which such charge is pending, whichever date last occurs. If a defendant consents in writing to be tried before a magistrate [United States magistrate judge] on a complaint, the trial shall commence within seventy days from the date of such consent.

(2) Unless the defendant consents in writing to the contrary, the trial shall not commence less than thirty days from the date on which the defendant first appears through counsel or expressly waives counsel and elects to proceed pro se.

(d) (1) If any indictment or information is dismissed upon motion of the defendant, or any charge contained in a complaint filed against an individual is dismissed or otherwise dropped, and thereafter a complaint is filed against such defendant or individual charging him with the same offense or an offense based on the same conduct or arising from the same criminal episode, or an information or indictment is filed charging such defendant with the same offense or an offense based on the same conduct or arising from the same criminal episode, the provisions of subsections (b) and (c) of this section shall be applicable with respect to such subsequent complaint, indictment, or information, as the case may be.

(2) If the defendant is to be tried upon an indictment or information dismissed by a trial court and reinstated following an appeal, the trial shall commence within seventy days from the date the action occasioning the trial becomes final, except that the court retrying the case may extend the period for trial not to exceed one hundred and eighty days from the date the action occasioning the trial becomes final if the unavailability of witnesses or other factors resulting from the passage of time shall make trial within seventy days impractical. The periods of delay enumerated in section 3161(h) are excluded in computing the time limitations specified in this section. The sanctions of section 3162 apply to this subsection.

(e) If the defendant is to be tried again following a declaration by the trial judge of a mistrial or following an order of such judge for a new trial, the trial shall commence within seventy days from the date the action occasioning the retrial becomes final. If the defendant is to be tried again following an appeal or a collateral attack, the trial shall commence within seventy days from the date the action occasioning the retrial becomes final, except that the court retrying the case may extend the period for retrial not to exceed one hundred and eighty days from the date the action occasioning the retrial becomes final if unavailability of witnesses or other factors resulting from passage of time shall make trial within seventy days impractical. The periods of delay enumerated in section 3161(h) are excluded in computing the time limitations specified in this section. The sanctions of section 3162 apply to this subsection.

(f) Notwithstanding the provisions of subsection (b) of this section, for the first twelve-calendar-month period following the effective date of this section as set forth in section 3163(a) of this chapter[,] the time limit imposed with respect to the period between arrest and indictment by subsection (b) of this section shall be sixty days, for the second such twelve-month period such time limit shall be forty-five days and for the third such period such time limit shall be thirty-five days.

(g) Notwithstanding the provisions of subsection (c) of this section, for the first twelve-calendar-month period following the effective date of this section as set forth in section 3163(b) of this chapter, the time limit with respect to the period between arraignment and trial imposed by subsection (c) of this section shall be one hundred and eighty days, for the second such twelve-month period such time limit shall be one hundred and twenty days, and for the third such period such time limit with respect to the period between arraignment and trial shall be eighty days.

(h) The following periods of delay shall be excluded in computing the time within which an information or an indictment must be filed, or in computing the time within which the trial of any such offense must commence:

(1) Any period of delay resulting from other proceedings concerning the defendant, including but not limited to —

(A) delay resulting from any proceeding, including any examinations, to determine the mental competency or physical capacity of the defendant;

(B) delay resulting from trial with respect to other charges against the defendant;

(C) delay resulting from any interlocutory appeal;

(D) delay resulting from any pretrial motion, from the filing of the motion through the conclusion of the hearing on, or other prompt disposition of, such motion;

(E) delay resulting from any proceeding relating to the transfer of a case or the removal of any defendant from another district under the Federal Rules of Criminal Procedure;

(F) delay resulting from transportation of any defendant from another district, or to and from places of examination or hospitalization, except that any time consumed in excess of ten days from the date an order of removal or an order directing such transportation, and the defendant's arrival at the destination shall be presumed to be unreasonable;

(G) delay resulting from consideration by the court of a proposed plea agreement to be entered into by the defendant and the attorney for the Government; and

(H) delay reasonably attributable to any period, not to exceed thirty days, during which any proceeding concerning the defendant is actually under advisement by the court.

(2) Any period of delay during which prosecution is deferred by the attorney for the Government pursuant to written agreement with the defendant, with the approval of the court, for the purpose of allowing the defendant to demonstrate his good conduct.

(3)(A) Any period of delay resulting from the absence or unavailability of the defendant or an essential witness.

(B) For purposes of subparagraph (A) of this paragraph, a defendant or an essential witness shall be considered absent when his whereabouts are unknown and, in addition, he is attempting to avoid apprehension or prosecution or his whereabouts cannot be determined by due diligence. For purposes of such subparagraph, a defendant or an essential witness shall be considered unavailable whenever his whereabouts are known but his presence for trial cannot be obtained by due diligence or he resists appearing at or being returned for trial.

(4) Any period of delay resulting from the fact that the defendant is mentally incompetent or physically unable to stand trial.

(5) If the information or indictment is dismissed upon motion of the attorney for the Government and thereafter a charge is filed against the defendant for the same offense, or any offense required to be joined with that offense, any period of delay from the date the charge was dismissed to the date the time limitation would commence to run as to the subsequent charge had there been no previous charge.

(6) A reasonable period of delay when the defendant is joined for trial with a codefendant as to whom the time for trial has not run and no motion for severance has been granted.

(7)(A) Any period of delay resulting from a continuance granted by any judge on his own motion or at the request of the defendant or his counsel or at the request of the attorney for the Government, if the judge granted such continuance on the basis of his findings that the ends of justice served by taking such action outweigh the best interest of the public and the defendant in a speedy trial. No such period of delay resulting from a continuance granted by the court in accordance with this paragraph shall be excludable under this subsection unless the court sets forth, in the record of the case, either orally or in writing, its reasons for finding that the ends of justice served by the granting of such continuance outweigh the best interests of the public and the defendant in a speedy trial.

(B) The factors, among others, which a judge shall consider in determining whether to grant a continuance under subparagraph (A) of this paragraph in any case are as follows:

(i) Whether the failure to grant such a continuance in the proceeding would be likely to make a continuation of such proceeding impossible, or result in a miscarriage of justice.

(ii) Whether the case is so unusual or so complex, due to the number of defendants, the nature of the prosecution, or the existence of novel questions of fact or law, that it is unreasonable to expect adequate preparation for pretrial proceedings or for the trial itself within the time limits established by this section.

(iii) Whether, in a case in which arrest precedes indictment, delay in the filing of the indictment is caused because the arrest occurs at a time such that it is unreasonable to expect return and filing of the indictment within the period specified in section 3161(b) or because the facts upon which the grand jury must base its determination are unusual or complex.

(iv) Whether the failure to grant such a continuance in a case that, taken as a whole, is not so unusual or so complex as to fall within clause (ii), would deny the defendant reasonable time to obtain counsel, would unreasonably deny the defendant or the Government continuity of counsel, or would deny counsel for the defendant or the attorney for the Government the reasonable time necessary for effective preparation, taking into account the exercise of due diligence.

(C) No continuance under subparagraph (A) of this paragraph shall be granted because of general congestion of the court's calendar, or lack of diligent preparation or failure to obtain available witnesses on the part of the attorney for the Government.

(8) Any period of delay, not to exceed one year, ordered by a district court upon an application of a party and a finding by a preponderance of the evidence that an official request, as defined in section 3292 of this title, has been made for evidence of any such offense and that it reasonably appears, or reasonably appeared at the time the request was made, that such evidence is, or was, in such foreign country.

(i) If trial did not commence within the time limitation specified in section 3161 because the defendant had entered a plea of guilty or nolo contendere subsequently withdrawn to any or all charges in an indictment or information, the defendant shall be deemed indicted with respect to all charges therein contained within the meaning of section 3161 on the day the order permitting withdrawal of the plea becomes final.

(j)(1) If the attorney for the Government knows that a person charged with an offense is serving a term of imprisonment in any penal institution, he shall promptly —

(A) undertake to obtain the presence of the prisoner for trial; or

(B) cause a detainer to be filed with the person having custody of the prisoner and request him to so advise the prisoner and to advise the prisoner of his right to demand trial.

(2) If the person having custody of such prisoner receives a detainer, he shall promptly advise the prisoner of the charge and of the prisoner's right to demand trial. If at any time thereafter the prisoner informs the person having custody that he does demand trial, such person shall cause notice to that effect to be sent promptly to the attorney for the Government who caused the detainer to be filed.

(3) Upon receipt of such notice, the attorney for the Government shall promptly seek to obtain the presence of the prisoner for trial.

(4) When the person having custody of the prisoner receives from the attorney for the Government a properly supported request for temporary custody of such prisoner for trial, the prisoner shall be made available to that attorney for the Government (subject, in cases of interjurisdictional transfer, to any right of the prisoner to contest the legality of his delivery).

(k)(1) If the defendant is absent (as defined by subsection (h)(3)) on the day set for trial, and the defendant's subsequent appearance before the court on a bench warrant or other process or surrender to the court occurs more than twenty-one days after the day set for trial, the defendant shall be deemed to have first appeared before a judicial officer of the court in which the information or indictment is pending within the meaning of subsection (c) on the date of the defendant's subsequent appearance before the court.

(2) If the defendant is absent (as defined by subsection (h)(3)) on the day set for trial, and the defendant's subsequent appearance before the court on a bench warrant or other process or surrender to the court occurs not more than twenty-one days after the day set for trial, the time limit required by subsection (c), as extended by subsection (h), shall be further extended by twenty-one days.

18 U.S.C. §3162. Sanctions

(a)(1) If, in the case of any individual against whom a complaint is filed charging such individual with an offense, no indictment or information is filed within the time limit required by section 3161(b) as extended by section 3161(h) of this chapter, such charge against that individual contained in such complaint shall be dismissed or otherwise dropped. In determining whether to dismiss the case with or without prejudice, the court shall consider, among others, each of the following factors: the seriousness of the offense; the facts and circumstances of the case which led to the dismissal; and the impact of a reprosecution on the administration of this chapter [18 U.S.C. §§ 3161 et seq.] and on the administration of justice.

(2) If a defendant is not brought to trial within the time limit required by section 3161(c) as extended by section 3161(h), the information or indictment shall be dismissed on motion of the defendant. The defendant shall have the burden of proof of supporting such motion but the Government shall have the burden of going forward with the evidence in connection with any exclusion of time under subparagraph 3161(h)(3).

In determining whether to dismiss the case with or without prejudice, the court shall consider, among others, each of the following factors: the seriousness of the offense; the facts and circumstances of the case which led to the dismissal; and the impact of a reprosecution on the administration of this chapter [18 U.S.C. §§ 3161 et seq.] and on the administration of justice. Failure of the defendant to move for dismissal prior to trial or entry of a plea of guilty or nolo contendere shall constitute a waiver of the right to dismissal under this section.

(b) In any case in which counsel for the defendant or the attorney for the Government

(1) knowingly allows the case to be set for trial without disclosing the fact that a necessary witness would be unavailable for trial;

(2) files a motion solely for the purpose of delay, which he knows is totally frivolous and without merit;

(3) makes a statement for the purpose of obtaining a continuance that he knows to be false and that is material to the granting of a continuance; or

(4) otherwise willfully fails to proceed to trial without justification consistent with section 3161 of this chapter, the court may punish any such counsel or attorney, as follows:

(A) in the case of an appointed defense counsel, by reducing the amount of compensation that otherwise would have been paid to such counsel pursuant to section 3006A of this title in an amount not to exceed 25 per centum thereof;

(B) in the case of a counsel retained in connection with the defense of a defendant, by imposing on such counsel a fine of not to exceed 25 per centum of the compensation to which he is entitled in connection with his defense of such defendant;

(C) by imposing on any attorney for the Government a fine of not to exceed $250;

(D) by denying any such counsel or attorney for the Government the right to practice before the court considering such case for a period of not to exceed 90 days; or

(E) by filing a report with an appropriate disciplinary committee.

The authority to punish provided for by this subsection shall be in addition to any other authority or power available to such court.

(c) The court shall follow procedures established in the Federal Rules of Criminal Procedure in punishing any counsel or attorney for the Government pursuant to this section.

18 U.S.C. §3164. Persons Detained or Designated As Being of High Risk

(a) The trial or other disposition of cases involving —

(1) a detained person who is being held in detention solely because he is awaiting trial, and

(2) a released person who is awaiting trial and has been designated by the attorney for the Government as being of high risk, shall be accorded priority.

(b) The trial of any person described in subsection (a)(1) or (a)(2) of this section shall commence not later than ninety days following the beginning of such continuous detention or designation of high risk by the attorney for the Government. The periods of delay enumerated in section 3161(h) are excluded in computing the time limitation specified in this section.

(c) Failure to commence trial of a detainee as specified in subsection (b), through no fault of the accused or his counsel, or failure to commence trial of a designated releasee as specified in subsection (b), through no fault of the attorney for the Government, shall result in the automatic review by the court of the conditions of release. No detainee, as defined in subsection (a), shall be held in custody pending trial after the expiration of such ninety-day period required for the commencement of his trial. A designated releasee, as defined in subsection (a), who is found by the court to have intentionally delayed the trial of his case shall be subject to an order of the court modifying his nonfinancial conditions of release under this title to insure that he shall appear at trial as required.

18 U.S.C. §3173. Sixth Amendment Rights

No provision of this chapter [18 U.S.C. §§ 3161 et seq.] shall be interpreted as a bar to any claim of denial of speedy trial as required by amendment VI of the Constitution.

Jencks Act

18 U.S.C. §3500. Demands for production of statements and reports of witnesses

(a) In any criminal prosecution brought by the United States, no statement or report in the possession of the United States which was made by a Government witness or prospective Government witness (other than the defendant) shall be the subject of subpena, discovery, or inspection until said witness has testified on direct examination in the trial of the case.

(b) After a witness called by the United States has testified on direct examination, the court shall, on motion of the defendant, order the United States to produce any statement (as hereinafter defined) of the witness in the possession of the United States which relates to the subject matter as to which the witness has testified. If the entire contents of any such statement relate to the subject matter of the testimony of the witness, the court shall order it to be delivered directly to the defendant for his examination and use.

(c) If the United States claims that any statement ordered to be produced under this section contains matter which does not relate to the subject matter of the testimony of the witness, the court shall order the United States to deliver such statement for the inspection of the court in camera. Upon such delivery the court shall excise the portions of such statement which do not relate to the subject matter of the testimony of the witness. With such material excised, the court shall then direct delivery of such statement to the defendant for his use. If, pursuant to such procedure, any portion of such statement is withheld from the defendant and the defendant objects to such withholding, and the trial is continued to an adjudication of the guilt of the defendant, the entire text of such statement shall be preserved by the United States and, in the event the defendant appeals, shall be made available to the appellate court for the purpose of determining the correctness of the ruling of the trial judge. Whenever any statement is delivered to a defendant pursuant to this section, the court in its discretion, upon application of said defendant, may recess proceedings in the trial for such time as it may determine to be reasonably required for the examination of such statement by said defendant and his preparation for its use in the trial.

(d) If the United States elects not to comply with an order of the court under subsection (b) or (c) hereof to deliver to the defendant any such statement, or such portion thereof as the court may direct, the court shall strike from the record the testimony of the witness, and the trial shall proceed unless the court in its discretion shall determine that the interests of justice require that a mistrial be declared.

(e) The term "statement," as used in subsections (b), (c), and (d) of this section in relation to any witness called by the United States, means—

(1) a written statement made by said witness and signed or otherwise adopted or approved by him;

(2) a stenographic, mechanical, electrical, or other recording, or a transcription thereof, which is a substantially verbatim recital of an oral statement made by said witness and recorded contemporaneously with the making of such oral statement; or

(3) a statement, however taken or recorded, or a transcription thereof, if any, made by said witness to a grand jury.

Criminal Appeals Act of 1970 (as amended)

18 U.S.C. §3731. Appeal by United States

In a criminal case an appeal by the United States shall lie to a court of appeals from a decision, judgment, or order of a district court dismissing an indictment or information or granting a new trial after verdict or judgment, as to any one or more counts, or any part thereof, except that no appeal shall lie where the double jeopardy clause of the United States Constitution prohibits further prosecution.

An appeal by the United States shall lie to a court of appeals from a decision or order of a district court suppressing or excluding evidence or requiring the return of seized property in a criminal proceeding, not made after the defendant has been put in jeopardy and before the verdict or finding on an indictment or information, if the United States attorney certifies to the district court that the appeal is not taken for purpose of delay and that the evidence is a substantial proof of a fact material in the proceeding.

An appeal by the United States shall lie to a court of appeals from a decision or order, entered by a district court of the United States, granting the release of a person charged with or convicted of an offense, or denying a motion for revocation of, or modification of the conditions of, a decision or order granting release.

The appeal in all such cases shall be taken within thirty days after the decision, judgment, or order has been rendered and shall be diligently prosecuted.

The provisions of this section shall be liberally construed to effectuate its purposes.

Crime Victims' Rights Act

18 U.S.C. §3771. Crime victims' rights

(a) Rights of Crime Victims. — A crime victim has the following rights:

(1) The right to be reasonably protected from the accused.

(2) The right to reasonable, accurate, and timely notice of any public court proceeding, or any parole proceeding, involving the crime or of any release or escape of the accused.

(3) The right not to be excluded from any such public court proceeding, unless the court, after receiving clear and convincing evidence, determines that testimony by the victim would be materially altered if the victim heard other testimony at that proceeding.

(4) The right to be reasonably heard at any public proceeding in the district court involving release, plea, sentencing, or any parole proceeding.

(5) The reasonable right to confer with the attorney for the Government in the case.

(6) The right to full and timely restitution as provided in law.

(7) The right to proceedings free from unreasonable delay.

(8) The right to be treated with fairness and with respect for the victim's dignity and privacy.

(b) Rights Afforded. —

(1) In general. — In any court proceeding involving an offense against a crime victim, the court shall ensure that the crime victim is afforded the rights described in subsection (a). Before making a determination described in subsection (a)(3), the court shall make every effort to permit the fullest attendance possible by the victim and shall consider reasonable alternatives to the exclusion of the victim from the criminal proceeding. The reasons for any decision denying relief under this chapter shall be clearly stated on the record.

(2) Habeas corpus proceedings. —

(A) In general. — In a Federal habeas corpus proceeding arising out of a State conviction, the court shall ensure that a crime victim is afforded the rights described in paragraphs (3), (4), (7), and (8) of subsection (a).

(B) Enforcement. —

(i) In general. — These rights may be enforced by the crime victim or the crime victim's lawful representative in the manner described in paragraphs (1) and (3) of subsection (d).

(ii) Multiple victims. — In a case involving multiple victims, subsection (d)(2) shall also apply.

(C) Limitation. — This paragraph relates to the duties of a court in relation to the rights of a crime victim in Federal habeas corpus proceedings arising out of a State conviction, and does not give rise to any obligation or requirement applicable to personnel of any agency of the Executive Branch of the Federal Government.

(D) Definition. — For purposes of this paragraph, the term "crime victim" means the person against whom the State offense is committed or, if that person is killed or incapacitated, that person's family member or other lawful representative.

(c) Best Efforts to Accord Rights. —

(1) Government. — Officers and employees of the Department of Justice and other departments and agencies of the United States engaged in the detection, investigation, or prosecution of crime shall make their best efforts to see that crime victims are notified of, and accorded, the rights described in subsection (a).

(2) Advice of attorney. — The prosecutor shall advise the crime victim that the crime victim can seek the advice of an attorney with respect to the rights described in subsection (a).

(3) Notice. — Notice of release otherwise required pursuant to this chapter shall not be given if such notice may endanger the safety of any person.

(d) Enforcement and Limitations. —

(1) Rights. — The crime victim or the crime victim's lawful representative, and the attorney for the Government may assert the rights described in subsection (a). A person accused of the crime may not obtain any form of relief under this chapter.

(2) Multiple crime victims. — In a case where the court finds that the number of crime victims makes it impracticable to accord all of the crime victims the rights described in subsection (a), the court shall fashion a reasonable procedure to give effect to this chapter that does not unduly complicate or prolong the proceedings.

(3) Motion for relief and writ of mandamus. — The rights described in subsection (a) shall be asserted in the district court in which a defendant is being prosecuted for the crime or, if no prosecution is underway, in the district court in the district in which the crime occurred. The district court shall take up and decide any motion asserting a victim's right forthwith. If the district court denies the relief sought, the movant may petition the court of appeals for a writ of mandamus. The court of appeals may issue the writ on the order of a single judge pursuant to circuit rule or the Federal Rules of Appellate Procedure. The court of appeals shall take up and decide such application forthwith within 72 hours after the petition has been filed. In no event shall proceedings be stayed or subject to a continuance of more than five days for purposes of enforcing this chapter. If the court of appeals denies the relief sought, the reasons for the denial shall be clearly stated on the record in a written opinion.

(4) Error. — In any appeal in a criminal case, the Government may assert as error the district court's denial of any crime victim's right in the proceeding to which the appeal relates.

(5) Limitation on relief. — In no case shall a failure to afford a right under this chapter provide grounds for a new trial. A victim may make a motion to re-open a plea or sentence only if—

(A) the victim has asserted the right to be heard before or during the proceeding at issue and such right was denied;

(B) the victim petitions the court of appeals for a writ of mandamus within 14 days; and

(C) in the case of a plea, the accused has not pled to the highest offense charged. This paragraph does not affect the victim's right to restitution as provided in title 18, United States Code.

(6) No cause of action.— Nothing in this chapter shall be construed to authorize a cause of action for damages or to create, to enlarge, or to imply any duty or obligation to any victim or other person for the breach of which the United States or any of its officers or employees could be held liable in damages. Nothing in this chapter shall be construed to impair the prosecutorial discretion of the Attorney General or any officer under his direction.

(e) Definitions.— For the purposes of this chapter, the term "crime victim" means a person directly and proximately harmed as a result of the commission of a Federal offense or an offense in the District of Columbia. In the case of a crime victim who is under 18 years of age, incompetent, incapacitated, or deceased, the legal guardians of the crime victim or the representatives of the crime victim's estate, family members, or any other persons appointed as suitable by the court, may assume the crime victim's rights under this chapter, but in no event shall the defendant be named as such guardian or representative.

(f) Procedures to Promote Compliance.—

(1) Regulations.— Not later than 1 year after the date of enactment of this chapter, the Attorney General of the United States shall promulgate regulations to enforce the rights of crime victims and to ensure compliance by responsible officials with the obligations described in law respecting crime victims.

(2) Contents.— The regulations promulgated under paragraph (1) shall—

(A) designate an administrative authority within the Department of Justice to receive and investigate complaints relating to the provision or violation of the rights of a crime victim;

(B) require a course of training for employees and offices of the Department of Justice that fail to comply with provisions of Federal law pertaining to the treatment of crime victims, and otherwise assist such employees and offices in responding more effectively to the needs of crime victims;

(C) contain disciplinary sanctions, including suspension or termination from employment, for employees of the Department of Justice who willfully or wantonly fail to comply with provisions of Federal law pertaining to the treatment of crime victims; and

(D) provide that the Attorney General, or the designee of the Attorney General, shall be the final arbiter of the complaint, and that there shall be no judicial review of the final decision of the Attorney General by a complainant.

Habeas Corpus Act of 1867 (as amended by Antiterrorism and Effective Death Penalty Act of 1996)

28 U.S.C. §2241. Power to Grant Writ

(a) Writs of habeas corpus may be granted by the Supreme Court, any justice thereof, the district courts, and any circuit judge within their respective jurisdictions. The order of a circuit judge shall be entered in the records of the district court of the district wherein the restraint complained of is had.

(b) The Supreme Court, any justice thereof, and any circuit judge may decline to entertain an application for a writ of habeas corpus and may transfer the application for hearing and determination to the district court having jurisdiction to entertain it.

(c) The writ of habeas corpus shall not extend to a prisoner unless —

(1) He is in custody under or by color of the authority of the United States or is committed for trial before some court thereof; or

(2) He is in custody for an act done or omitted in pursuance of an Act of Congress, or an order, process, judgment or decree of a court or judge of the United States; or

(3) He is in custody in violation of the Constitution or laws or treaties of the United States; or

(4) He, being a citizen of a foreign state and domiciled therein, is in custody for an act done or omitted under any alleged right, title, authority, privilege, protection, or exemption claimed under the commission, order or sanction of any foreign state, or under color thereof, the validity and effect of which depend upon the law of nations; or

(5) It is necessary to bring him into court to testify or for trial.

(d) Where an application for a writ of habeas corpus is made by a person in custody under the judgment and sentence of a State court of a State which contains two or more Federal judicial districts, the application may be filed in the district court for the district wherein such person is in custody or in the district court for the district within which the State court was held which convicted and sentenced him and each of such district courts shall have concurrent jurisdiction to entertain the application. The district court for the district wherein such an application is filed in the exercise of its discretion and in furtherance of justice may transfer the application to the other district court for hearing and determination.

(e) [**NOTE**—This provision, which was added to the statute as part of the Detainee Treatment Act of 2005 and which purported to deny access to habeas corpus for aliens detained by the U.S. Department of Defense at Guantanamo Bay as alleged "enemy combatants," was held unconstitutional by the U.S. Supreme Court in Boumediene v. Bush, 553 U.S. 723 (2008). See the main casebook, Chapter 17, pages 1602-1603, for further discussion of *Boumediene*.—Eds.]

28 U.S.C. §2242. Application

Application for a writ of habeas corpus shall be in writing signed and verified by the person for whose relief it is intended or by someone acting in his behalf.

It shall allege the facts concerning the applicant's commitment or detention, the name of the person who has custody over him and by virtue of what claim or authority, if known.

It may be amended or supplemented as provided in the rules of procedure applicable to civil actions.

If addressed to the Supreme Court, a justice thereof, or a circuit judge, it shall state the reasons for not making application to the district court of the district in which the applicant is held.

28 U.S.C. §2243. Issuance of Writ; Return; Hearing; Decision

A court, justice, or judge entertaining an application for a writ of habeas corpus shall forthwith award the writ or issue an order directing the respondent to show cause why the writ should not be granted, unless it appears from the application that the applicant or person detained is not entitled thereto.

The writ, or order to show cause, shall be directed to the person having custody of the person detained. It shall be returned within three days unless for good cause additional time, not exceeding twenty days, is allowed.

The person to whom the writ or order is directed shall make a return certifying the true cause of the detention.

When the writ or order is returned a day shall be set for hearing, not more than five days after the return unless for good cause additional time is allowed.

Unless the application for the writ and the return present only issues of law, the person to whom the writ is directed shall be required to produce at the hearing the body of the person detained.

The applicant or the person detained may, under oath, deny any of the facts set forth in the return or allege any other material facts.

The return and all suggestions made against it may be amended, by leave of court, before or after being filed.

The court shall summarily hear and determine the facts and dispose of the matter as law and justice require.

28 U.S.C. §2244. Finality of Determination

(a) No circuit or district judge shall be required to entertain an application for a writ of habeas corpus to inquire into the detention of a person pursuant to a judgment of a court of the United States if it appears that the legality of such detention has been determined by a judge or court of the United States on a prior application for a writ of habeas corpus, except as provided in section 2255.

(b)(1) A claim presented in a second or successive habeas corpus application under section 2254 that was presented in a prior application shall be dismissed.

(2) A claim presented in a second or successive habeas corpus application under section 2254 that was not presented in a prior application shall be dismissed unless —

(A) the applicant shows that the claim relies on a new rule of constitutional law, made retroactive to cases on collateral review by the Supreme Court, that was previously unavailable; or

(B)(i) the factual predicate for the claim could not have been discovered previously through the exercise of due diligence; and

(ii) the facts underlying the claim, if proven and viewed in light of the evidence as a whole, would be sufficient to establish by clear and convincing evidence that, but for constitutional error, no reasonable factfinder would have found the applicant guilty of the underlying offense.

(3)(A) Before a second or successive application permitted by this section is filed in the district court, the applicant shall move in the appropriate court of appeals for an order authorizing the district court to consider the application.

(B) A motion in the court of appeals for an order authorizing the district court to consider a second or successive application shall be determined by a three-judge panel of the court of appeals.

(C) The court of appeals may authorize the filing of a second or successive application only if it determines that the application makes a prima facie showing that the application satisfies the requirements of this subsection.

(D) The court of appeals shall grant or deny the authorization to file a second or successive application not later than 30 days after the filing of the motion.

(E) The grant or denial of an authorization by a court of appeals to file a second or successive application shall not be appealable and shall not be the subject of a petition for rehearing or for a writ of certiorari.

(4) A district court shall dismiss any claim presented in a second or successive application that the court of appeals has authorized to be filed unless the applicant shows that the claim satisfies the requirements of this section.

(c) In a habeas corpus proceeding brought in behalf of a person in custody pursuant to the judgment of a State court, a prior judgment of the Supreme Court of the United States on an appeal or review by a writ of certiorari at the instance of the prisoner of the decision of such State court, shall be conclusive as to all issues of fact or law with respect to an asserted denial of a Federal right which constitutes ground for discharge in a habeas corpus proceeding, actually adjudicated by the Supreme Court therein, unless the applicant for the writ of habeas corpus shall plead and the court shall find the existence of a material and controlling fact which did not appear in the record of the proceeding in the Supreme Court and the court shall further find that the applicant for the writ of habeas corpus could not have caused such fact to appear in such record by the exercise of reasonable diligence.

(d)(1) A one-year period of limitation shall apply to an application for a writ of habeas corpus by a person in custody pursuant to the judgment of a State court. The limitation period shall run from the latest of —

(A) the date on which the judgment became final by the conclusion of direct review or the expiration of the time for seeking such review;

(B) the date on which the impediment to filing an application created by State action in violation of the Constitution or laws of the United States is removed, if the applicant was prevented from filing by such State action;

(C) the date on which the constitutional right asserted was initially recognized by the Supreme Court, if the right has been newly recognized by the Supreme Court and made retroactively applicable to cases on collateral review; or

(D) the date on which the factual predicate of the claim or claims presented could have been discovered through the exercise of due diligence.

(2) The time during which a properly filed application for State post-conviction or other collateral review with respect to the pertinent judgment or claim is pending shall not be counted toward any period of limitation under this subsection.

28 U.S.C. §2253. Appeal

(a) In a habeas corpus proceeding or a proceeding under section 2255 before a district judge, the final order shall be subject to review, on appeal, by the court of appeals for the circuit in which the proceeding is held.

(b) There shall be no right of appeal from a final order in a proceeding to test the validity of a warrant to remove to another district or place for commitment or trial a person charged with a criminal offense against the United States, or to test the validity of such person's detention pending removal proceedings.

(c)(1) Unless a circuit justice or judge issues a certificate of appealability, an appeal may not be taken to the court of appeals from —

(A) the final order in a habeas corpus proceeding in which the detention complained of arises out of process issued by a State court; or

(B) the final order in a proceeding under section 2255.

(2) A certificate of appealability may issue under paragraph (1) only if the applicant has made a substantial showing of the denial of a constitutional right.

(3) The certificate of appealability under paragraph (1) shall indicate which specific issue or issues satisfy the showing required by paragraph (2).

28 U.S.C. §2254. State Custody; Remedies in Federal Courts

(a) The Supreme Court, a Justice thereof, a circuit judge, or a district court shall entertain an application for a writ of habeas corpus in behalf of a person in custody pursuant to the judgment of a State court only on the ground that he is in custody in violation of the Constitution or laws or treaties of the United States.

(b)(1) An application for a writ of habeas corpus on behalf of a person in custody pursuant to the judgment of a State court shall not be granted unless it appears that —

(A) the applicant has exhausted the remedies available in the courts of the State; or

(B) (i) there is an absence of available State corrective process; or

(ii) circumstances exist that render such process ineffective to protect the rights of the applicant.

(2) An application for a writ of habeas corpus may be denied on the merits, notwithstanding the failure of the applicant to exhaust the remedies available in the courts of the State.

(3) A State shall not be deemed to have waived the exhaustion requirement or be estopped from reliance upon the requirement unless the State, through counsel, expressly waives the requirement.

(c) An applicant shall not be deemed to have exhausted the remedies available in the courts of the State, within the meaning of this section, if he has the right under the law of the State to raise, by any available procedure, the question presented.

(d) An application for a writ of habeas corpus on behalf of a person in custody pursuant to the judgment of a State court shall not be granted with respect to any claim that was adjudicated on the merits in State court proceedings unless the adjudication of the claim —

(1) resulted in a decision that was contrary to, or involved an unreasonable application of, clearly established Federal law, as determined by the Supreme Court of the United States; or

(2) resulted in a decision that was based on an unreasonable determination of the facts in light of the evidence presented in the State court proceeding.

(e)(1) In a proceeding instituted by an application for a writ of habeas corpus by a person in custody pursuant to the judgment of a State court, a determination of a factual issue made by a State court shall be presumed to be correct. The applicant shall have the burden of rebutting the presumption of correctness by clear and convincing evidence.

(2) If the applicant has failed to develop the factual basis of a claim in State court proceedings, the court shall not hold an evidentiary hearing on the claim unless the applicant shows that —

(A) the claim relies on —

(i) a new rule of constitutional law, made retroactive to cases on collateral review by the Supreme Court, that was previously unavailable; or

(ii) a factual predicate that could not have been previously discovered through the exercise of due diligence; and

(B) the facts underlying the claim would be sufficient to establish by clear and convincing evidence that but for constitutional error, no reasonable factfinder would have found the applicant guilty of the underlying offense.

(f) If the applicant challenges the sufficiency of the evidence adduced in such State court proceeding to support the State court's determination of a factual issue made therein, the applicant, if able, shall produce that part of the record pertinent to a determination of the sufficiency of the evidence to support such determination. If the applicant, because of indigency or other reason is unable to produce such part of the record, then the State shall produce such part of the record and the Federal court shall direct the State to do so by order directed to an appropriate State official. If the State cannot provide such pertinent part of the record, then the court shall determine under the existing facts and circumstances what weight shall be given to the State court's factual determination.

(g) A copy of the official records of the State court, duly certified by the clerk of such court to be a true and correct copy of a finding, judicial opinion, or other reliable written indicia showing such a factual determination by the State court shall be admissible in the Federal court proceeding.

(h) Except as provided in section 408 of the Controlled Substance Acts [21 U.S.C. § 848], in all proceedings brought under this section, and any subsequent proceedings on review, the court may appoint counsel for an applicant who is or becomes financially unable to afford counsel, except as provided by a rule promulgated by the Supreme Court pursuant to statutory authority. Appointment of counsel under this section shall be governed by section 3006A of title 18.

(i) The ineffectiveness or incompetence of counsel during Federal or State collateral post-conviction proceedings shall not be a ground for relief in a proceeding arising under section 2254.

Collateral Review for Federal Prisoners

28 U.S.C. §2255. Federal Custody; Remedies on Motion Attacking Sentence

(a) A prisoner in custody under sentence of a court established by Act of Congress claiming the right to be released upon the ground that the sentence was imposed in violation of the Constitution or laws of the United States, or that the court was without jurisdiction to impose such sentence, or that the sentence was in excess of the maximum authorized by law, or is otherwise subject to collateral attack, may move the court which imposed the sentence to vacate, set aside or correct the sentence.

(b) Unless the motion and the files and records of the case conclusively show that the prisoner is entitled to no relief, the court shall cause notice thereof to be served upon the United States attorney, grant a prompt hearing thereon, determine the issues and make findings of fact and conclusions of law with respect thereto. If the court finds that the judgment was rendered without jurisdiction, or that the sentence imposed was not authorized by law or otherwise open to collateral attack, or that there has been such a denial or infringement of the constitutional rights of the prisoner as to render the judgment vulnerable to collateral attack, the court shall vacate and set the judgment aside and shall discharge the prisoner or resentence him or grant a new trial or correct the sentence as may appear appropriate.

(c) A court may entertain and determine such motion without requiring the production of the prisoner at the hearing.

(d) An appeal may be taken to the court of appeals from the order entered on the motion as from the final judgment on application for a writ of habeas corpus.

(e) An application for a writ of habeas corpus in behalf of a prisoner who is authorized to apply for relief by motion pursuant to this section, shall not be entertained if it appears that the applicant has failed to apply for relief, by motion, to the court which sentenced him, or that such court has denied him relief, unless it also appears that the remedy by motion is inadequate or ineffective to test the legality of his detention.

(f) A one-year period of limitation shall apply to a motion under this section. The limitation period shall run from the latest of —

> (1) the date on which the judgment of conviction becomes final;

(2) the date on which the impediment to making a motion created by governmental action in violation of the Constitution or laws of the United States is removed, if the movant was prevented from making a motion by such governmental action;

(3) the date on which the right asserted was initially recognized by the Supreme Court, if that right has been newly recognized by the Supreme Court and made retroactively applicable to cases on collateral review; or

(4) the date on which the facts supporting the claim or claims presented could have been discovered through the exercise of due diligence.

(g) Except as provided in section 408 of the Controlled Substances Act [21 U.S.C. § 848], in all proceedings brought under this section, and any subsequent proceedings on review, the court may appoint counsel, except as provided by a rule promulgated by the Supreme Court pursuant to statutory authority. Appointment of counsel under this section shall be governed by section 3006A of title 18.

(h) A second or successive motion must be certified as provided in section 2244 by a panel of the appropriate court of appeals to contain —

(1) newly discovered evidence that, if proven and viewed in light of the evidence as a whole, would be sufficient to establish by clear and convincing evidence that no reasonable factfinder would have found the movant guilty of the offense; or

(2) a new rule of constitutional law, made retroactive to cases on collateral review by the Supreme Court, that was previously unavailable.

Foreign Intelligence Surveillance Act

50 U.S.C. §1861. Access to certain business records for foreign intelligence and international terrorism investigations

(a) Application for order; conduct of investigation generally

(1) Subject to paragraph (3), the Director of the Federal Bureau of Investigation or a designee of the Director (whose rank shall be no lower than Assistant Special Agent in Charge) may make an application for an order requiring the production of any tangible

things (including books, records, papers, documents, and other items) for an investigation to obtain foreign intelligence information not concerning a United States person or to protect against international terrorism or clandestine intelligence activities, provided that such investigation of a United States person is not conducted solely upon the basis of activities protected by the first amendment to the Constitution.

(2) An investigation conducted under this section shall—

(A) be conducted under guidelines approved by the Attorney General under Executive Order 12333 (or a successor order); and

(B) not be conducted of a United States person solely upon the basis of activities protected by the first amendment to the Constitution of the United States.

(3) In the case of an application for an order requiring the production of library circulation records, library patron lists, book sales records, book customer lists, firearms sales records, tax return records, educational records, or medical records containing information that would identify a person, the Director of the Federal Bureau of Investigation may delegate the authority to make such application to either the Deputy Director of the Federal Bureau of Investigation or the Executive Assistant Director for National Security (or any successor position). The Deputy Director or the Executive Assistant Director may not further delegate such authority.

(b) Recipient and contents of application. Each application under this section—

(1) shall be made to—

(A) a judge of the court established by section 1803 (a) of this title; or

(B) a United States Magistrate Judge under chapter 43 of title 28, who is publicly designated by the Chief Justice of the United States to have the power to hear applications and grant orders for the production of tangible things under this section on behalf of a judge of that court; and

(2) shall include—

(A) a statement of facts showing that there are reasonable grounds to believe that the tangible things sought are relevant to an authorized investigation (other than a threat assessment) conducted in accordance with subsection (a)(2) to obtain foreign intelligence information not concerning a United States person or to protect against international terrorism or clandestine intelligence activities, such things being presumptively relevant to an authorized investigation if the applicant shows in the statement of the facts that they pertain to —

(i) a foreign power or an agent of a foreign power;

(ii) the activities of a suspected agent of a foreign power who is the subject of such authorized investigation; or

(iii) an individual in contact with, or known to, a suspected agent of a foreign power who is the subject of such authorized investigation; and

(B) an enumeration of the minimization procedures adopted by the Attorney General under subsection (g) that are applicable to the retention and dissemination by the Federal Bureau of Investigation of any tangible things to be made available to the Federal Bureau of Investigation based on the order requested in such application.

(c) Ex parte judicial order of approval

(1) Upon an application made pursuant to this section, if the judge finds that the application meets the requirements of subsections (a) and (b), the judge shall enter an ex parte order as requested, or as modified, approving the release of tangible things. Such order shall direct that minimization procedures adopted pursuant to subsection (g) be followed.

(2) An order under this subsection —

(A) shall describe the tangible things that are ordered to be produced with sufficient particularity to permit them to be fairly identified;

(B) shall include the date on which the tangible things must be provided, which shall allow a reasonable period of time within which the tangible things can be assembled and made available;

(C) shall provide clear and conspicuous notice of the principles and procedures described in subsection (d);

(D) may only require the production of a tangible thing if such thing can be obtained with a subpoena duces tecum issued by a court of the United States in aid of a grand jury investigation or with any other order issued by a court of the United States directing the production of records or tangible things; and

(E) shall not disclose that such order is issued for purposes of an investigation described in subsection (a).

(d) Nondisclosure

(1) No person shall disclose to any other person that the Federal Bureau of Investigation has sought or obtained tangible things pursuant to an order under this section, other than to —

(A) those persons to whom disclosure is necessary to comply with such order;

(B) an attorney to obtain legal advice or assistance with respect to the production of things in response to the order; or

(C) other persons as permitted by the Director of the Federal Bureau of Investigation or the designee of the Director.

(2)(A) A person to whom disclosure is made pursuant to paragraph (1) shall be subject to the nondisclosure requirements applicable to a person to whom an order is directed under this section in the same manner as such person.

(B) Any person who discloses to a person described in subparagraph (A), (B), or (C) of paragraph (1) that the Federal Bureau of Investigation has sought or obtained tangible things pursuant to an order under this section shall notify such person of the nondisclosure requirements of this subsection.

(C) At the request of the Director of the Federal Bureau of Investigation or the designee of the Director, any person making or intending to make a disclosure under subparagraph (A) or (C) of paragraph (1) shall identify to the Director or such designee the person to whom such disclosure will be made or to whom such disclosure was made prior to the request.

(e) Liability for good faith disclosure; waiver. A person who, in good faith, produces tangible things under an order pursuant to this section shall not be liable to any other person for such production. Such production shall not be deemed to constitute a waiver of any privilege in any other proceeding or context.

(f) Judicial review of FISA orders

(1) In this subsection —

(A) the term "production order" means an order to produce any tangible thing under this section; and

(B) the term "nondisclosure order" means an order imposed under subsection (d).

(2)(A)(i) A person receiving a production order may challenge the legality of that order by filing a petition with the pool established by section 1803(e)(1) of this title. Not less than 1 year after the date of the issuance of the production order, the recipient of a production order may challenge the nondisclosure order imposed in connection with such production order by filing a petition to modify or set aside such nondisclosure order, consistent with the requirements of subparagraph (C), with the pool established by section 1803(e)(1) of this title.

(ii) The presiding judge shall immediately assign a petition under clause (i) to 1 of the judges serving in the pool established by section 1803(e)(1) of this title. Not later than 72 hours after the assignment of such petition, the assigned judge shall conduct an initial review of the petition. If the assigned judge determines that the petition is frivolous, the assigned judge shall immediately deny the petition and affirm the production order or nondisclosure order. If the assigned judge determines the petition is not frivolous, the assigned judge shall promptly consider the petition in accordance with the procedures established under section 1803(e)(2) of this title.

(iii) The assigned judge shall promptly provide a written statement for the record of the reasons for any determination under this subsection. Upon the request of the Government, any order setting aside a nondisclosure order shall be stayed pending review pursuant to paragraph (3).

(B) A judge considering a petition to modify or set aside a production order may grant such petition only if the judge finds that such order does not meet the requirements of this section or is otherwise unlawful. If the judge does not modify or set aside the production order, the judge shall immediately affirm such order, and order the recipient to comply therewith.

(C)(i) A judge considering a petition to modify or set aside a nondisclosure order may grant such petition only if the judge finds that there is no reason to believe that disclosure may endanger the national security of the United States, interfere with a criminal, counterterrorism, or counterintelligence investigation, interfere with diplomatic relations, or endanger the life or physical safety of any person.

(ii) If, upon filing of such a petition, the Attorney General, Deputy Attorney General, an Assistant Attorney General, or the Director of the Federal Bureau of Investigation certifies that disclosure may endanger the national security of the United States or interfere with diplomatic relations, such certification shall be treated as conclusive, unless the judge finds that the certification was made in bad faith.

(iii) If the judge denies a petition to modify or set aside a nondisclosure order, the recipient of such order shall be precluded for a period of 1 year from filing another such petition with respect to such nondisclosure order.

(D) Any production or nondisclosure order not explicitly modified or set aside consistent with this subsection shall remain in full effect.

(3) A petition for review of a decision under paragraph (2) to affirm, modify, or set aside an order by the Government or any person receiving such order shall be made to the court of review established under section 1803(b) of this title, which shall have jurisdiction to consider such petitions. The court of review shall provide for the record a written statement of the reasons for its decision and, on petition by the Government or any person receiving such order for writ of certiorari, the record shall be transmitted under seal to the Supreme Court of the United States, which shall have jurisdiction to review such decision.

(4) Judicial proceedings under this subsection shall be concluded as expeditiously as possible. The record of proceedings, including petitions filed, orders granted, and statements of reasons for decision, shall be maintained under security measures established by the Chief Justice of the United States, in consultation with the Attorney General and the Director of National Intelligence.

(5) All petitions under this subsection shall be filed under seal. In any proceedings under this subsection, the court shall, upon request of the Government, review ex parte and in camera any Government submission, or portions thereof, which may include classified information.

(g) Minimization procedures

(1) In general. Not later than 180 days after March 9, 2006, the Attorney General shall adopt specific minimization procedures governing the retention and dissemination by the Federal Bureau of Investigation of any tangible things, or information therein, received by the Federal Bureau of Investigation in response to an order under this subchapter.

(2) Defined. In this section, the term "minimization procedures" means —

(A) specific procedures that are reasonably designed in light of the purpose and technique of an order for the production of tangible things, to minimize the retention, and prohibit the dissemination, of nonpublicly available information concerning unconsenting United States persons consistent with the need of the United States to obtain, produce, and disseminate foreign intelligence information;

(B) procedures that require that nonpublicly available information, which is not foreign intelligence information, as defined in section 1801(e)(1) of this title, shall not be disseminated in a manner that identifies any United States person, without such person's consent, unless such person's identity is necessary to understand foreign intelligence information or assess its importance; and

(C) notwithstanding subparagraphs (A) and (B), procedures that allow for the retention and dissemination of information that is evidence of a crime which has been, is being, or is about to be committed and that is to be retained or disseminated for law enforcement purposes.

(h) Use of information. Information acquired from tangible things received by the Federal Bureau of Investigation in response to an order under this subchapter concerning any United States person may be used and disclosed by Federal officers and employees without the consent of the United States person only in accordance with the minimization procedures adopted pursuant to subsection (g). No otherwise privileged information acquired from tangible things received by the Federal Bureau of Investigation in accordance with the provisions of this subchapter shall lose its privileged character. No information acquired from tangible things received by the Federal Bureau of Investigation in response to an order under this subchapter may be used or disclosed by Federal officers or employees except for lawful purposes.